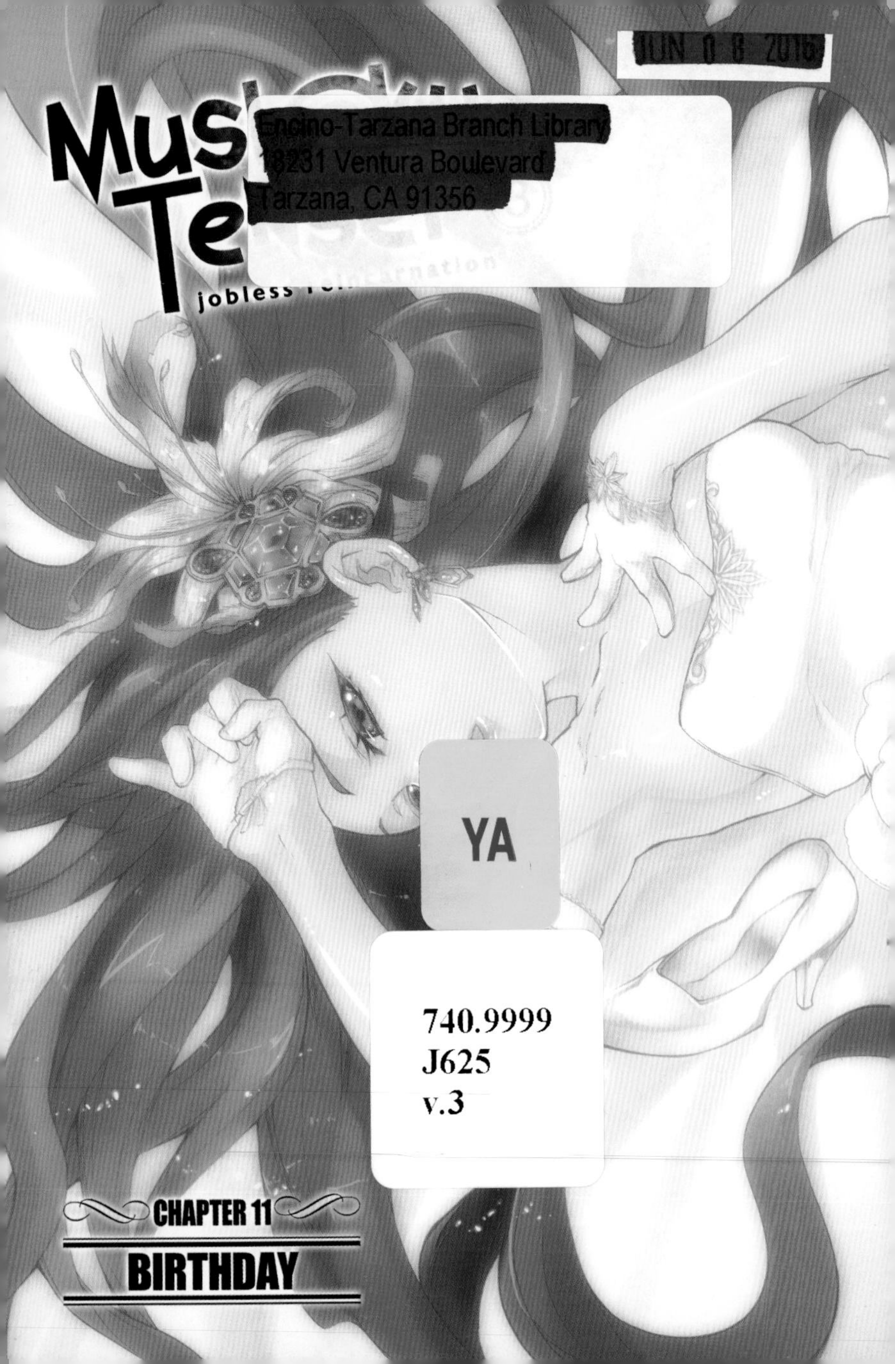

Mushoku Tensei

jobless reincarnation

CHAPTER 11

BIRTHDAY

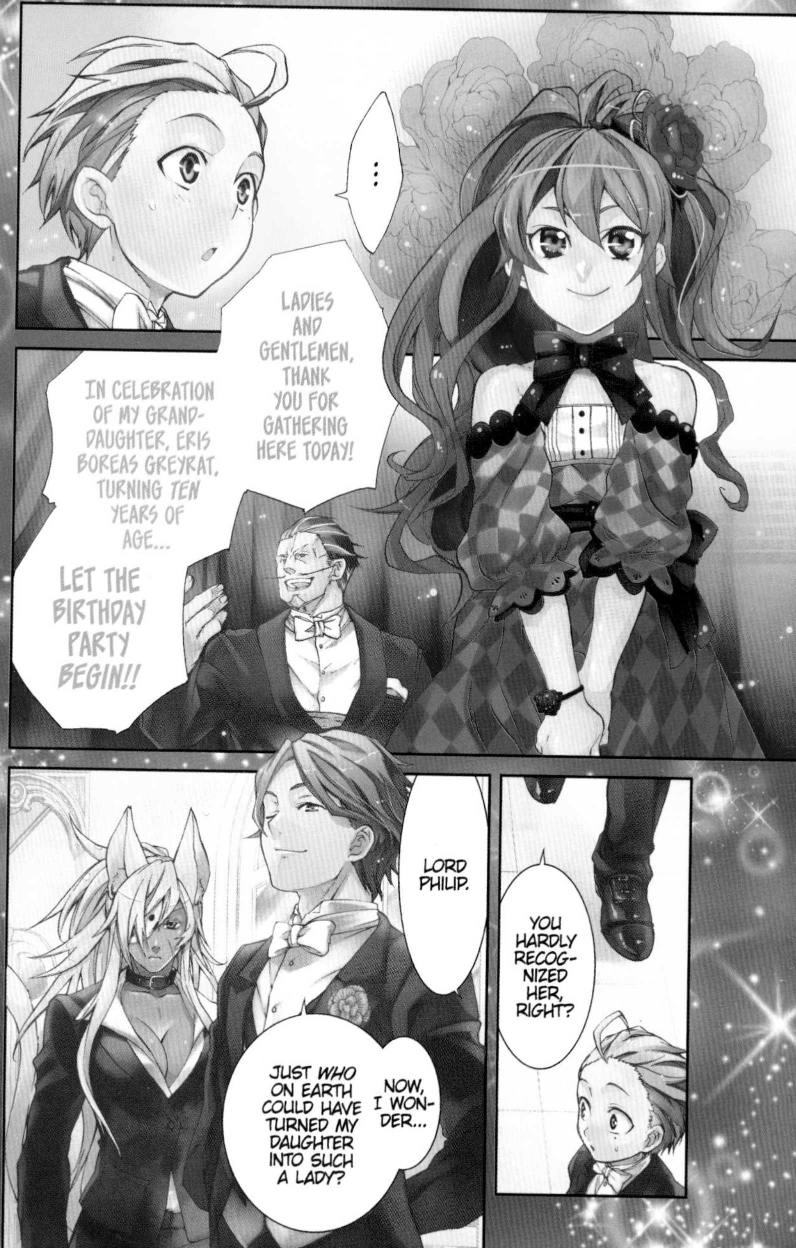
...
LADIES AND GENTLEMEN, THANK YOU FOR GATHERING HERE TODAY!
IN CELEBRATION OF MY GRAND-DAUGHTER, ERIS BOREAS GREYRAT, TURNING *TEN* YEARS OF AGE...
LET THE BIRTHDAY PARTY *BEGIN!!*
YOU HARDLY RECOG-NIZED HER, RIGHT?
LORD PHILIP.
NOW, I WON-DER...
JUST *WHO* ON EARTH COULD HAVE TURNED MY DAUGHTER INTO SUCH A LADY?

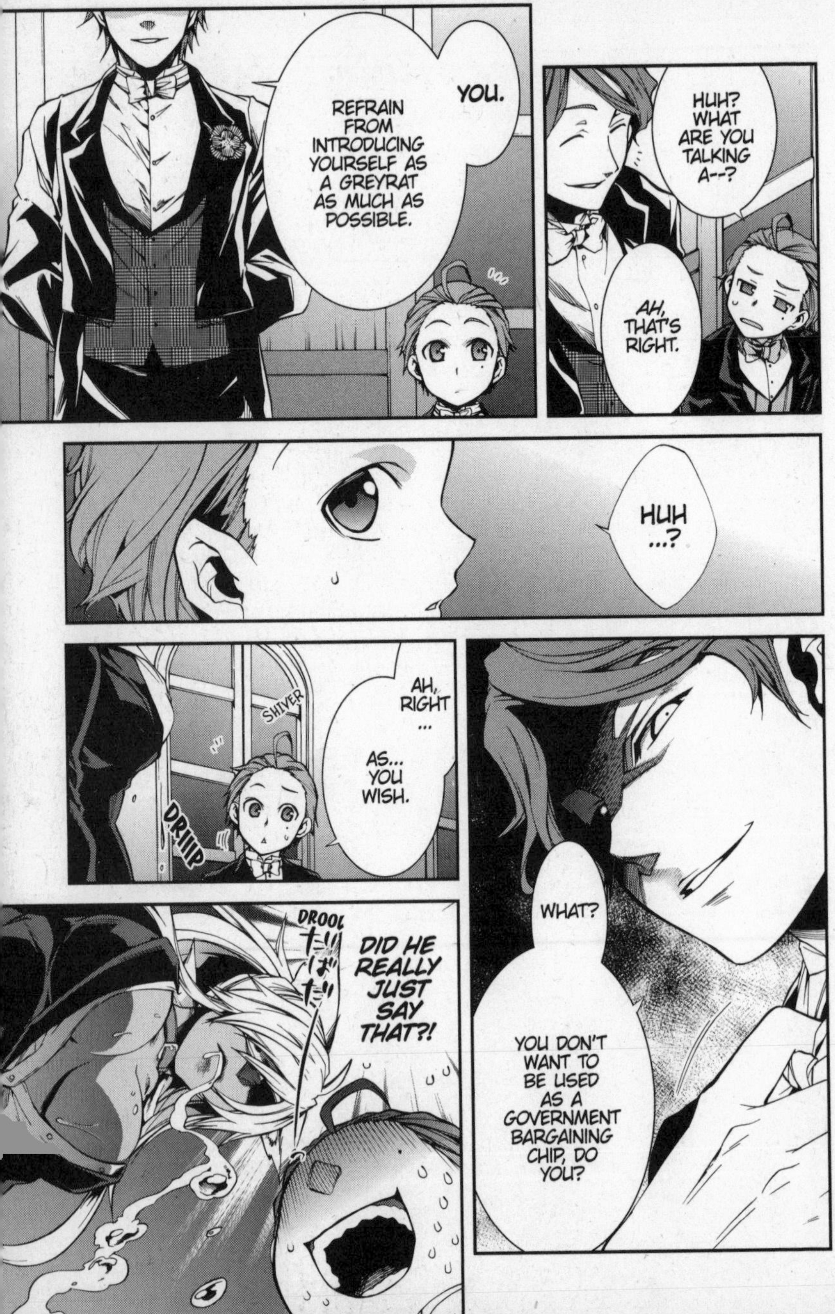
HUH? WHAT ARE YOU TALKING A--?
AH, THAT'S RIGHT.
YOU.
REFRAIN FROM INTRODUCING YOURSELF AS A GREYRAT AS MUCH AS POSSIBLE.
HUH ...?
WHAT?
YOU DON'T WANT TO BE USED AS A GOVERNMENT BARGAINING CHIP, DO YOU?
SHIVER
AH, RIGHT ...
AS... YOU WISH.
DRIIIP
DROOL
DID HE REALLY JUST SAY THAT?!

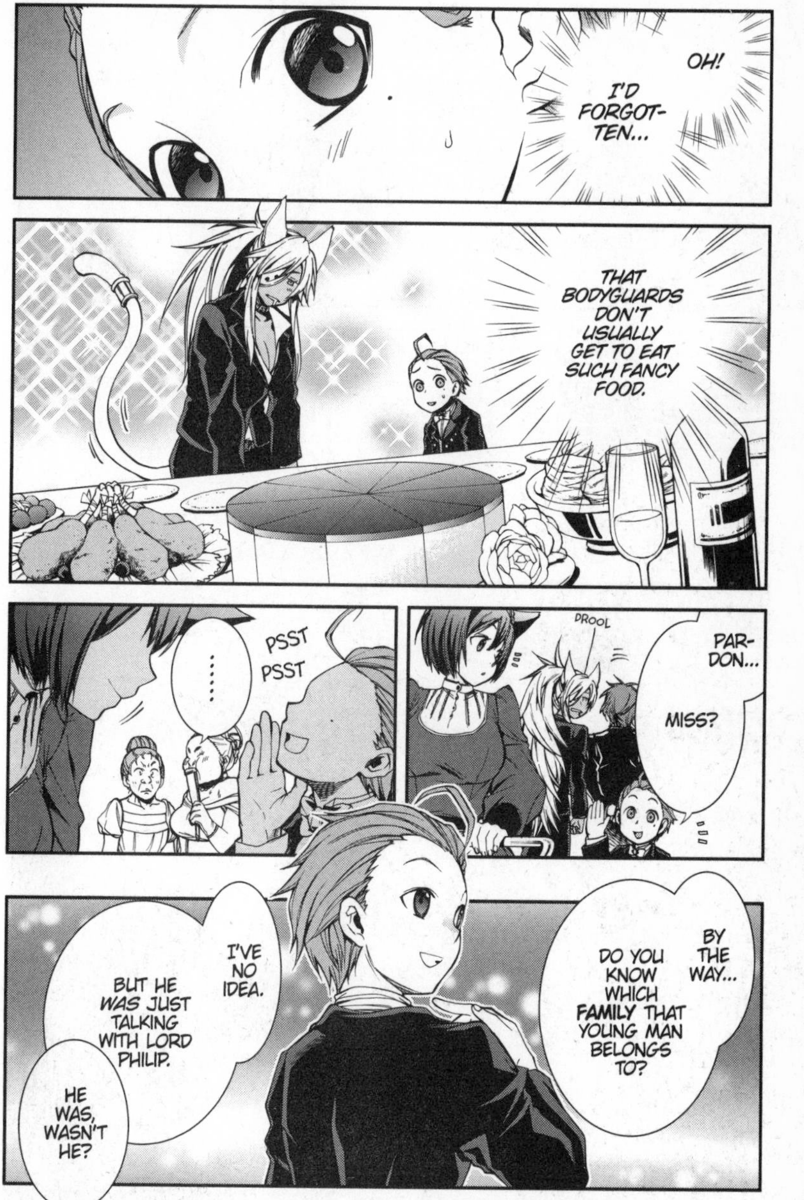
OH!
I'D FORGOT-TEN...
THAT BODYGUARDS DON'T USUALLY GET TO EAT SUCH FANCY FOOD.
DROOL
PAR-DON...
MISS?
PSST PSST
......
BY THE WAY...
DO YOU KNOW WHICH **FAMILY** THAT YOUNG MAN BELONGS TO?
I'VE NO IDEA.
BUT HE *WAS* JUST TALKING WITH LORD PHILIP.
HE WAS, WASN'T HE?

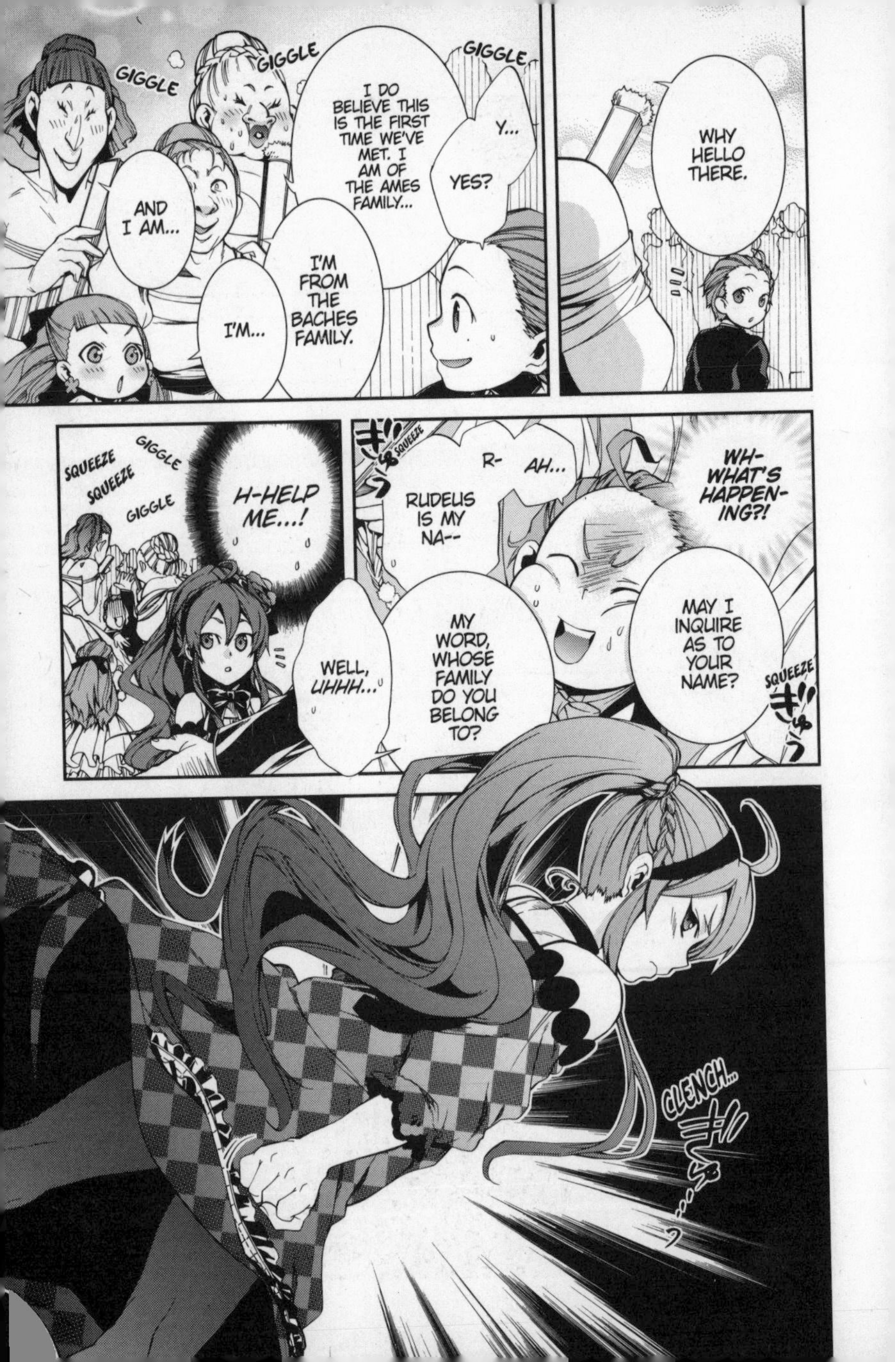
WHY HELLO THERE.
GIGGLE
Y... YES?
I DO BELIEVE THIS IS THE FIRST TIME WE'VE MET. I AM OF THE AMES FAMILY...
GIGGLE
GIGGLE
I'M FROM THE BACHES FAMILY.
AND I AM...
I'M...
WH- WHAT'S HAPPENING?!
AH...
R- RUDEUS IS MY NA--
SQUEEZE
MAY I INQUIRE AS TO YOUR NAME?
SQUEEZE
MY WORD, WHOSE FAMILY DO YOU BELONG TO?
WELL, UHHH...
H-HELP ME...!
GIGGLE
SQUEEZE
SQUEEZE
GIGGLE
CLENCH...

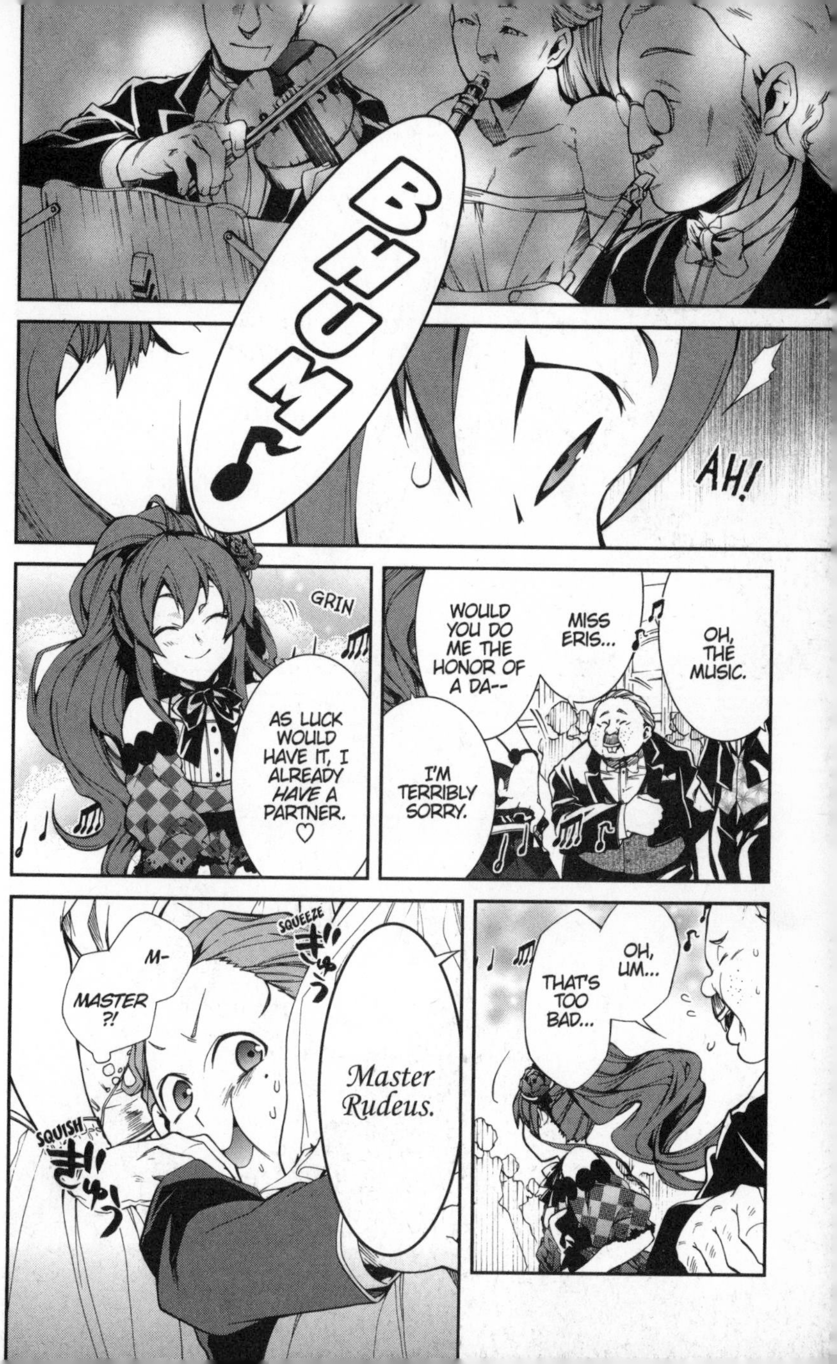
BHUM♪
AH!
OH, THE MUSIC.
MISS ERIS...
WOULD YOU DO ME THE HONOR OF A DA--
I'M TERRIBLY SORRY.
GRIN
AS LUCK WOULD HAVE IT, I ALREADY HAVE A PARTNER. ♡
OH, UM... THAT'S TOO BAD...
SQUEEZE
Master Rudeus.
M- MASTER?!
SQUISH

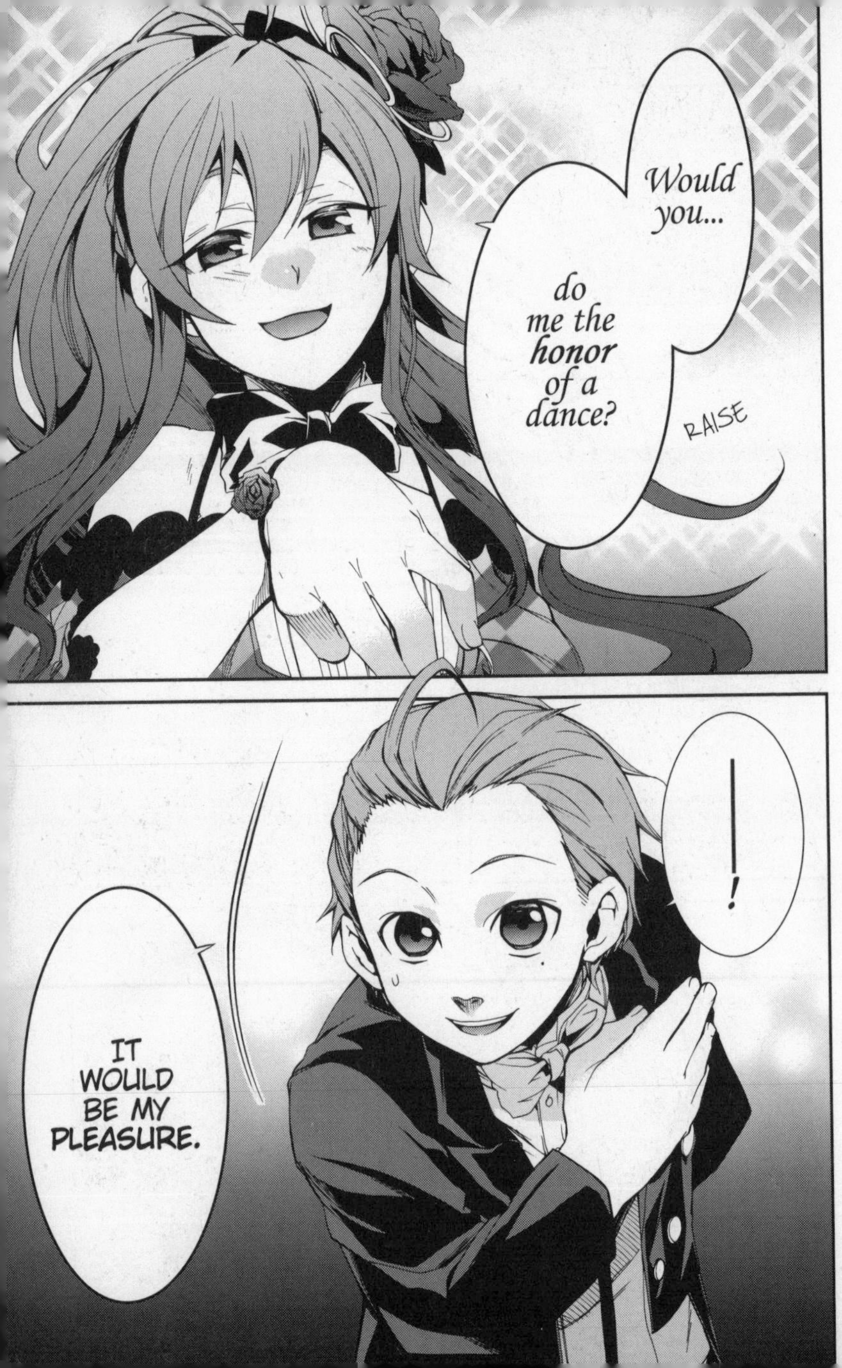
Would you...
do me the *honor* of a dance?
RAISE
—!
IT WOULD BE MY PLEASURE.

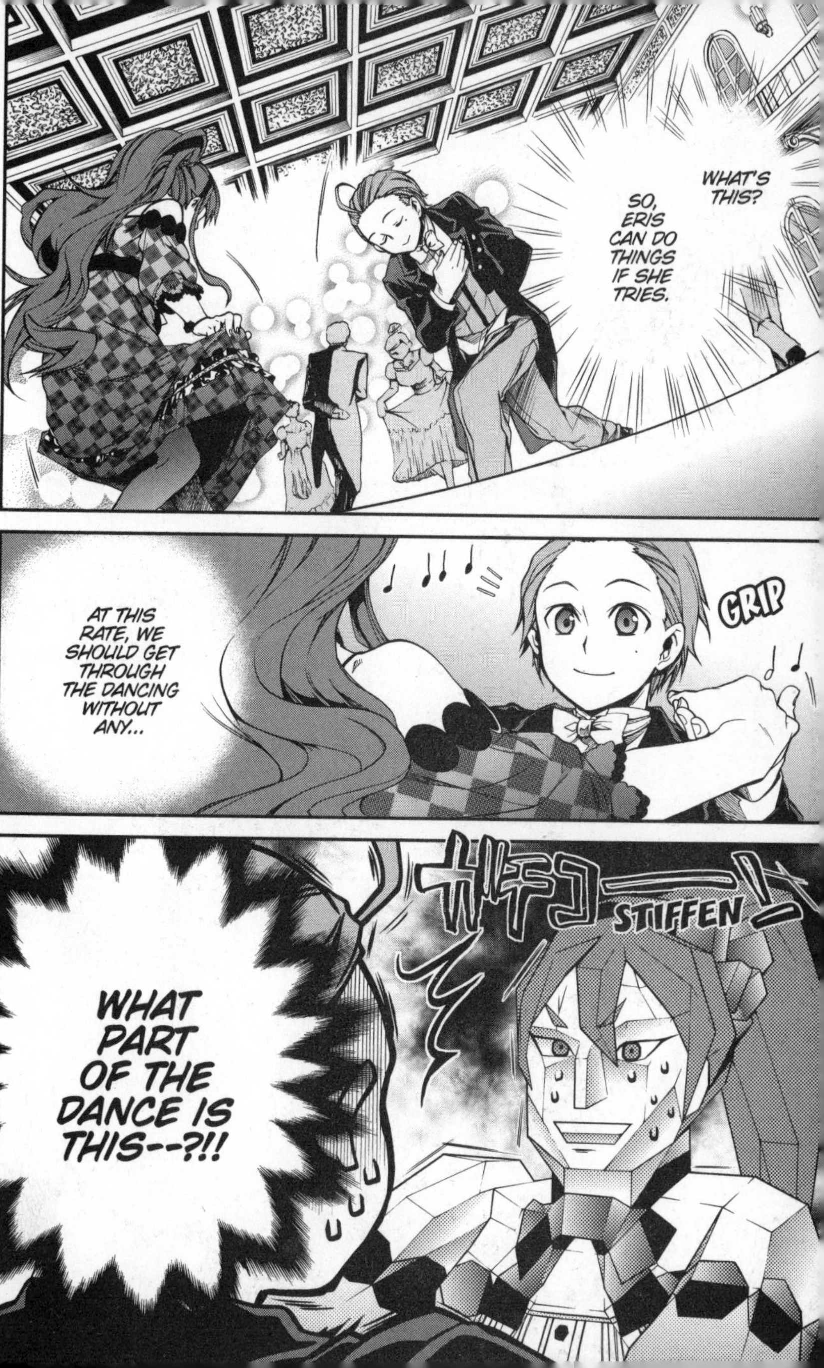
WHAT'S THIS?
SO, ERIS CAN DO THINGS IF SHE TRIES.
GRIP
AT THIS RATE, WE SHOULD GET THROUGH THE DANCING WITHOUT ANY...
STIFFEN
WHAT PART OF THE DANCE IS THIS--?!!

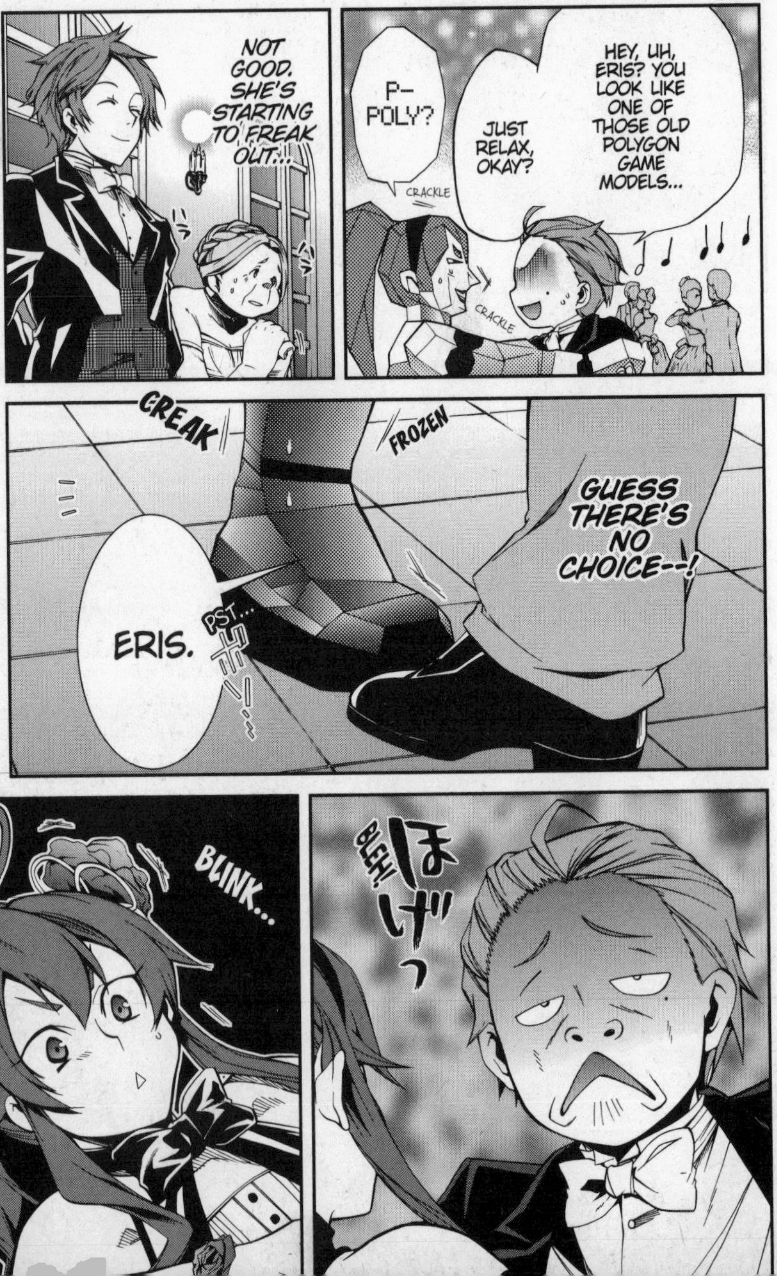
HEY, UH, ERIS? YOU LOOK LIKE ONE OF THOSE OLD POLYGON GAME MODELS...
JUST RELAX, OKAY?
P-POLY?
CRACKLE
CRACKLE
NOT GOOD. SHE'S STARTING TO FREAK OUT...
FROZEN
GUESS THERE'S NO CHOICE--!
CREAK
ERIS.
PST...
BLEH!
ほげっ
BLINK...

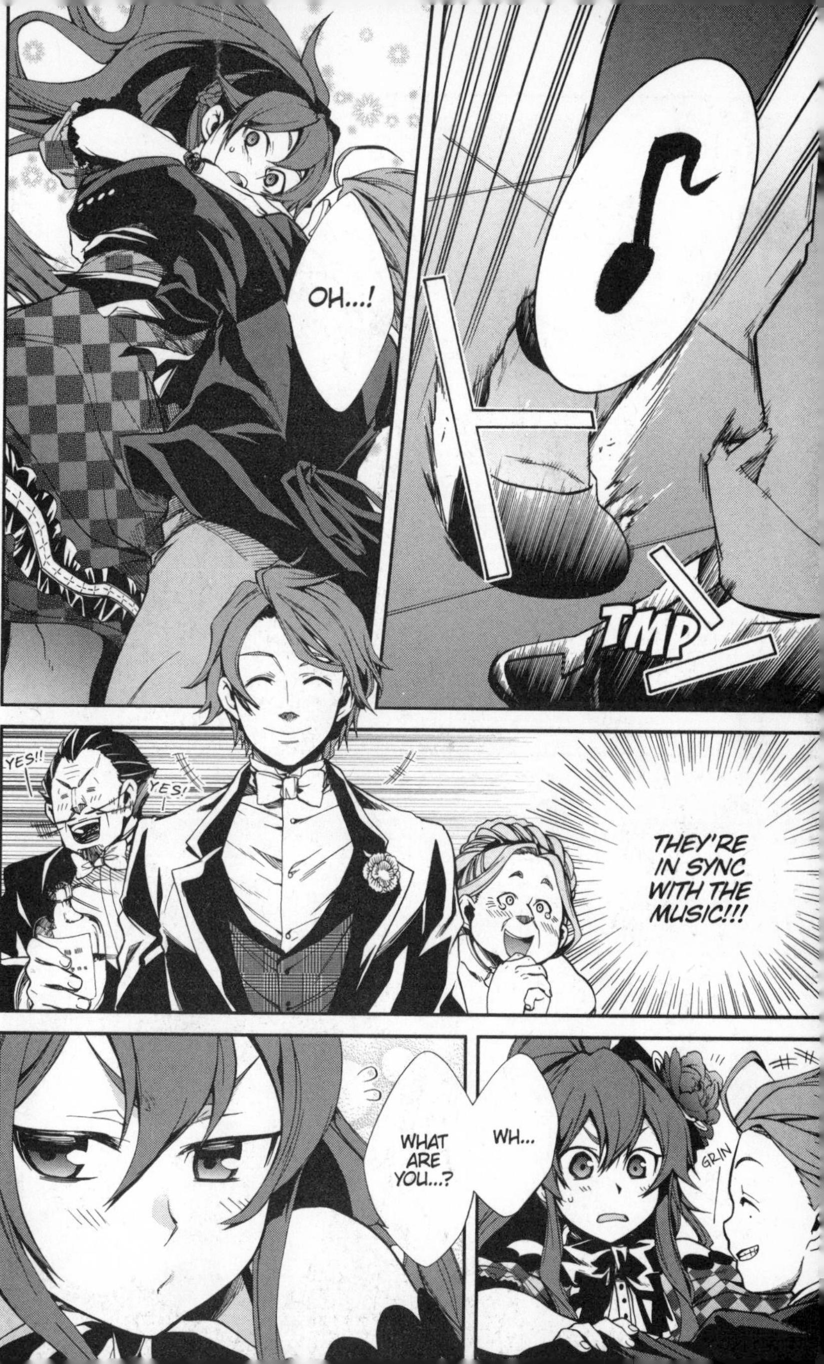
TMP
OH...!
THEY'RE IN SYNC WITH THE MUSIC!!!
YES!
YES!!
WH...
GRIN
WHAT ARE YOU...?

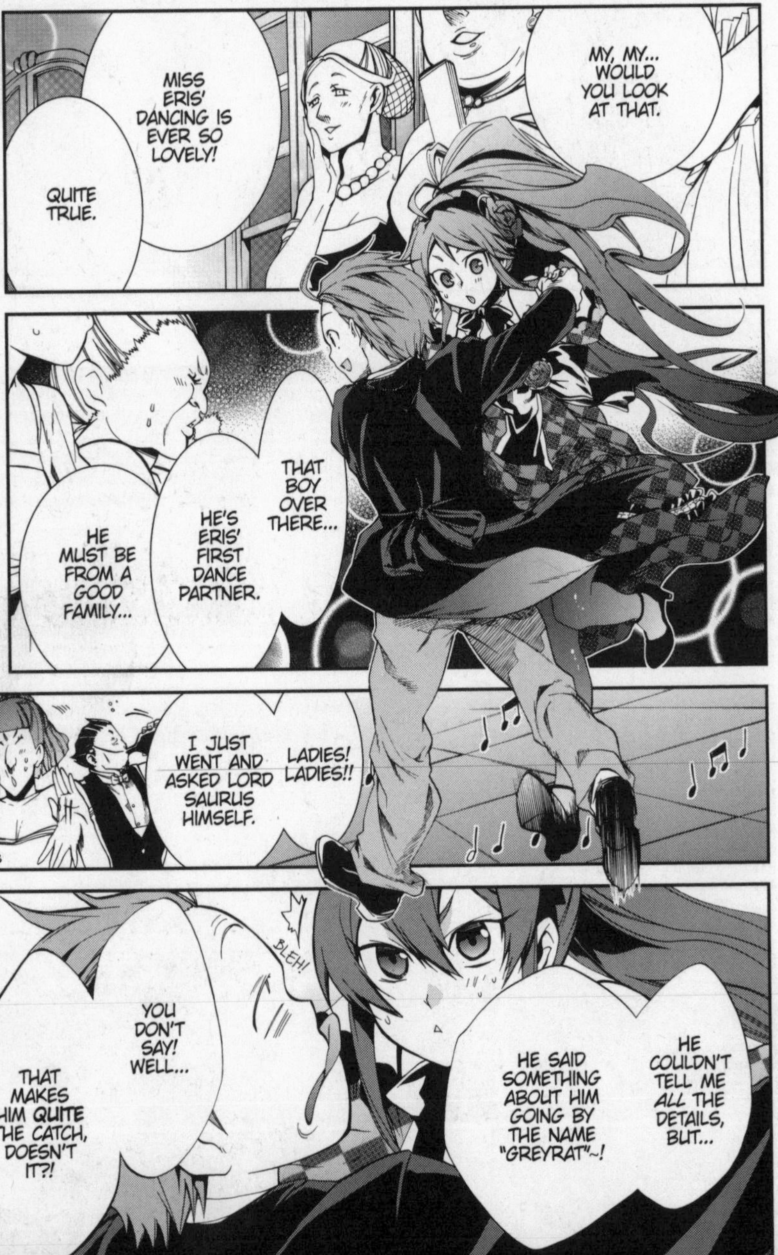
MY, MY... WOULD YOU LOOK AT THAT.
MISS ERIS' DANCING IS EVER SO LOVELY!
QUITE TRUE.
THAT BOY OVER THERE...
HE'S ERIS' FIRST DANCE PARTNER.
HE MUST BE FROM A GOOD FAMILY...
LADIES! LADIES!!
I JUST WENT AND ASKED LORD SAURUS HIMSELF.
HE COULDN'T TELL ME *ALL* THE DETAILS, BUT...
HE SAID SOMETHING ABOUT HIM GOING BY THE NAME "GREYRAT"~!
BLEH!
YOU DON'T SAY! WELL...
THAT MAKES HIM QUITE THE CATCH, DOESN'T IT?!

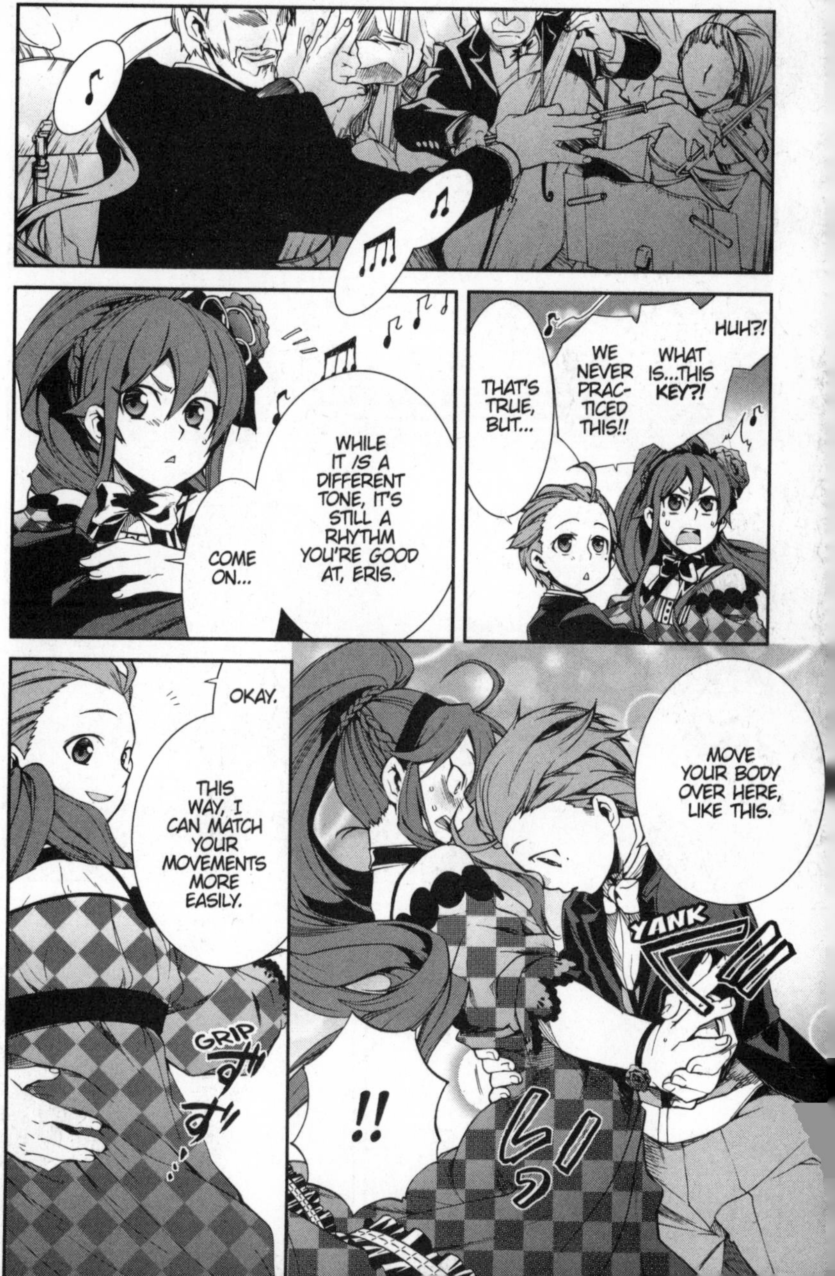
HUH?!
WHAT IS...THIS KEY?!
WE NEVER PRACTICED THIS!!
THAT'S TRUE, BUT...
WHILE IT IS A DIFFERENT TONE, IT'S STILL A RHYTHM YOU'RE GOOD AT, ERIS.
COME ON...
MOVE YOUR BODY OVER HERE, LIKE THIS.
YANK
!!
OKAY.
THIS WAY, I CAN MATCH YOUR MOVEMENTS MORE EASILY.
GRIP

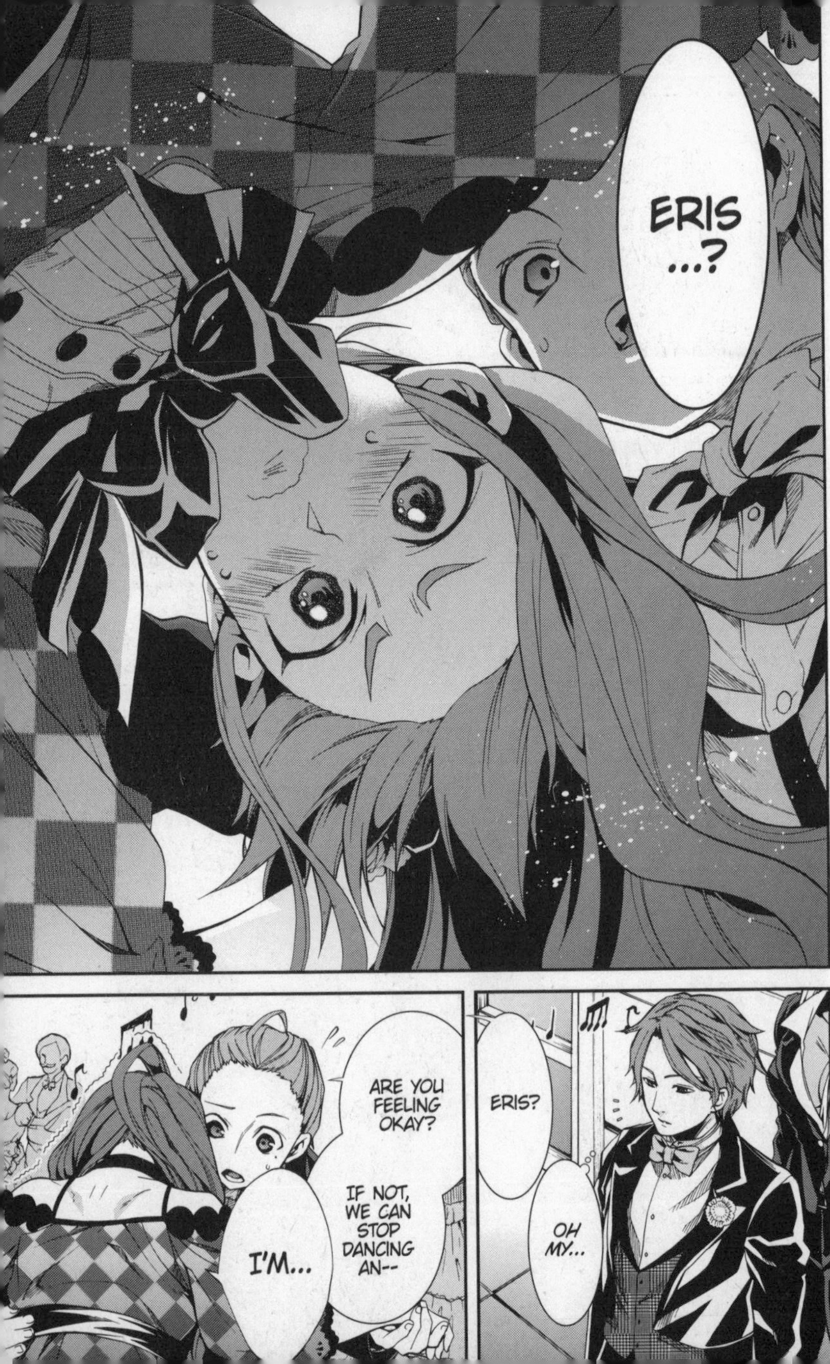
ERIS ...?
ERIS?
OH MY...
ARE YOU FEELING OKAY?
IF NOT, WE CAN STOP DANCING AN--
I'M...

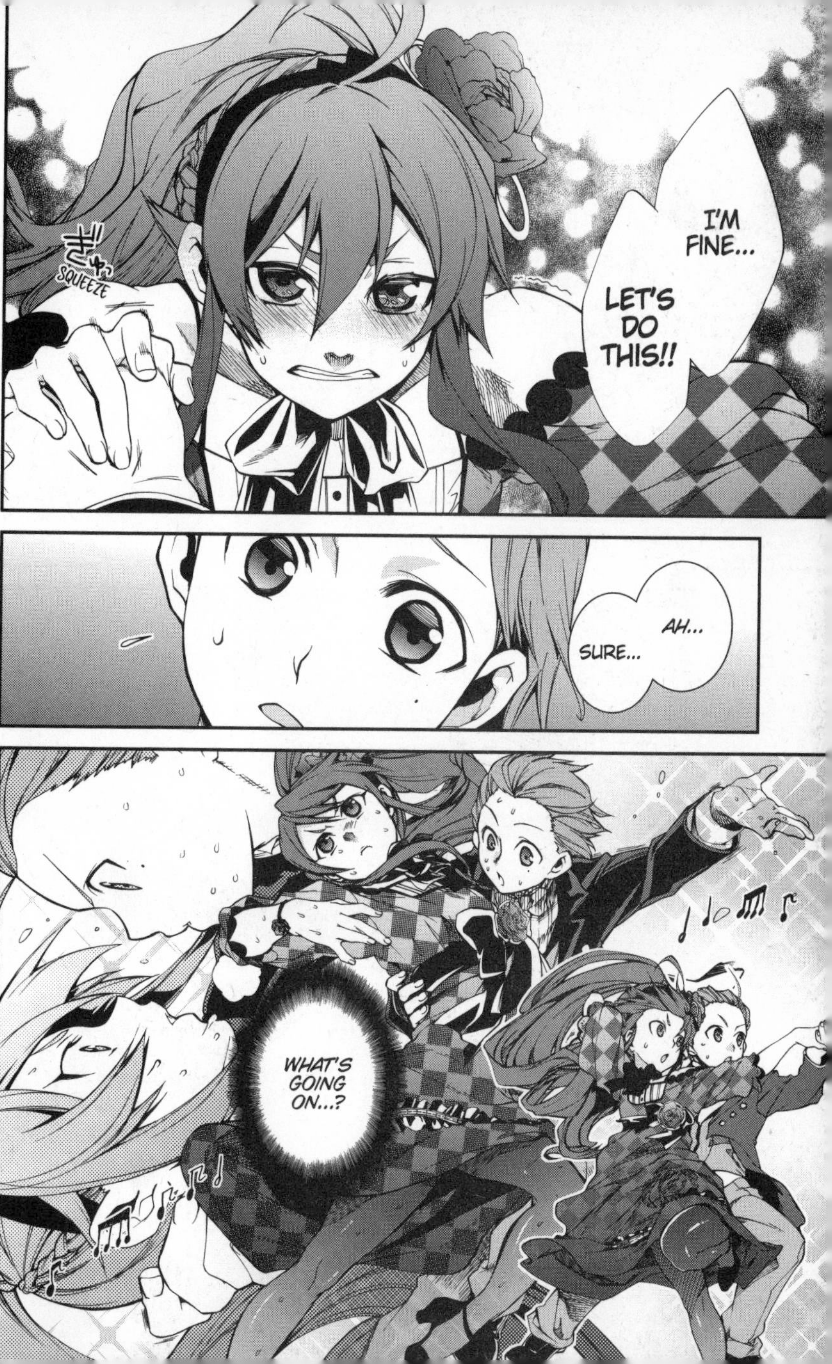
I'M FINE...
LET'S DO THIS!!
ぎゅっ
SQUEEZE
AH... SURE...
WHAT'S GOING ON...?

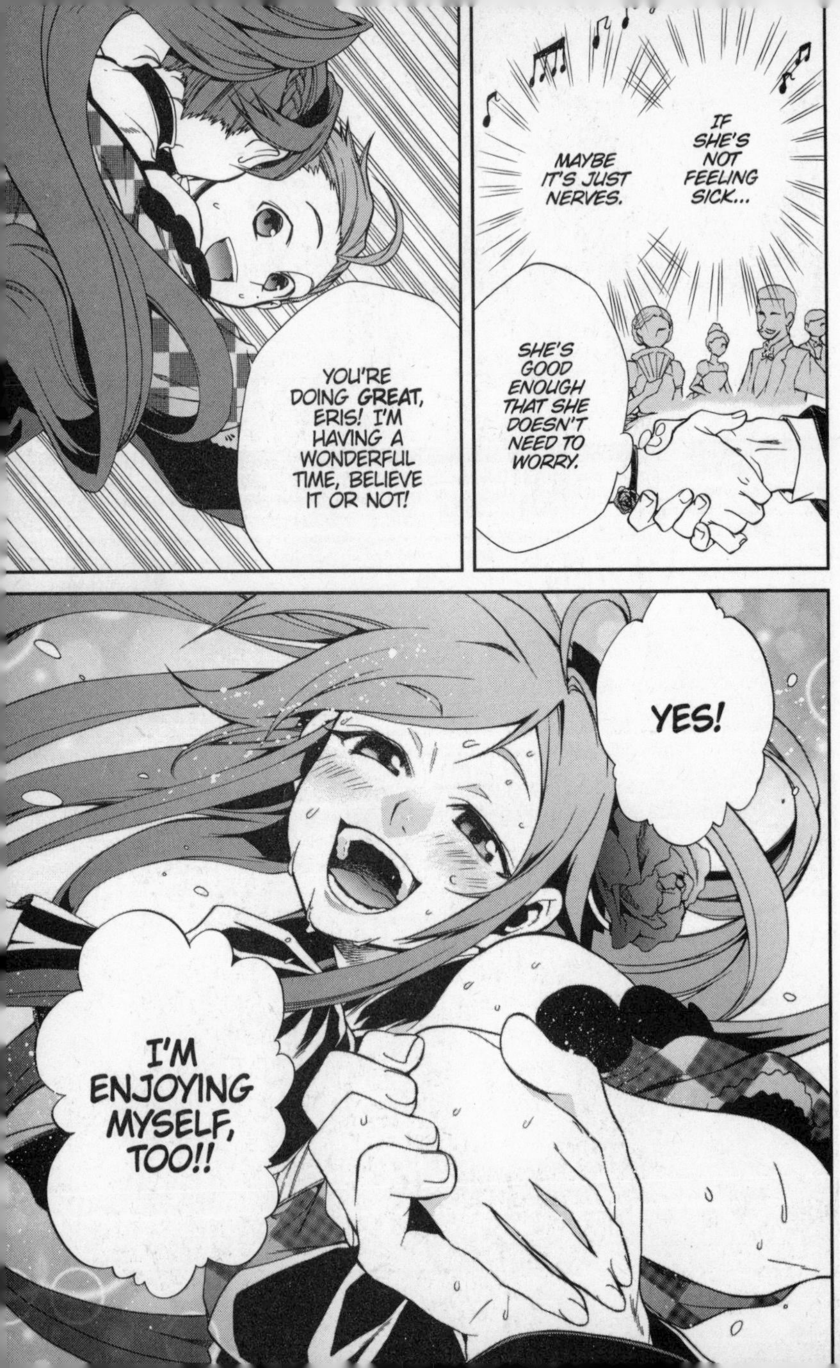
IF SHE'S NOT FEELING SICK...
MAYBE IT'S JUST NERVES.
SHE'S GOOD ENOUGH THAT SHE DOESN'T NEED TO WORRY.
YOU'RE DOING GREAT, ERIS! I'M HAVING A WONDERFUL TIME, BELIEVE IT OR NOT!
YES!
I'M ENJOYING MYSELF, TOO!!

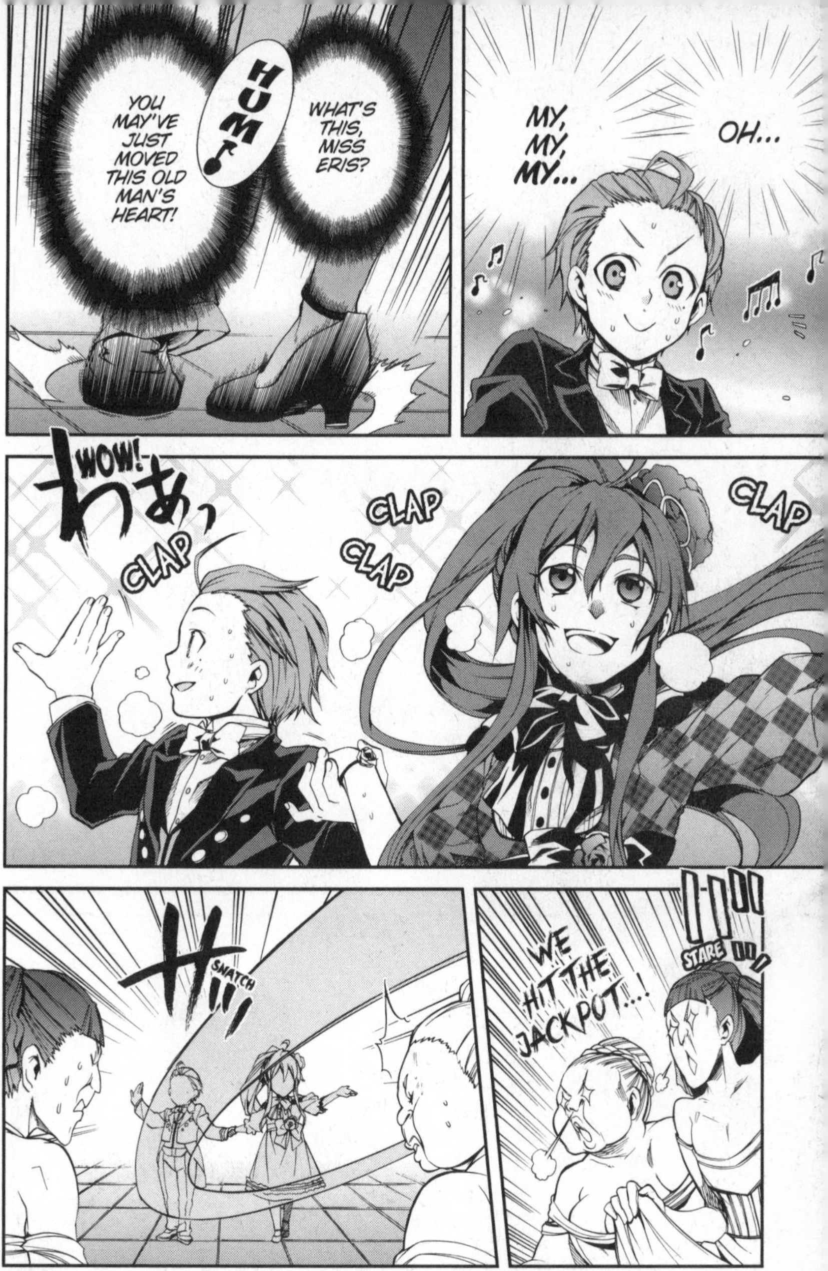
OH...
MY, MY, MY...
WHAT'S THIS, MISS ERIS?
HUM♪
YOU MAY'VE JUST MOVED THIS OLD MAN'S HEART!
CLAP
CLAP
CLAP
CLAP
WOW!
わあっ
STARE
WE HIT THE JACKPOT...!
SNATCH
サッ

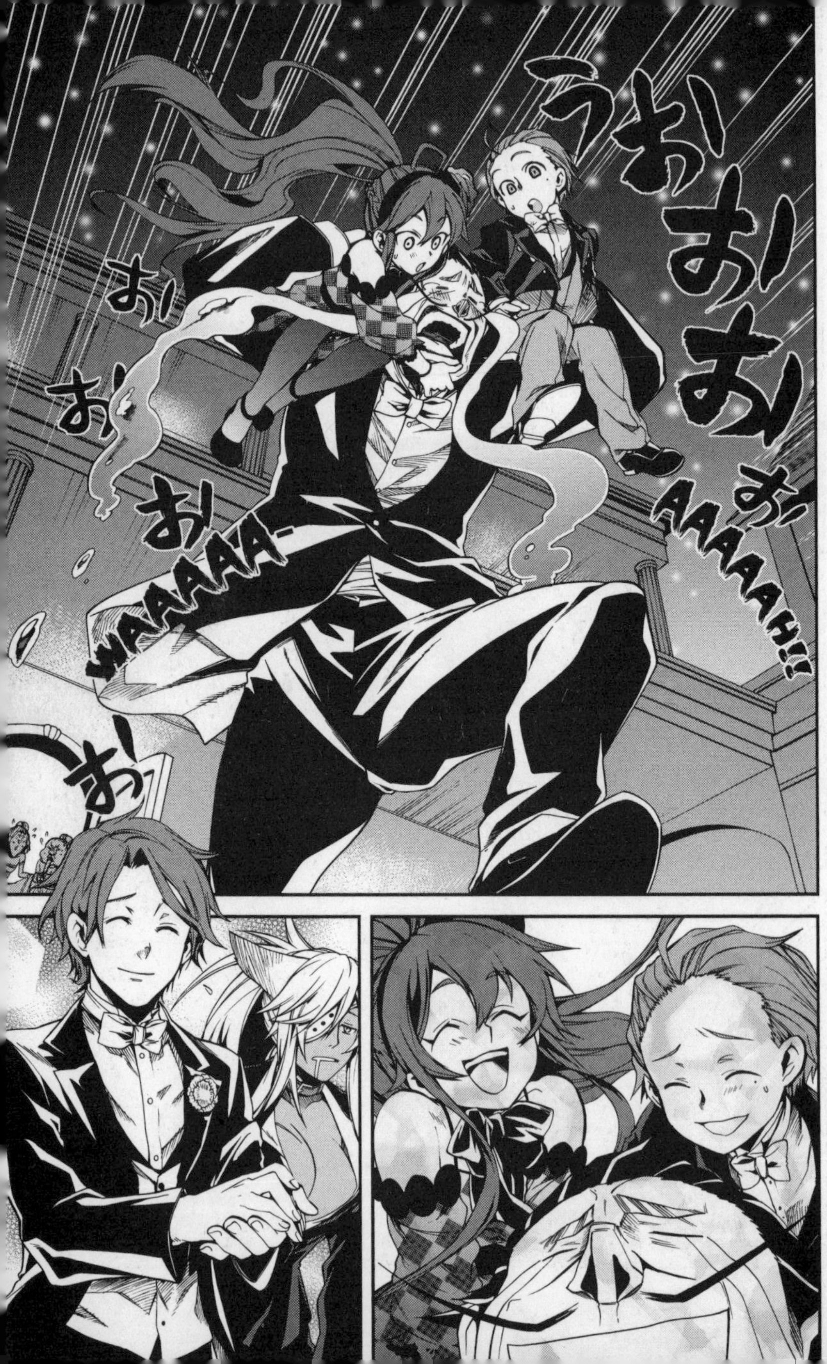
うおおおお
WAAAAAA-
AAAAAAH!!
おおおお

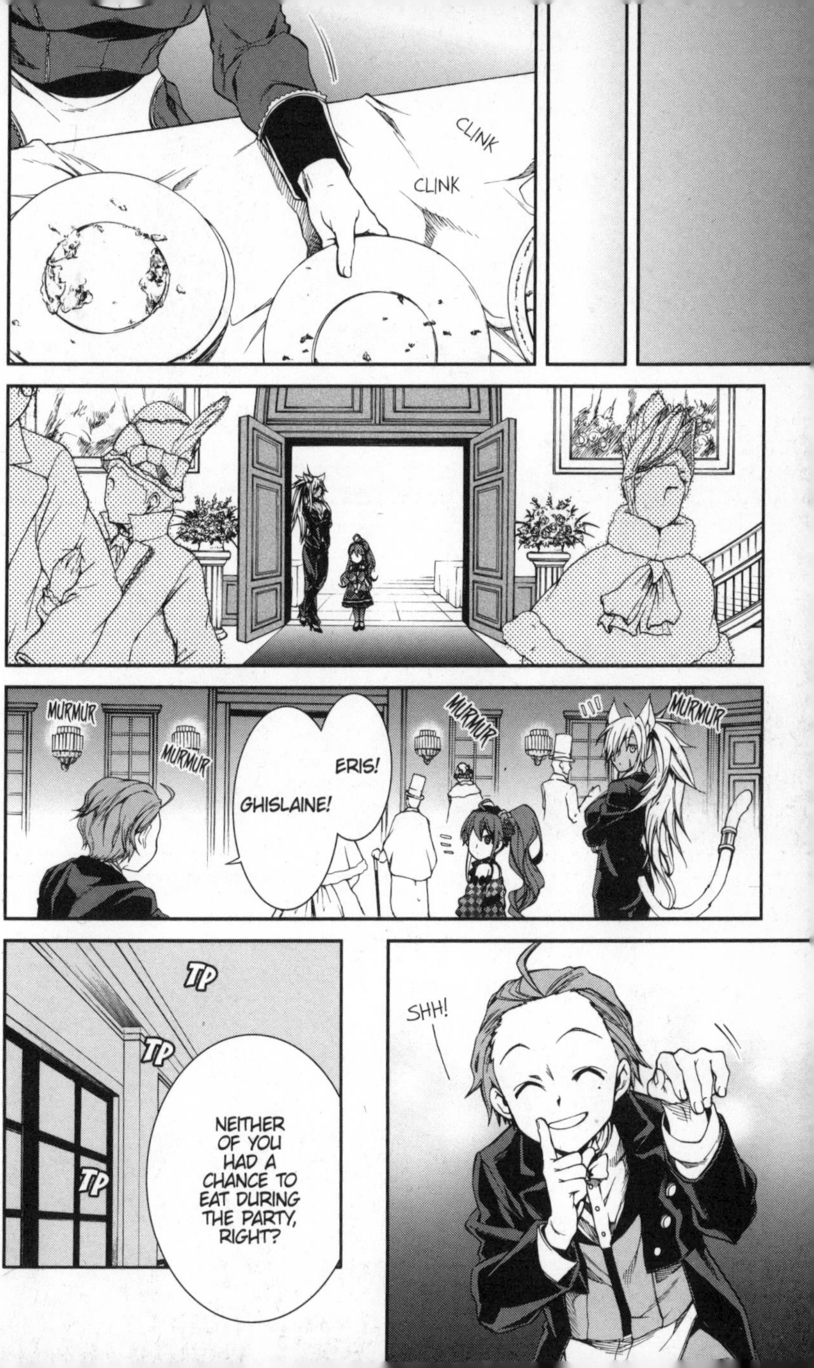
CLINK
CLINK
MURMUR
MURMUR
ERIS!
GHISLAINE!
MURMUR
MURMUR
SHH!
TP
TP
TP
NEITHER OF YOU HAD A CHANCE TO EAT DURING THE PARTY, RIGHT?

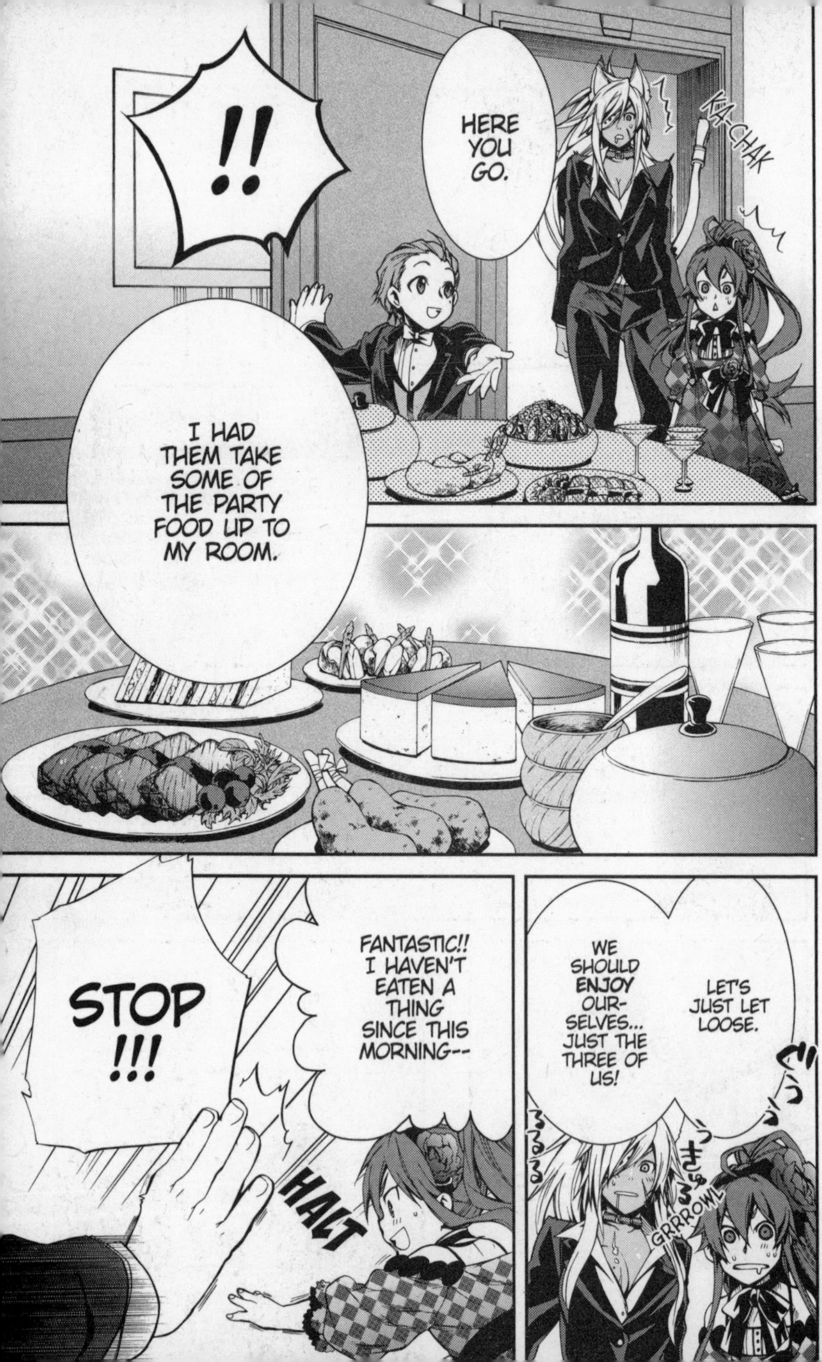
KA-CHAK
HERE YOU GO.
!!
I HAD THEM TAKE SOME OF THE PARTY FOOD UP TO MY ROOM.
LET'S JUST LET LOOSE.
WE SHOULD ENJOY OURSELVES... JUST THE THREE OF US!
GRRROWL
FANTASTIC!! I HAVEN'T EATEN A THING SINCE THIS MORNING--
STOP !!!
HALT

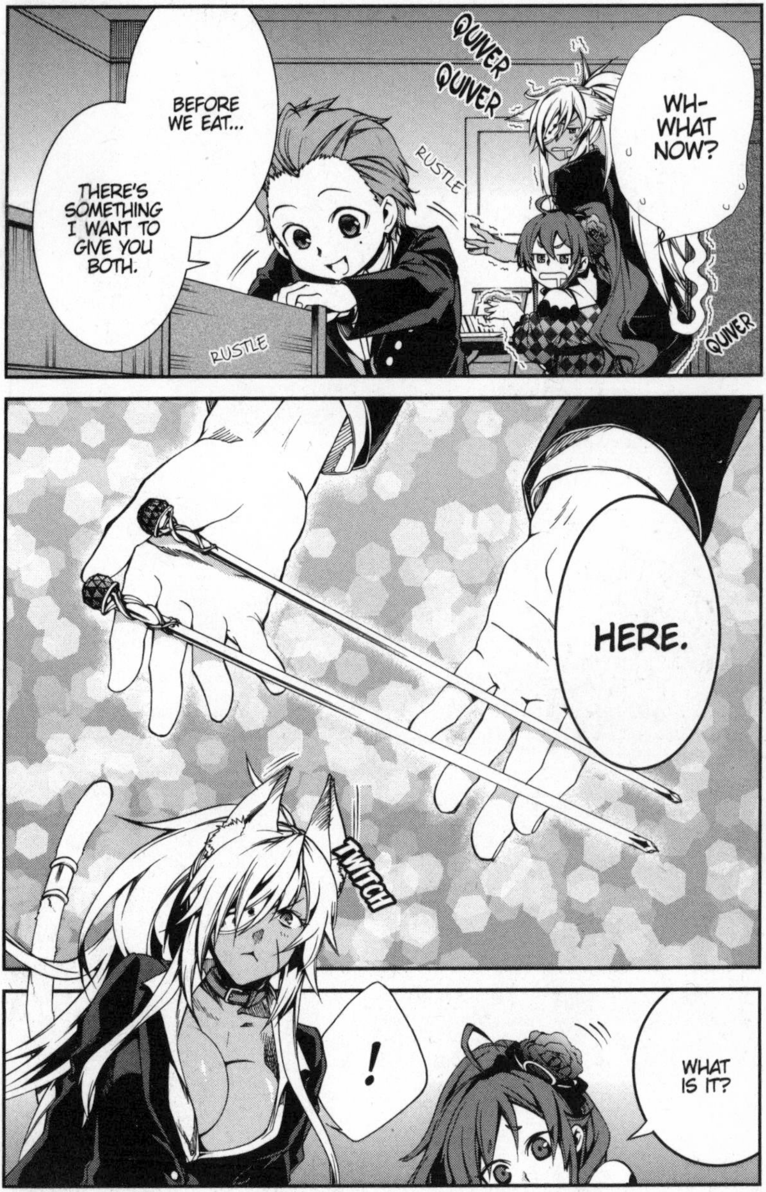
WH- WHAT NOW?
QUIVER QUIVER
QUIVER
RUSTLE
BEFORE WE EAT...
THERE'S SOMETHING I WANT TO GIVE YOU BOTH.
RUSTLE
HERE.
TWITCH
WHAT IS IT?
!

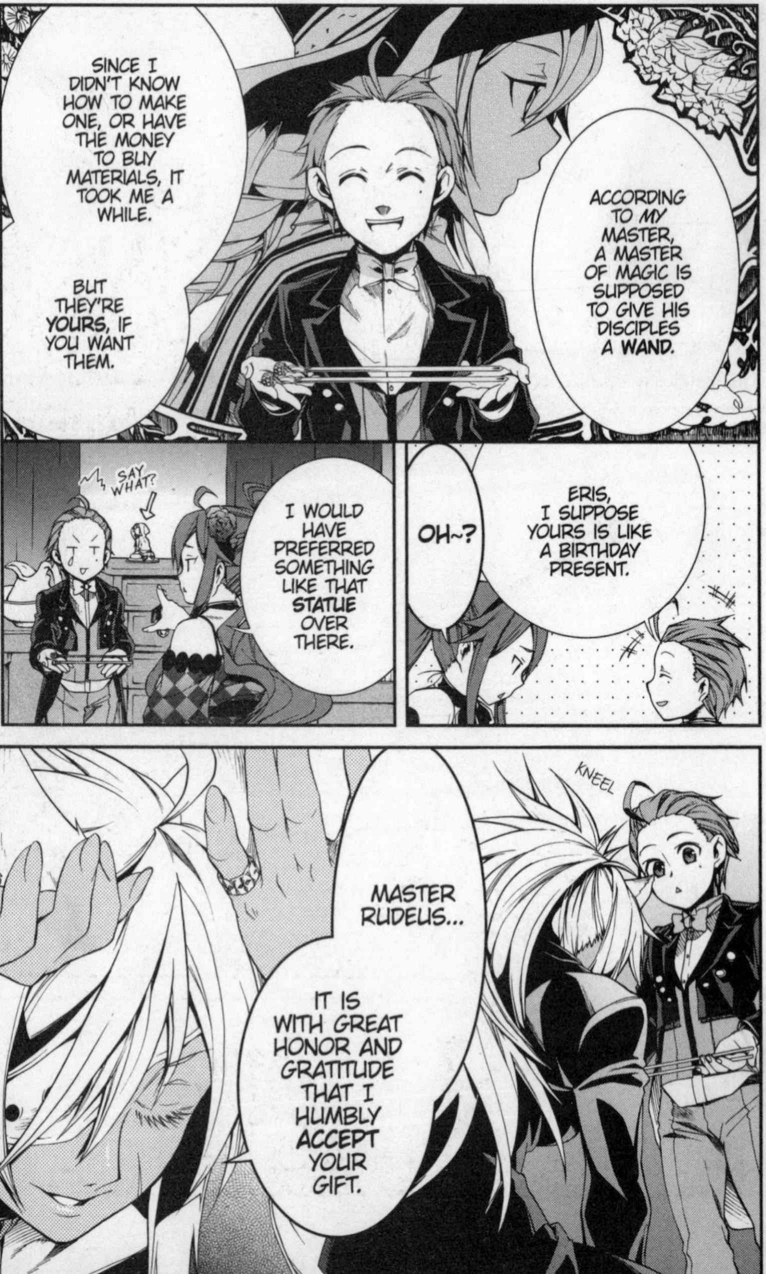
ACCORDING TO MY MASTER, A MASTER OF MAGIC IS SUPPOSED TO GIVE HIS DISCIPLES A WAND.
SINCE I DIDN'T KNOW HOW TO MAKE ONE, OR HAVE THE MONEY TO BUY MATERIALS, IT TOOK ME A WHILE.
BUT THEY'RE YOURS, IF YOU WANT THEM.
ERIS, I SUPPOSE YOURS IS LIKE A BIRTHDAY PRESENT.
OH~?
I WOULD HAVE PREFERRED SOMETHING LIKE THAT STATUE OVER THERE.
SAY WHAT?
KNEEL
MASTER RUDEUS...
IT IS WITH GREAT HONOR AND GRATITUDE THAT I HUMBLY ACCEPT YOUR GIFT.

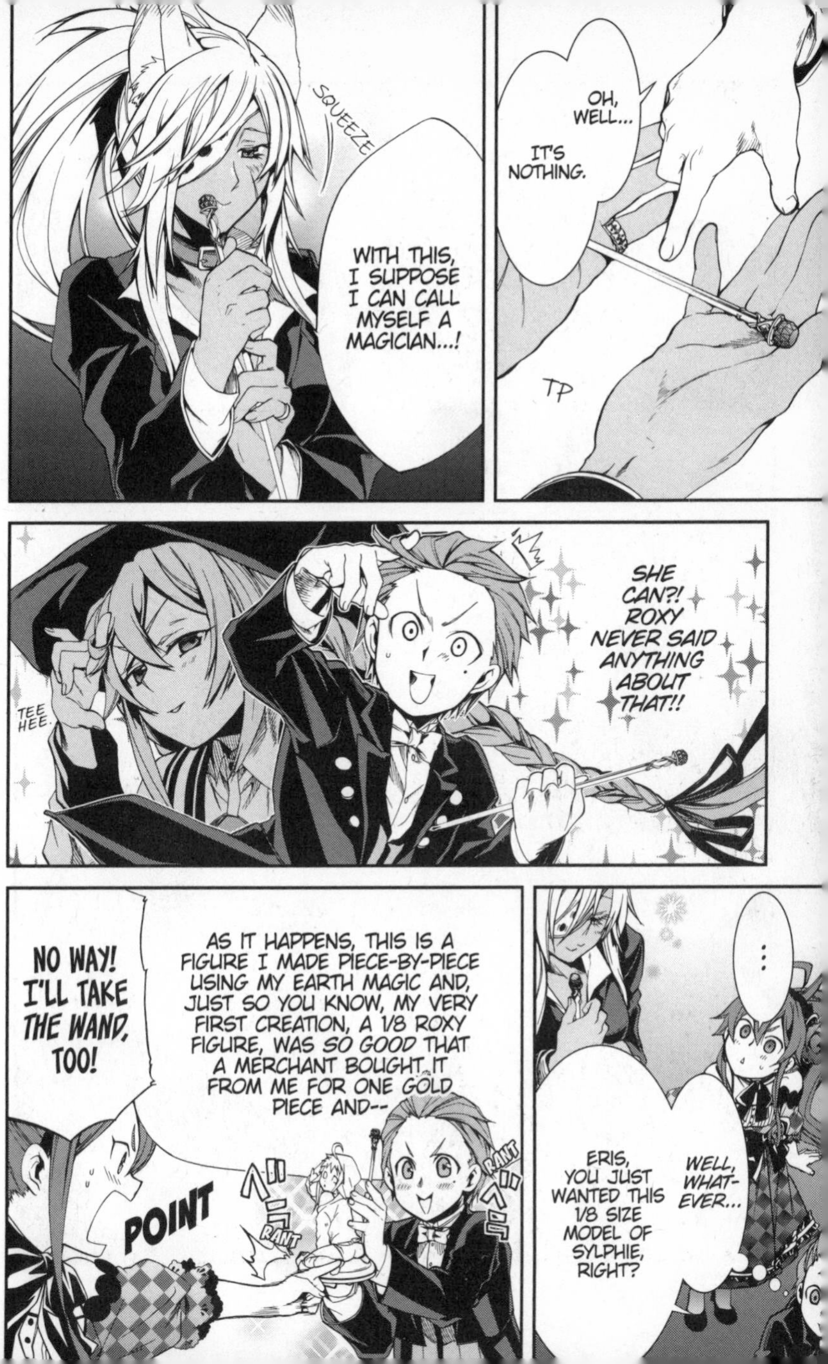

OH, WELL...
IT'S NOTHING.
TP
SQUEEZE
WITH THIS, I SUPPOSE I CAN CALL MYSELF A MAGICIAN...!
SHE CAN?! ROXY NEVER SAID ANYTHING ABOUT THAT!!
TEE HEE.
...
WELL, WHAT-EVER...
ERIS, YOU JUST WANTED THIS 1/8 SIZE MODEL OF SYLPHIE, RIGHT?
AS IT HAPPENS, THIS IS A FIGURE I MADE PIECE-BY-PIECE USING MY EARTH MAGIC AND, JUST SO YOU KNOW, MY VERY FIRST CREATION, A 1/8 ROXY FIGURE, WAS SO GOOD THAT A MERCHANT BOUGHT IT FROM ME FOR ONE GOLD PIECE AND--
RANT
RANT
NO WAY! I'LL TAKE THE WAND, TOO!
POINT

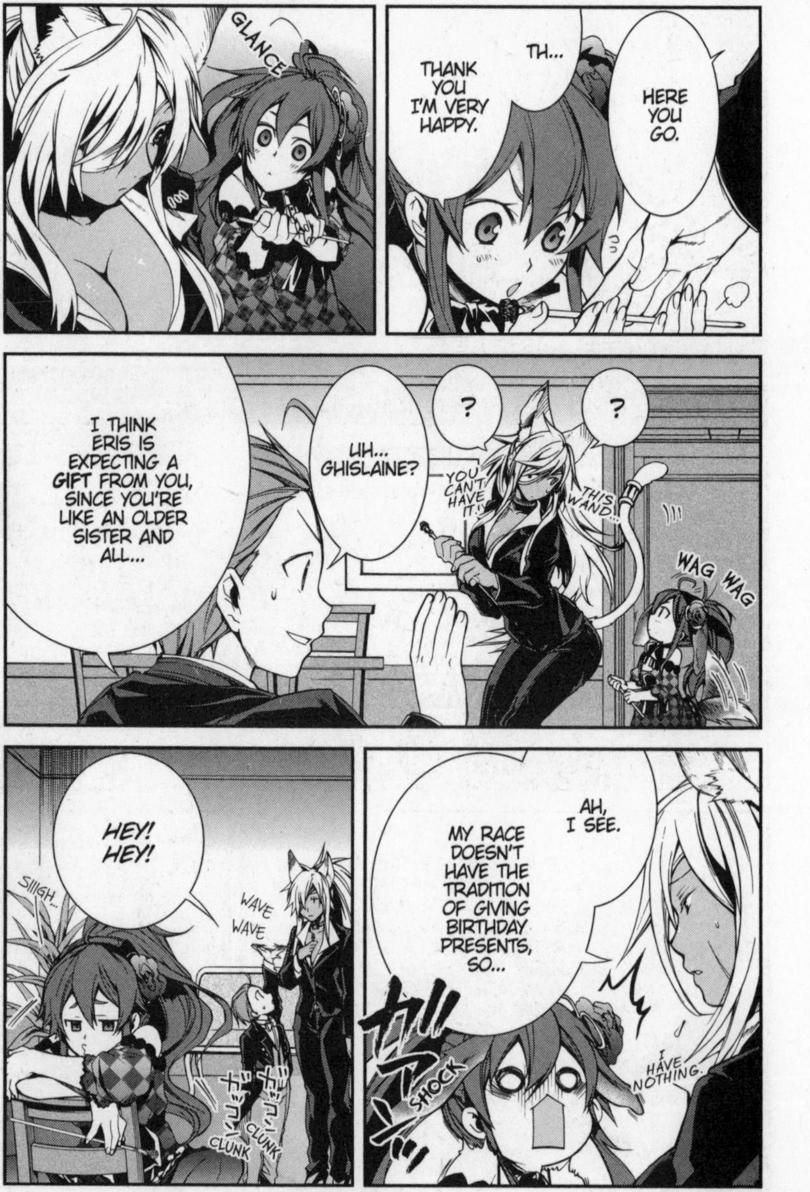
HERE YOU GO.
TH...
THANK YOU I'M VERY HAPPY.
GLANCE
?
?
THIS WAND...
YOU CAN'T HAVE IT.
WAG WAG
UH... GHISLAINE?
I THINK ERIS IS EXPECTING A GIFT FROM YOU, SINCE YOU'RE LIKE AN OLDER SISTER AND ALL...
AH, I SEE.
MY RACE DOESN'T HAVE THE TRADITION OF GIVING BIRTHDAY PRESENTS, SO...
I HAVE NOTHING.
SHOCK
HEY! HEY!
WAVE WAVE
SIIIGH...
CLUNK
CLUNK

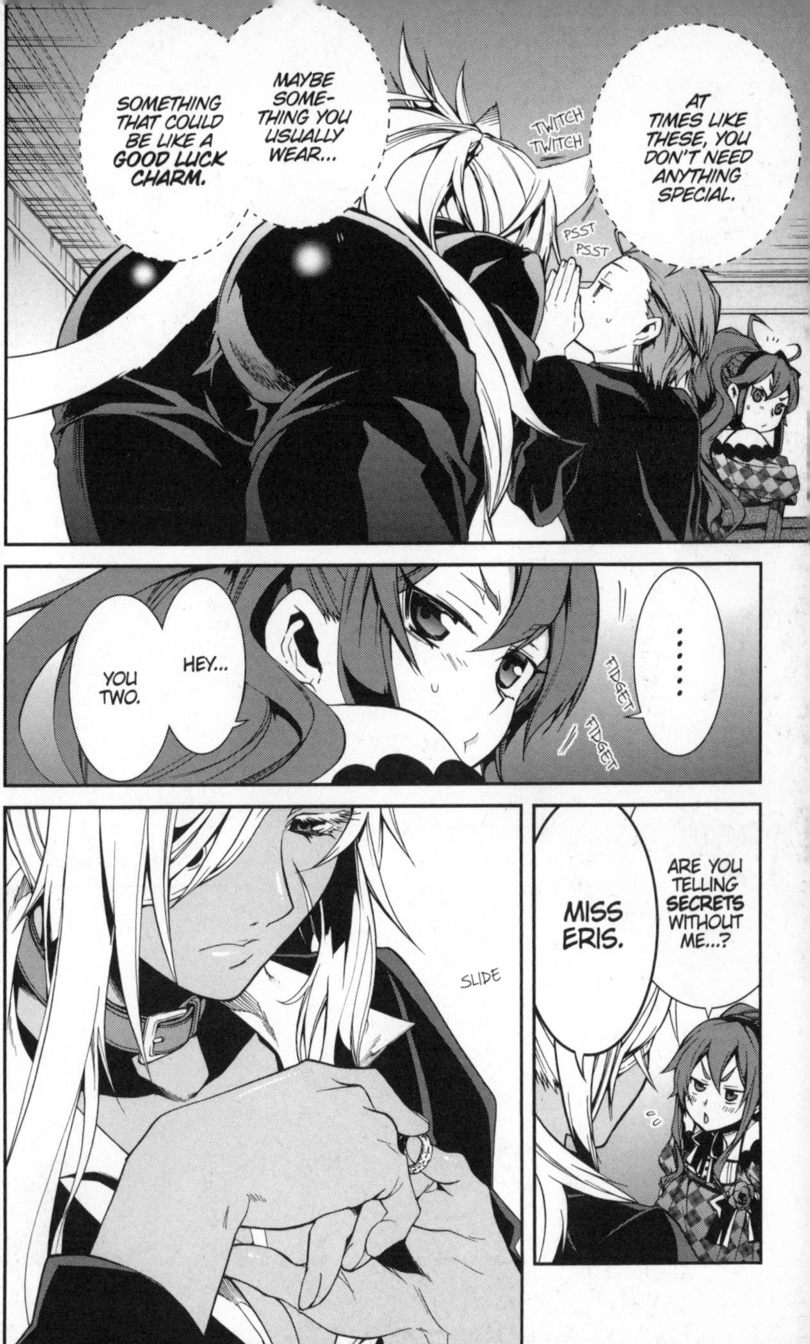
AT TIMES LIKE THESE, YOU DON'T NEED ANYTHING SPECIAL.
TWITCH TWITCH
PSST PSST
MAYBE SOME-THING YOU USUALLY WEAR...
SOMETHING THAT COULD BE LIKE A GOOD LUCK CHARM.
......
FIDGET FIDGET
HEY... YOU TWO.
ARE YOU TELLING SECRETS WITHOUT ME...?
MISS ERIS.
SLIDE

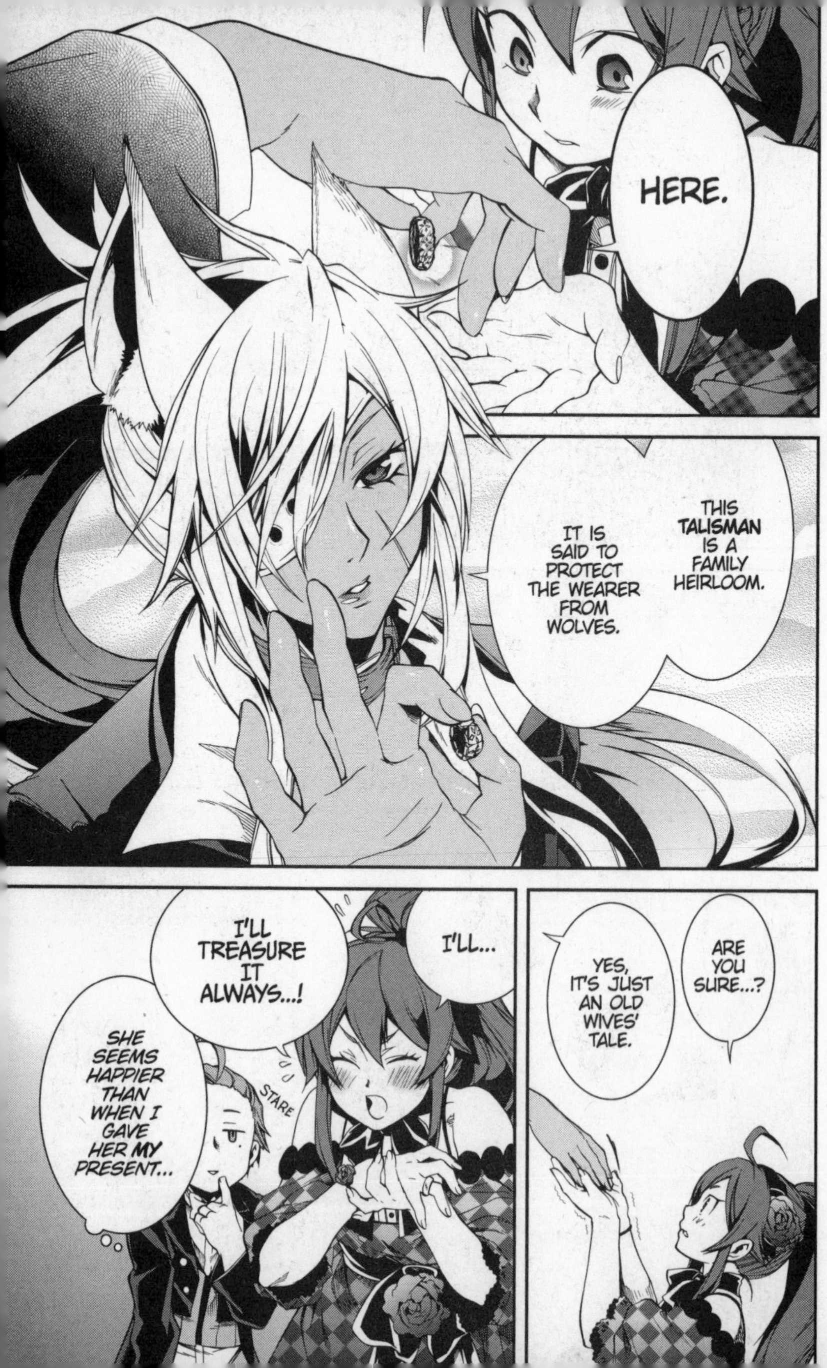
HERE.
THIS TALISMAN IS A FAMILY HEIRLOOM.
IT IS SAID TO PROTECT THE WEARER FROM WOLVES.
ARE YOU SURE...?
YES, IT'S JUST AN OLD WIVES' TALE.
I'LL...
I'LL TREASURE IT ALWAYS...!
STARE
SHE SEEMS HAPPIER THAN WHEN I GAVE HER MY PRESENT...

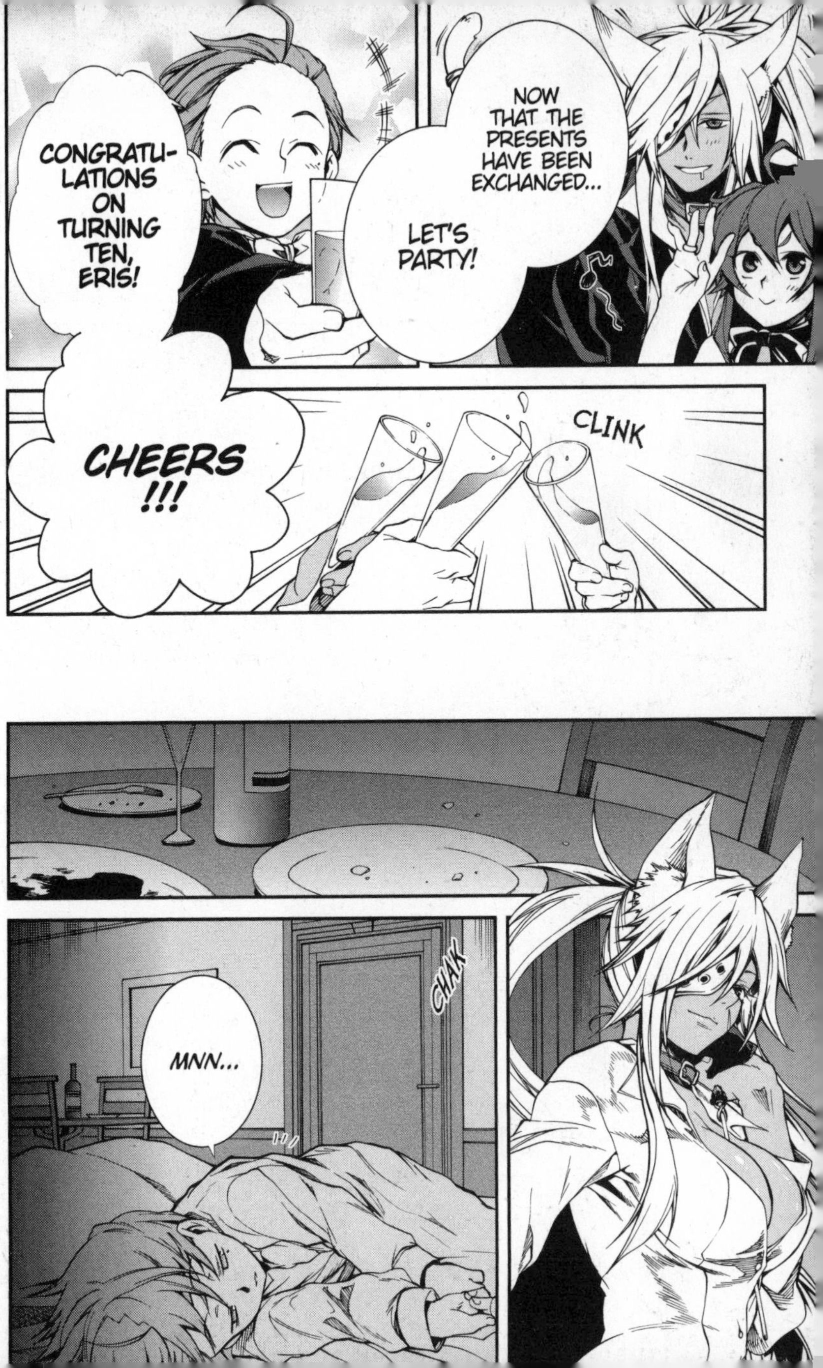
NOW THAT THE PRESENTS HAVE BEEN EXCHANGED...
LET'S PARTY!
CONGRATULATIONS ON TURNING TEN, ERIS!
CLINK
CHEERS !!!
CHAK
MNN...

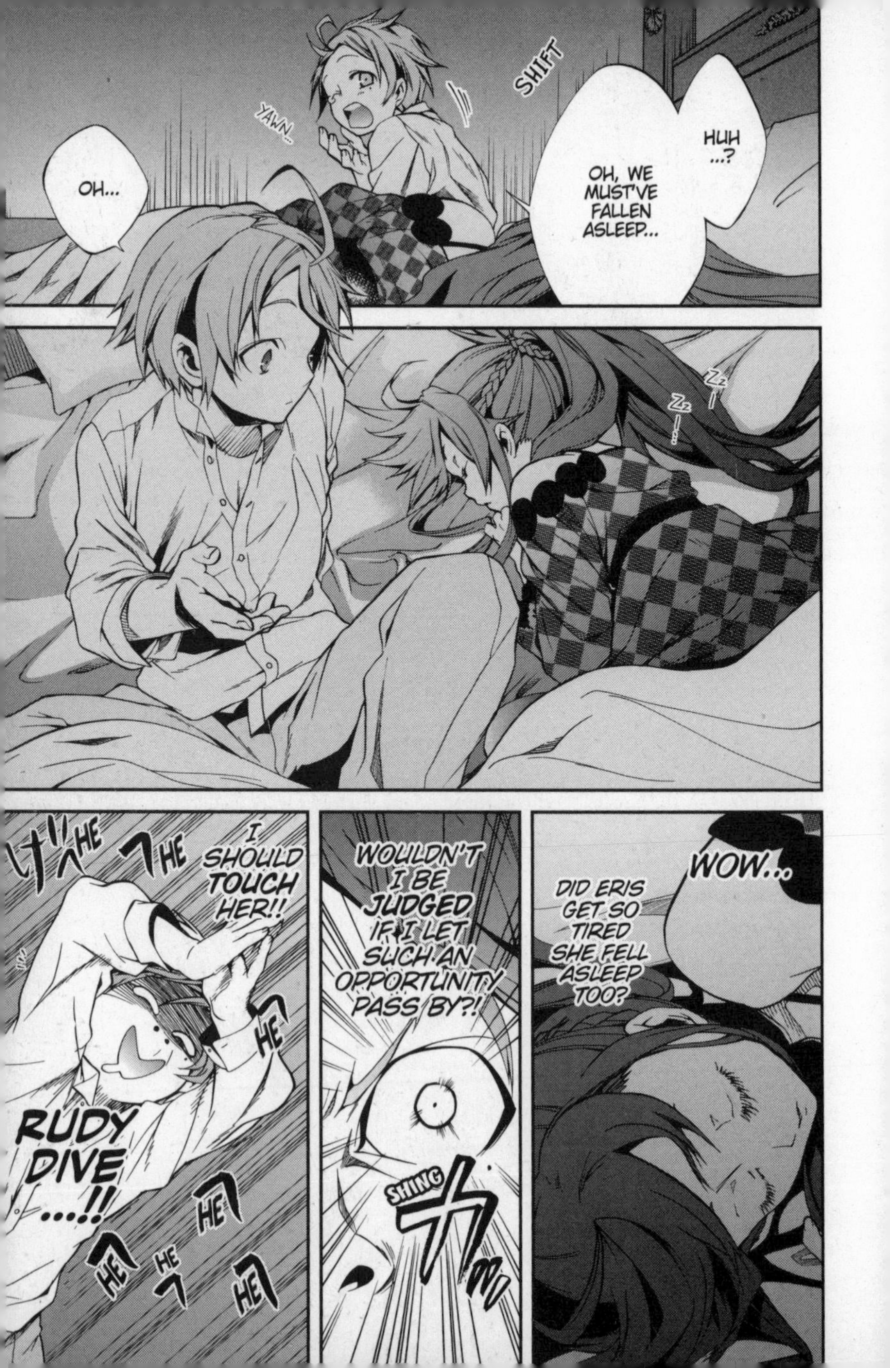
HUH ...?
OH, WE MUST'VE FALLEN ASLEEP...
SHIFT
YAWN...
OH...
Zz
Zz
WOW...
DID ERIS GET SO TIRED SHE FELL ASLEEP TOO?
WOULDN'T I BE JUDGED IF I LET SUCH AN OPPORTUNITY PASS BY?!
SHING
I SHOULD TOUCH HER!!
HE
HE
HE
RUDY DIVE ....!!
HE
HE
HE
HE

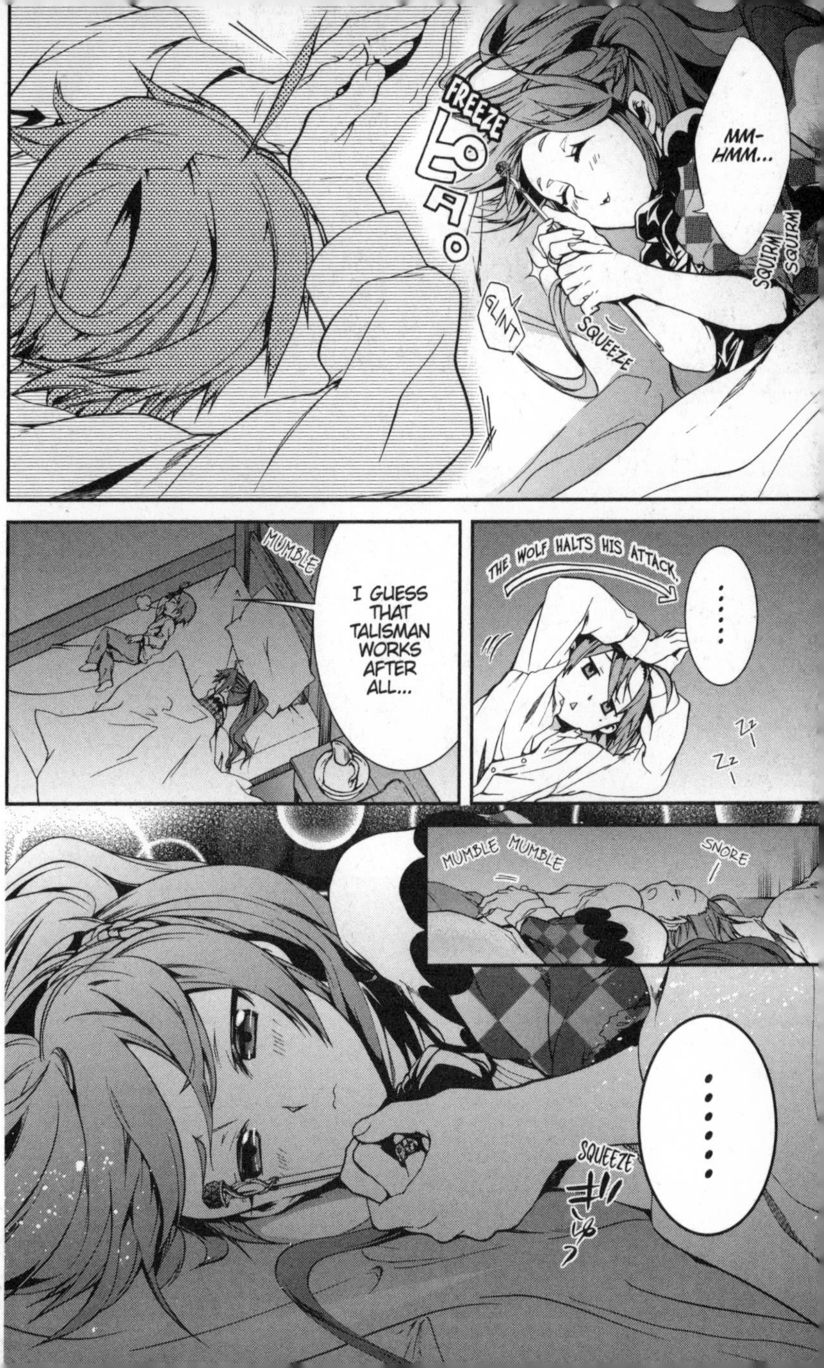
MM-HMM...
SQUIRM SQUIRM
FREEZE
GLINT
SQUEEZE
THE WOLF HALTS HIS ATTACK.
......
Zz Zz
I GUESS THAT TALISMAN WORKS AFTER ALL...
MUMBLE
SNORE
MUMBLE MUMBLE
......
SQUEEZE

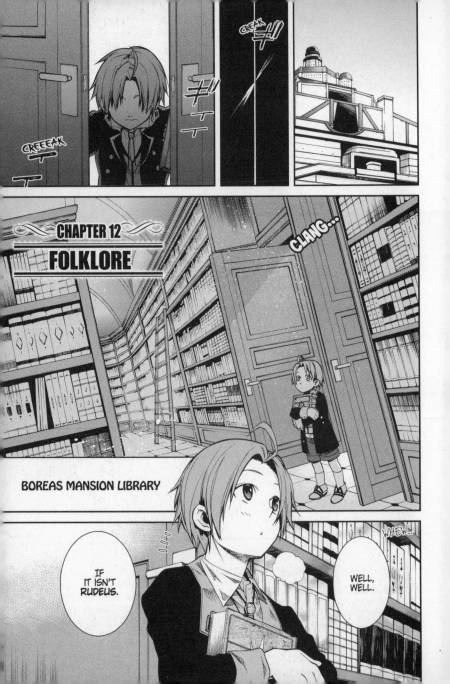

CREAK

CREEEAK

CLANG...

CHAPTER 12
FOLKLORE

BOREAS MANSION LIBRARY

IF IT ISN'T RUDEUS.

WHEW...

WELL, WELL.

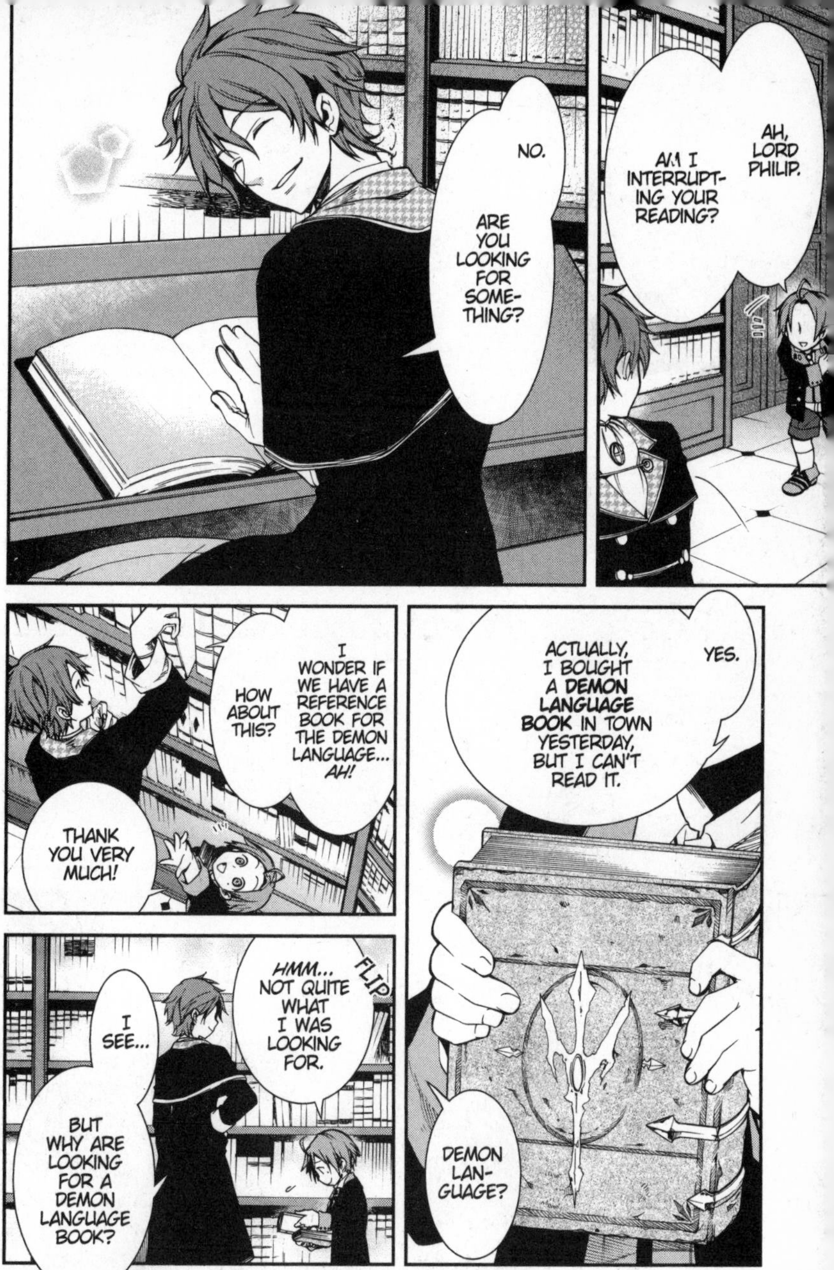
AH, LORD PHILIP.
AM I INTERRUPTING YOUR READING?
NO.
ARE YOU LOOKING FOR SOMETHING?
YES.
ACTUALLY, I BOUGHT A **DEMON LANGUAGE BOOK** IN TOWN YESTERDAY, BUT I CAN'T READ IT.
DEMON LANGUAGE?
I WONDER IF WE HAVE A REFERENCE BOOK FOR THE DEMON LANGUAGE... *AH!*
HOW ABOUT THIS?
THANK YOU VERY MUCH!
FLIP
HMM... NOT QUITE WHAT I WAS LOOKING FOR.
I SEE...
BUT WHY ARE LOOKING FOR A DEMON LANGUAGE BOOK?

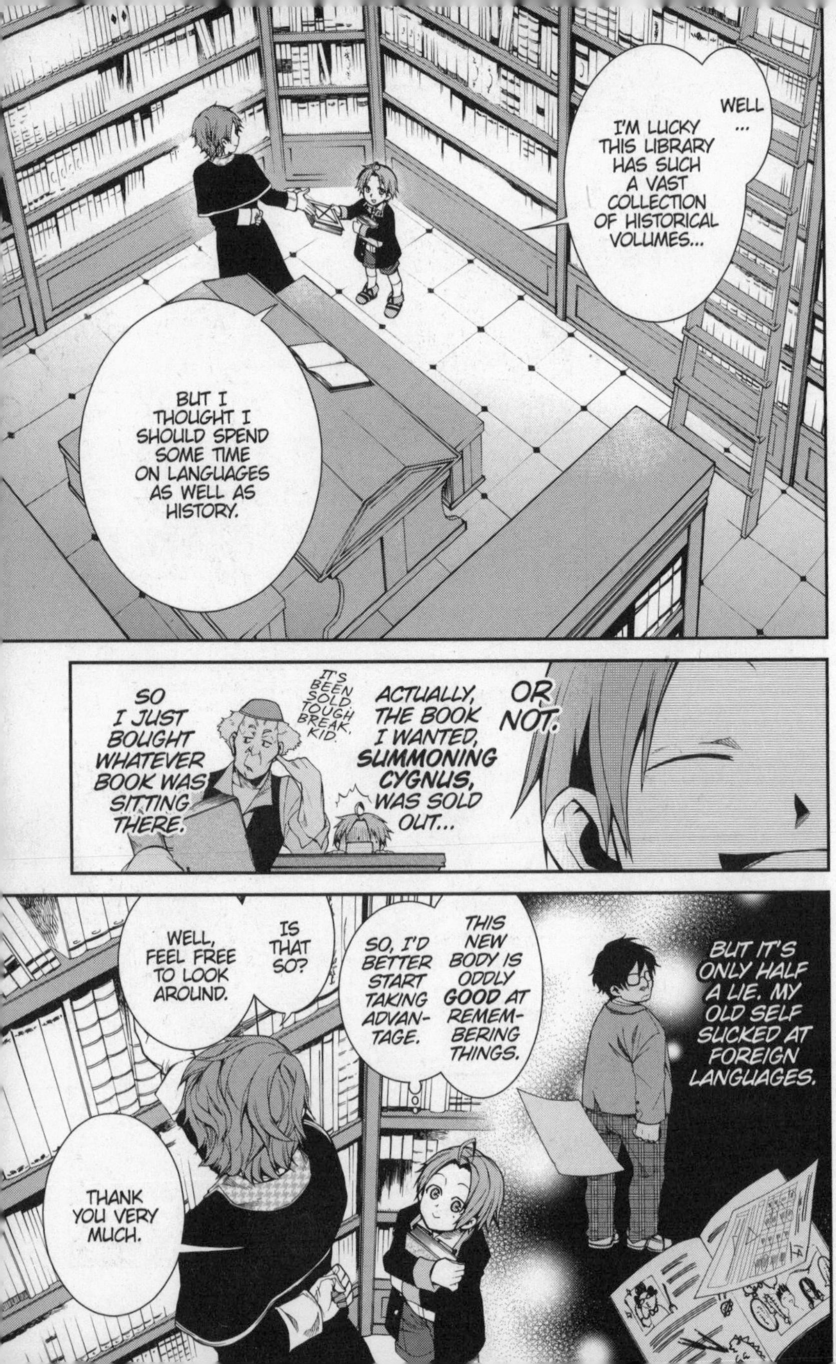
WELL... I'M LUCKY THIS LIBRARY HAS SUCH A VAST COLLECTION OF HISTORICAL VOLUMES...
BUT I THOUGHT I SHOULD SPEND SOME TIME ON LANGUAGES AS WELL AS HISTORY.
OR NOT.
ACTUALLY, THE BOOK I WANTED, SUMMONING CYGNUS, WAS SOLD OUT...
IT'S BEEN SOLD. TOUGH BREAK, KID.
SO I JUST BOUGHT WHATEVER BOOK WAS SITTING THERE.
BUT IT'S ONLY HALF A LIE. MY OLD SELF SUCKED AT FOREIGN LANGUAGES.
THIS NEW BODY IS ODDLY GOOD AT REMEMBERING THINGS.
SO, I'D BETTER START TAKING ADVANTAGE.
IS THAT SO?
WELL, FEEL FREE TO LOOK AROUND.
THANK YOU VERY MUCH.

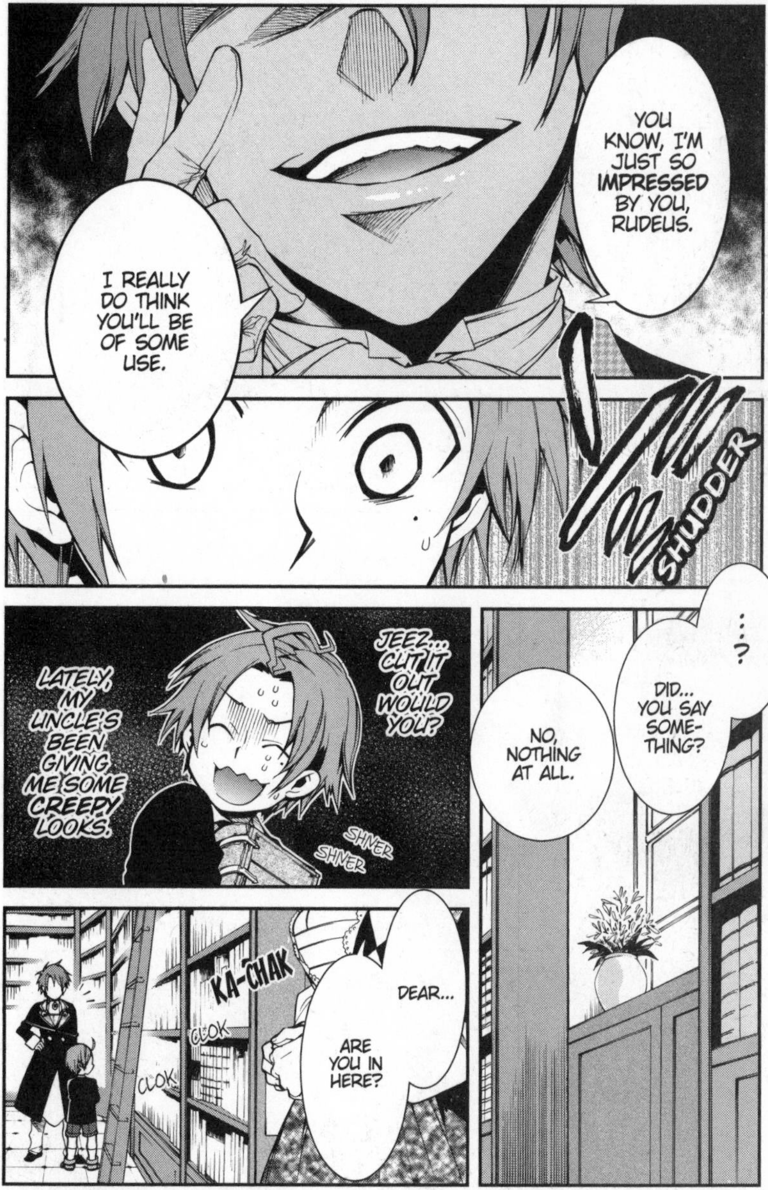
YOU KNOW, I'M JUST SO IMPRESSED BY YOU, RUDEUS.
I REALLY DO THINK YOU'LL BE OF SOME USE.
SHUDDER
...?
DID... YOU SAY SOME-THING?
NO, NOTHING AT ALL.
JEEZ... CUT IT OUT WOULD YOU?
LATELY, MY UNCLE'S BEEN GIVING ME SOME CREEPY LOOKS.
SHIVER
SHIVER
DEAR...
ARE YOU IN HERE?
KA-CHAK
CLOK
CLOK!

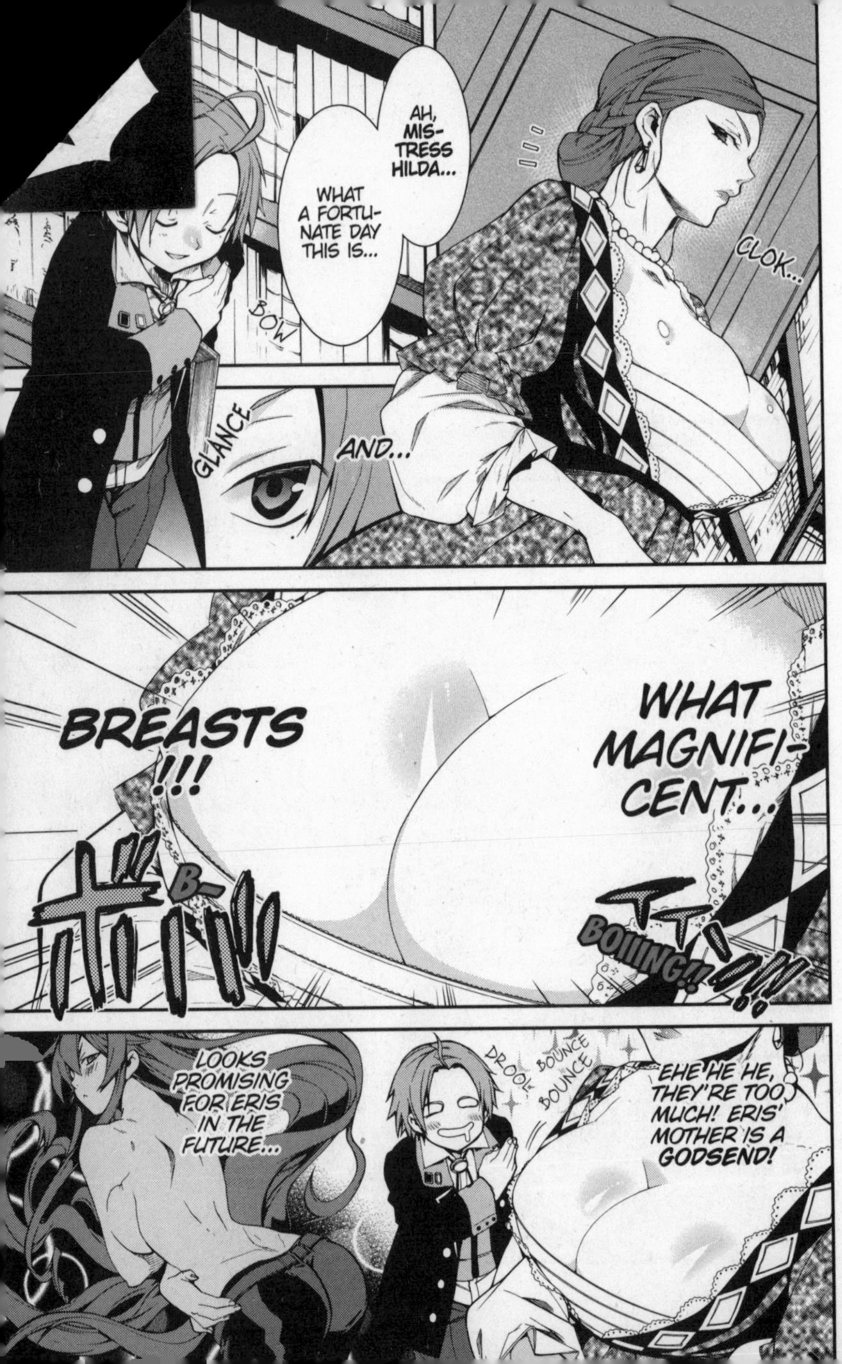
CLOK...
AH, MIS-TRESS HILDA...
WHAT A FORTU-NATE DAY THIS IS...
BOW
AND...
GLANCE
WHAT MAGNIFI-CENT...
BOIIING!!
BREASTS!!!
B-
EHE HE HE, THEY'RE TOO MUCH! ERIS' MOTHER IS A GODSEND!
BOUNCE BOUNCE
DROOL
LOOKS PROMISING FOR ERIS IN THE FUTURE...

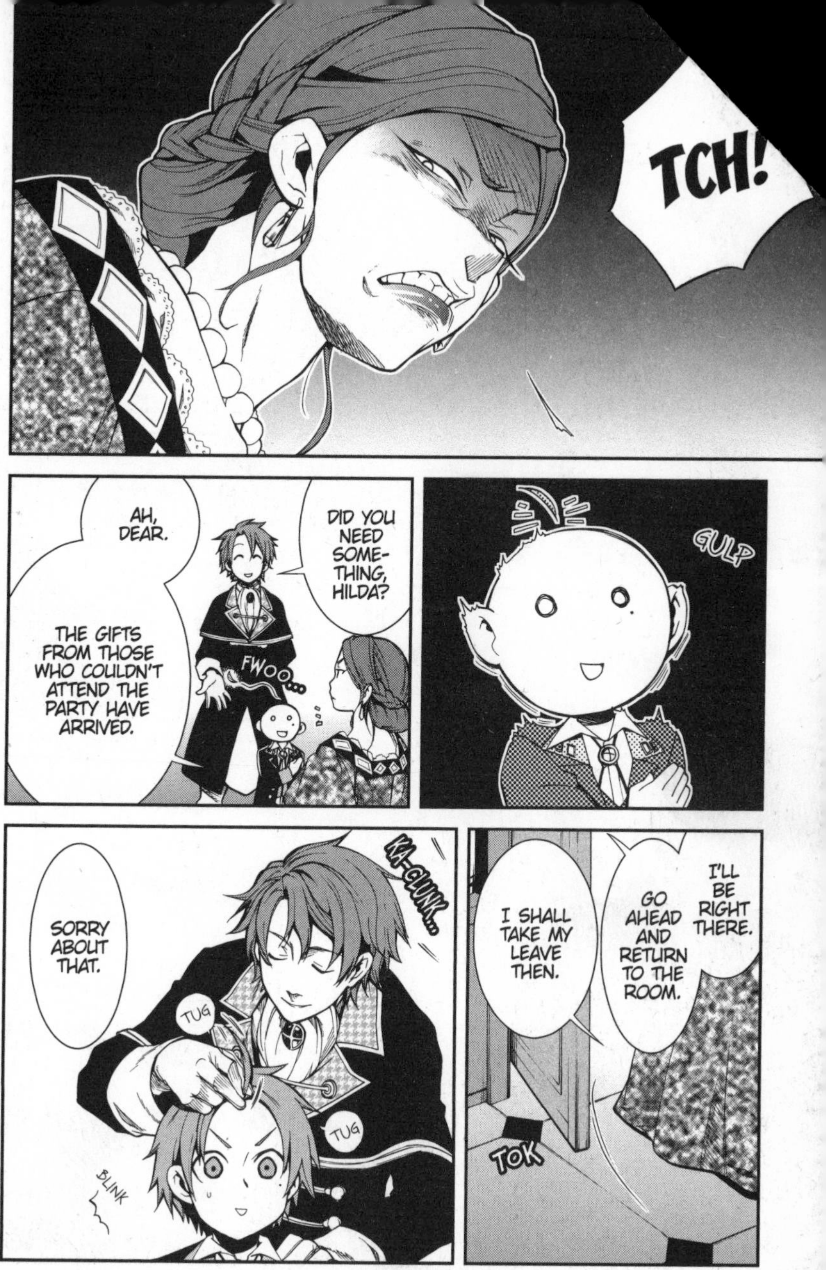
TCH!
GULP
DID YOU NEED SOME-THING, HILDA?
AH, DEAR.
THE GIFTS FROM THOSE WHO COULDN'T ATTEND THE PARTY HAVE ARRIVED.
FWOO...
I'LL BE RIGHT THERE.
GO AHEAD AND RETURN TO THE ROOM.
I SHALL TAKE MY LEAVE THEN.
TOK
KA-CLUNK...
SORRY ABOUT THAT.
TUG
TUG
BLINK

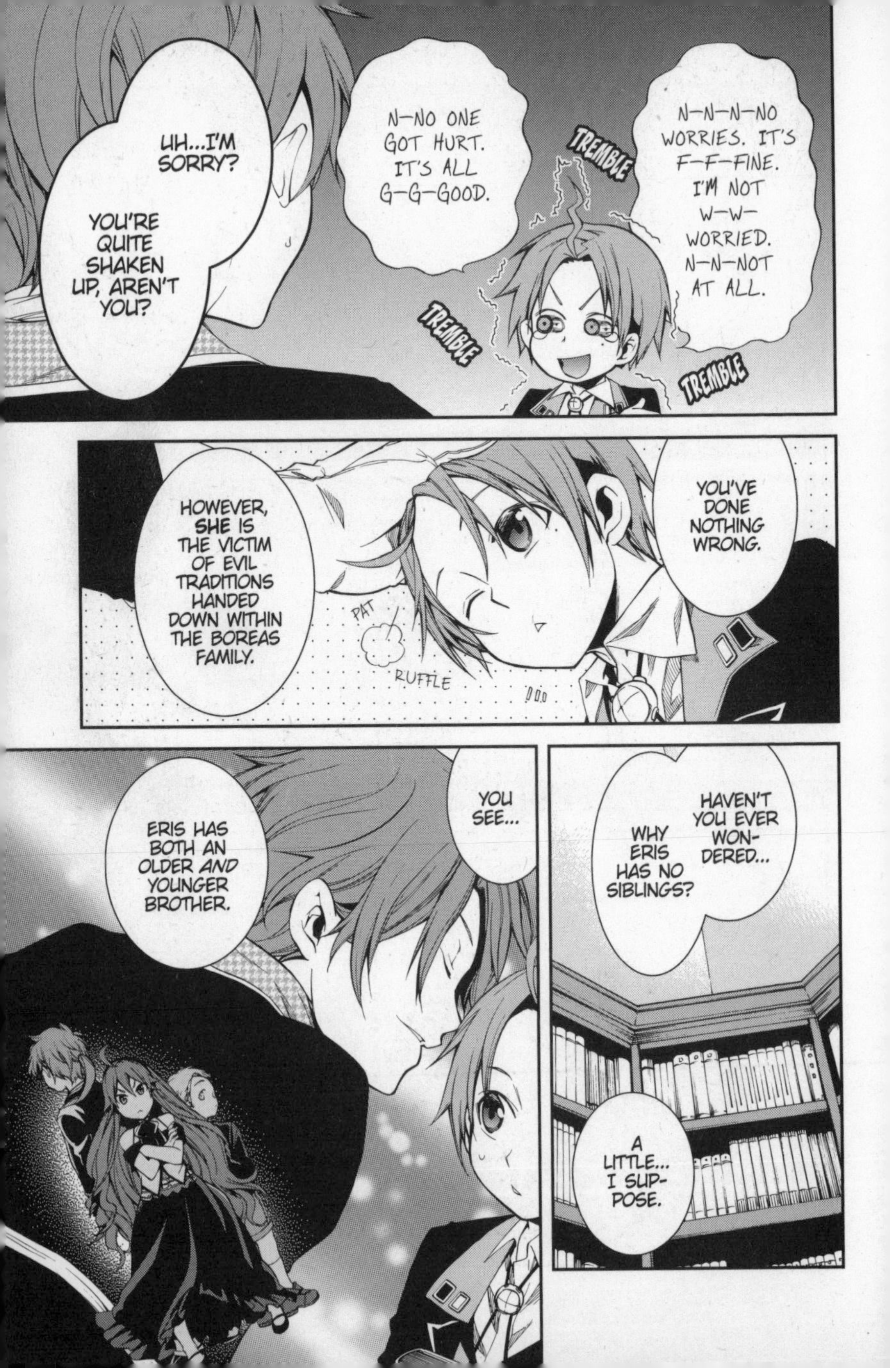
N-N-N-NO WORRIES. IT'S F-F-FINE. I'M NOT W-W-WORRIED. N-N-NOT AT ALL.
TREMBLE
N-NO ONE GOT HURT. IT'S ALL G-G-GOOD.
UH...I'M SORRY?
YOU'RE QUITE SHAKEN UP, AREN'T YOU?
TREMBLE
TREMBLE
YOU'VE DONE NOTHING WRONG.
PAT
RUFFLE
HOWEVER, SHE IS THE VICTIM OF EVIL TRADITIONS HANDED DOWN WITHIN THE BOREAS FAMILY.
HAVEN'T YOU EVER WONDERED...
WHY ERIS HAS NO SIBLINGS?
A LITTLE... I SUPPOSE.
YOU SEE...
ERIS HAS BOTH AN OLDER *AND* YOUNGER BROTHER.

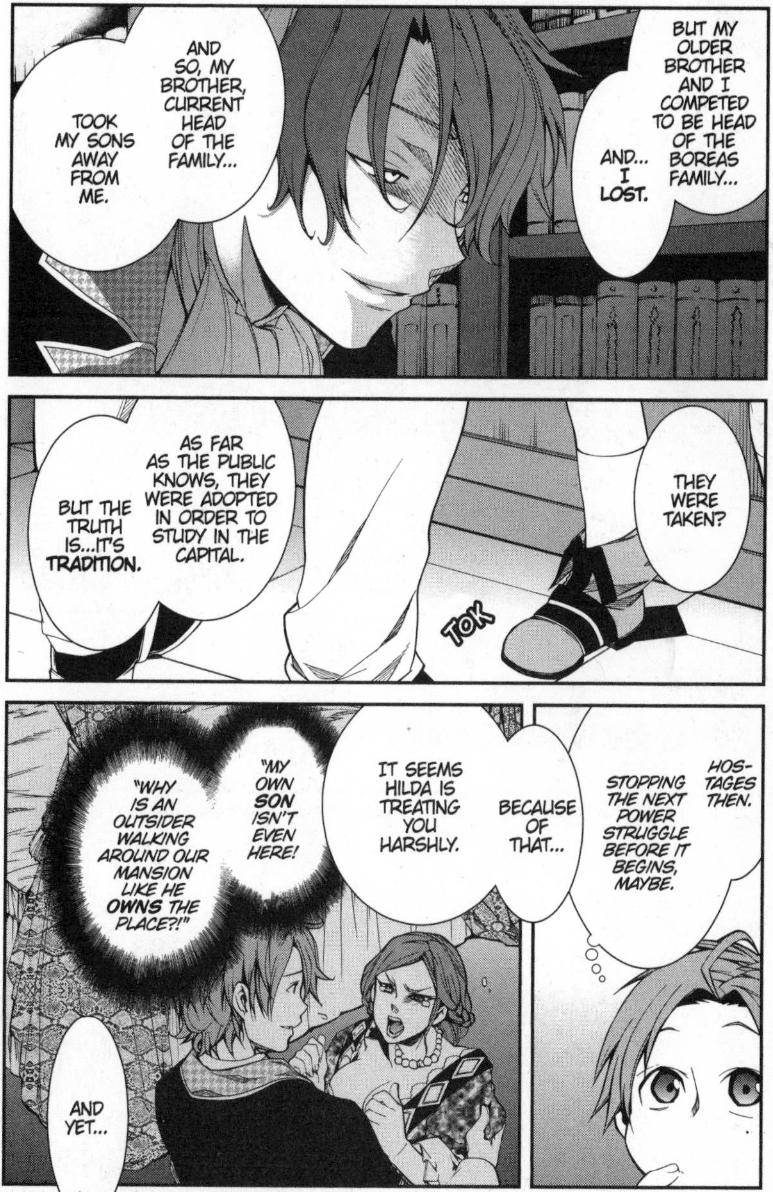
BUT MY OLDER BROTHER AND I COMPETED TO BE HEAD OF THE BOREAS FAMILY...
AND... I **LOST.**
AND SO, MY BROTHER, CURRENT HEAD OF THE FAMILY...
TOOK MY SONS AWAY FROM ME.
THEY WERE TAKEN?
TOK
AS FAR AS THE PUBLIC KNOWS, THEY WERE ADOPTED IN ORDER TO STUDY IN THE CAPITAL.
BUT THE TRUTH IS...IT'S **TRADITION.**
HOS-TAGES THEN.
STOPPING THE NEXT POWER STRUGGLE BEFORE IT BEGINS, MAYBE.
BECAUSE OF THAT...
IT SEEMS HILDA IS TREATING YOU HARSHLY.
"MY OWN **SON** ISN'T EVEN HERE!
"WHY IS AN OUTSIDER WALKING AROUND OUR MANSION LIKE HE **OWNS** THE PLACE?!"
AND YET...

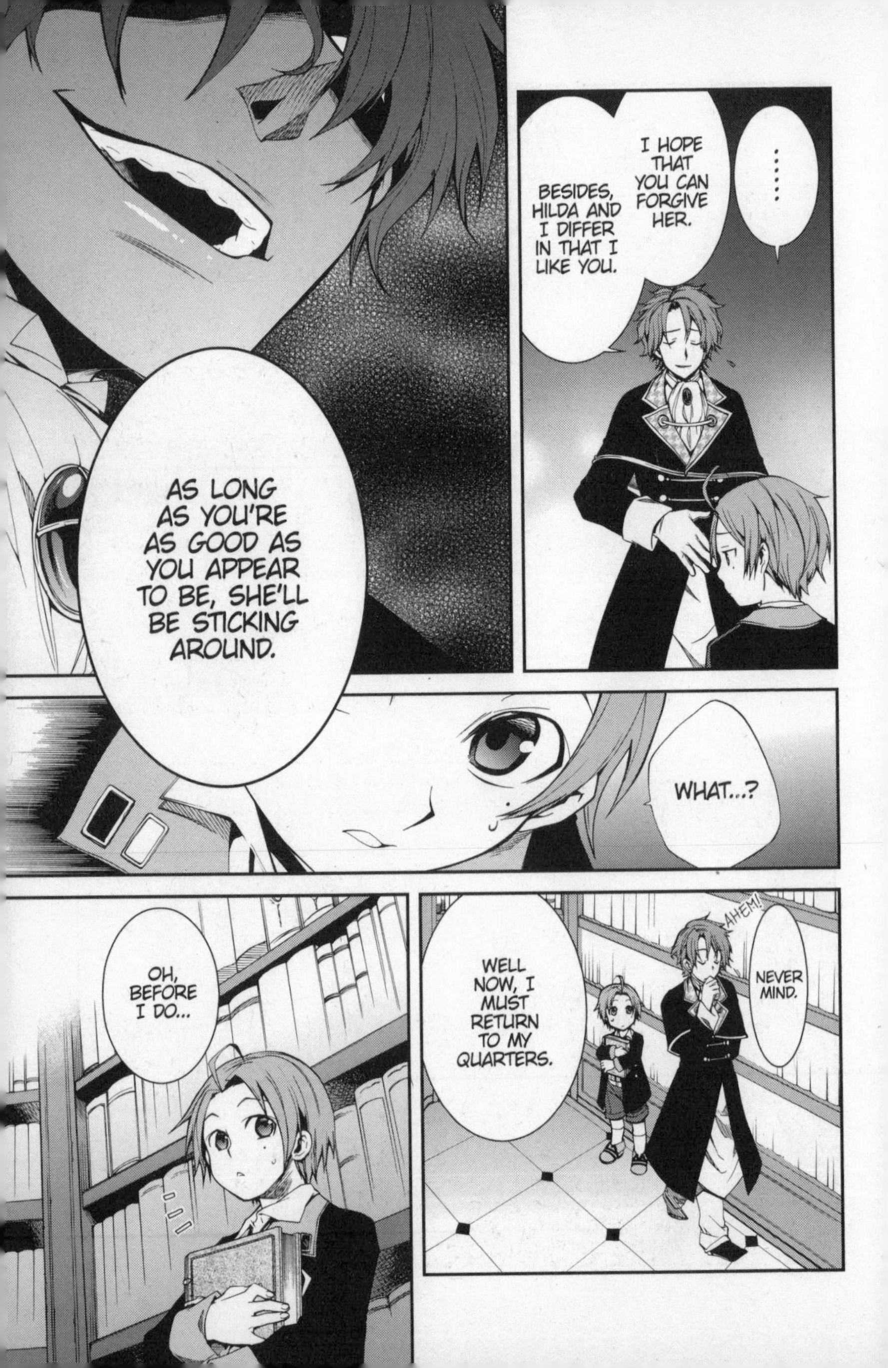
......
I HOPE THAT YOU CAN FORGIVE HER.
BESIDES, HILDA AND I DIFFER IN THAT I LIKE YOU.
AS LONG AS YOU'RE AS GOOD AS YOU APPEAR TO BE, SHE'LL BE STICKING AROUND.
WHAT...?
AHEM!
NEVER MIND.
WELL NOW, I MUST RETURN TO MY QUARTERS.
OH, BEFORE I DO...

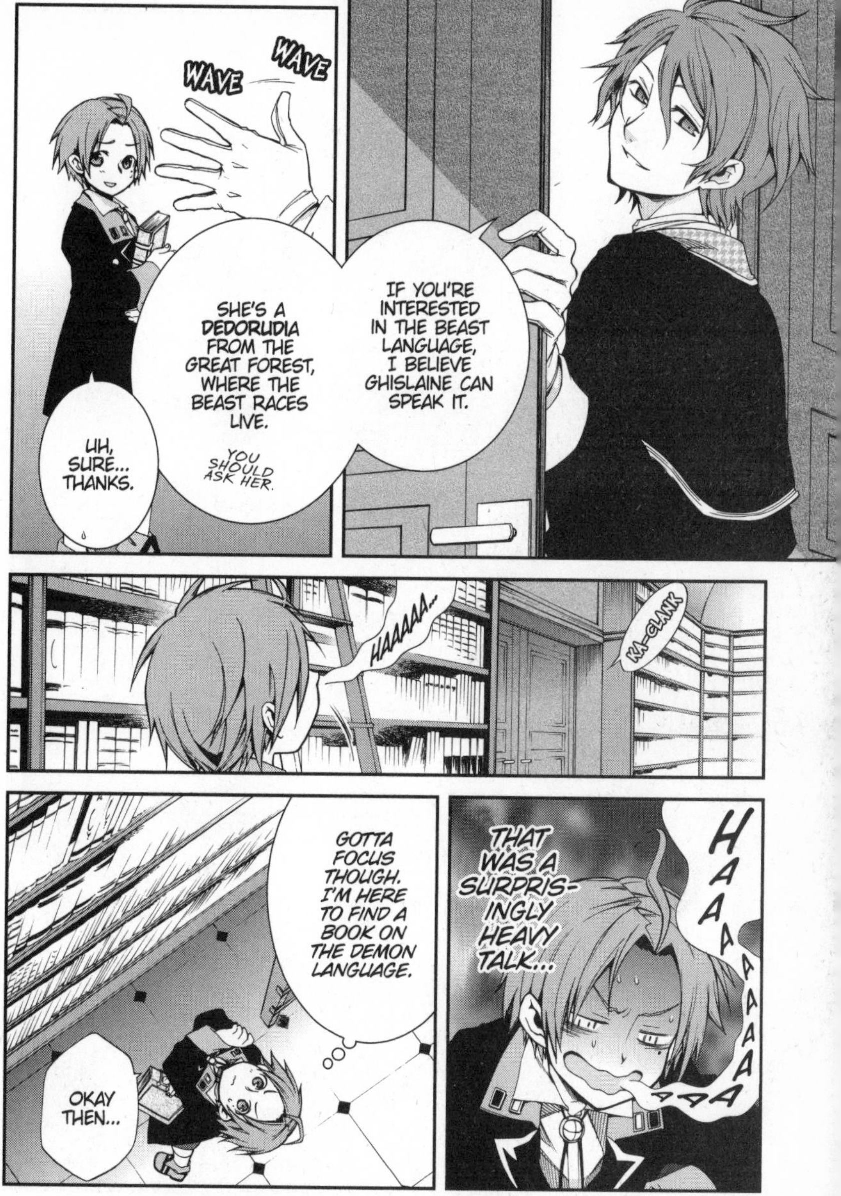
IF YOU'RE INTERESTED IN THE BEAST LANGUAGE, I BELIEVE GHISLAINE CAN SPEAK IT.
SHE'S A DEDORUDIA FROM THE GREAT FOREST, WHERE THE BEAST RACES LIVE.
YOU SHOULD ASK HER.
WAVE
WAVE
UH, SURE... THANKS.
KA-CLANK
HAAAAA...
HAAAAAAAAAAAAA
THAT WAS A SURPRISINGLY HEAVY TALK...
GOTTA FOCUS THOUGH. I'M HERE TO FIND A BOOK ON THE DEMON LANGUAGE.
OKAY THEN...

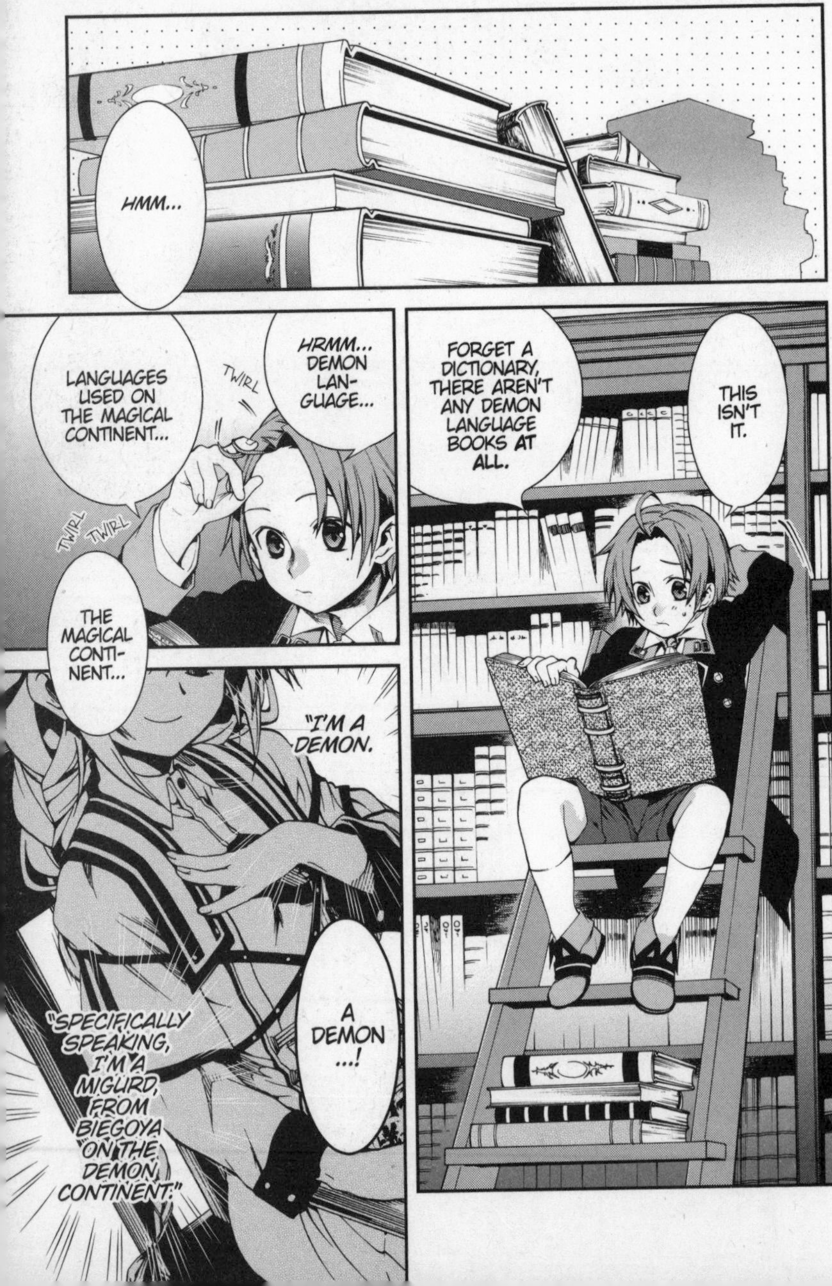
HMM...
THIS ISN'T IT.
FORGET A DICTIONARY, THERE AREN'T ANY DEMON LANGUAGE BOOKS AT ALL.
HRMM... DEMON LAN-GUAGE...
LANGUAGES USED ON THE MAGICAL CONTINENT...
TWIRL
TWIRL TWIRL
THE MAGICAL CONTI-NENT...
"I'M A DEMON.
A DEMON ...!
"SPECIFICALLY SPEAKING, I'M A MIGURD, FROM BIEGOYA ON THE DEMON CONTINENT."

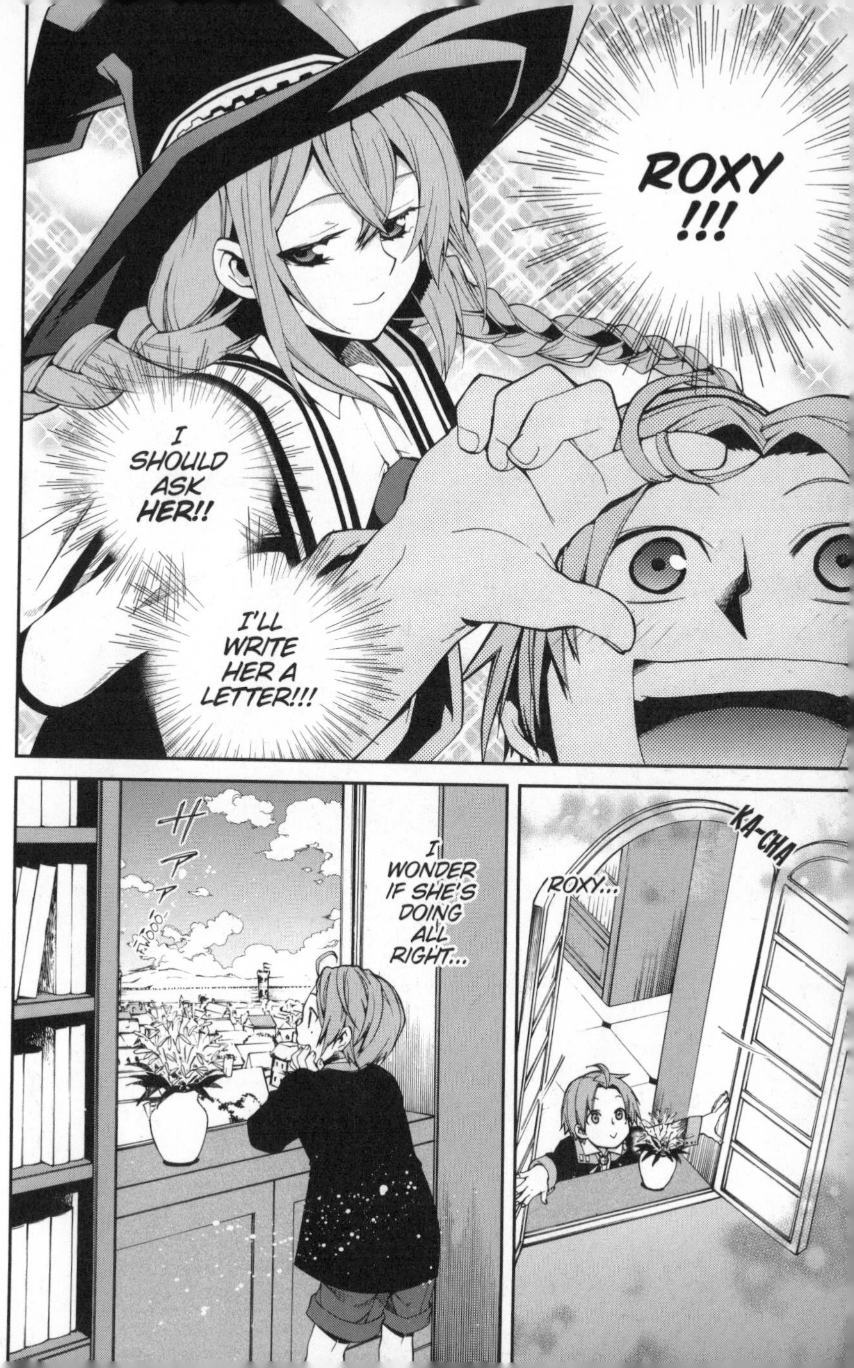
ROXY !!!
I SHOULD ASK HER!!
I'LL WRITE HER A LETTER!!!
KA-CHA
ROXY...
I WONDER IF SHE'S DOING ALL RIGHT...
ザァァ
FWOOO

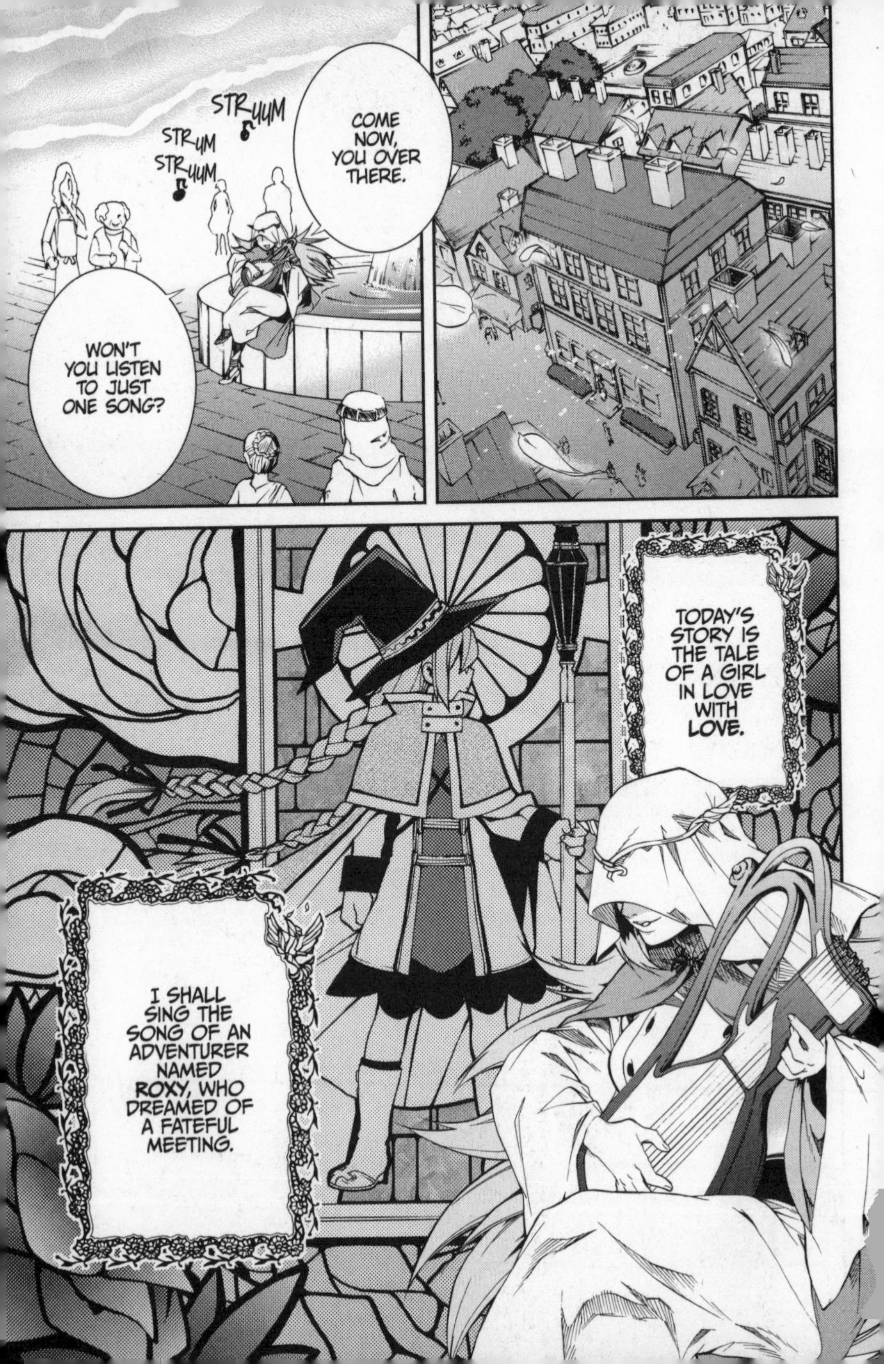
COME NOW, YOU OVER THERE.
STRUUM
STRUM STRUUM
WON'T YOU LISTEN TO JUST ONE SONG?
TODAY'S STORY IS THE TALE OF A GIRL IN LOVE WITH **LOVE.**
I SHALL SING THE SONG OF AN ADVENTURER NAMED **ROXY,** WHO DREAMED OF A FATEFUL MEETING.

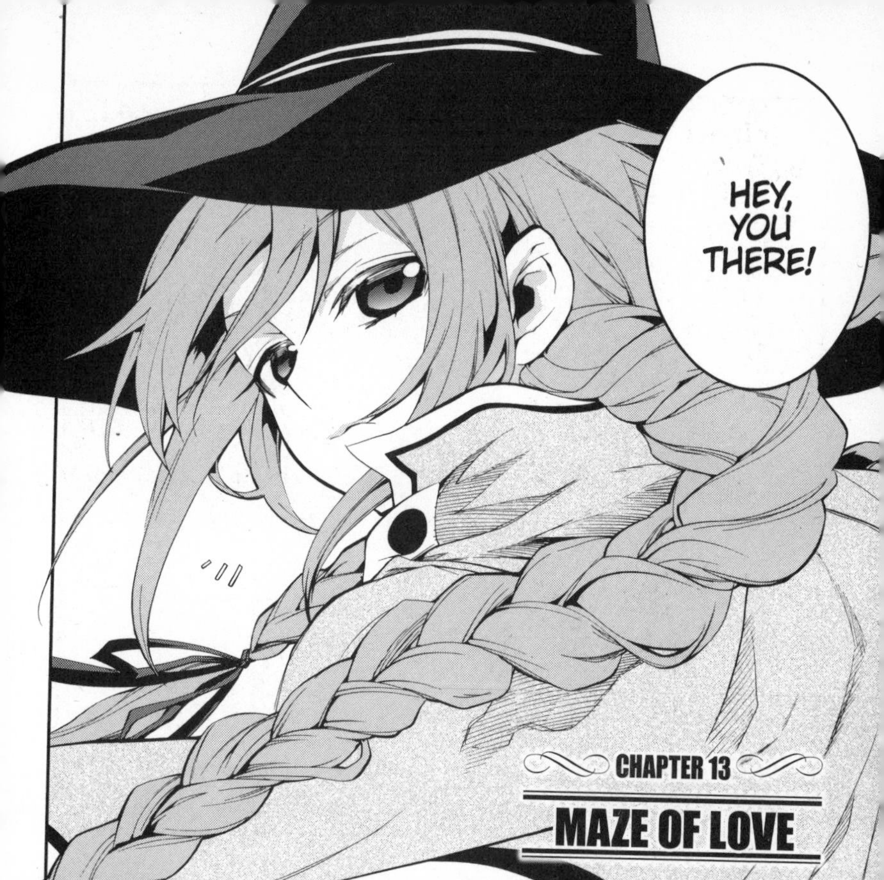
HEY, YOU THERE!
CHAPTER 13
MAZE OF LOVE

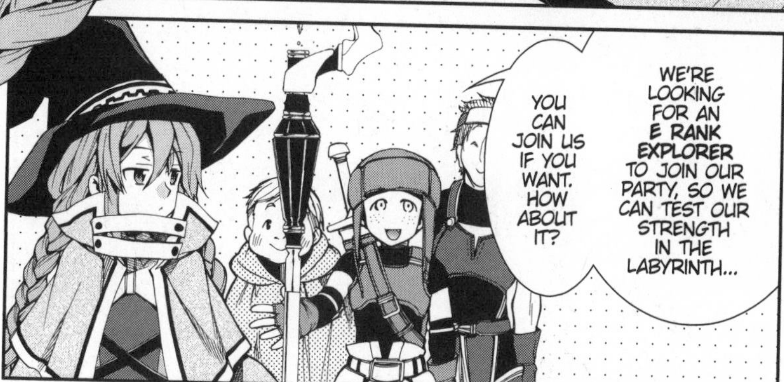
WE'RE LOOKING FOR AN E RANK EXPLORER TO JOIN OUR PARTY, SO WE CAN TEST OUR STRENGTH IN THE LABYRINTH...
YOU CAN JOIN US IF YOU WANT. HOW ABOUT IT?

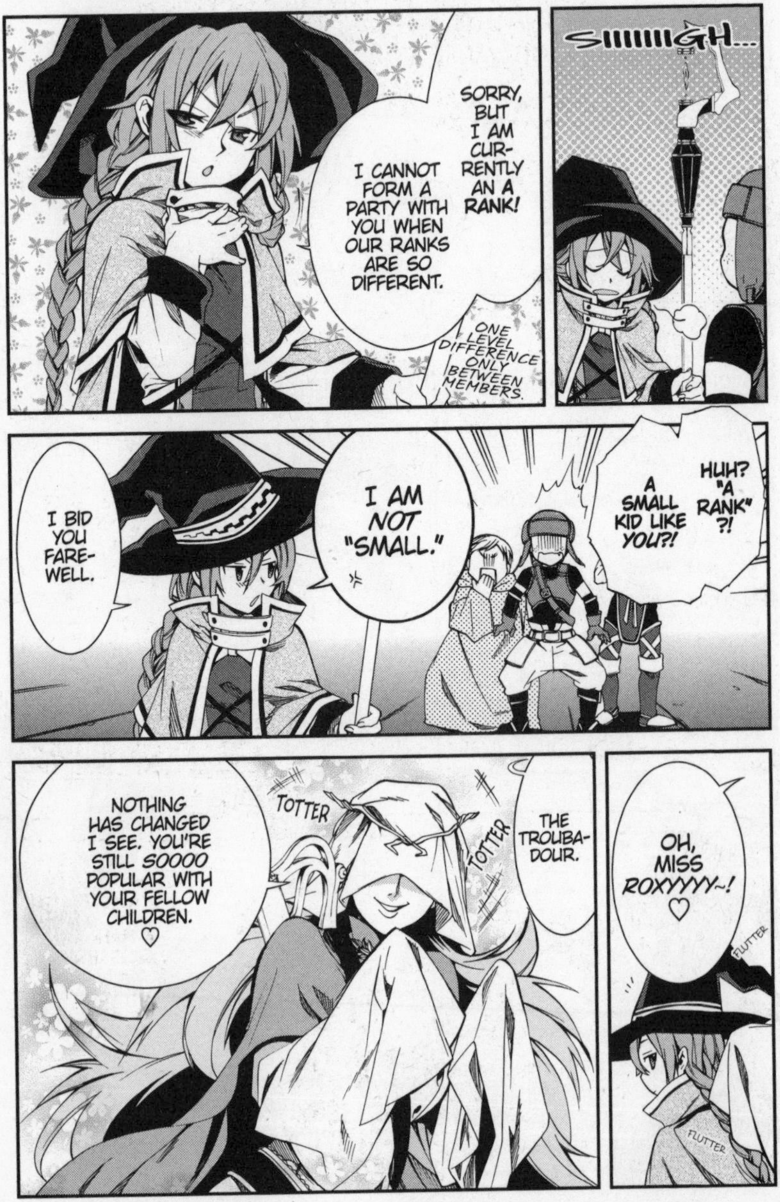
SIIIIIIGH...
SORRY, BUT I AM CURRENTLY AN A RANK!
I CANNOT FORM A PARTY WITH YOU WHEN OUR RANKS ARE SO DIFFERENT.
ONE LEVEL DIFFERENCE ONLY BETWEEN MEMBERS.
HUH? "A RANK" ?!
A SMALL KID LIKE YOU?!
I AM NOT "SMALL."
I BID YOU FAREWELL.
OH, MISS ROXYYYY~! ♡
FLUTTER
FLUTTER
TOTTER
TOTTER
THE TROUBADOUR.
NOTHING HAS CHANGED I SEE. YOU'RE STILL SOOOO POPULAR WITH YOUR FELLOW CHILDREN. ♡

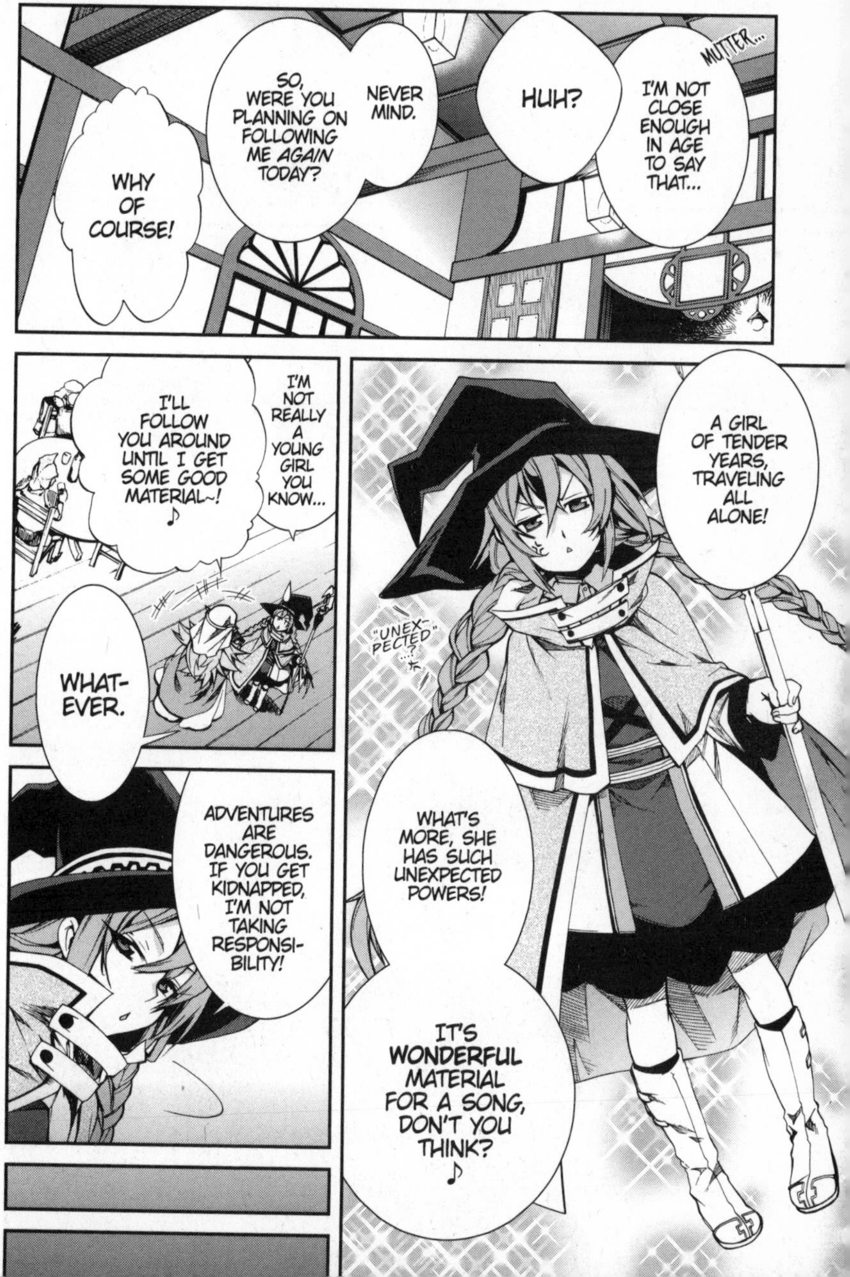
MUTTER...
I'M NOT CLOSE ENOUGH IN AGE TO SAY THAT...
HUH?
NEVER MIND.
SO, WERE YOU PLANNING ON FOLLOWING ME *AGAIN* TODAY?
WHY OF COURSE!
A GIRL OF TENDER YEARS, TRAVELING ALL ALONE!
"UNEXPECTED"...?
WHAT'S MORE, SHE HAS SUCH UNEXPECTED POWERS!
IT'S **WONDERFUL** MATERIAL FOR A SONG, DON'T YOU THINK? ♪
I'M NOT REALLY A YOUNG GIRL YOU KNOW...
I'LL FOLLOW YOU AROUND UNTIL I GET SOME GOOD MATERIAL~! ♪
WHAT-EVER.
ADVENTURES ARE DANGEROUS. IF YOU GET KIDNAPPED, I'M NOT TAKING RESPONSI-BILITY!

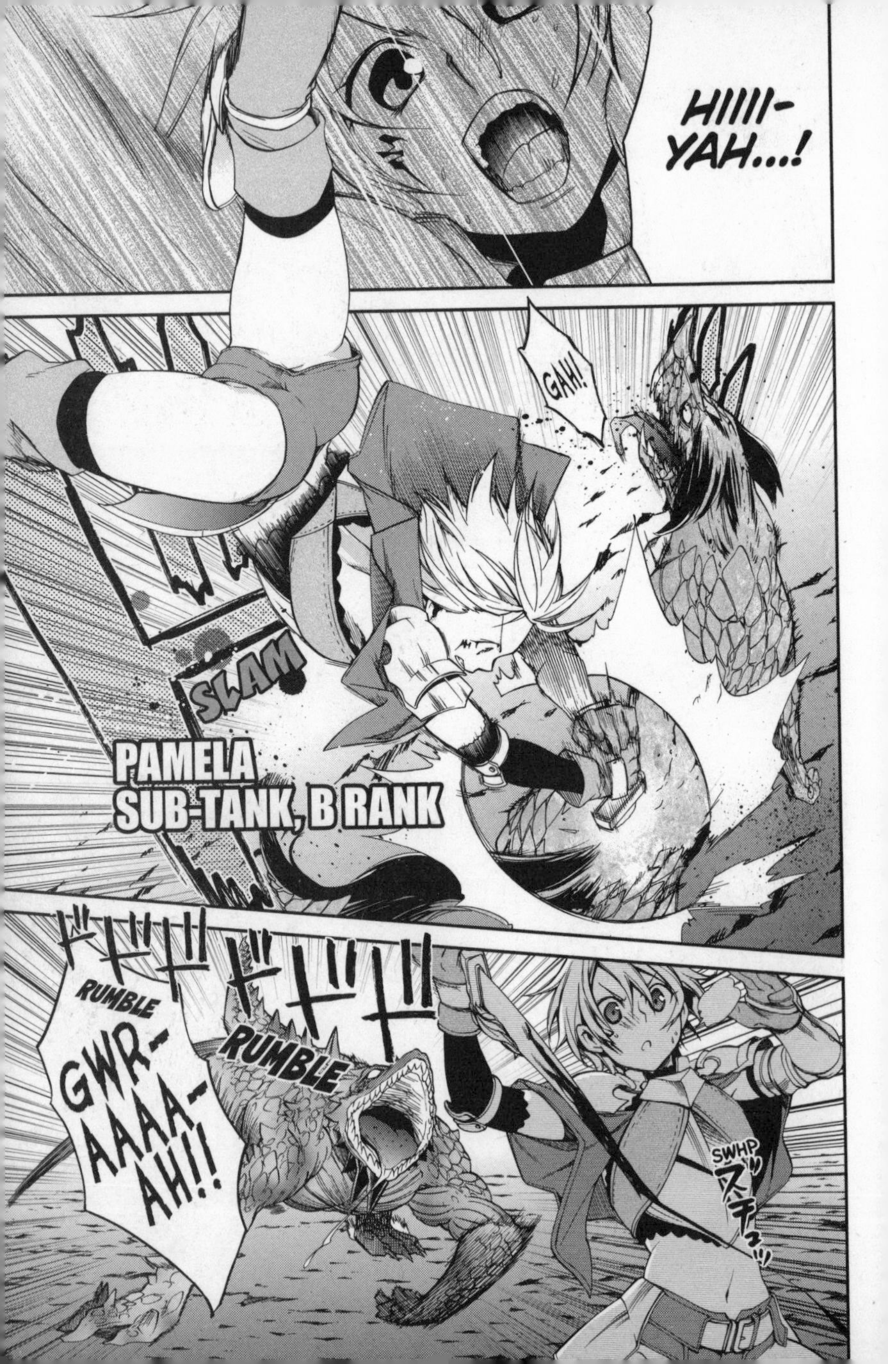
HIIII-
YAH...!
GAH!
SLAM
PAMELA
SUB-TANK, B RANK
SWHP
ズチュ!!
ドドドド
RUMBLE
RUMBLE
GWR-
AAAA-
AH!!

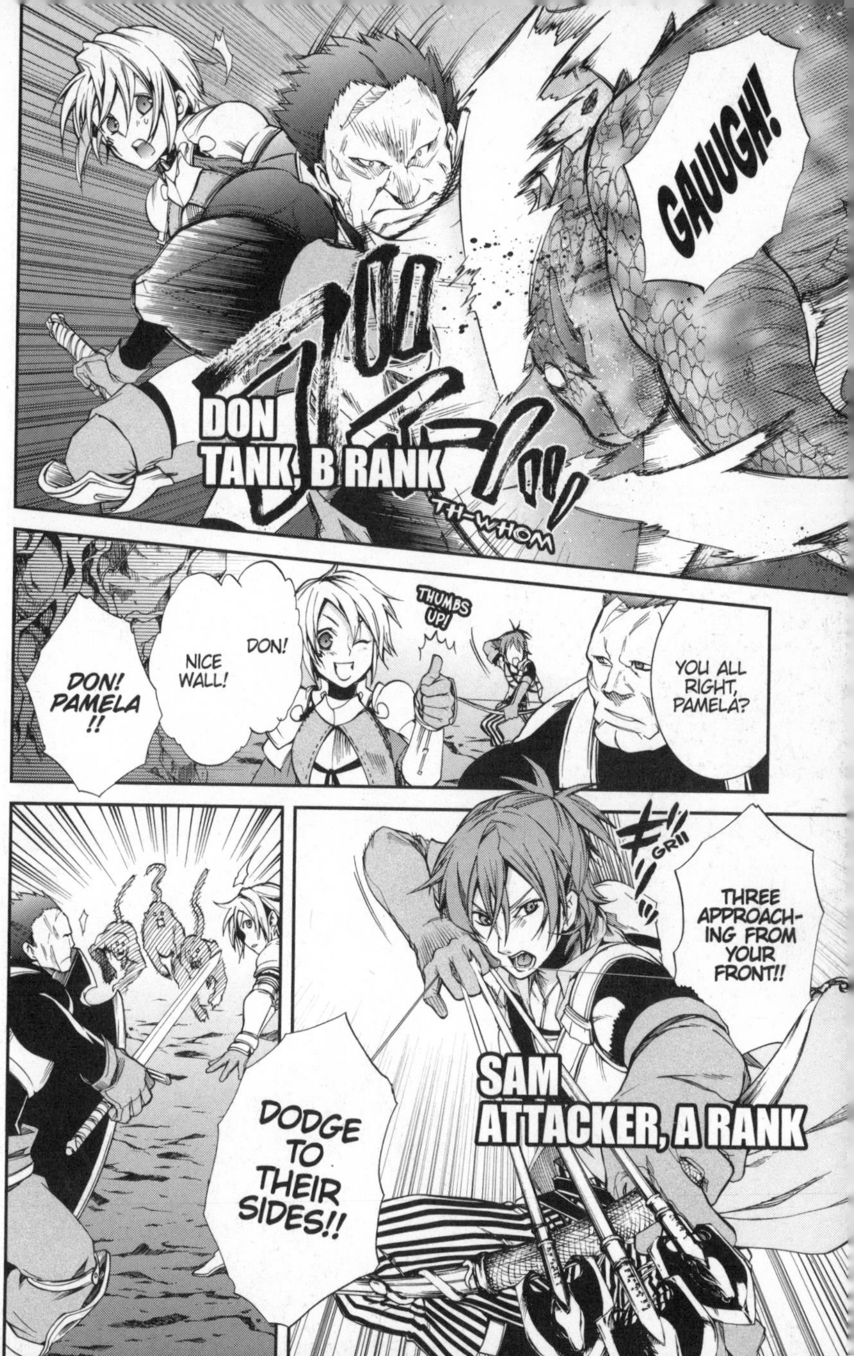
GAUUGH!
DON
TANK, B RANK
TH-WHOM
YOU ALL RIGHT, PAMELA?
THUMBS UP!
DON! NICE WALL!
DON! PAMELA !!
GRII
THREE APPROACHING FROM YOUR FRONT!!
SAM
ATTACKER, A RANK
DODGE TO THEIR SIDES!!

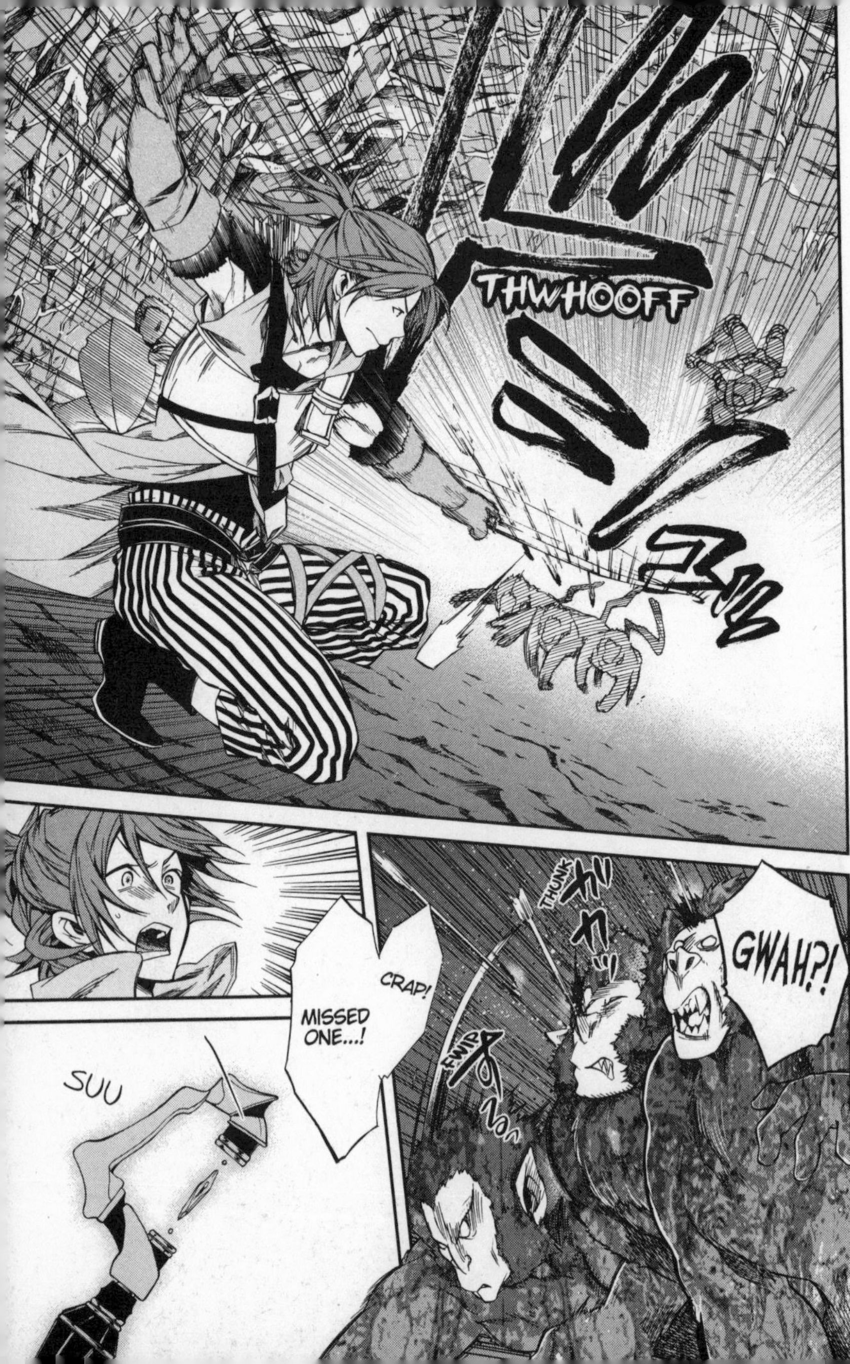
THWHOOFF
THUNK
GWAH?!
FWIP
CRAP!
MISSED ONE...!
SUU

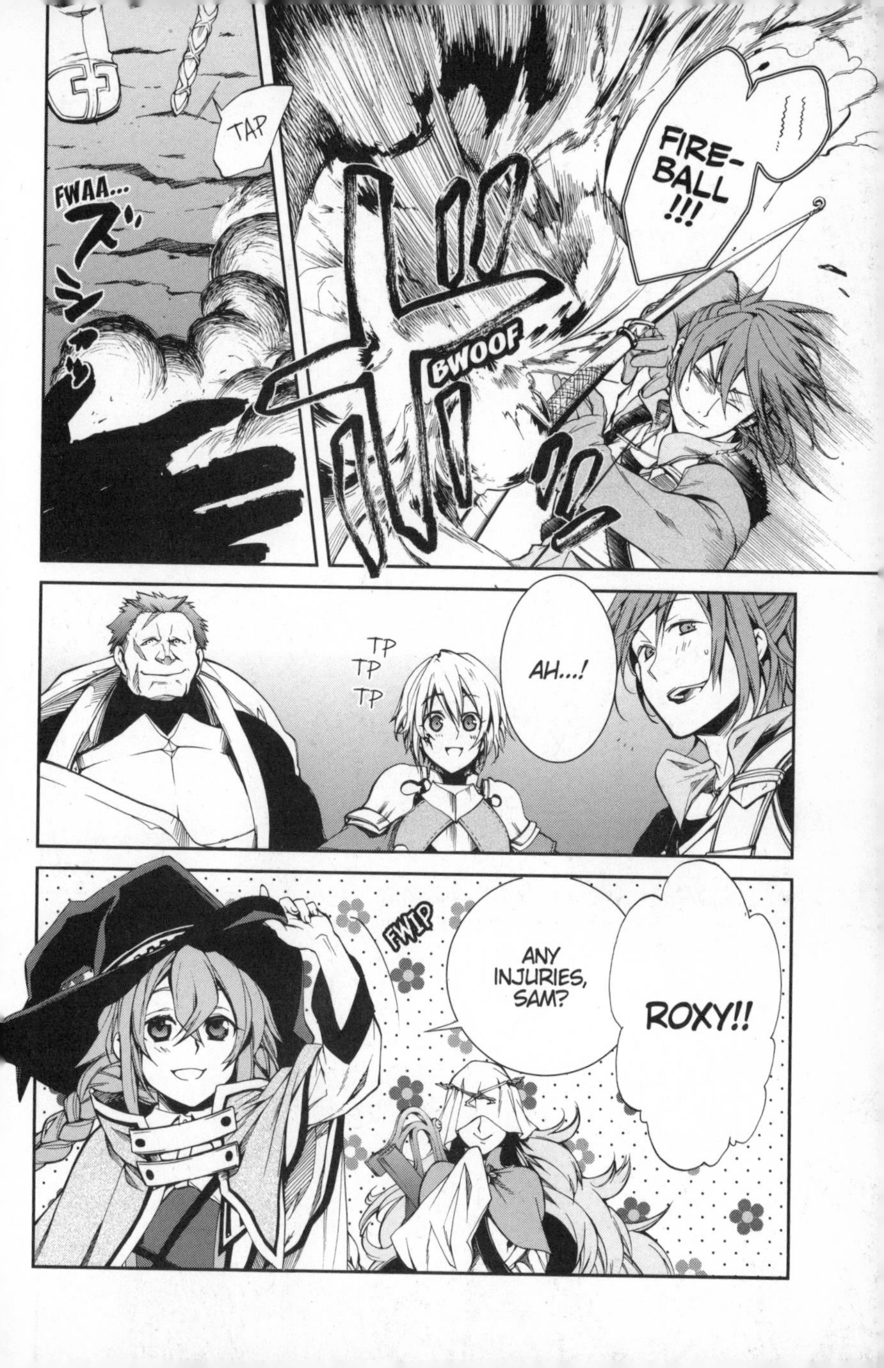
FIRE-BALL!!!
BWOOF
TAP
FWAA...
AH...!
TP TP TP
ROXY!!
ANY INJURIES, SAM?
FWIP

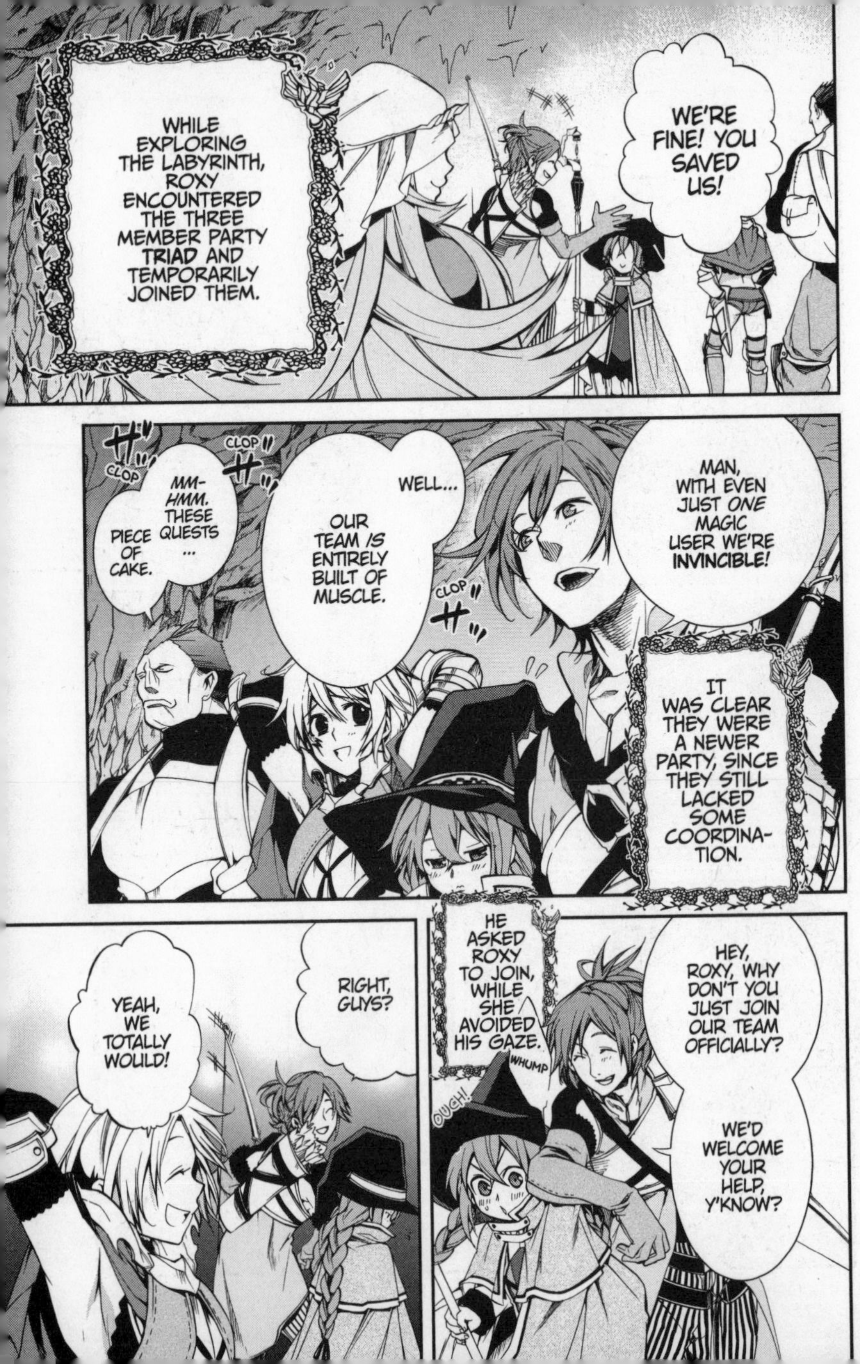
WE'RE FINE! YOU SAVED US!
WHILE EXPLORING THE LABYRINTH, ROXY ENCOUNTERED THE THREE MEMBER PARTY TRIAD AND TEMPORARILY JOINED THEM.
MAN, WITH EVEN JUST ONE MAGIC USER WE'RE INVINCIBLE!
WELL...
OUR TEAM IS ENTIRELY BUILT OF MUSCLE.
CLOP
CLOP
MM-HMM. THESE QUESTS...
PIECE OF CAKE.
CLOP
IT WAS CLEAR THEY WERE A NEWER PARTY, SINCE THEY STILL LACKED SOME COORDINATION.
HEY, ROXY, WHY DON'T YOU JUST JOIN OUR TEAM OFFICIALLY?
HE ASKED ROXY TO JOIN, WHILE SHE AVOIDED HIS GAZE.
WHUMP
OUCH!
WE'D WELCOME YOUR HELP, Y'KNOW?
RIGHT, GUYS?
YEAH, WE TOTALLY WOULD!

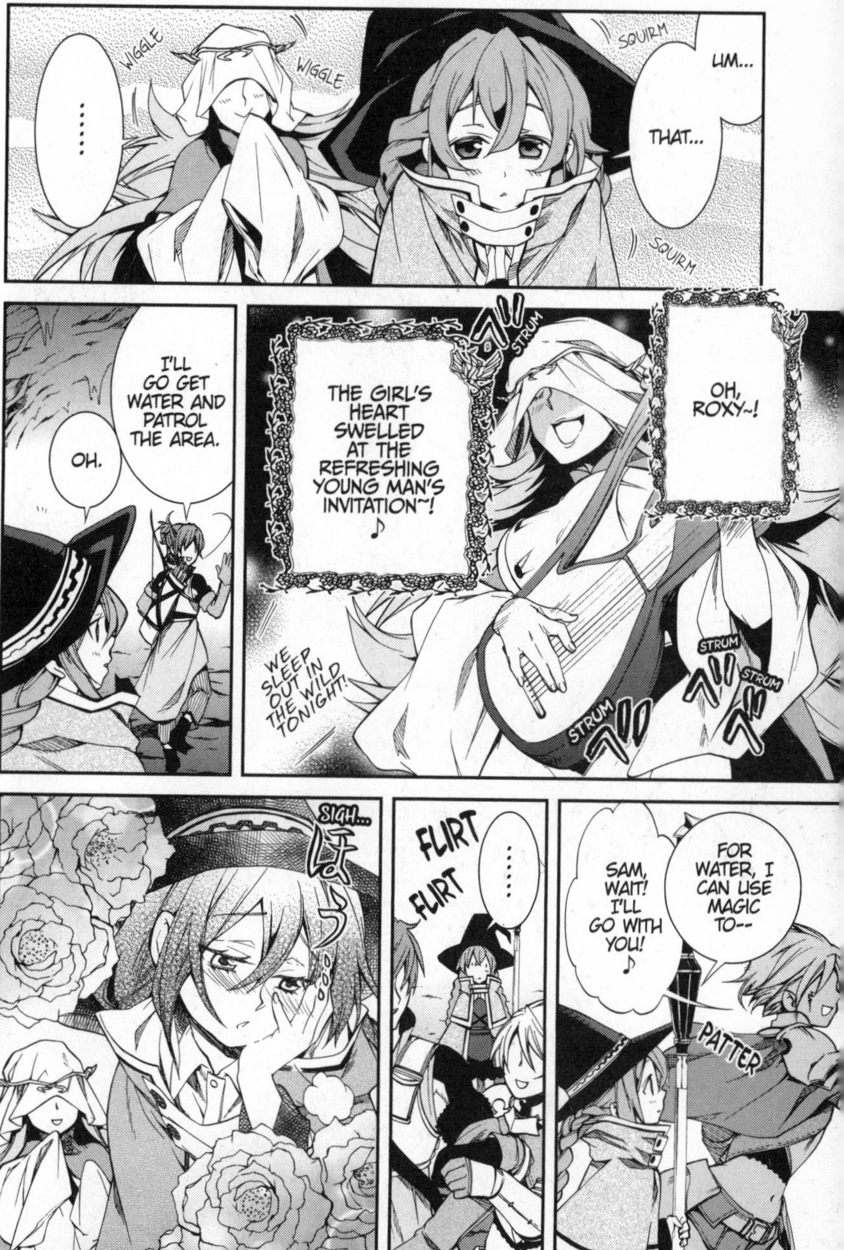
SQUIRM
UM...
THAT...
SQUIRM
WIGGLE
WIGGLE
......
OH, ROXY~!
STRUM
THE GIRL'S HEART SWELLED AT THE REFRESHING YOUNG MAN'S INVITATION~! ♪
STRUM
STRUM
STRUM
WE SLEEP OUT IN THE WILD TONIGHT!
I'LL GO GET WATER AND PATROL THE AREA.
OH.
FOR WATER, I CAN USE MAGIC TO--
SAM, WAIT! I'LL GO WITH YOU! ♪
PATTER
......
FLIRT
FLIRT
SIGH...

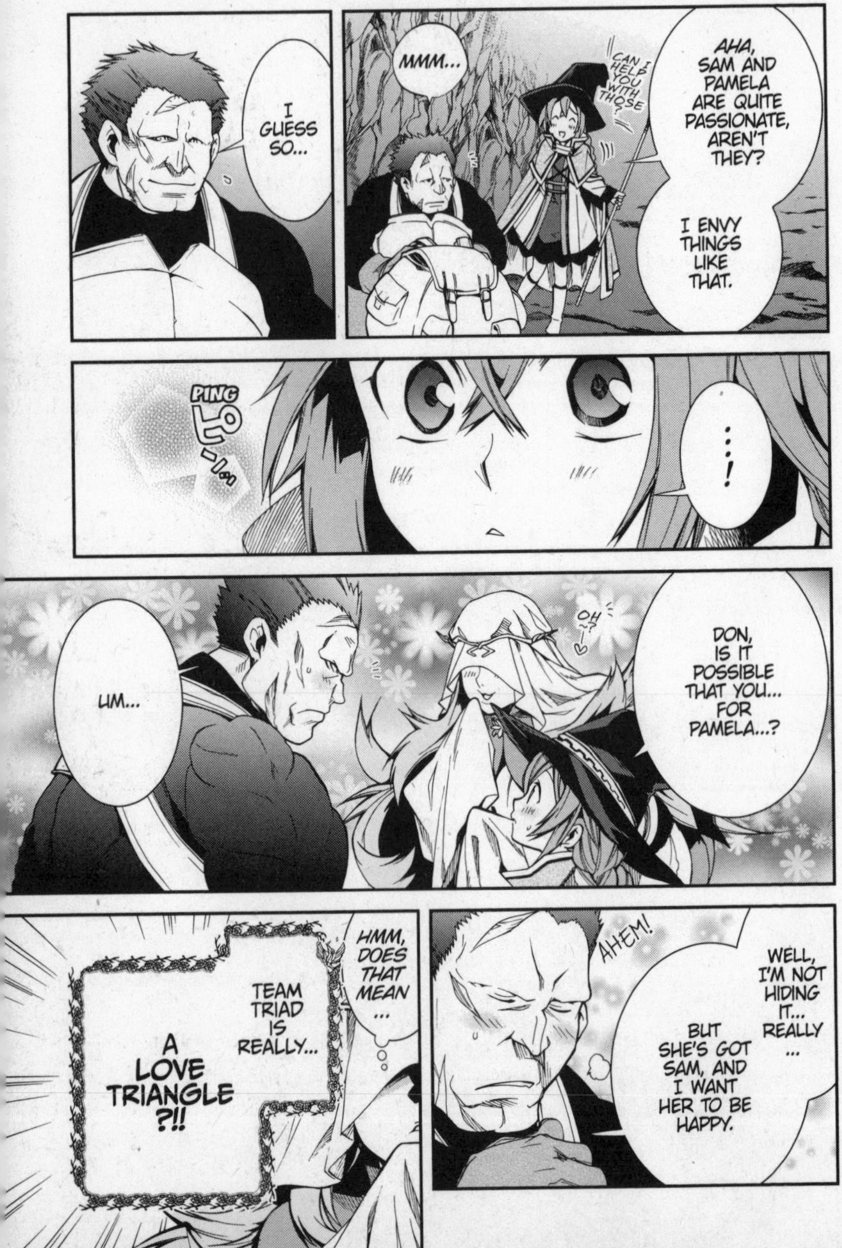
AHA, SAM AND PAMELA ARE QUITE PASSIONATE, AREN'T THEY?
I ENVY THINGS LIKE THAT.
CAN I HELP YOU WITH THOSE?
MMM...
I GUESS SO...
...!
PING
DON, IS IT POSSIBLE THAT YOU... FOR PAMELA...?
OH~?
UM...
AHEM!
WELL, I'M NOT HIDING IT... REALLY...
BUT SHE'S GOT SAM, AND I WANT HER TO BE HAPPY.
HMM, DOES THAT MEAN...
TEAM TRIAD IS REALLY...
A LOVE TRIANGLE?!!

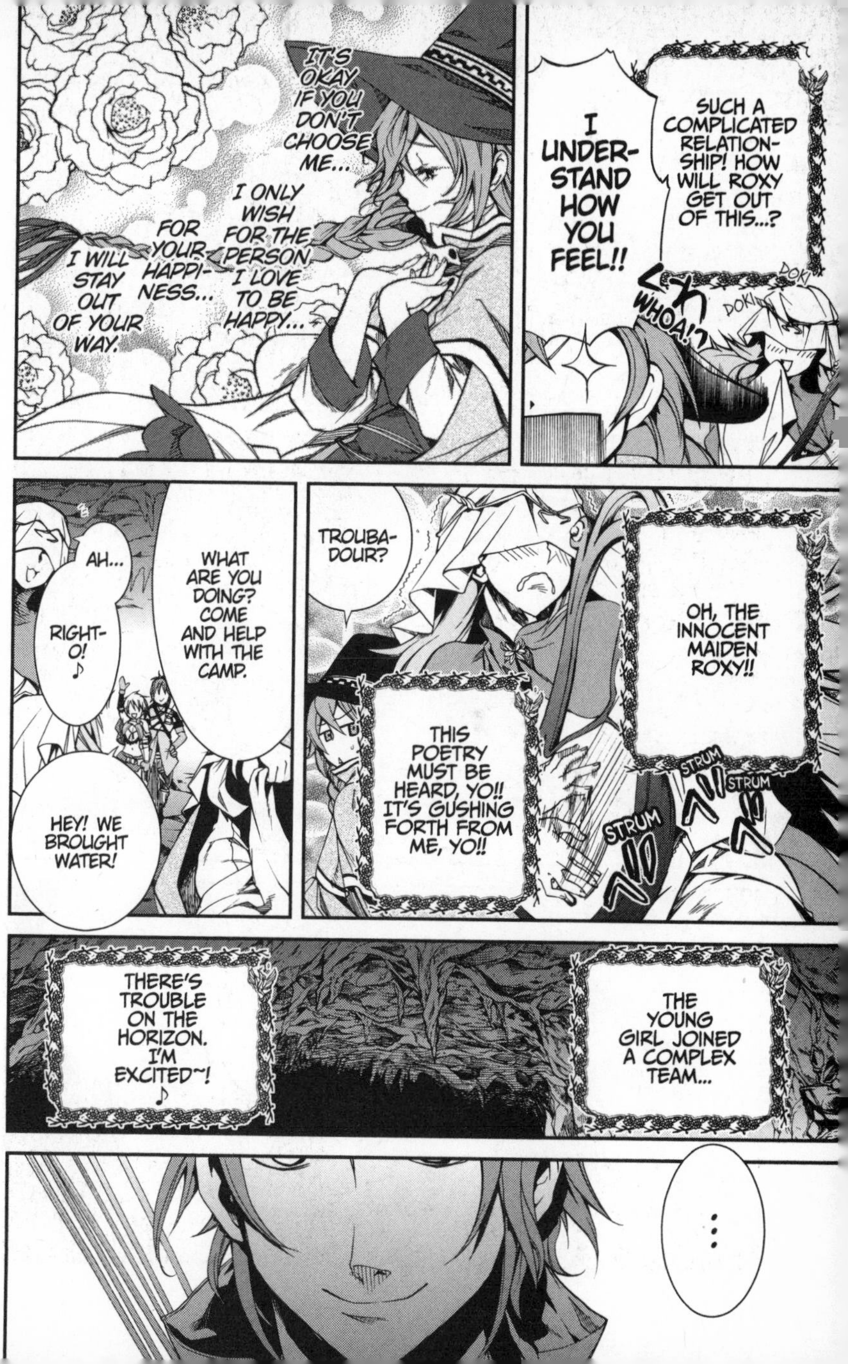
SUCH A COMPLICATED RELATIONSHIP! HOW WILL ROXY GET OUT OF THIS...?
I UNDERSTAND HOW YOU FEEL!!
WHOA!?
DOKI
DOKI
IT'S OKAY IF YOU DON'T CHOOSE ME...
I ONLY WISH FOR THE PERSON I LOVE TO BE HAPPY...
FOR YOUR HAPPINESS...
I WILL STAY OUT OF YOUR WAY.
OH, THE INNOCENT MAIDEN ROXY!!
STRUM
STRUM
STRUM
TROUBADOUR?
THIS POETRY MUST BE HEARD, YO!! IT'S GUSHING FORTH FROM ME, YO!!
WHAT ARE YOU DOING? COME AND HELP WITH THE CAMP.
AH...
RIGHT-O! ♪
HEY! WE BROUGHT WATER!
THE YOUNG GIRL JOINED A COMPLEX TEAM...
THERE'S TROUBLE ON THE HORIZON. I'M EXCITED~! ♪
...

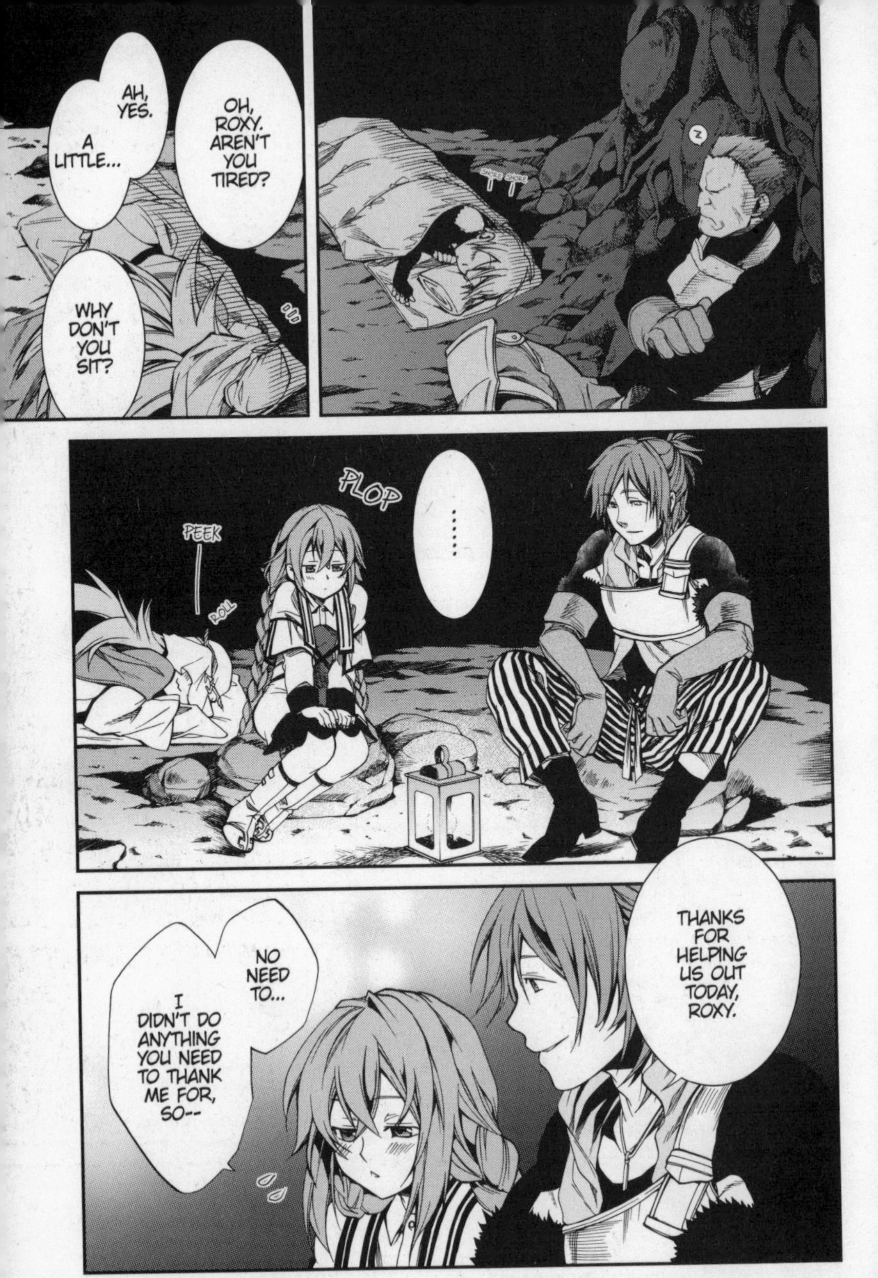
SNORE SNORE
OH, ROXY. AREN'T YOU TIRED?
AH, YES. A LITTLE...
WHY DON'T YOU SIT?
......
PLOP
PEEK
ROLL
THANKS FOR HELPING US OUT TODAY, ROXY.
NO NEED TO...
I DIDN'T DO ANYTHING YOU NEED TO THANK ME FOR, SO--

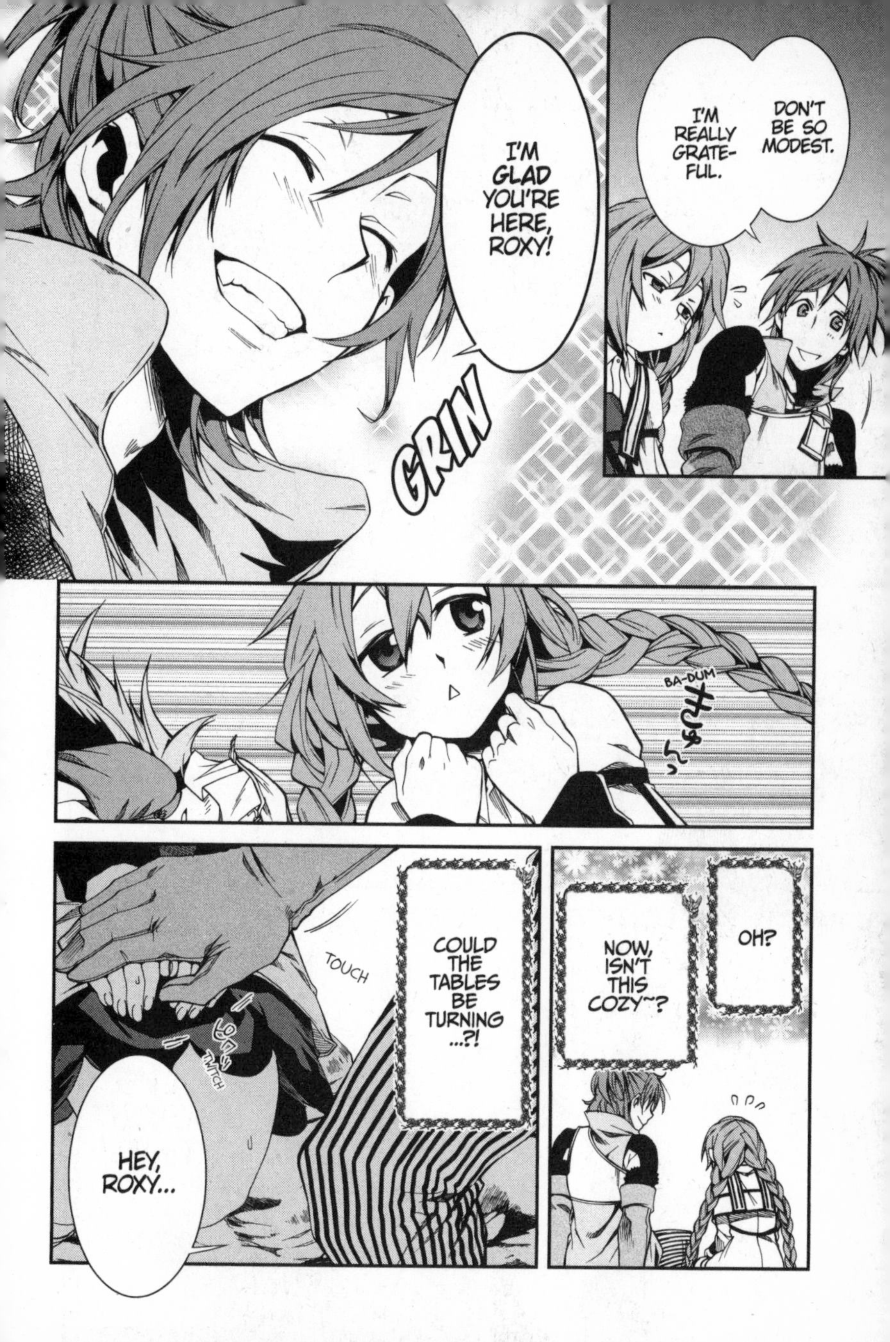
DON'T BE SO MODEST.
I'M REALLY GRATE-FUL.
I'M GLAD YOU'RE HERE, ROXY!
GRIN
BA-DUM
OH?
NOW, ISN'T THIS COZY~?
COULD THE TABLES BE TURNING...?!
TOUCH
TWITCH
HEY, ROXY...

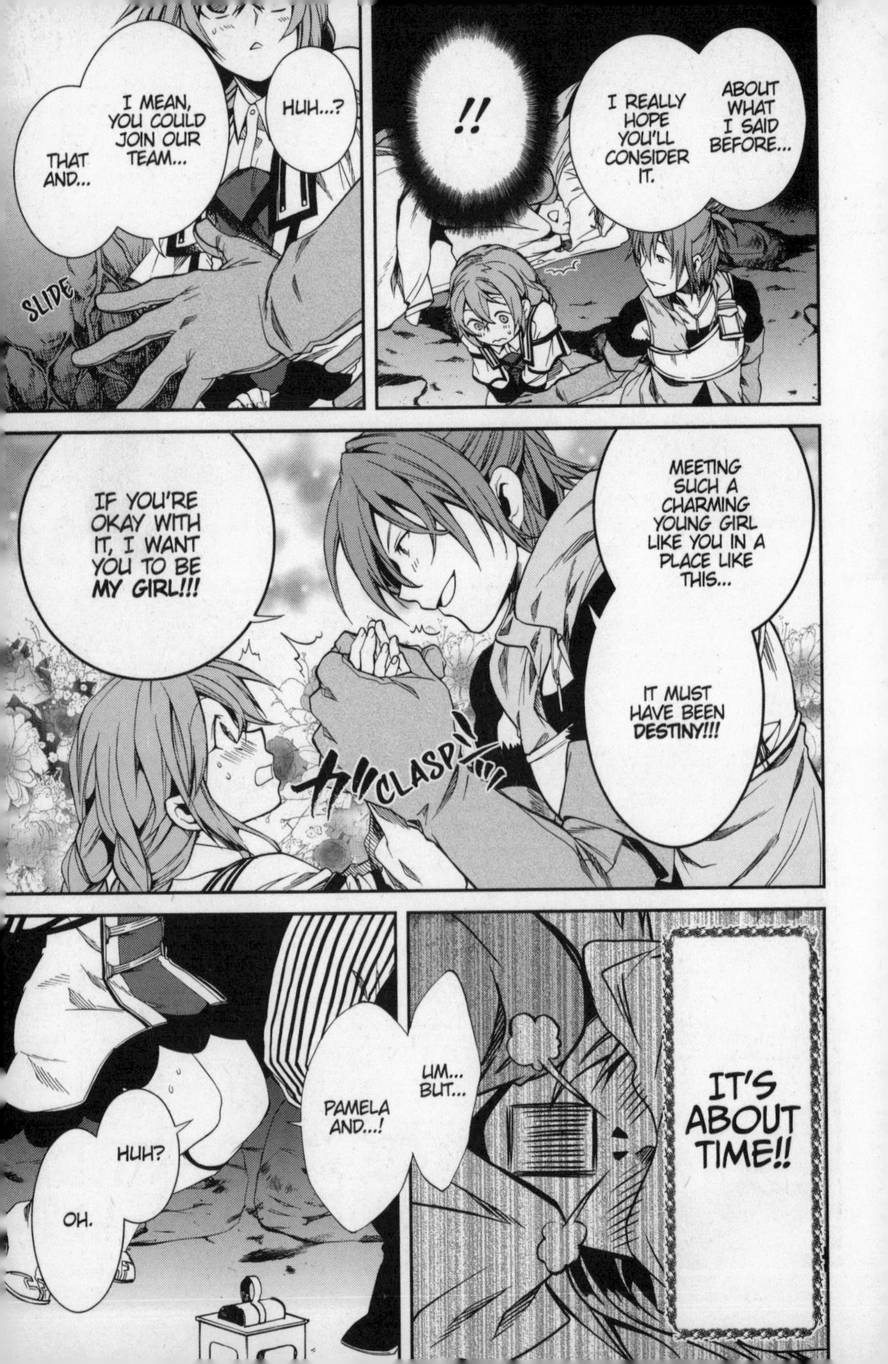
ABOUT WHAT I SAID BEFORE...
I REALLY HOPE YOU'LL CONSIDER IT.
!!
HUH...?
I MEAN, YOU COULD JOIN OUR TEAM...
THAT AND...
SLIDE
MEETING SUCH A CHARMING YOUNG GIRL LIKE YOU IN A PLACE LIKE THIS...
IT MUST HAVE BEEN DESTINY!!!
CLASP
IF YOU'RE OKAY WITH IT, I WANT YOU TO BE MY GIRL!!!
IT'S ABOUT TIME!!
UM... BUT...
PAMELA AND...!
HUH?
OH.

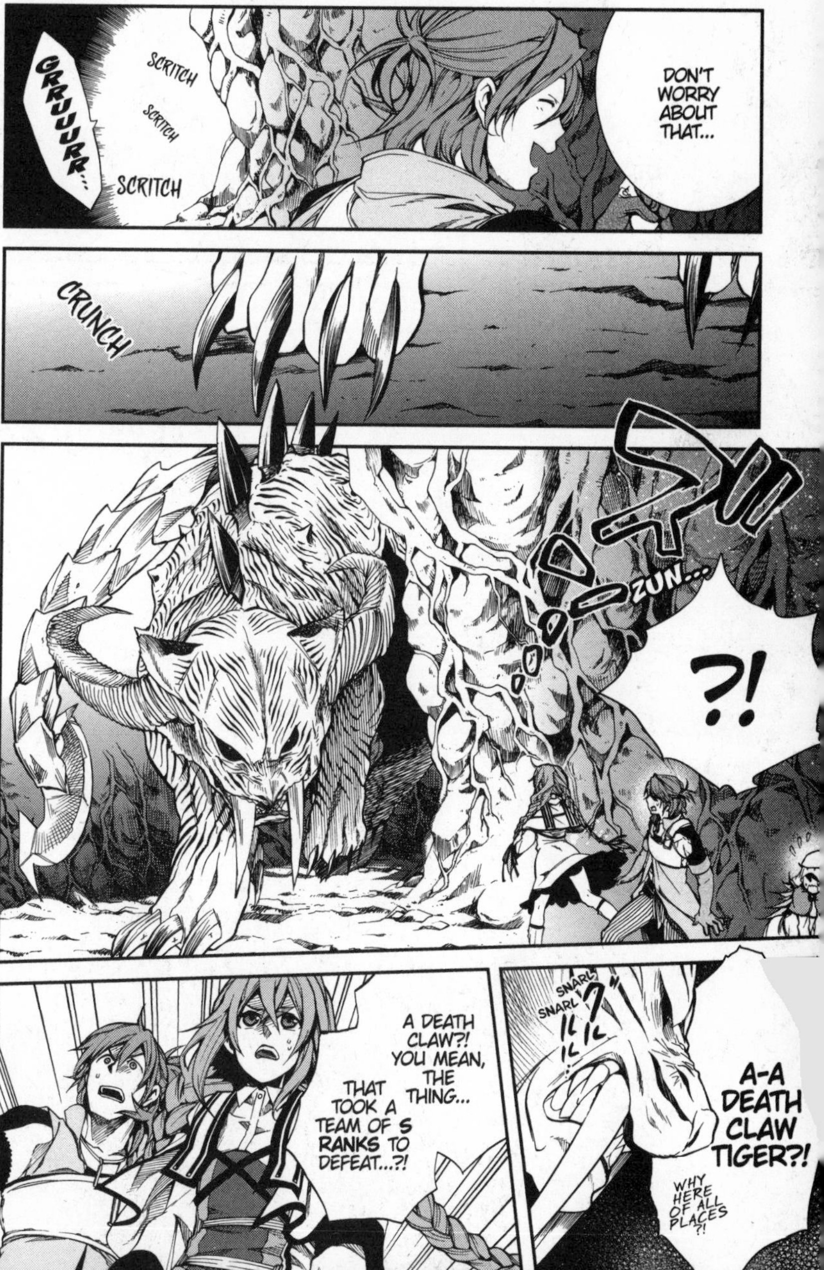
DON'T WORRY ABOUT THAT...
SCRITCH
SCRITCH
SCRITCH
GRRUUURR...
CRUNCH
ZUN...
?!
SNARL SNARL
A-A DEATH CLAW TIGER?!
WHY HERE OF ALL PLACES?!
A DEATH CLAW?! YOU MEAN, THE THING...
THAT TOOK A TEAM OF S RANKS TO DEFEAT...?!

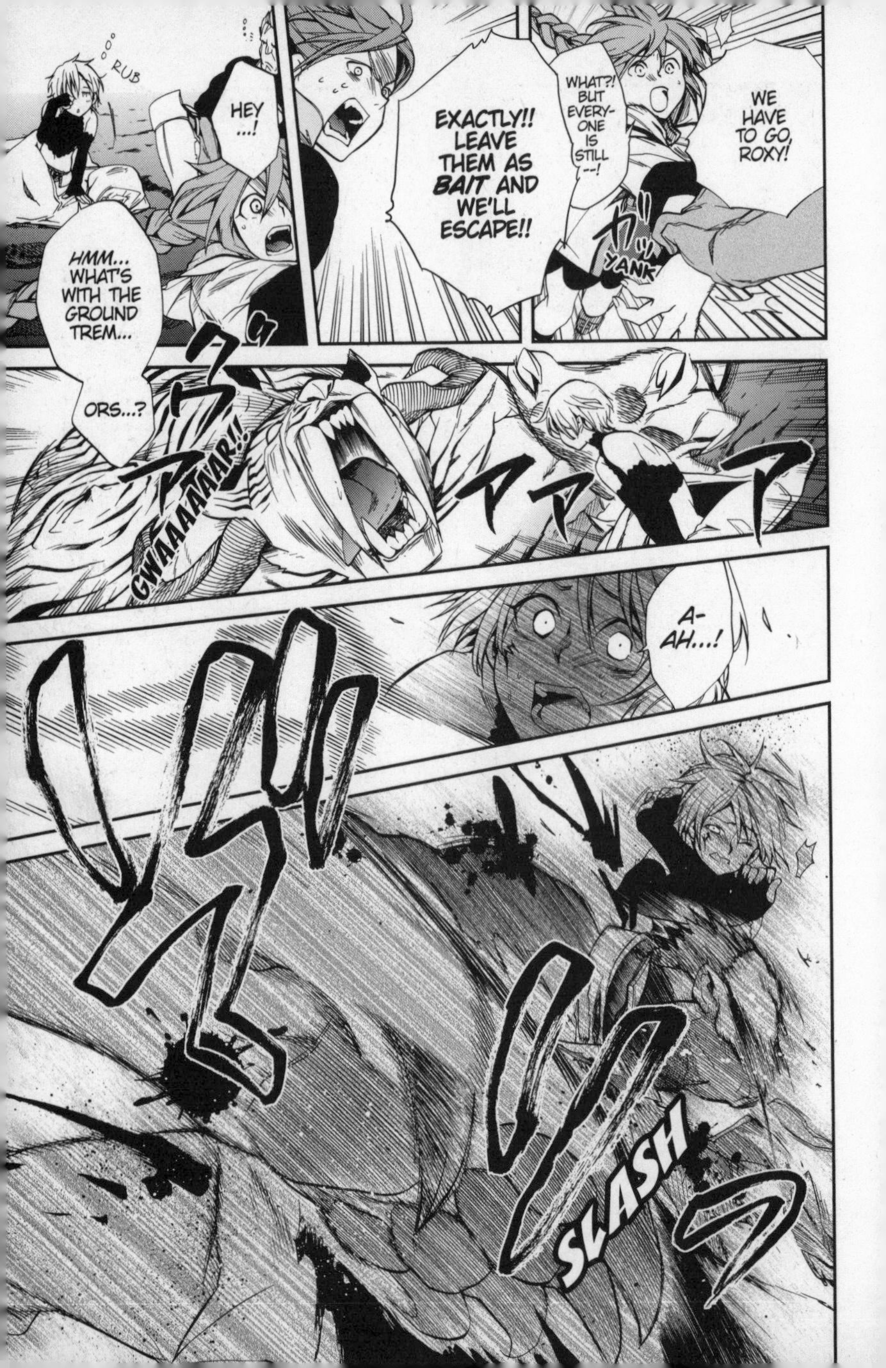
WE HAVE TO GO, ROXY!
WHAT?! BUT EVERY-ONE IS STILL --!
YANK
EXACTLY!! LEAVE THEM AS BAIT AND WE'LL ESCAPE!!
HEY ...!
RUB
HMM... WHAT'S WITH THE GROUND TREM...
ORS...?
GWAAAAAAR!!
A-AH...!
SLASH

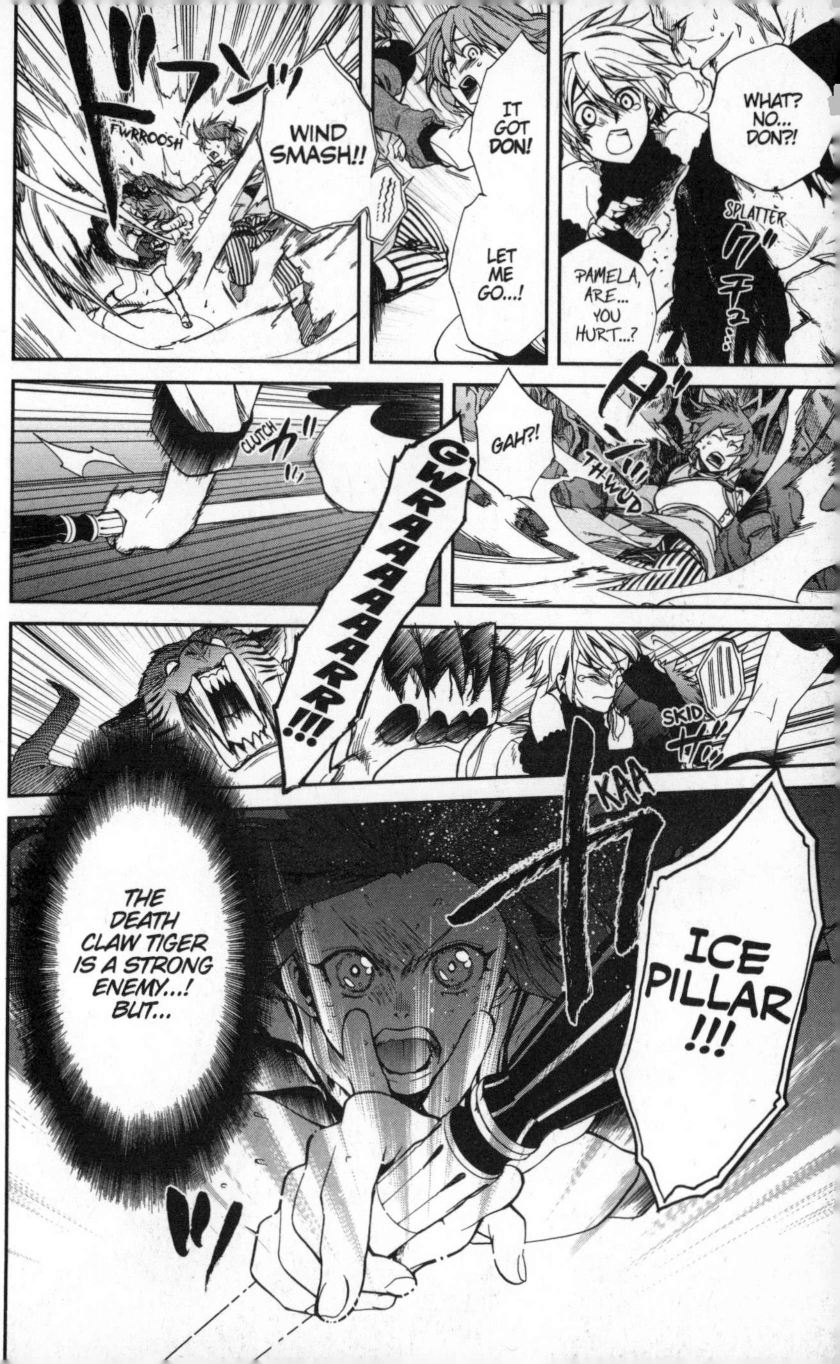
WHAT? NO... DON?!
SPLATTER
PAMELA, ARE... YOU HURT...?
IT GOT DON!
LET ME GO...!
WIND SMASH!!
FWRROOSH
GAH?!
THWUD
CLUTCH
GWRAAAAAAAARR!!!
SKID
KAA
ICE PILLAR!!!
THE DEATH CLAW TIGER IS A STRONG ENEMY...! BUT...

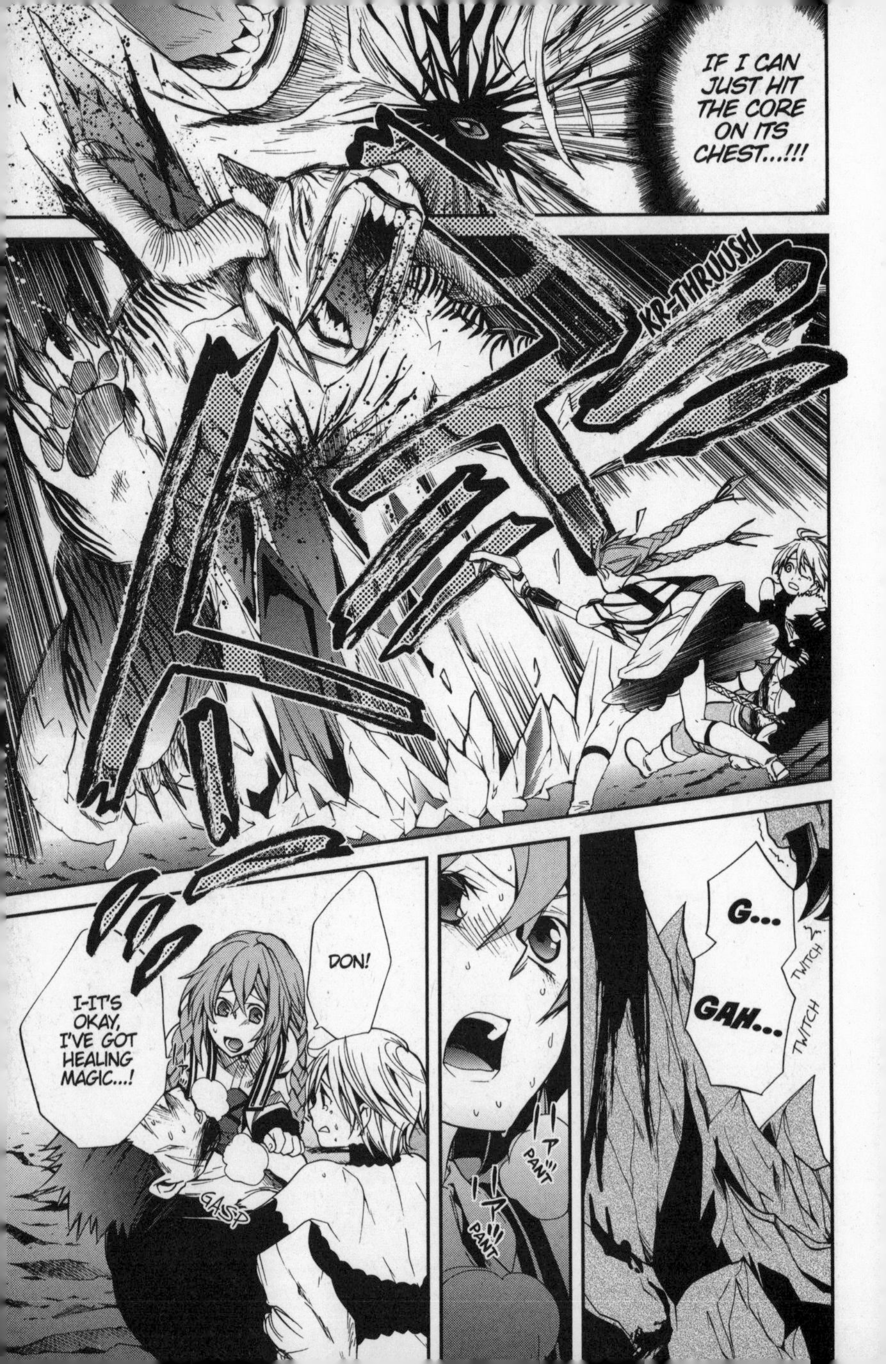
IF I CAN JUST HIT THE CORE ON ITS CHEST...!!!
KR-THRUUSH
G...
TWITCH
GAH...
TWITCH
PANT
PANT
DON!
I-IT'S OKAY, I'VE GOT HEALING MAGIC...!
GASP

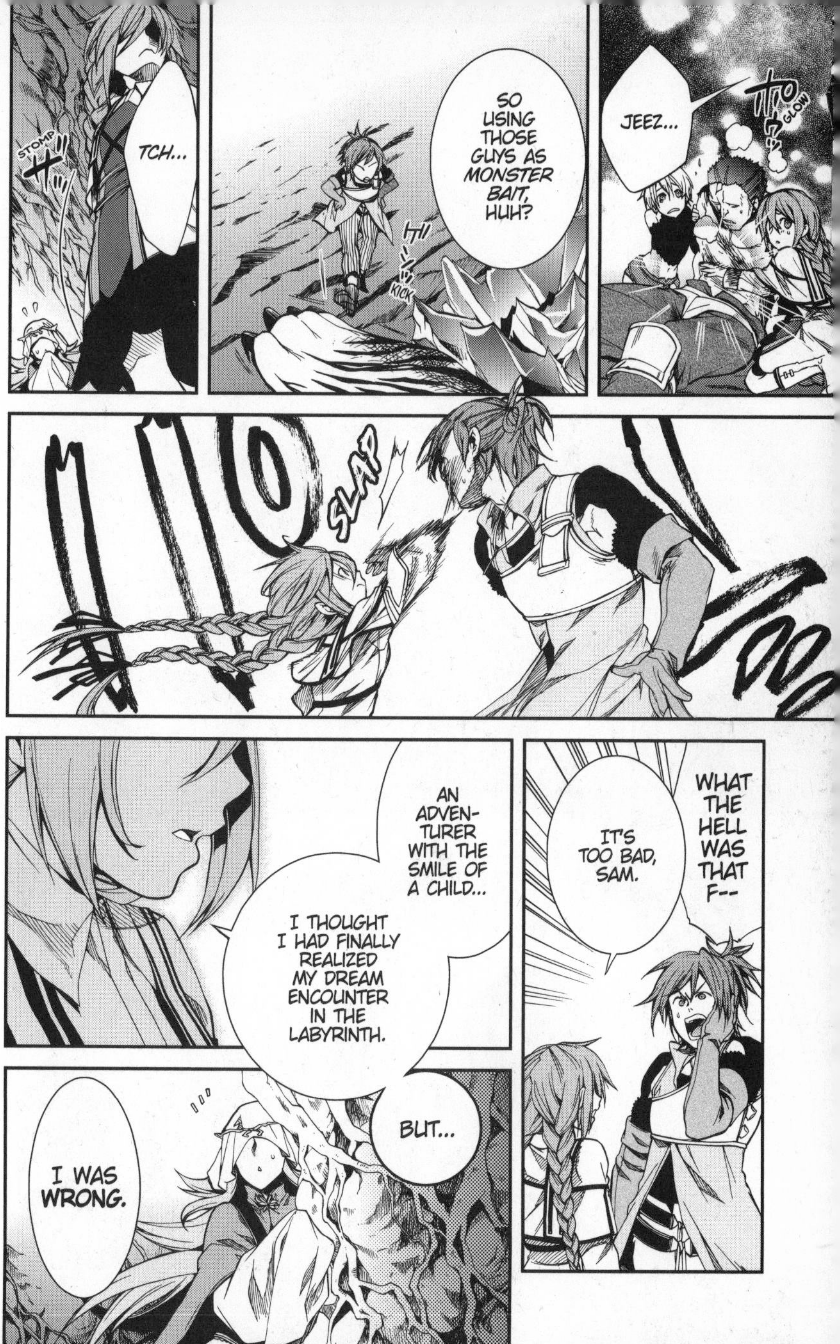
GLOW
JEEZ...
SO USING THOSE GUYS AS MONSTER BAIT, HUH?
KICK
TCH...
STOMP
SLAP
WHAT THE HELL WAS THAT F--
IT'S TOO BAD, SAM.
AN ADVEN-TURER WITH THE SMILE OF A CHILD...
I THOUGHT I HAD FINALLY REALIZED MY DREAM ENCOUNTER IN THE LABYRINTH.
BUT...
I WAS WRONG.

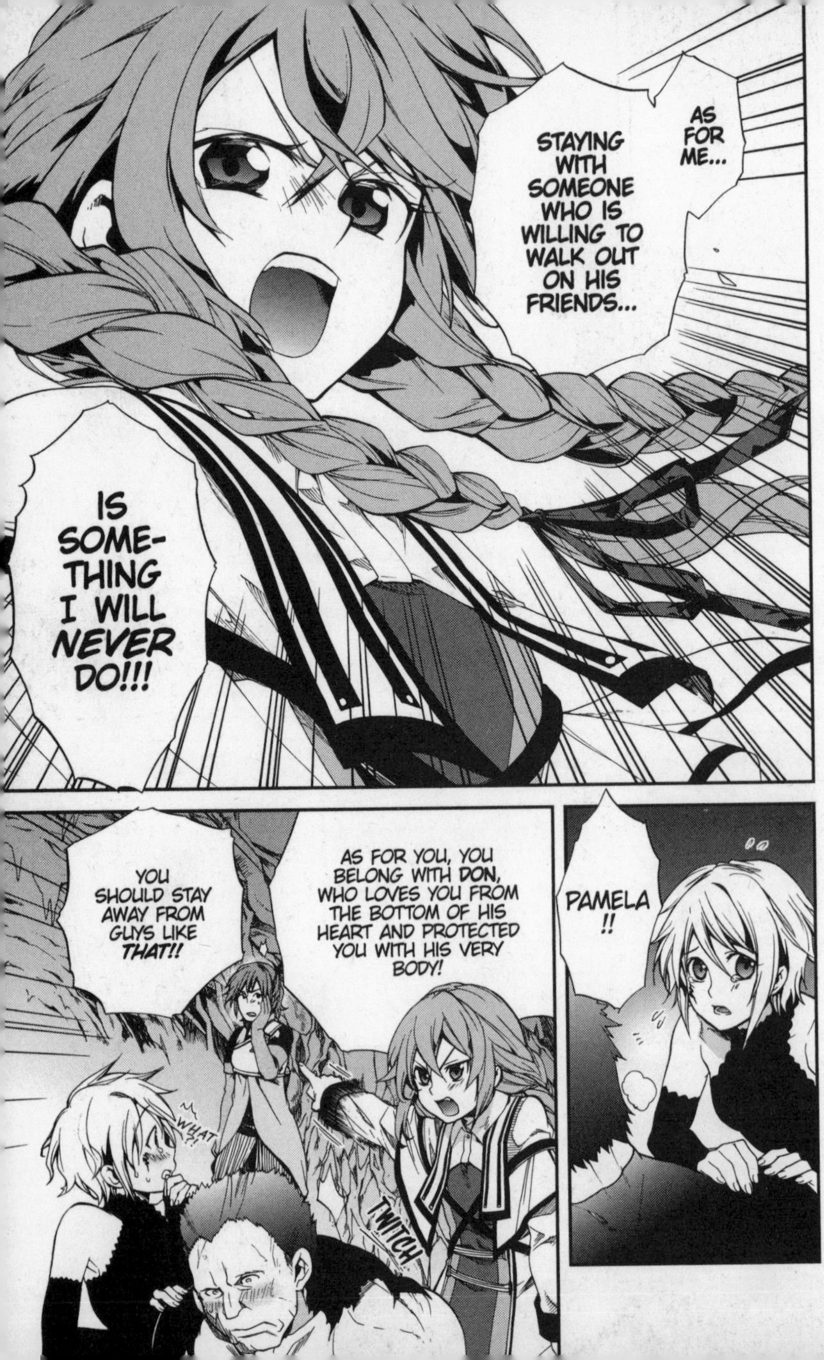
AS FOR ME...
STAYING WITH SOMEONE WHO IS WILLING TO WALK OUT ON HIS FRIENDS...
IS SOME-THING I WILL *NEVER* DO!!!
PAMELA !!
AS FOR YOU, YOU BELONG WITH DON, WHO LOVES YOU FROM THE BOTTOM OF HIS HEART AND PROTECTED YOU WITH HIS VERY BODY!
YOU SHOULD STAY AWAY FROM GUYS LIKE *THAT*!!
WHAT ?!
TWITCH

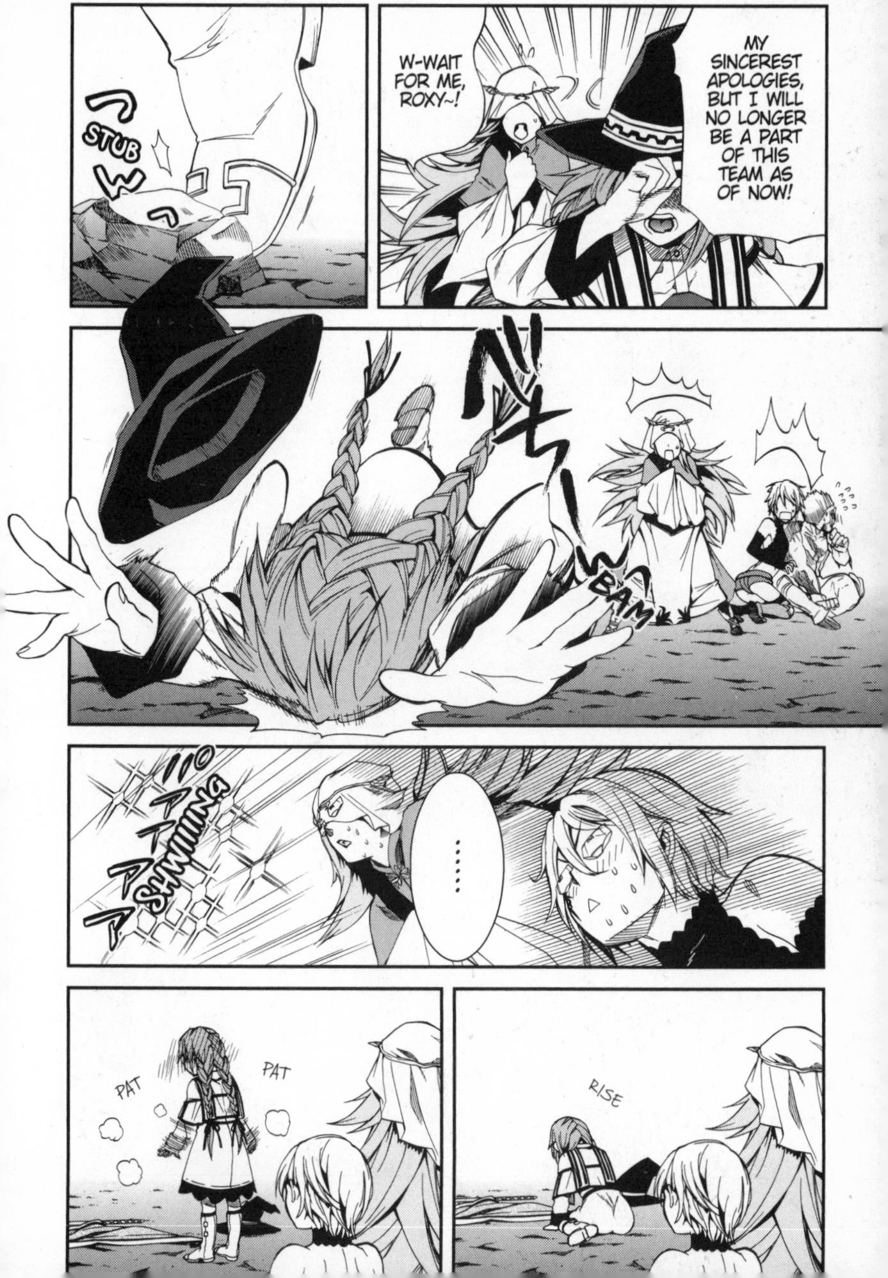

MY SINCEREST APOLOGIES, BUT I WILL NO LONGER BE A PART OF THIS TEAM AS OF NOW!
W-WAIT FOR ME, ROXY~!
STUB
BAM
......
SHWIIIING
RISE
PAT
PAT

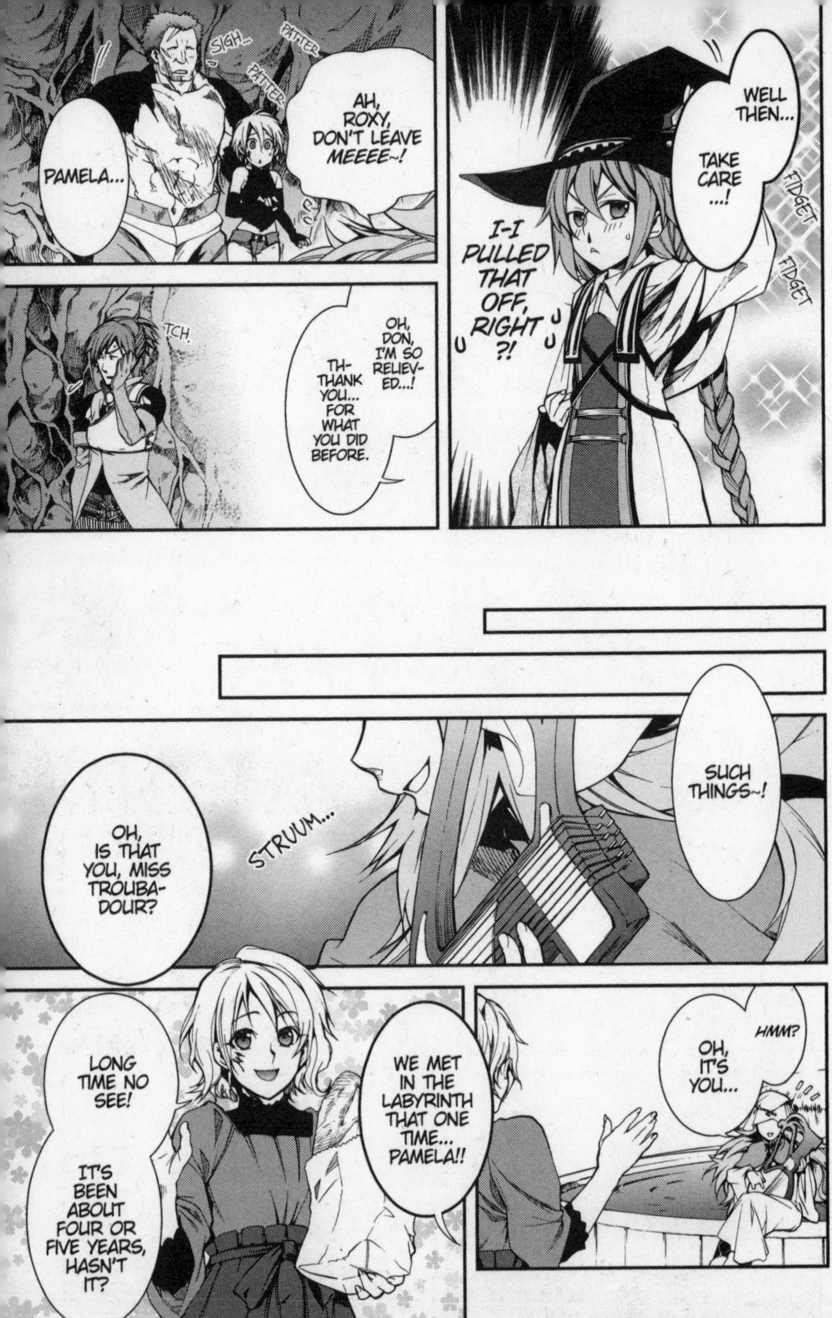
WELL THEN...
TAKE CARE ...!
FIDGET
FIDGET
I-I PULLED THAT OFF, RIGHT?!
AH, ROXY, DON'T LEAVE MEEEE~!
PATTER
PATTER
SIGH...
PAMELA...
OH, DON, I'M SO RELIEVED...!
TH-THANK YOU... FOR WHAT YOU DID BEFORE.
TCH.
SUCH THINGS~!
STRUUM...
OH, IS THAT YOU, MISS TROUBADOUR?
HMM?
OH, IT'S YOU...
WE MET IN THE LABYRINTH THAT ONE TIME... PAMELA!!
LONG TIME NO SEE!
IT'S BEEN ABOUT FOUR OR FIVE YEARS, HASN'T IT?

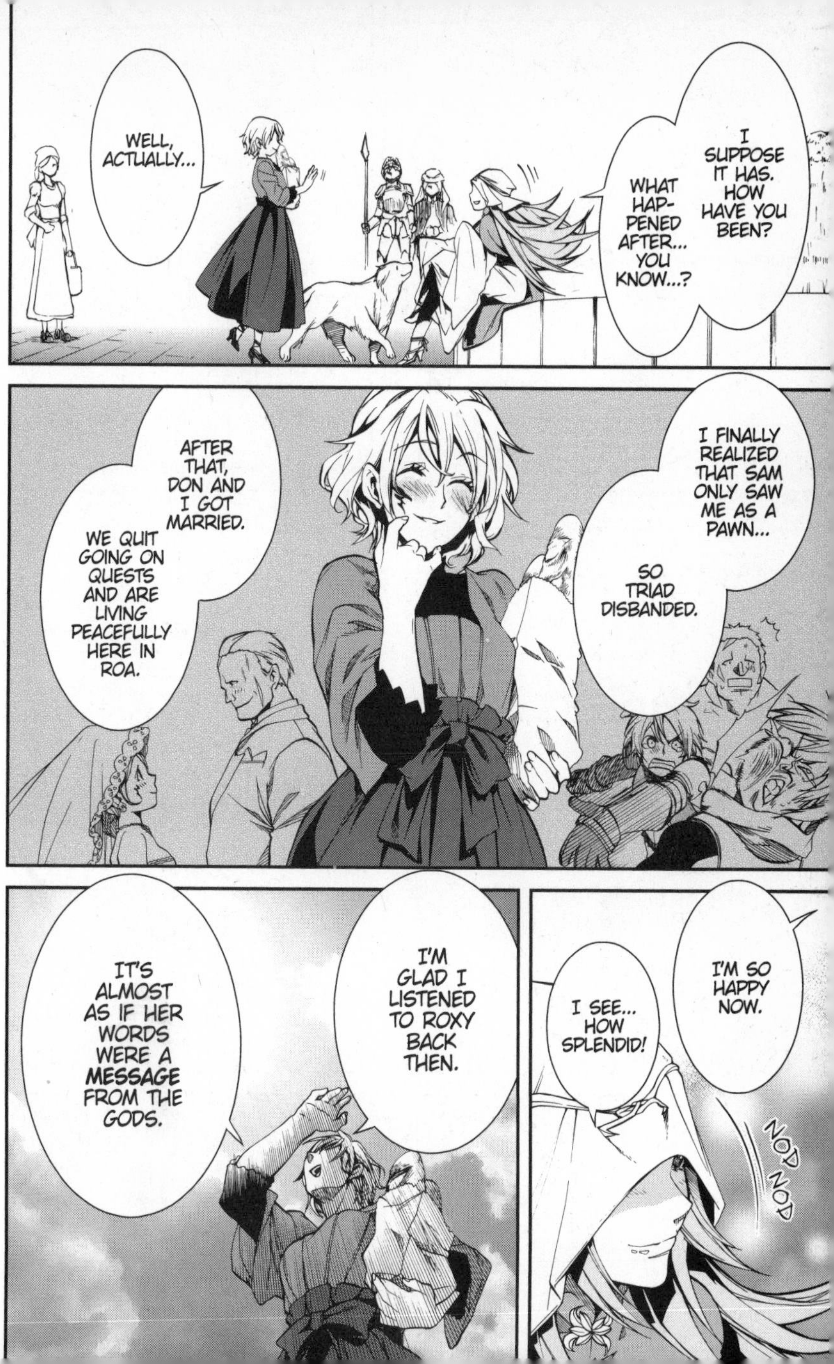
I SUPPOSE IT HAS. HOW HAVE YOU BEEN?
WHAT HAP-PENED AFTER... YOU KNOW...?
WELL, ACTUALLY...
I FINALLY REALIZED THAT SAM ONLY SAW ME AS A PAWN...
SO TRIAD DISBANDED.
AFTER THAT, DON AND I GOT MARRIED.
WE QUIT GOING ON QUESTS AND ARE LIVING PEACEFULLY HERE IN ROA.
I'M SO HAPPY NOW.
I SEE... HOW SPLENDID!
NOD NOD
I'M GLAD I LISTENED TO ROXY BACK THEN.
IT'S ALMOST AS IF HER WORDS WERE A MESSAGE FROM THE GODS.

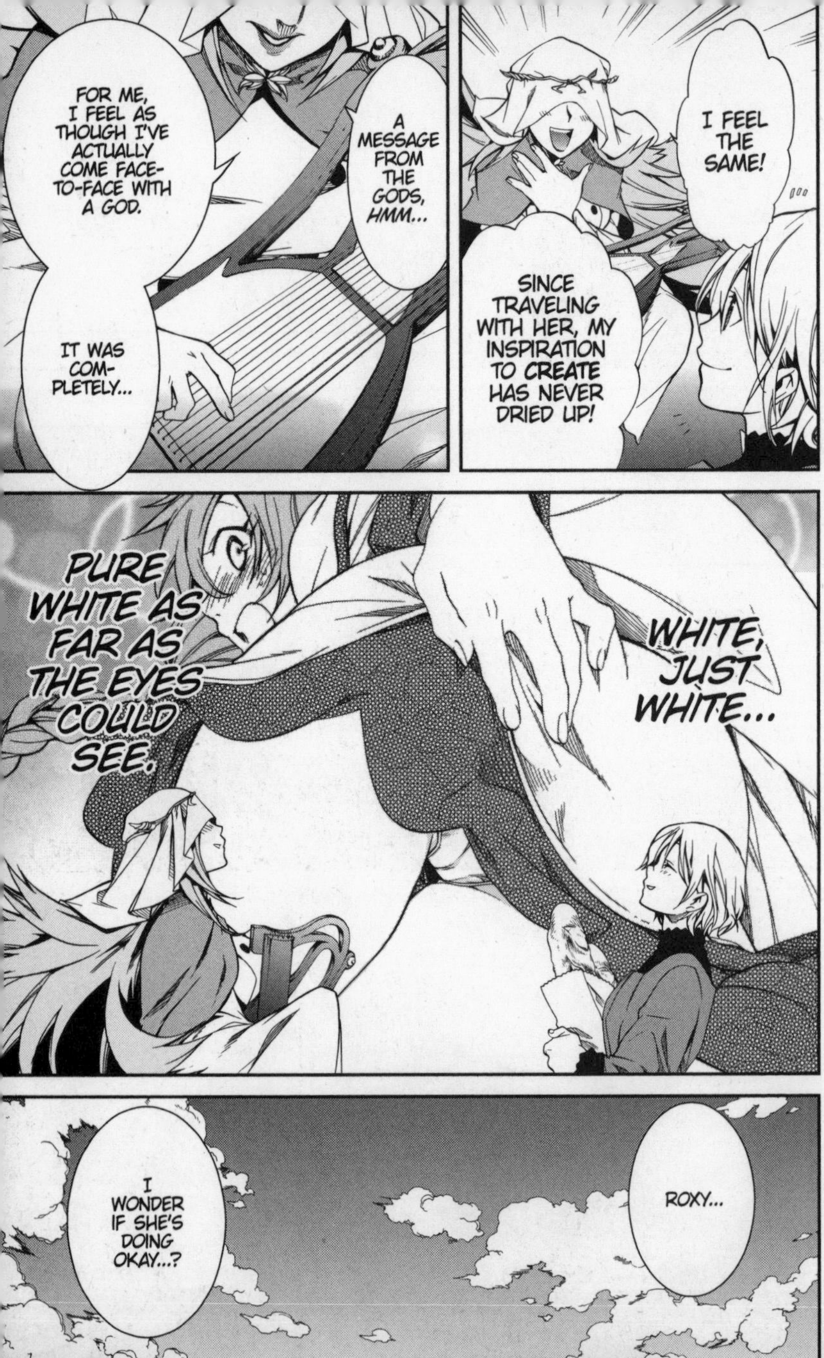
I FEEL THE SAME!
SINCE TRAVELING WITH HER, MY INSPIRATION TO CREATE HAS NEVER DRIED UP!
A MESSAGE FROM THE GODS, HMM...
FOR ME, I FEEL AS THOUGH I'VE ACTUALLY COME FACE-TO-FACE WITH A GOD.
IT WAS COM-PLETELY...
WHITE, JUST WHITE...
PURE WHITE AS FAR AS THE EYES COULD SEE.
ROXY...
I WONDER IF SHE'S DOING OKAY...?

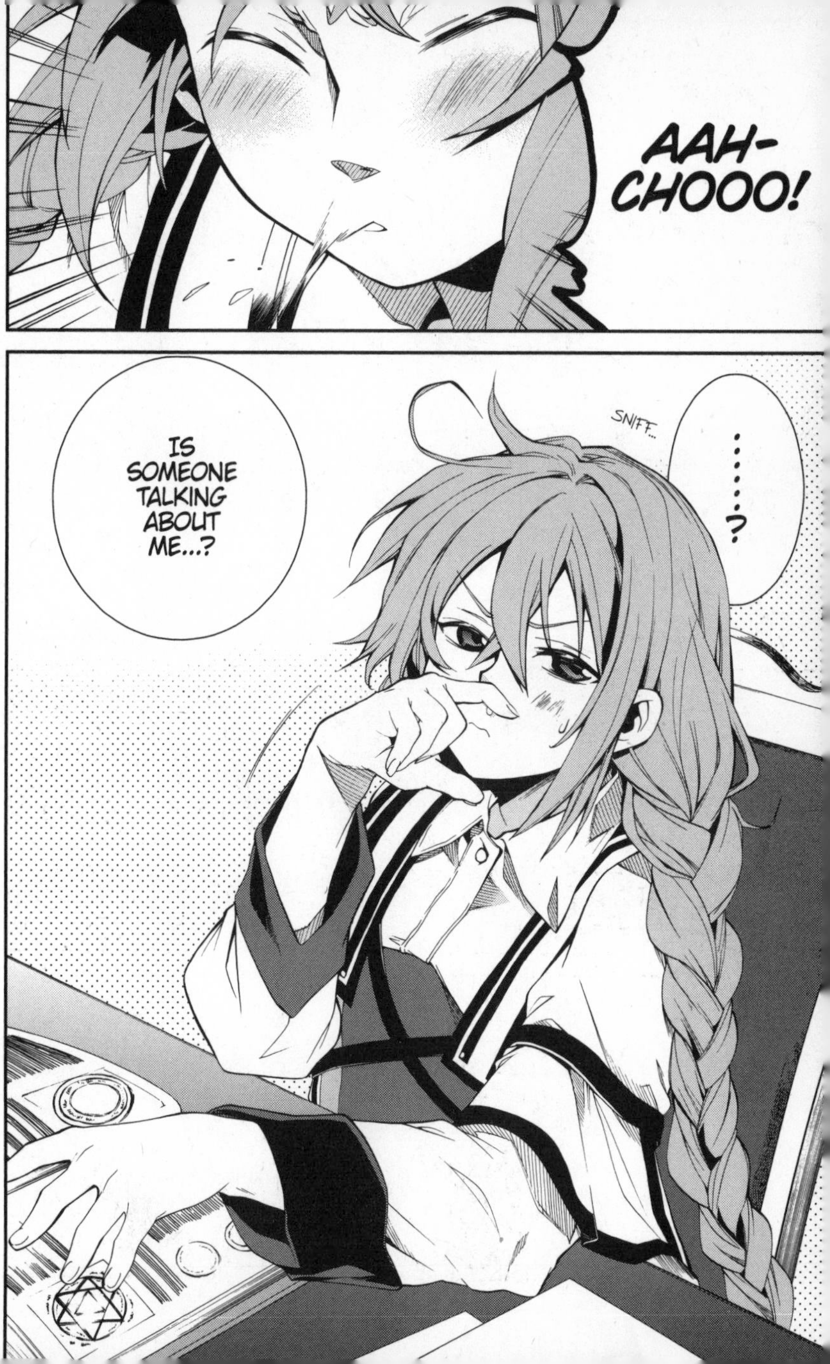
AAH-CHOOO!
SNIFF...
......?
IS SOMEONE TALKING ABOUT ME...?

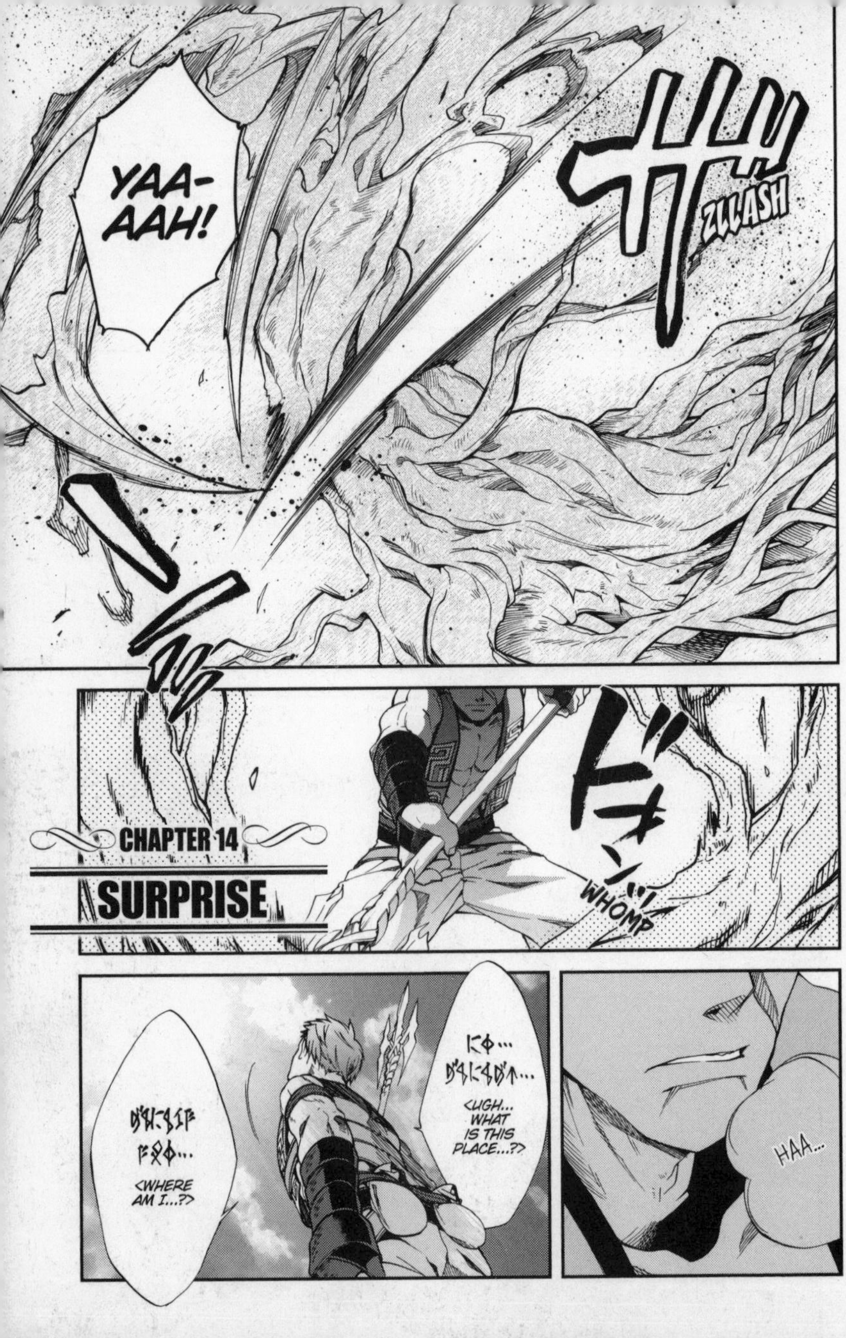
YAA-AAH!
ZULLASH
CHAPTER 14
SURPRISE
WHOMP
HAA...
<UGH... WHAT IS THIS PLACE...?>
<WHERE AM I...?>

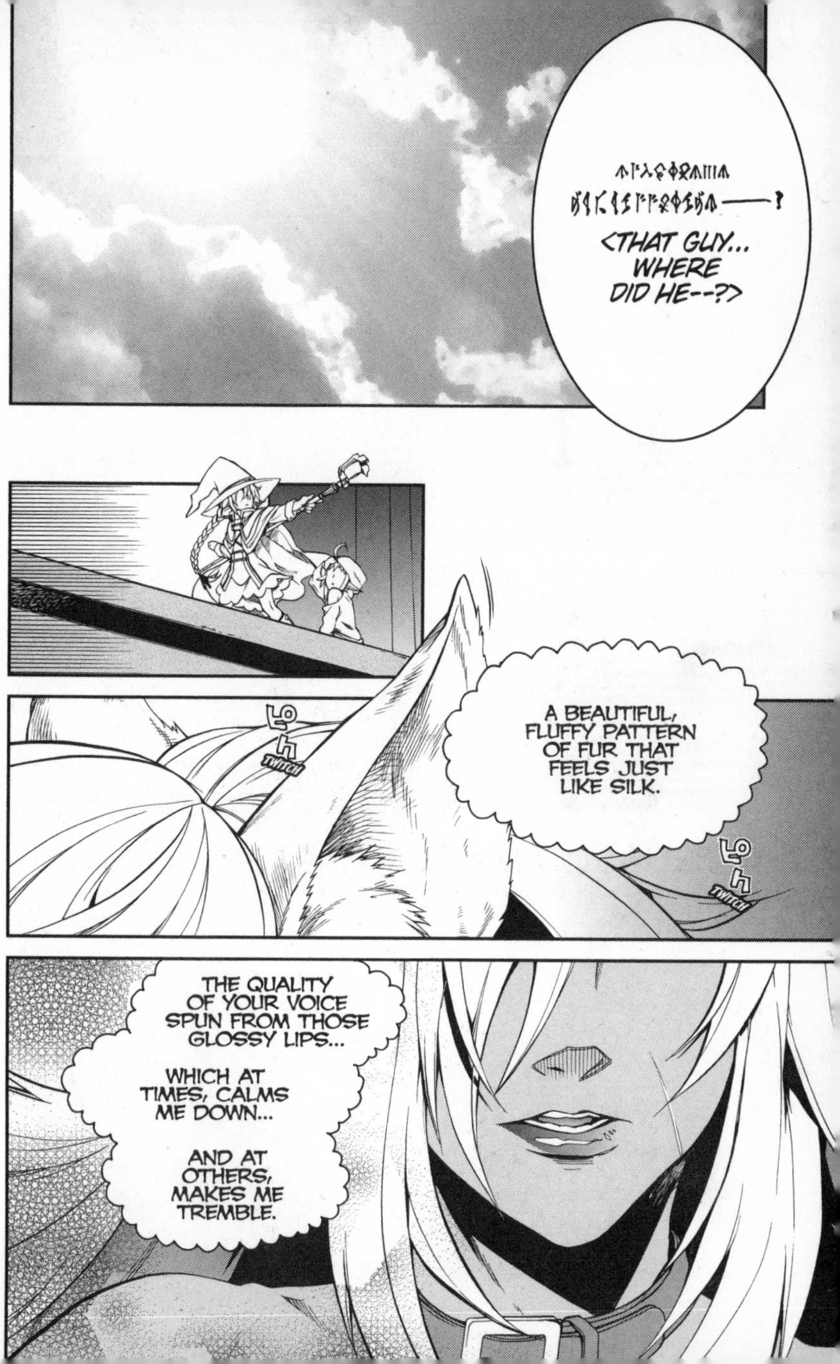
<THAT GUY... WHERE DID HE--?>
A BEAUTIFUL, FLUFFY PATTERN OF FUR THAT FEELS JUST LIKE SILK.
TWITCH
TWITCH
THE QUALITY OF YOUR VOICE SPUN FROM THOSE GLOSSY LIPS...
WHICH AT TIMES, CALMS ME DOWN...
AND AT OTHERS, MAKES ME TREMBLE.

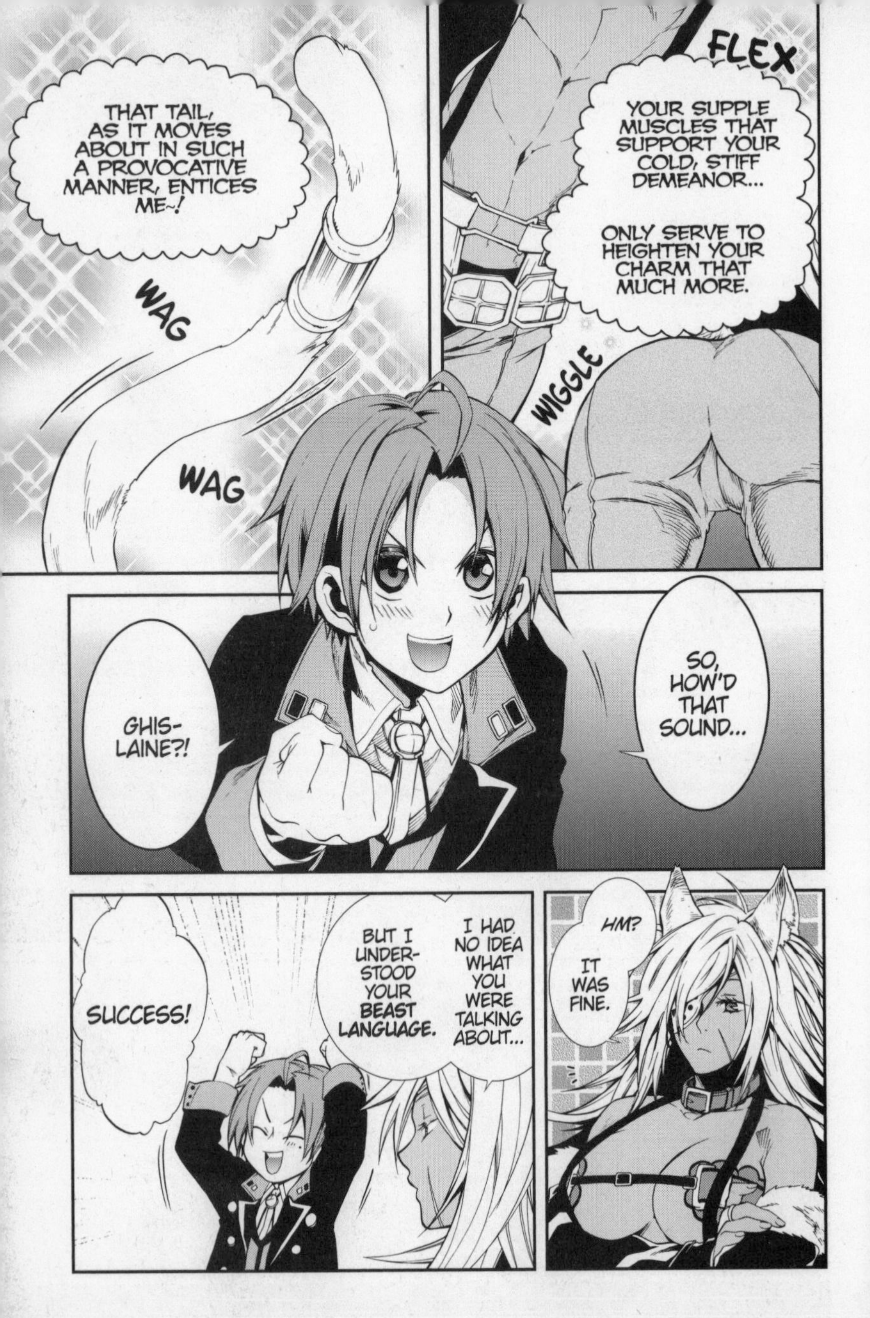
FLEX
YOUR SUPPLE MUSCLES THAT SUPPORT YOUR COLD, STIFF DEMEANOR...
ONLY SERVE TO HEIGHTEN YOUR CHARM THAT MUCH MORE.
WIGGLE
THAT TAIL, AS IT MOVES ABOUT IN SUCH A PROVOCATIVE MANNER, ENTICES ME~!
WAG
WAG
SO, HOW'D THAT SOUND...
GHIS-LAINE?!
HM?
IT WAS FINE.
I HAD NO IDEA WHAT YOU WERE TALKING ABOUT...
BUT I UNDER-STOOD YOUR BEAST LANGUAGE.
SUCCESS!

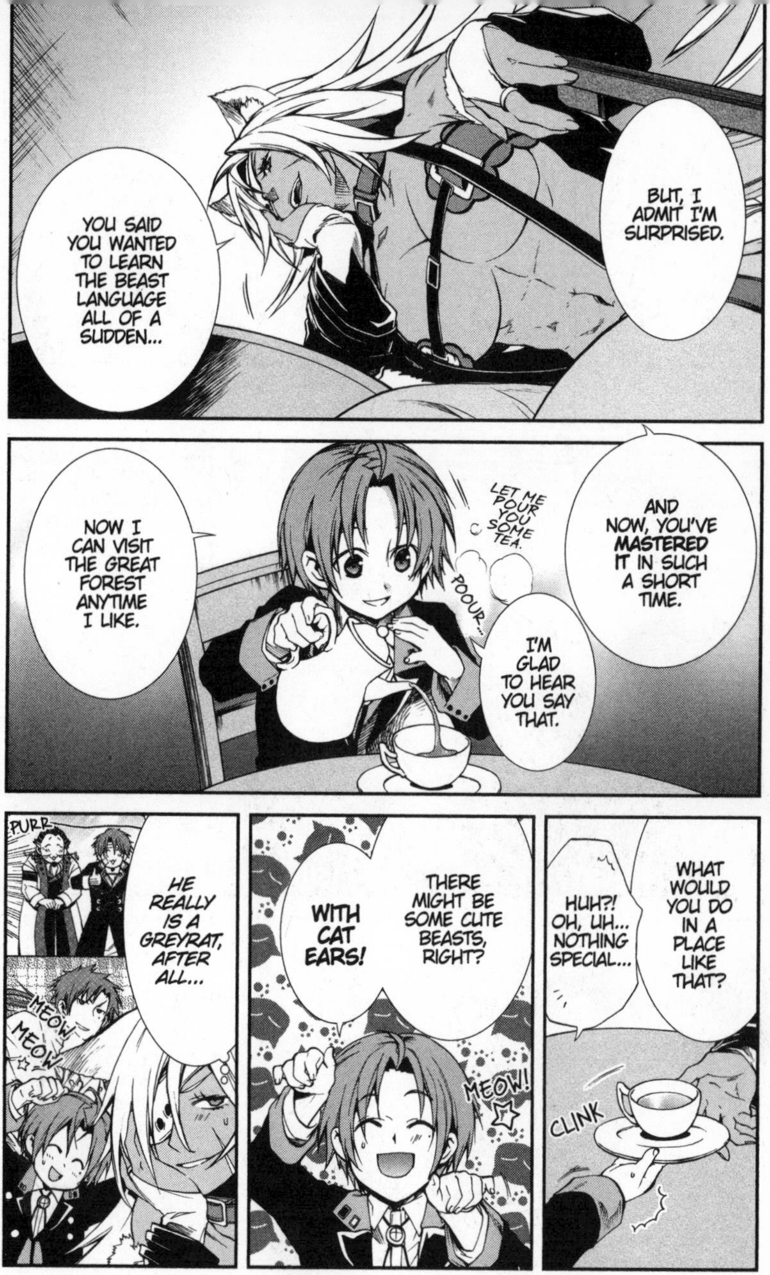
BUT, I ADMIT I'M SURPRISED.
YOU SAID YOU WANTED TO LEARN THE BEAST LANGUAGE ALL OF A SUDDEN...
AND NOW, YOU'VE MASTERED IT IN SUCH A SHORT TIME.
LET ME POUR YOU SOME TEA.
POOUR...
I'M GLAD TO HEAR YOU SAY THAT.
NOW I CAN VISIT THE GREAT FOREST ANYTIME I LIKE.
WHAT WOULD YOU DO IN A PLACE LIKE THAT?
HUH?! OH, UH... NOTHING SPECIAL...
CLINK
THERE MIGHT BE SOME CUTE BEASTS, RIGHT?
WITH CAT EARS!
MEOW!
HE REALLY IS A GREYRAT, AFTER ALL...
PURR
MEOW
MEOW

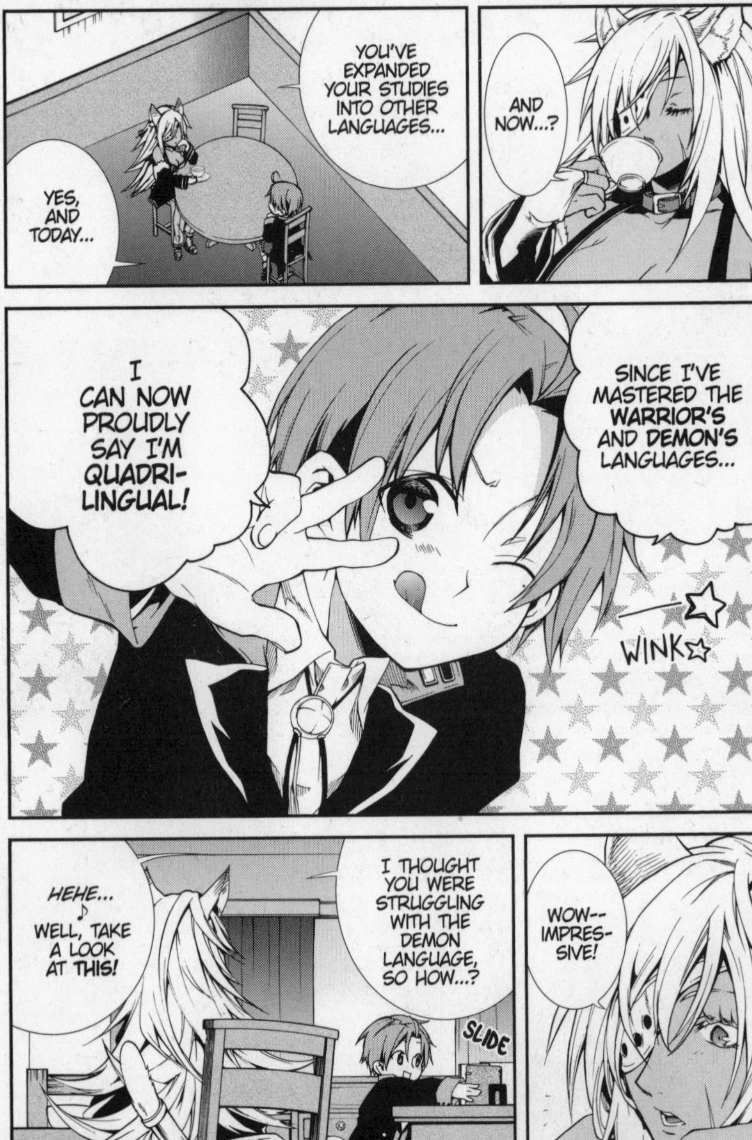
AND NOW...?
YOU'VE EXPANDED YOUR STUDIES INTO OTHER LANGUAGES...
YES, AND TODAY...
SINCE I'VE MASTERED THE **WARRIOR'S** AND **DEMON'S** LANGUAGES...
I CAN NOW PROUDLY SAY I'M QUADRI-LINGUAL!
WINK☆
WOW-- IMPRES-SIVE!
I THOUGHT YOU WERE STRUGGLING WITH THE DEMON LANGUAGE, SO HOW...?
SLIDE
HEHE... ♪ WELL, TAKE A LOOK AT **THIS!**

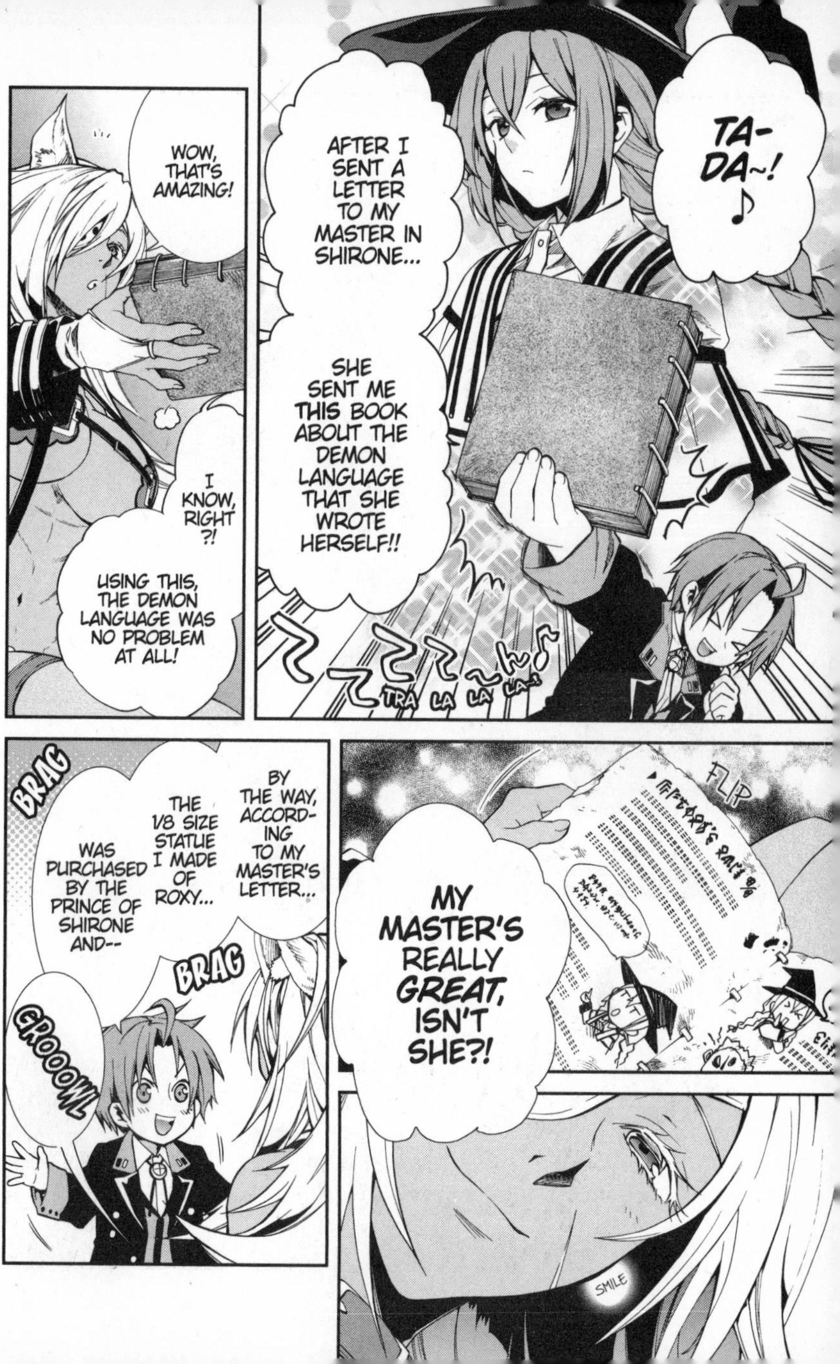
TA-DA~! ♪
AFTER I SENT A LETTER TO MY MASTER IN SHIRONE...
SHE SENT ME THIS BOOK ABOUT THE DEMON LANGUAGE THAT SHE WROTE HERSELF!!
TRA LA LA LA~
WOW, THAT'S AMAZING!
I KNOW, RIGHT?!
USING THIS, THE DEMON LANGUAGE WAS NO PROBLEM AT ALL!
FLIP
MY MASTER'S REALLY GREAT, ISN'T SHE?!
SMILE
BRAG
BY THE WAY, ACCORDING TO MY MASTER'S LETTER...
THE 1/8 SIZE STATUE I MADE OF ROXY...
WAS PURCHASED BY THE PRINCE OF SHIRONE AND--
BRAG
GROOOWL

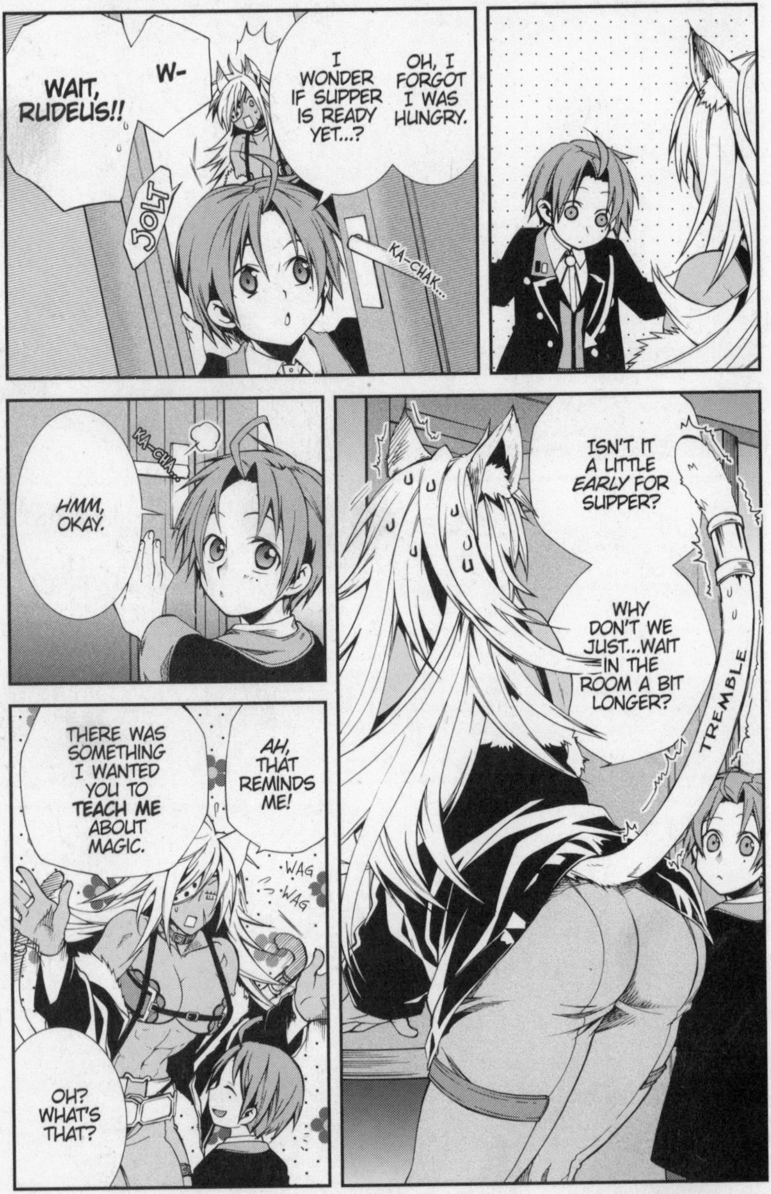

OH, I FORGOT I WAS HUNGRY.
I WONDER IF SUPPER IS READY YET...?
W-
WAIT, RUDEUS!!
JOLT
KA-CHAK...
ISN'T IT A LITTLE *EARLY* FOR SUPPER?
WHY DON'T WE JUST...WAIT IN THE ROOM A BIT LONGER?
TREMBLE
KA-CHA...
HMM, OKAY.
AH, THAT REMINDS ME!
THERE WAS SOMETHING I WANTED YOU TO **TEACH ME** ABOUT MAGIC.
WAG WAG
OH? WHAT'S THAT?

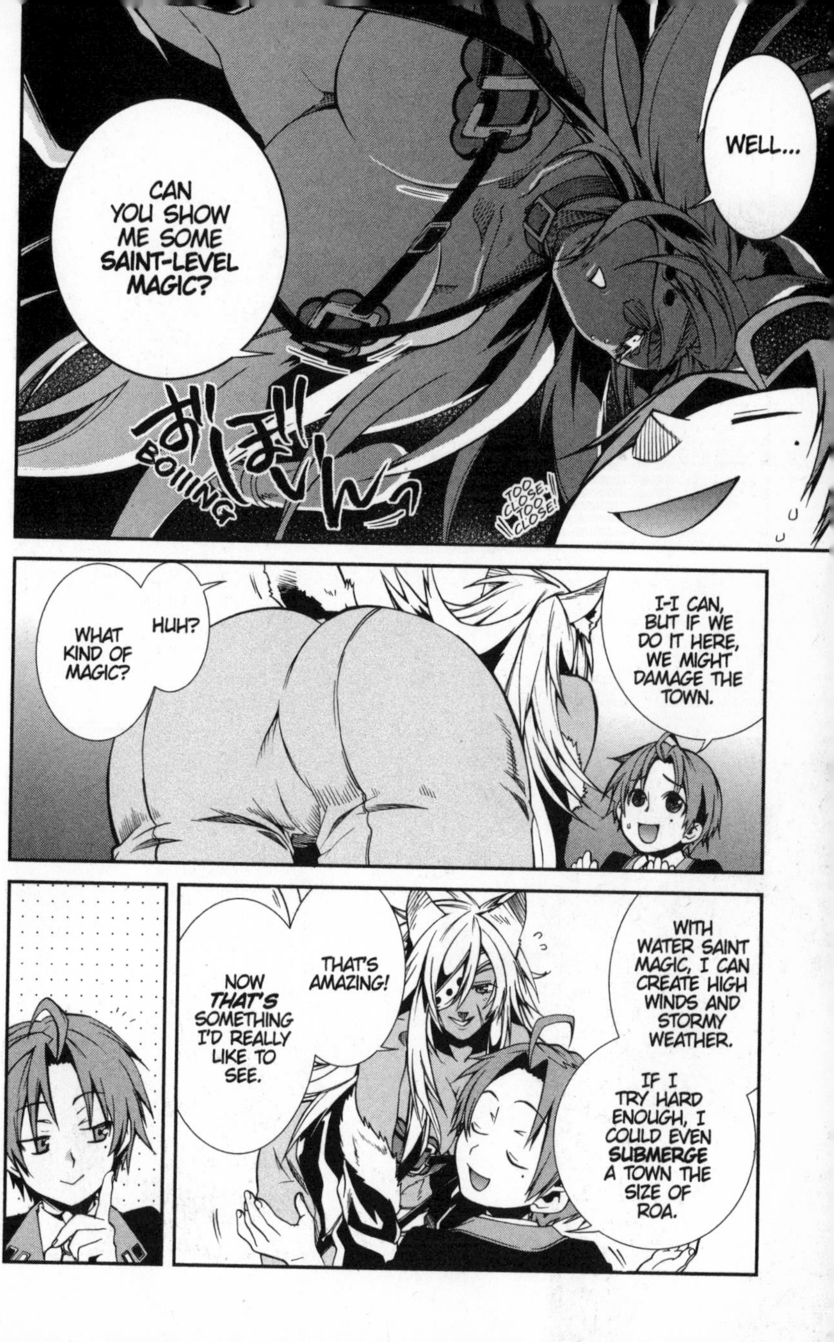
WELL...
CAN YOU SHOW ME SOME SAINT-LEVEL MAGIC?
BOIIING
TOO CLOSE! TOO CLOSE!
I-I CAN, BUT IF WE DO IT HERE, WE MIGHT DAMAGE THE TOWN.
HUH?
WHAT KIND OF MAGIC?
WITH WATER SAINT MAGIC, I CAN CREATE HIGH WINDS AND STORMY WEATHER.
IF I TRY HARD ENOUGH, I COULD EVEN SUBMERGE A TOWN THE SIZE OF ROA.
THAT'S AMAZING!
NOW *THAT'S* SOMETHING I'D REALLY LIKE TO SEE.

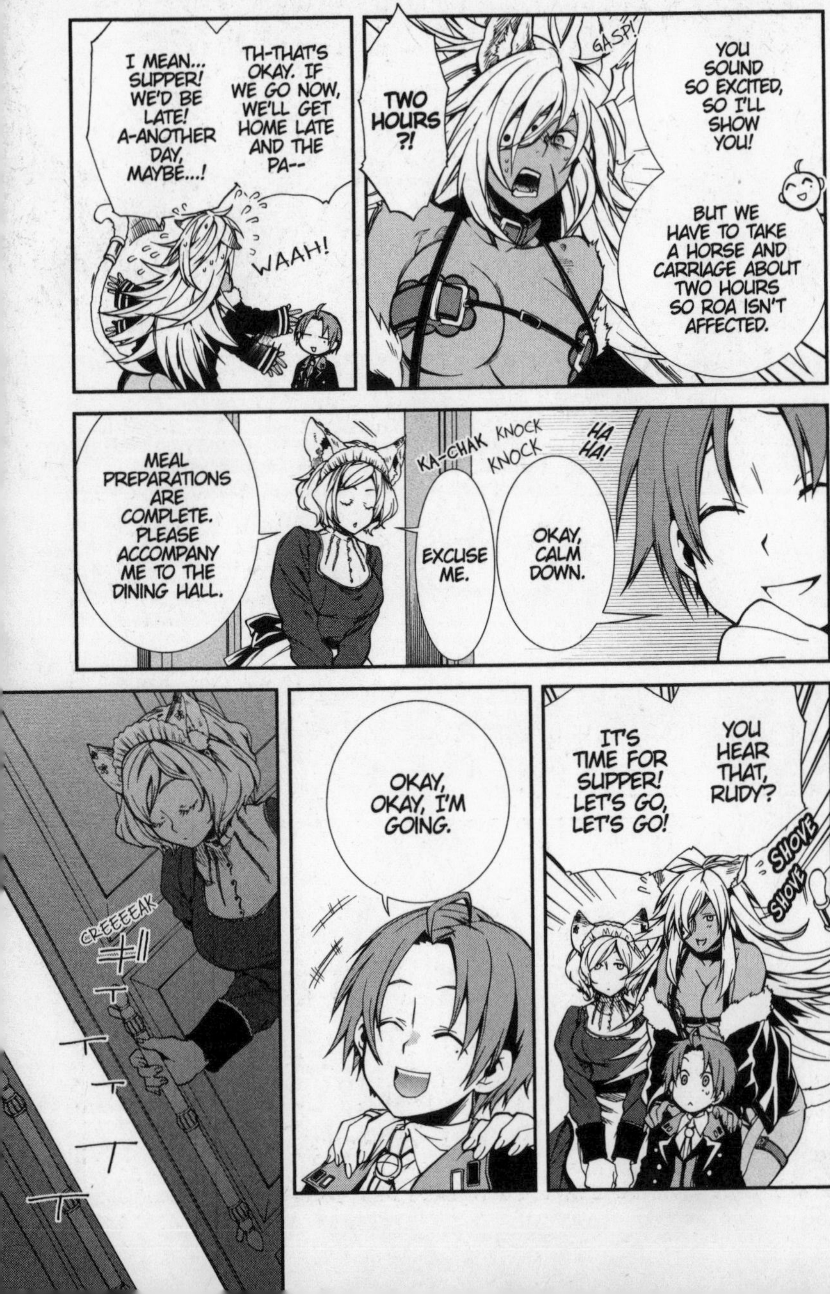
GASP!
YOU SOUND SO EXCITED, SO I'LL SHOW YOU!
BUT WE HAVE TO TAKE A HORSE AND CARRIAGE ABOUT TWO HOURS SO ROA ISN'T AFFECTED.
TWO HOURS?!
TH-THAT'S OKAY. IF WE GO NOW, WE'LL GET HOME LATE AND THE PA--
I MEAN... SUPPER! WE'D BE LATE! A-ANOTHER DAY, MAYBE...!
WAAH!
HA HA!
OKAY, CALM DOWN.
KNOCK KNOCK
KA-CHAK
EXCUSE ME.
MEAL PREPARATIONS ARE COMPLETE. PLEASE ACCOMPANY ME TO THE DINING HALL.
YOU HEAR THAT, RUDY?
IT'S TIME FOR SUPPER! LET'S GO, LET'S GO!
SHOVE SHOVE
OKAY, OKAY, I'M GOING.
CREEEEAK

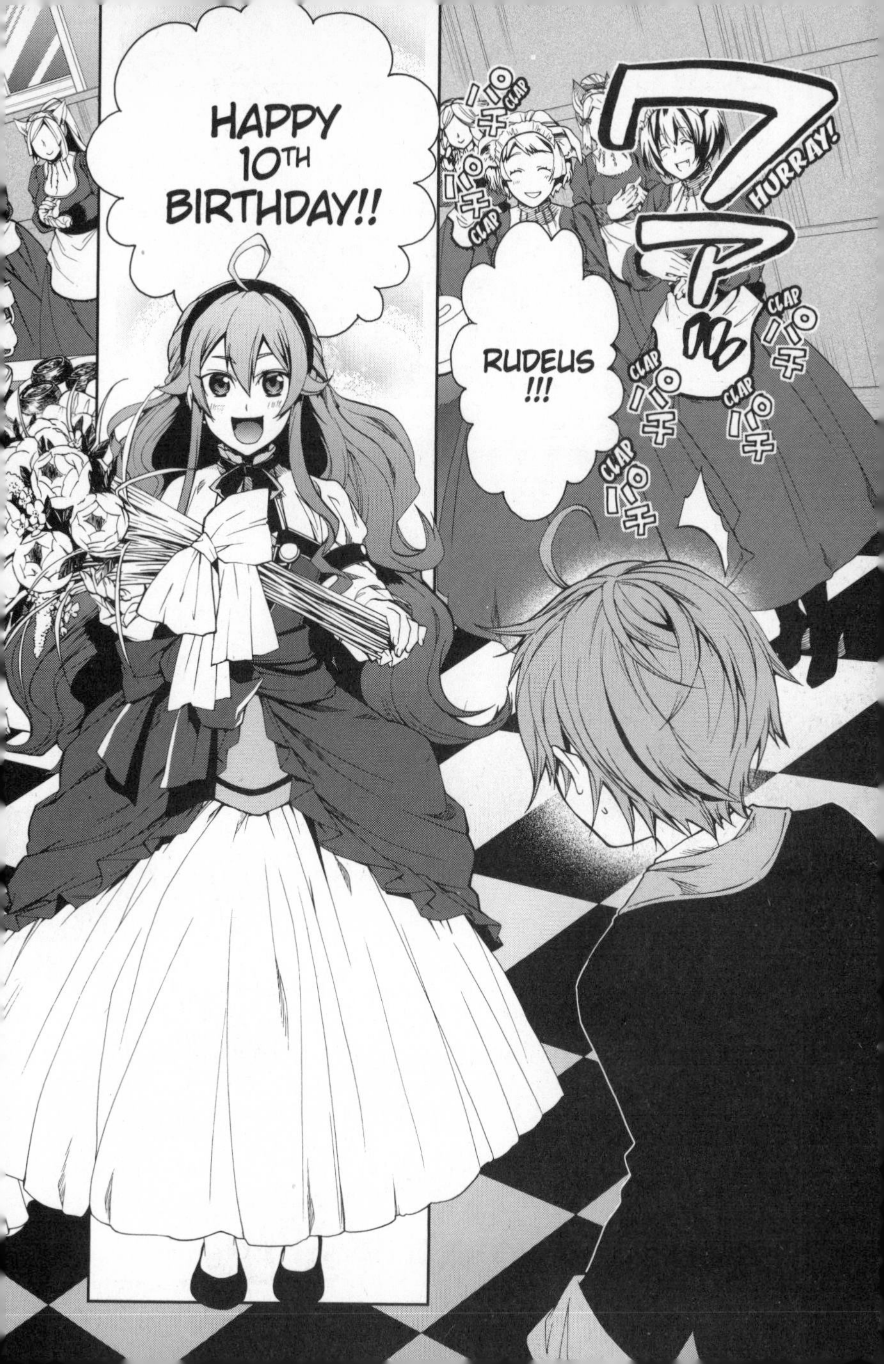

HURRAY!
CLAP パチ
CLAP パチ
CLAP パチ
CLAP パチ
CLAP パチ
CLAP パチ
RUDEUS !!!
HAPPY 10TH BIRTHDAY!!

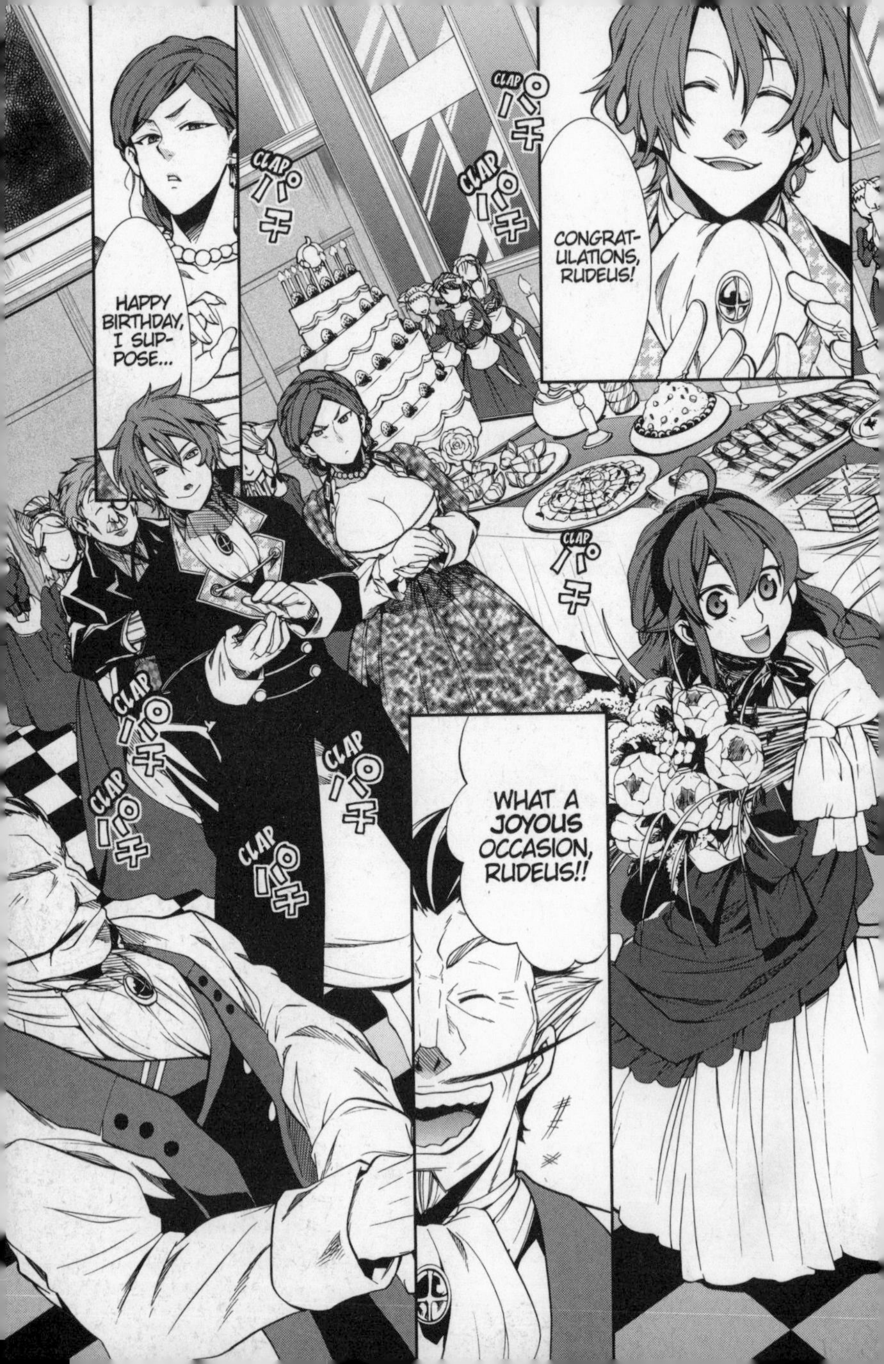
CONGRAT-
ULATIONS,
RUDEUS!
CLAP パチ
CLAP パチ
CLAP パチ
HAPPY
BIRTHDAY,
I SUP-
POSE...
CLAP パチ
CLAP パチ
CLAP パチ
CLAP パチ
CLAP パチ
WHAT A
JOYOUS
OCCASION,
RUDEUS!!

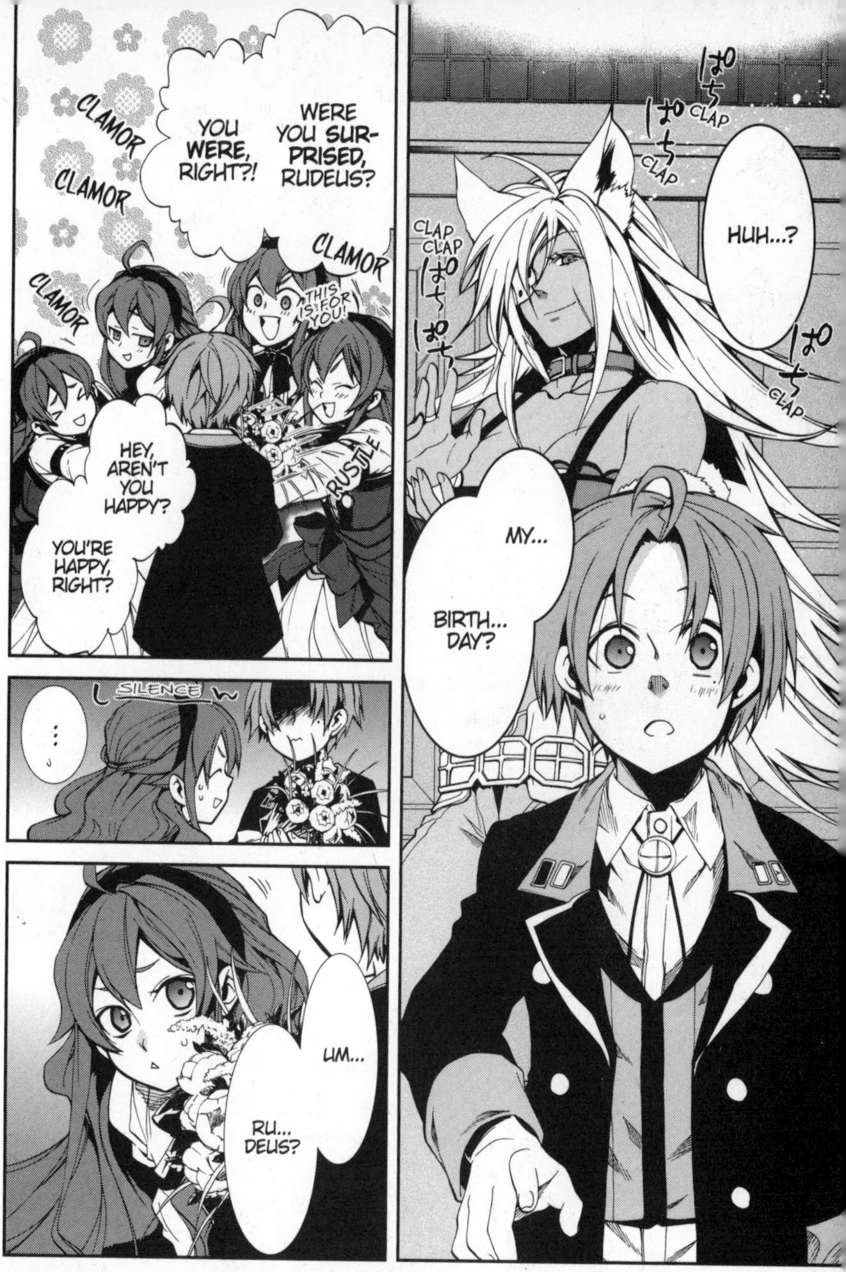
ぱち
CLAP
ぱち
CLAP
HUH...?
CLAP CLAP
ぱちぱち
ぱち
CLAP
MY...
BIRTH... DAY?
CLAMOR
CLAMOR
WERE YOU SUR-PRISED, RUDEUS?
YOU WERE, RIGHT?!
CLAMOR
CLAMOR
THIS IS FOR YOU!
HEY, AREN'T YOU HAPPY?
YOU'RE HAPPY, RIGHT?
RUSTLE
SILENCE
...
UM...
RU... DEUS?

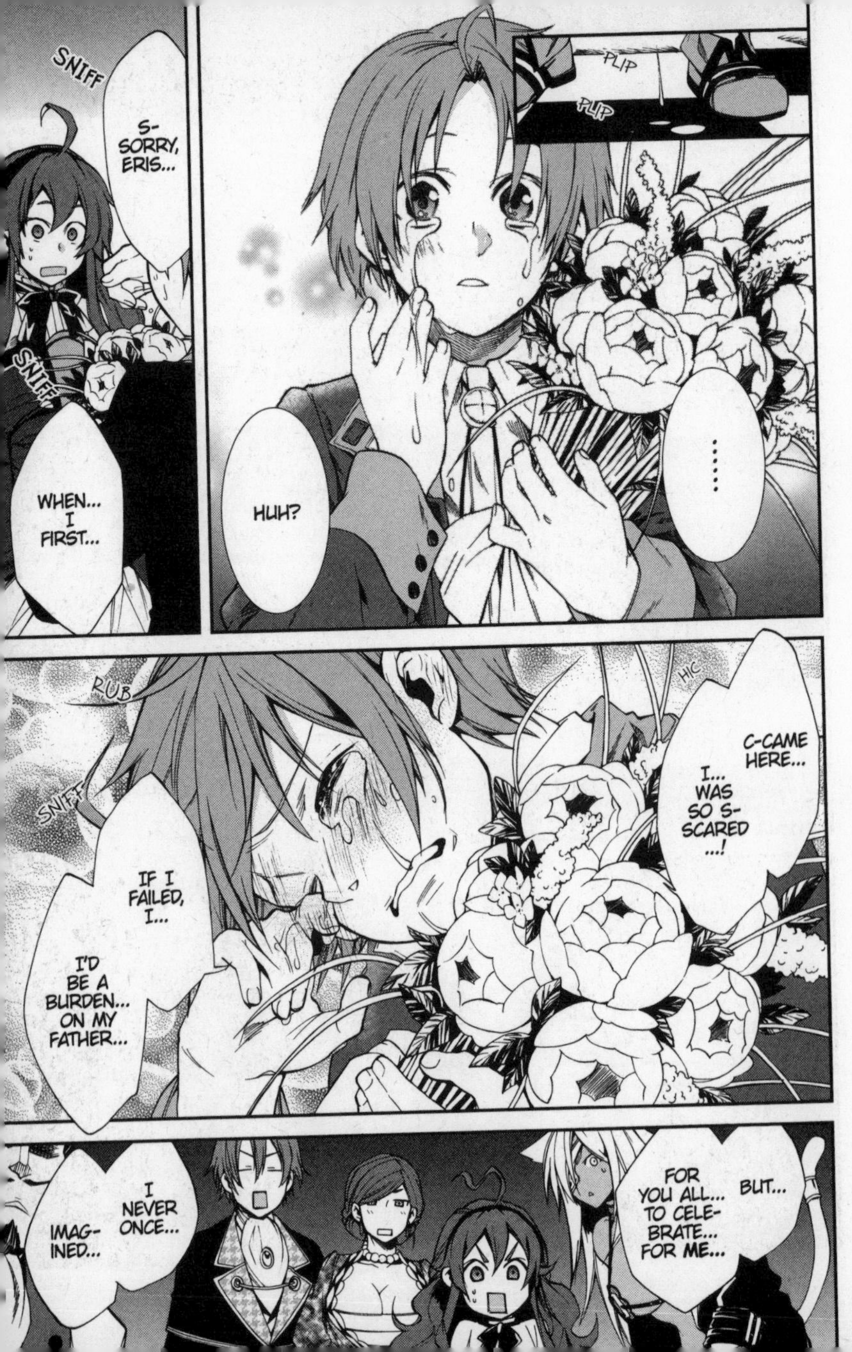
PLIP
PLIP
......
HUH?
SNIFF
S-SORRY, ERIS...
SNIFF
WHEN... I FIRST...
HIC
C-CAME HERE...
I... WAS SO S-SCARED...!
RUB
SNIFF
IF I FAILED, I...
I'D BE A BURDEN... ON MY FATHER...
BUT...
FOR YOU ALL... TO CELE-BRATE... FOR ME...
I NEVER ONCE...
IMAG-INED...

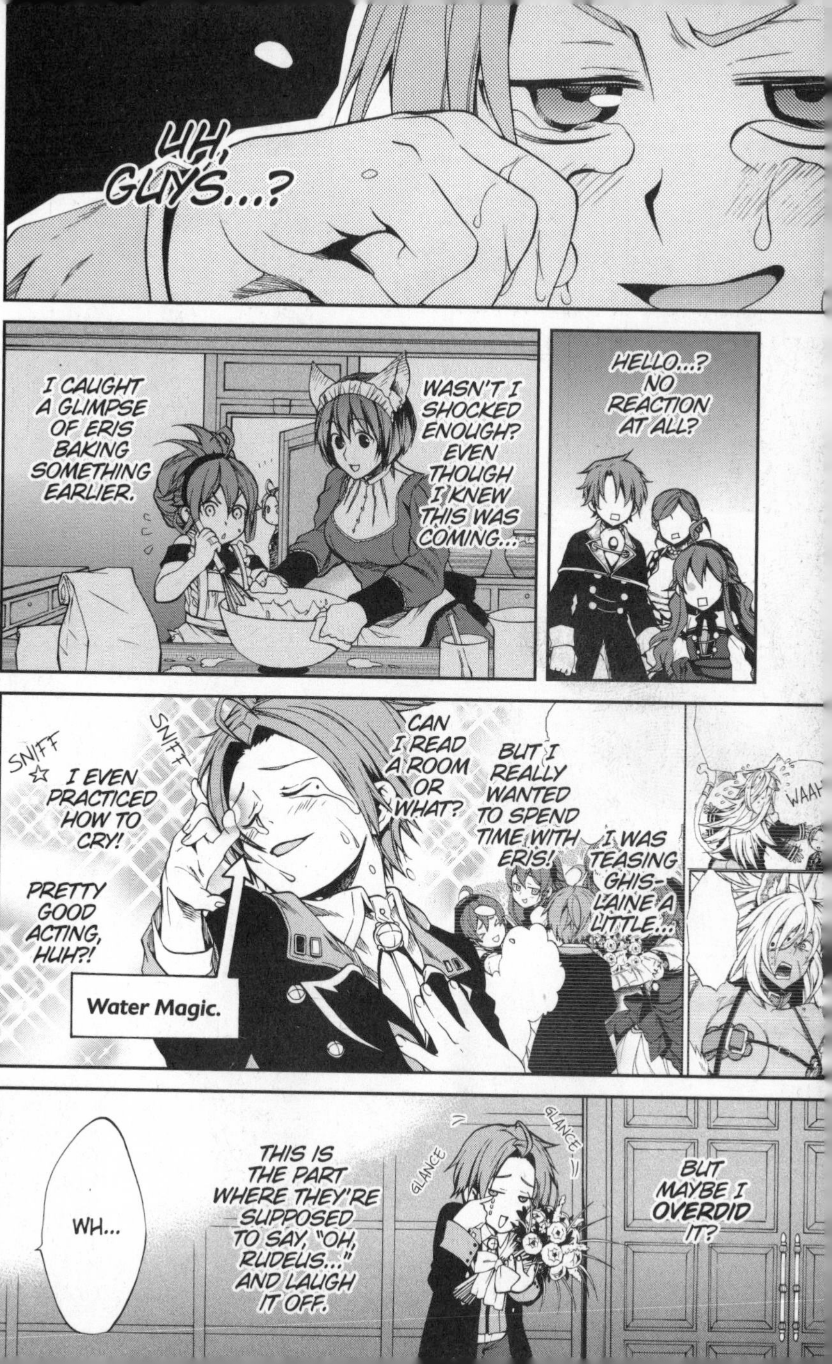
UH, GUYS...?
HELLO...? NO REACTION AT ALL?
WASN'T I SHOCKED ENOUGH? EVEN THOUGH I KNEW THIS WAS COMING...
I CAUGHT A GLIMPSE OF ERIS BAKING SOMETHING EARLIER.
WAAH
I WAS TEASING GHIS-LAINE A LITTLE...
BUT I REALLY WANTED TO SPEND TIME WITH ERIS!
CAN I READ A ROOM OR WHAT?
SNIFF
SNIFF ☆
I EVEN PRACTICED HOW TO CRY!
PRETTY GOOD ACTING, HUH?!
Water Magic.
BUT MAYBE I OVERDID IT?
GLANCE
GLANCE
THIS IS THE PART WHERE THEY'RE SUPPOSED TO SAY, "OH, RUDEUS..." AND LAUGH IT OFF.
WH...

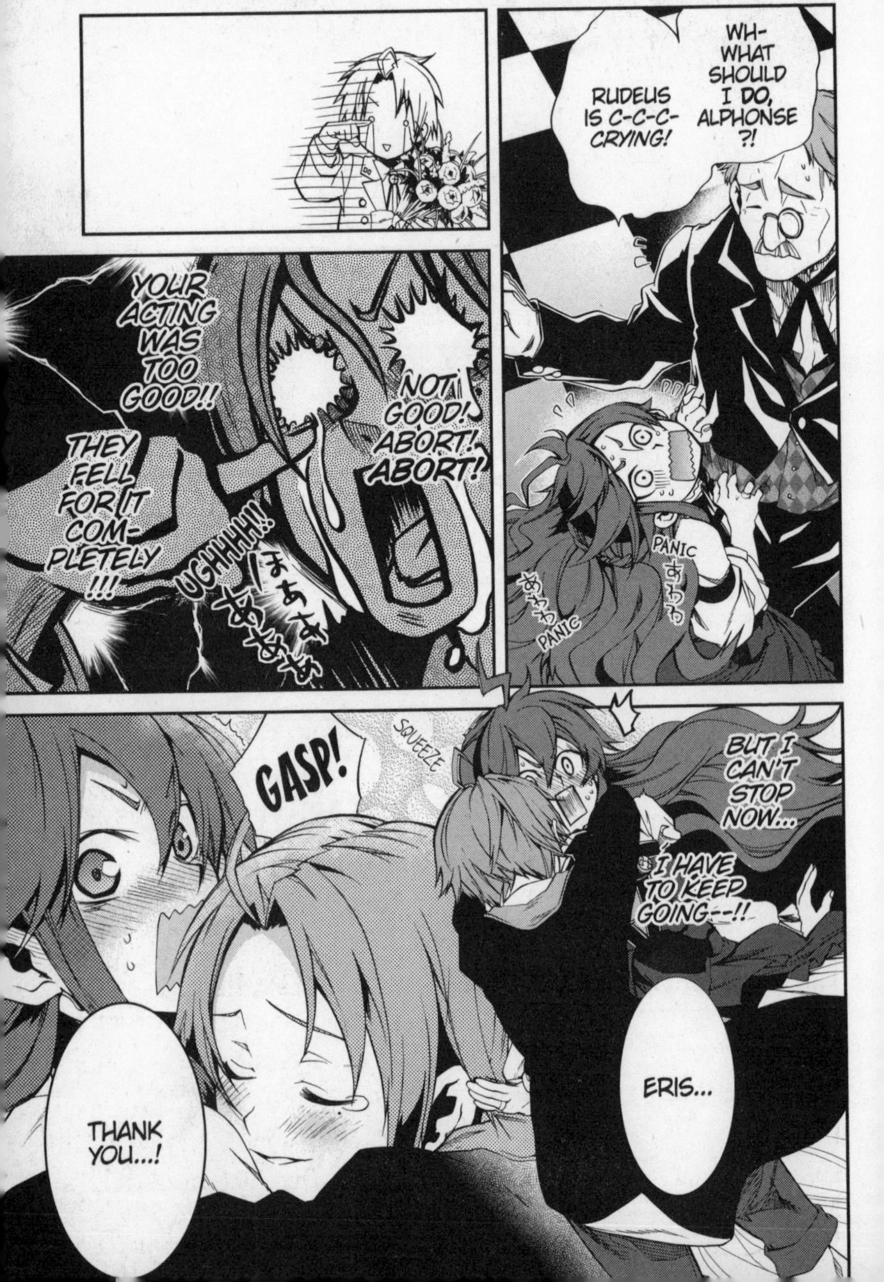
WH-WHAT SHOULD I DO, ALPHONSE?!
RUDEUS IS C-C-C-CRYING!
PANIC あわわ
あわわ PANIC
NOT GOOD! ABORT! ABORT!
YOUR ACTING WAS TOO GOOD!!
THEY FELL FOR IT COM-PLETELY!!!
UGHHHH!!
BUT I CAN'T STOP NOW...
I HAVE TO KEEP GOING--!!
SQUEEZE
GASP!
ERIS...
THANK YOU...!

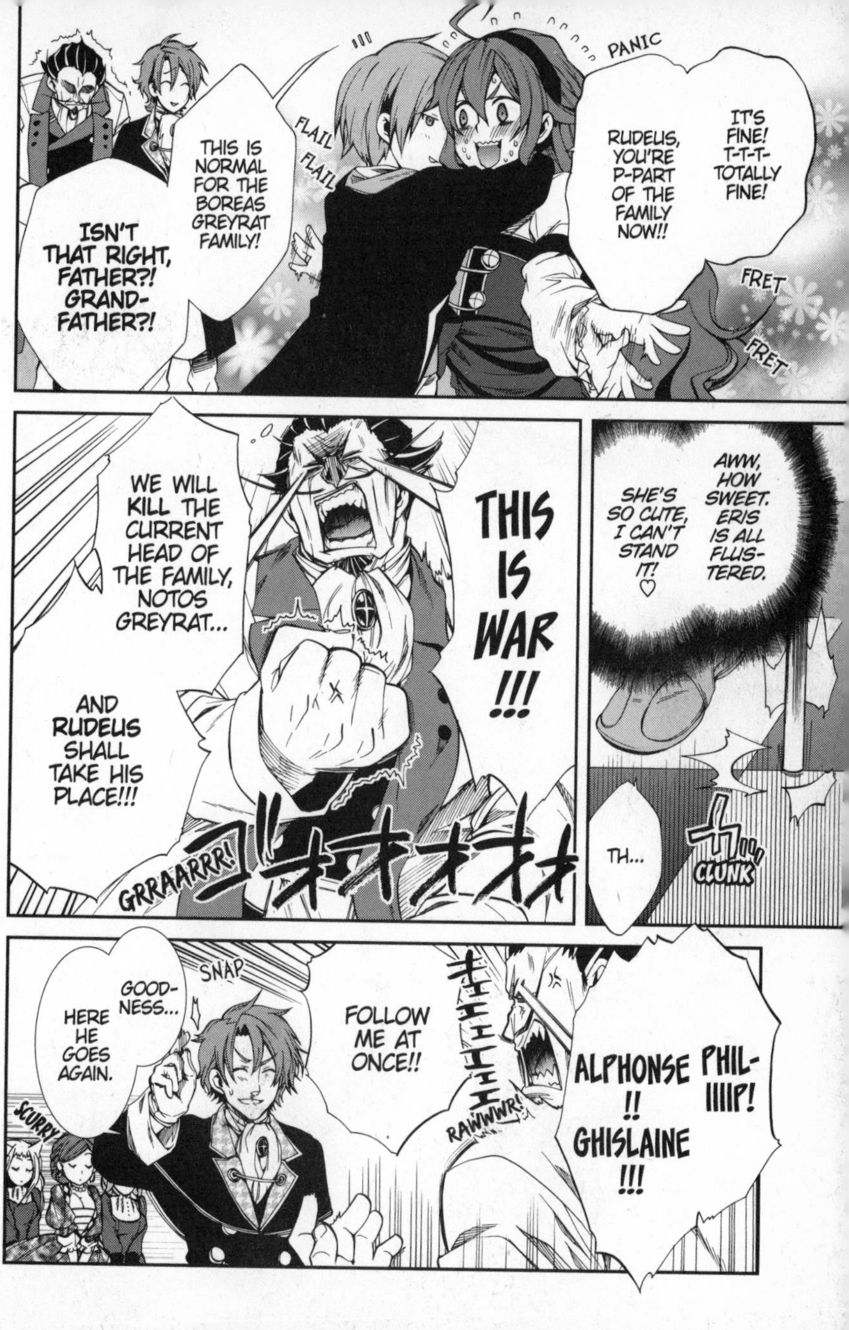
PANIC
IT'S FINE! T-T-T-TOTALLY FINE!
RUDEUS, YOU'RE P-PART OF THE FAMILY NOW!!
FRET
FRET
FLAIL
FLAIL
THIS IS NORMAL FOR THE BOREAS GREYRAT FAMILY!
ISN'T THAT RIGHT, FATHER?! GRAND-FATHER?!
AWW, HOW SWEET. ERIS IS ALL FLUS-TERED.
SHE'S SO CUTE, I CAN'T STAND IT! ♡
TH...
CLUNK
THIS IS WAR!!!
WE WILL KILL THE CURRENT HEAD OF THE FAMILY, NOTOS GREYRAT...
AND RUDEUS SHALL TAKE HIS PLACE!!!
GRRAARRR!
PHIL-IIIIP!
ALPHONSE!! GHISLAINE!!!
RAWWWR!
FOLLOW ME AT ONCE!!
SNAP
GOOD-NESS...
HERE HE GOES AGAIN.
SCURRY

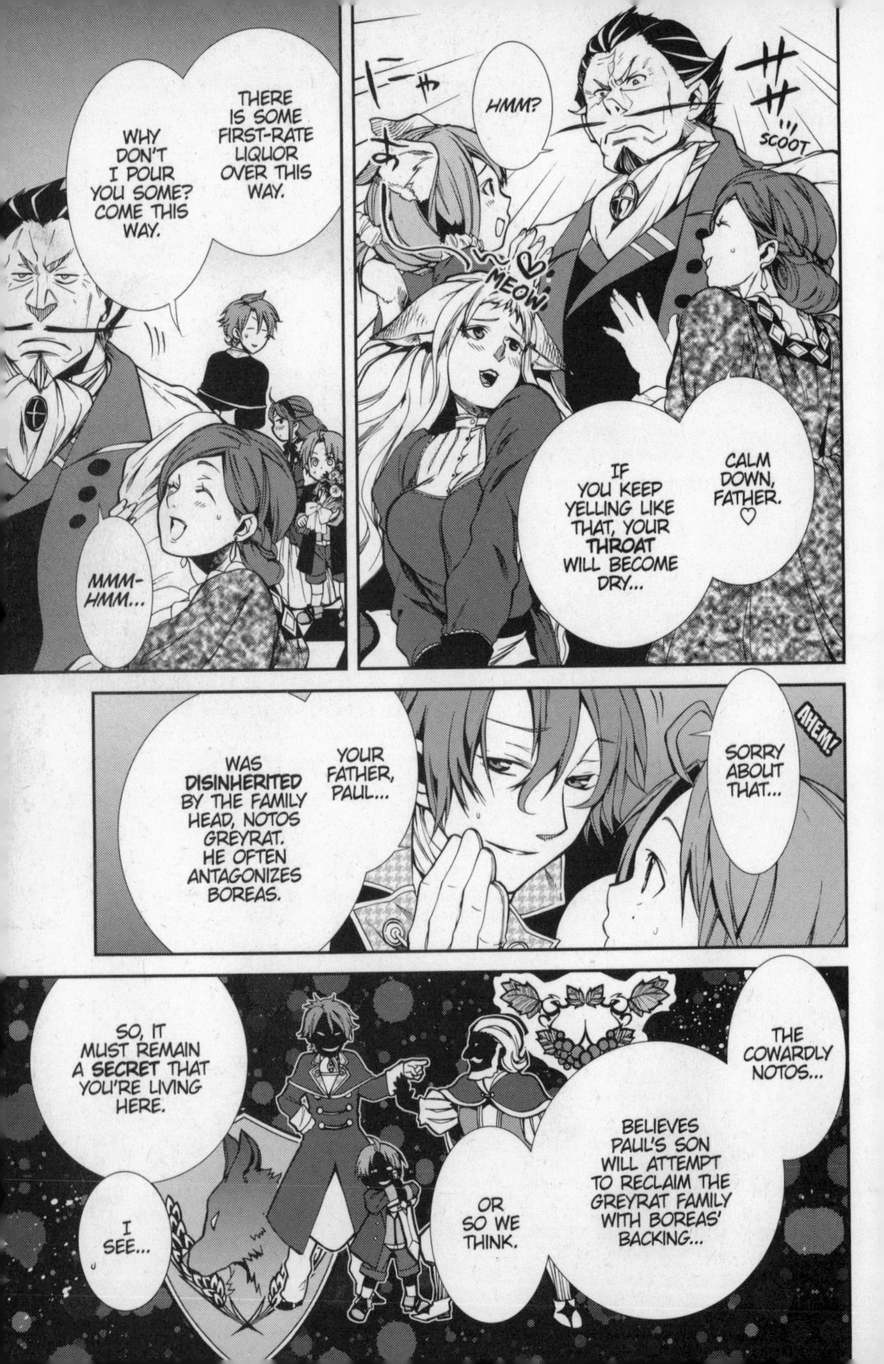
SCOOT
HMM?
MEOW
CALM DOWN, FATHER. ♡
IF YOU KEEP YELLING LIKE THAT, YOUR THROAT WILL BECOME DRY...
THERE IS SOME FIRST-RATE LIQUOR OVER THIS WAY.
WHY DON'T I POUR YOU SOME? COME THIS WAY.
MMM-HMM...
AHEM!
SORRY ABOUT THAT...
YOUR FATHER, PAUL...
WAS DISINHERITED BY THE FAMILY HEAD, NOTOS GREYRAT. HE OFTEN ANTAGONIZES BOREAS.
THE COWARDLY NOTOS...
BELIEVES PAUL'S SON WILL ATTEMPT TO RECLAIM THE GREYRAT FAMILY WITH BOREAS' BACKING...
OR SO WE THINK.
SO, IT MUST REMAIN A SECRET THAT YOU'RE LIVING HERE.
I SEE...

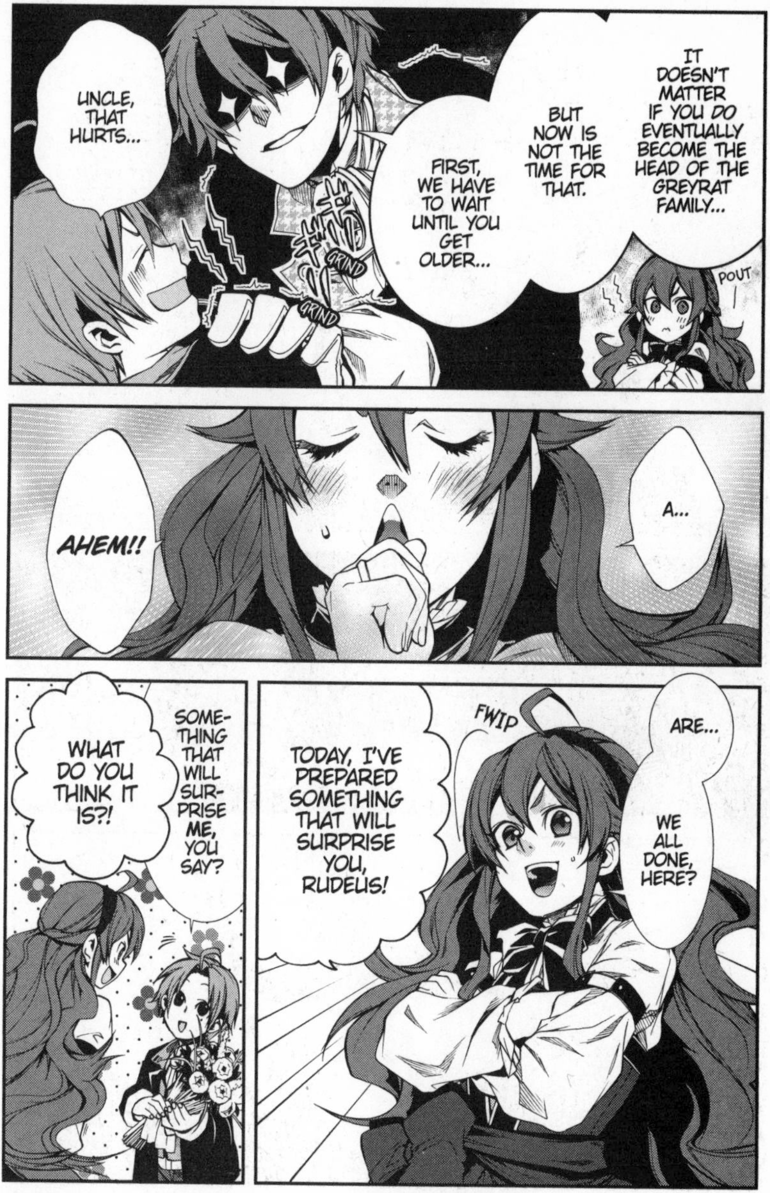
IT DOESN'T MATTER IF YOU *DO* EVENTUALLY BECOME THE HEAD OF THE GREYRAT FAMILY...
POUT
BUT NOW IS NOT THE TIME FOR THAT.
FIRST, WE HAVE TO WAIT UNTIL YOU GET OLDER...
GRIND
GRIND
UNCLE, THAT HURTS...
A...
AHEM!!
ARE...
WE ALL DONE, HERE?
FWIP
TODAY, I'VE PREPARED SOMETHING THAT WILL SURPRISE YOU, RUDEUS!
SOMETHING THAT WILL SURPRISE ME, YOU SAY?
WHAT DO YOU THINK IT IS?!

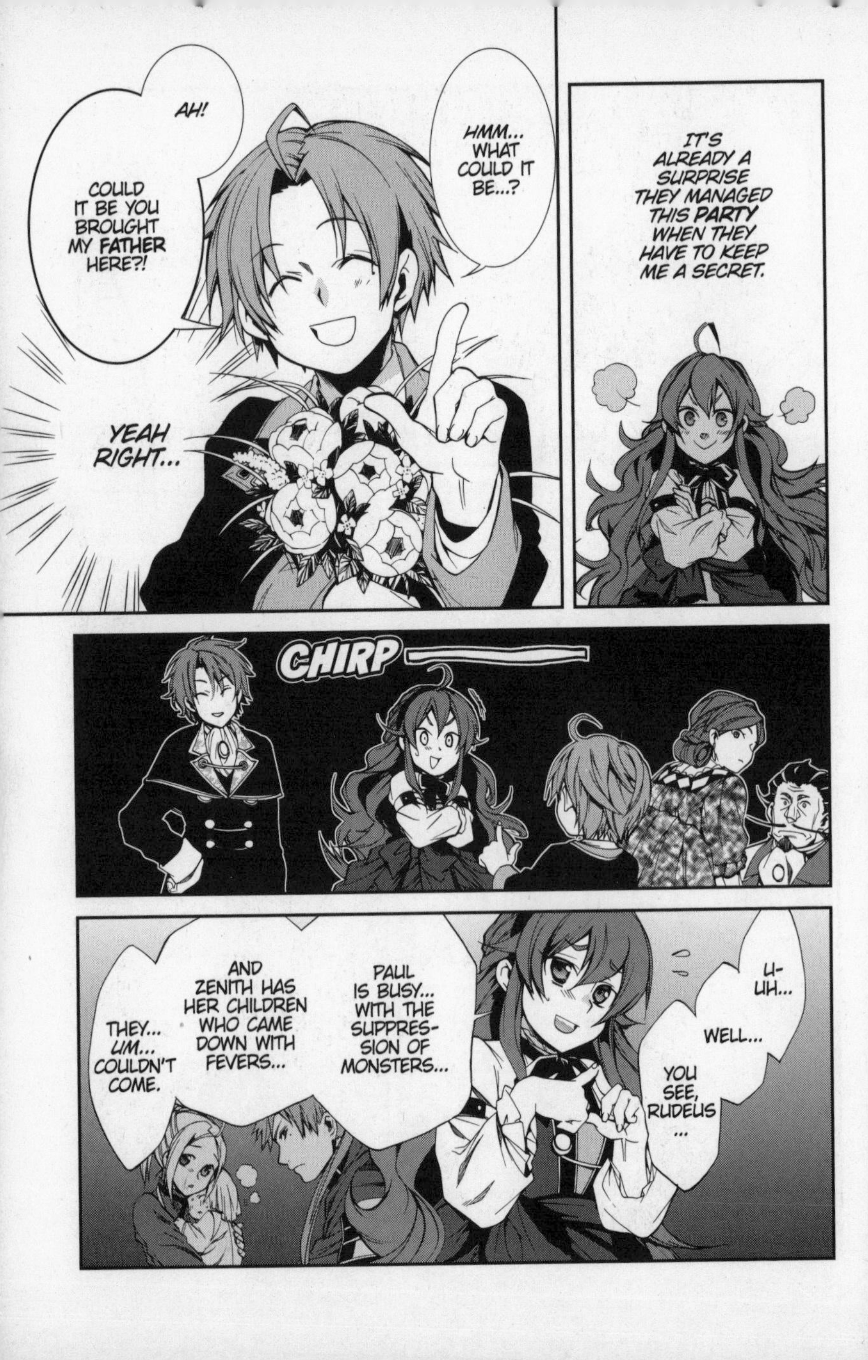
IT'S ALREADY A SURPRISE THEY MANAGED THIS PARTY WHEN THEY HAVE TO KEEP ME A SECRET.
HMM... WHAT COULD IT BE...?
AH!
COULD IT BE YOU BROUGHT MY FATHER HERE?!
YEAH RIGHT...
CHIRP
U-UH...
WELL...
YOU SEE, RUDEUS...
PAUL IS BUSY... WITH THE SUPPRESSION OF MONSTERS...
AND ZENITH HAS HER CHILDREN WHO CAME DOWN WITH FEVERS...
THEY... UM... COULDN'T COME.

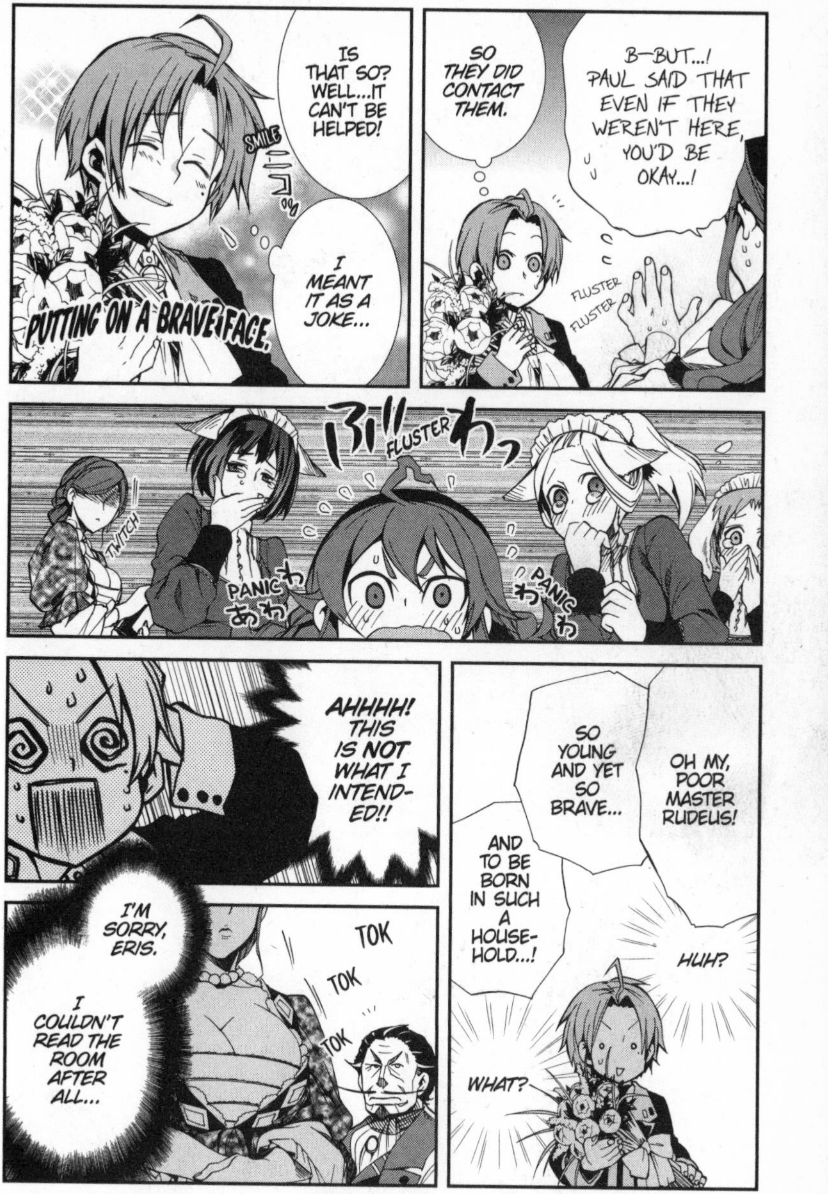
B—BUT...! PAUL SAID THAT EVEN IF THEY WEREN'T HERE, YOU'D BE OKAY...!
SO THEY DID CONTACT THEM.
FLUSTER FLUSTER
IS THAT SO? WELL...IT CAN'T BE HELPED!
SMILE
I MEANT IT AS A JOKE...
PUTTING ON A BRAVE FACE.
FLUSTER
PANIC
PANIC
TWITCH
OH MY, POOR MASTER RUDEUS!
SO YOUNG AND YET SO BRAVE...
AND TO BE BORN IN SUCH A HOUSE-HOLD...!
HUH?
WHAT?
AHHHH! THIS IS NOT WHAT I INTEND-ED!!
TOK
TOK
TOK
I'M SORRY, ERIS.
I COULDN'T READ THE ROOM AFTER ALL...

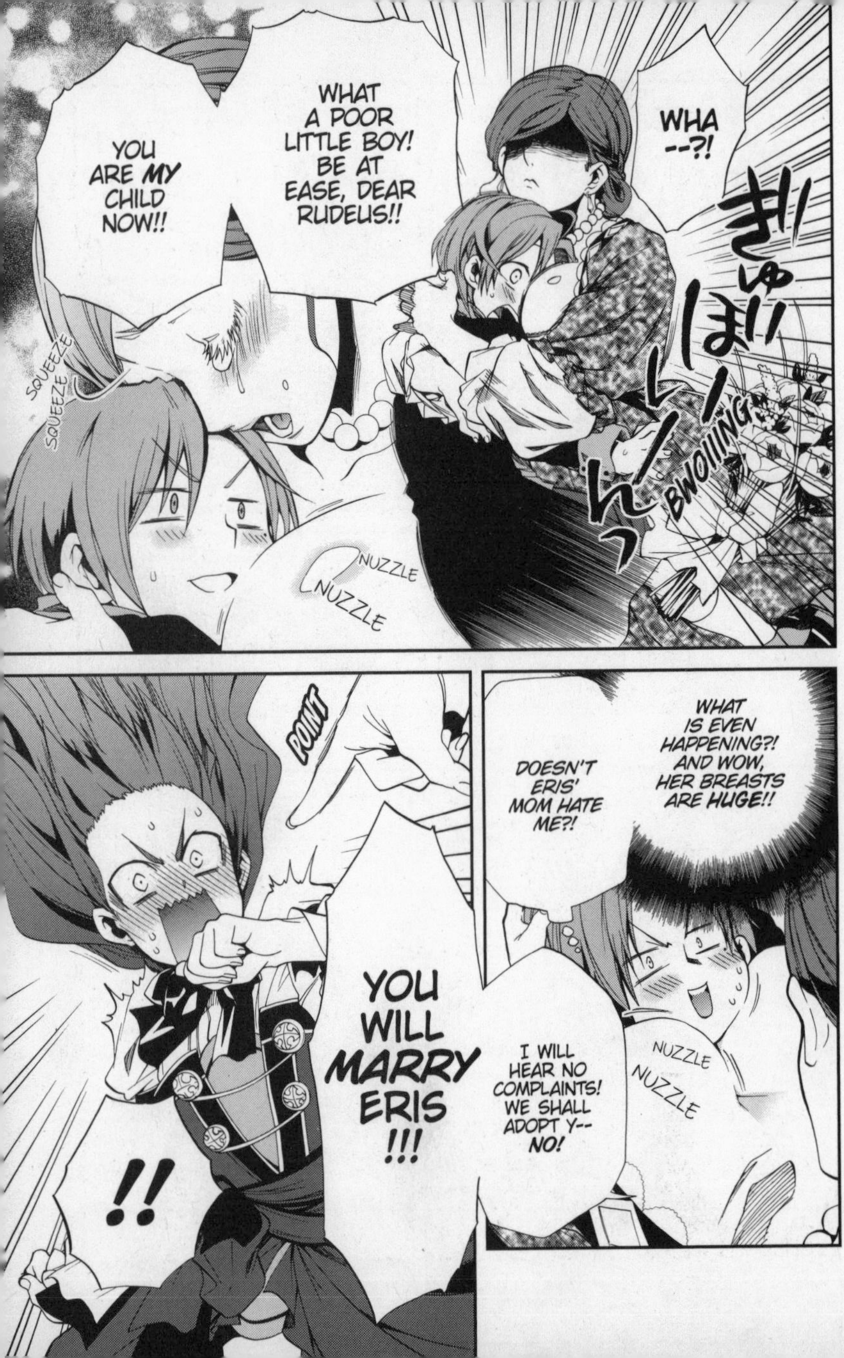
WHA --?!
ぎゅ
ぼい～ん
BWOIIING
WHAT A POOR LITTLE BOY! BE AT EASE, DEAR RUDEUS!!
YOU ARE MY CHILD NOW!!
SQUEEZE SQUEEZE
NUZZLE NUZZLE
WHAT IS EVEN HAPPENING?! AND WOW, HER BREASTS ARE HUGE!!
DOESN'T ERIS' MOM HATE ME?!
I WILL HEAR NO COMPLAINTS! WE SHALL ADOPT Y-- NO!
NUZZLE NUZZLE
POINT
YOU WILL MARRY ERIS !!!
!!

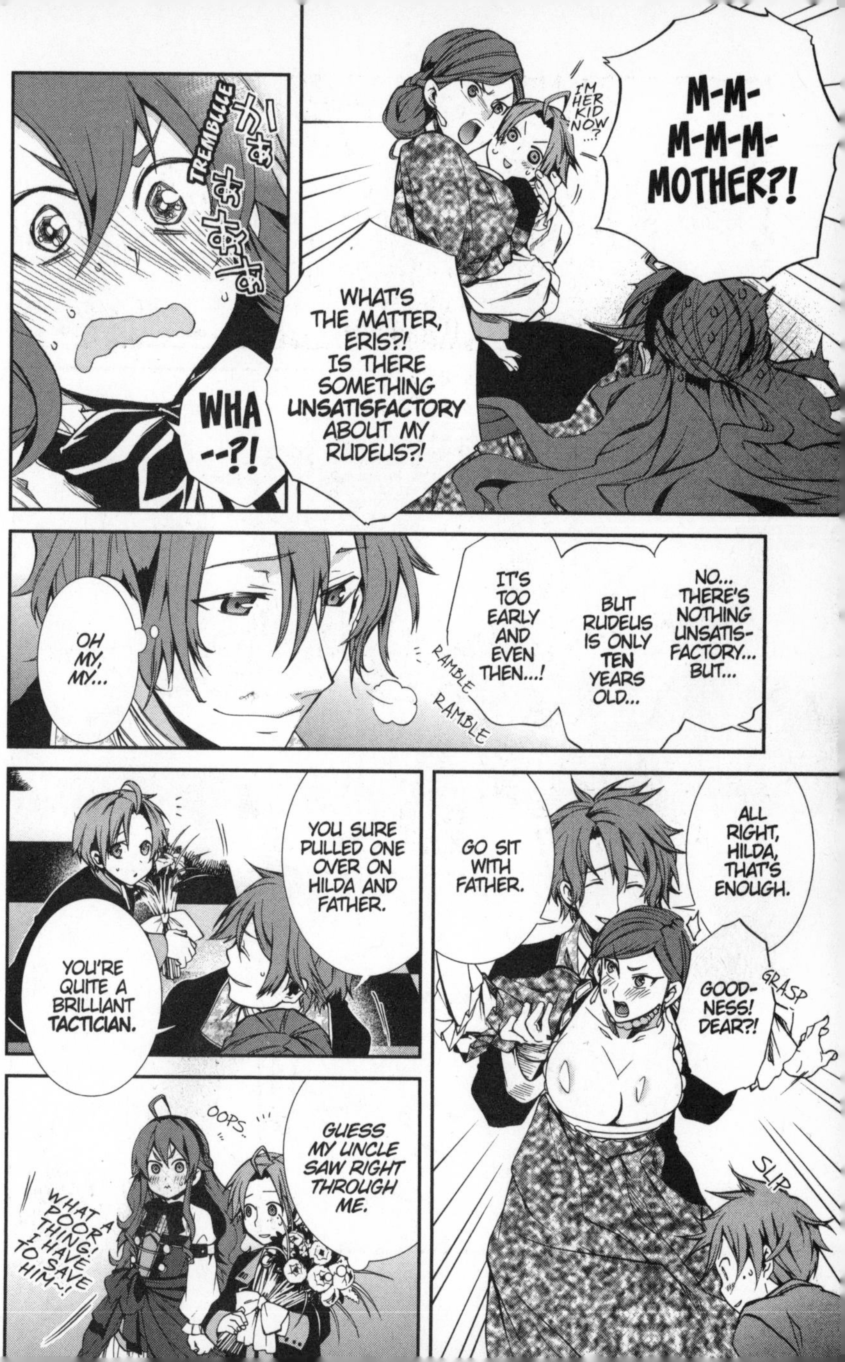
M-M-M-M-M-MOTHER?!
I'M HER KID NOW...?
WHAT'S THE MATTER, ERIS?! IS THERE SOMETHING UNSATISFACTORY ABOUT MY RUDEUS?!
TREMBLLLE
かぁぁぁぁぁ
WHA--?!
NO... THERE'S NOTHING UNSATIS-FACTORY... BUT...
BUT RUDEUS IS ONLY TEN YEARS OLD...
IT'S TOO EARLY AND EVEN THEN...!
RAMBLE
RAMBLE
OH MY, MY...
ALL RIGHT, HILDA, THAT'S ENOUGH.
GO SIT WITH FATHER.
GOOD-NESS! DEAR?!
GRASP
SLIP
YOU SURE PULLED ONE OVER ON HILDA AND FATHER.
YOU'RE QUITE A BRILLIANT TACTICIAN.
GUESS MY UNCLE SAW RIGHT THROUGH ME.
OOPS
WHAT A POOR THING! I HAVE TO SAVE HIM~!

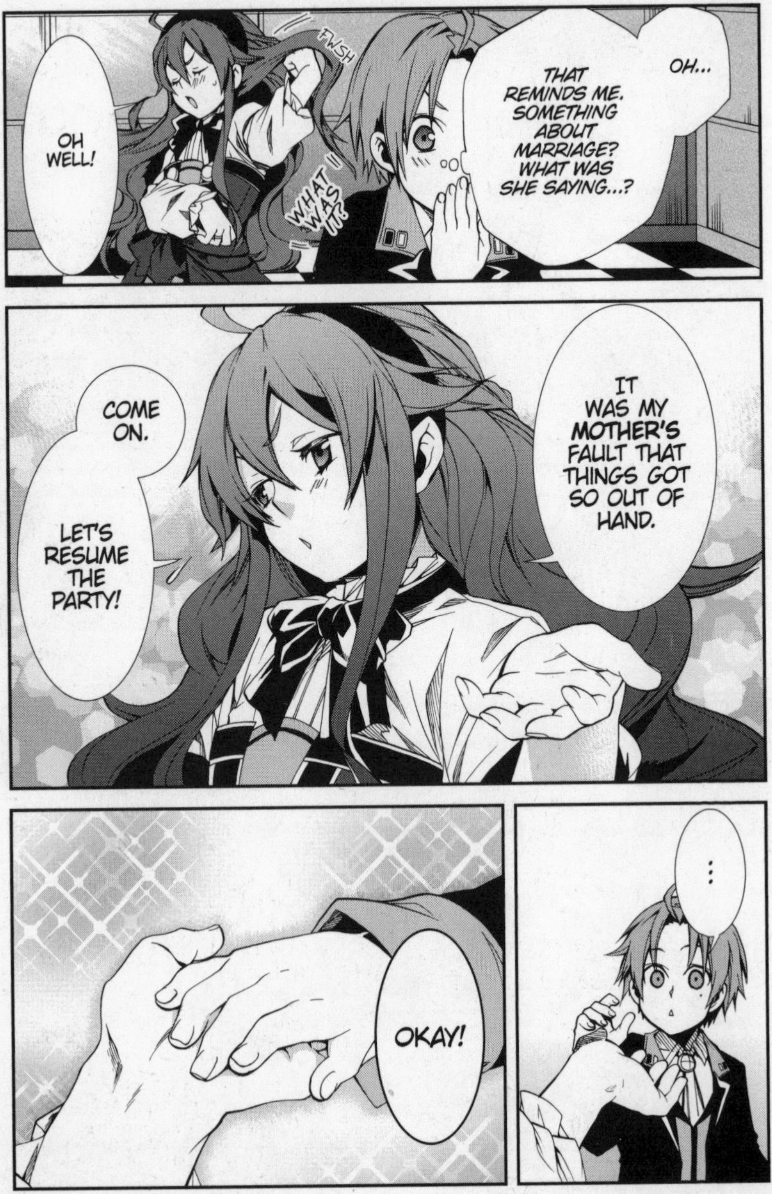
OH...
THAT REMINDS ME. SOMETHING ABOUT MARRIAGE? WHAT WAS SHE SAYING...?
FWSH
WHAT WAS IT?
OH WELL!
IT WAS MY MOTHER'S FAULT THAT THINGS GOT SO OUT OF HAND.
COME ON.
LET'S RESUME THE PARTY!
...
OKAY!

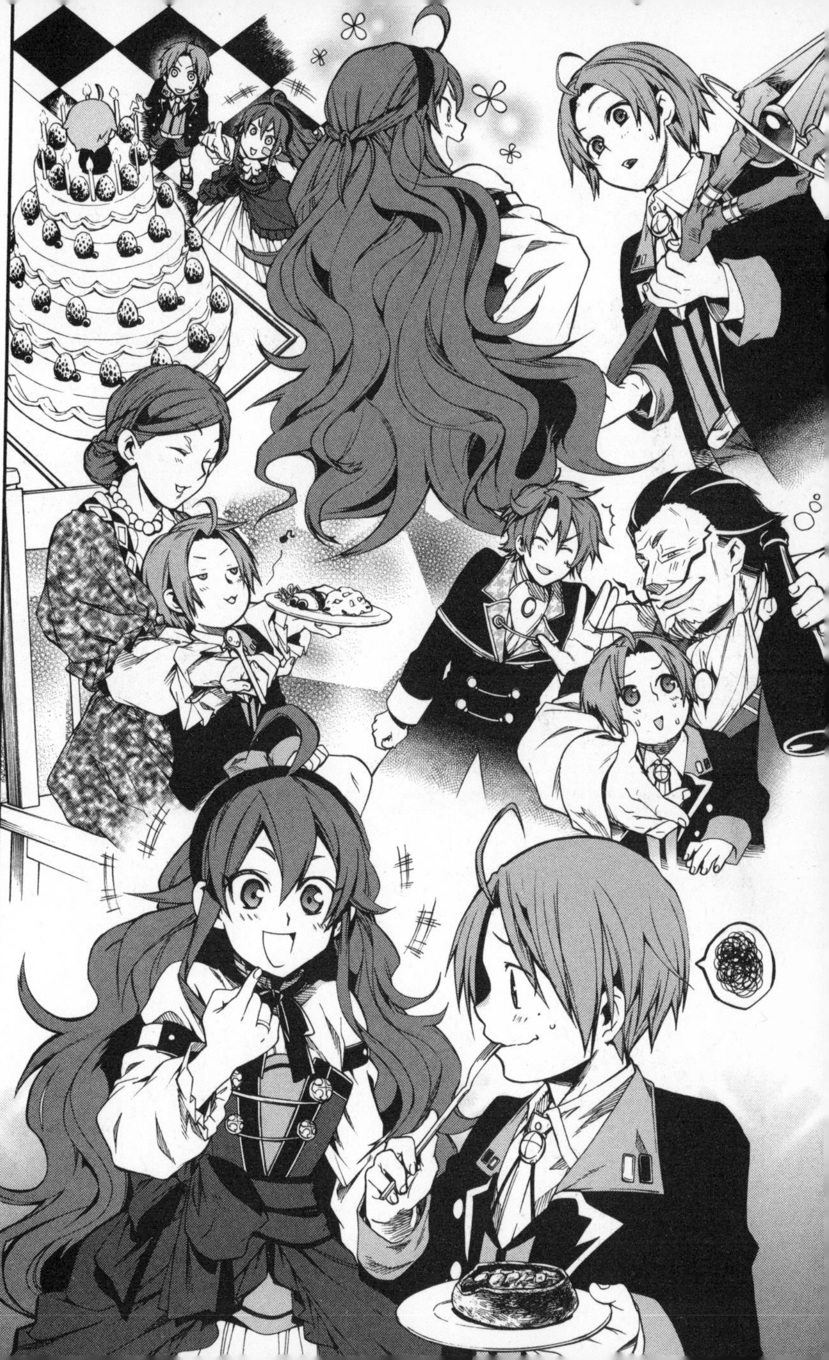

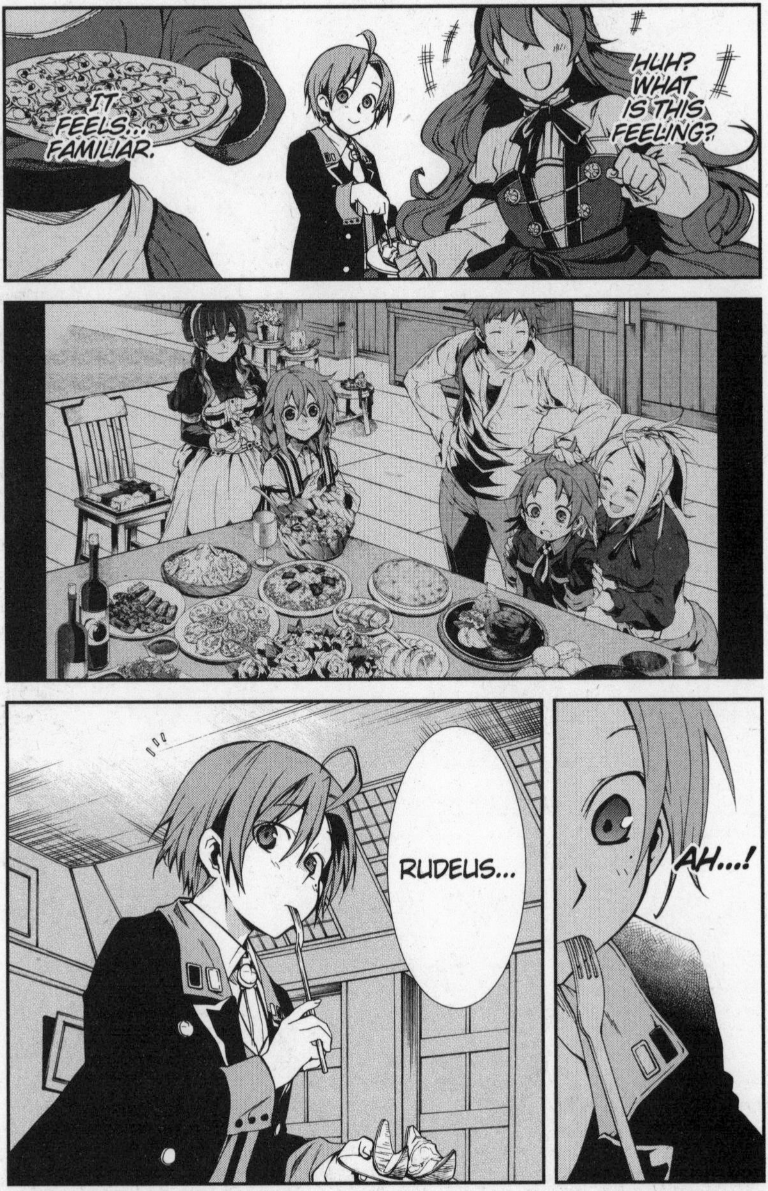
HUH? WHAT IS THIS FEELING?
IT FEELS... FAMILIAR.
AH...!
RUDEUS...

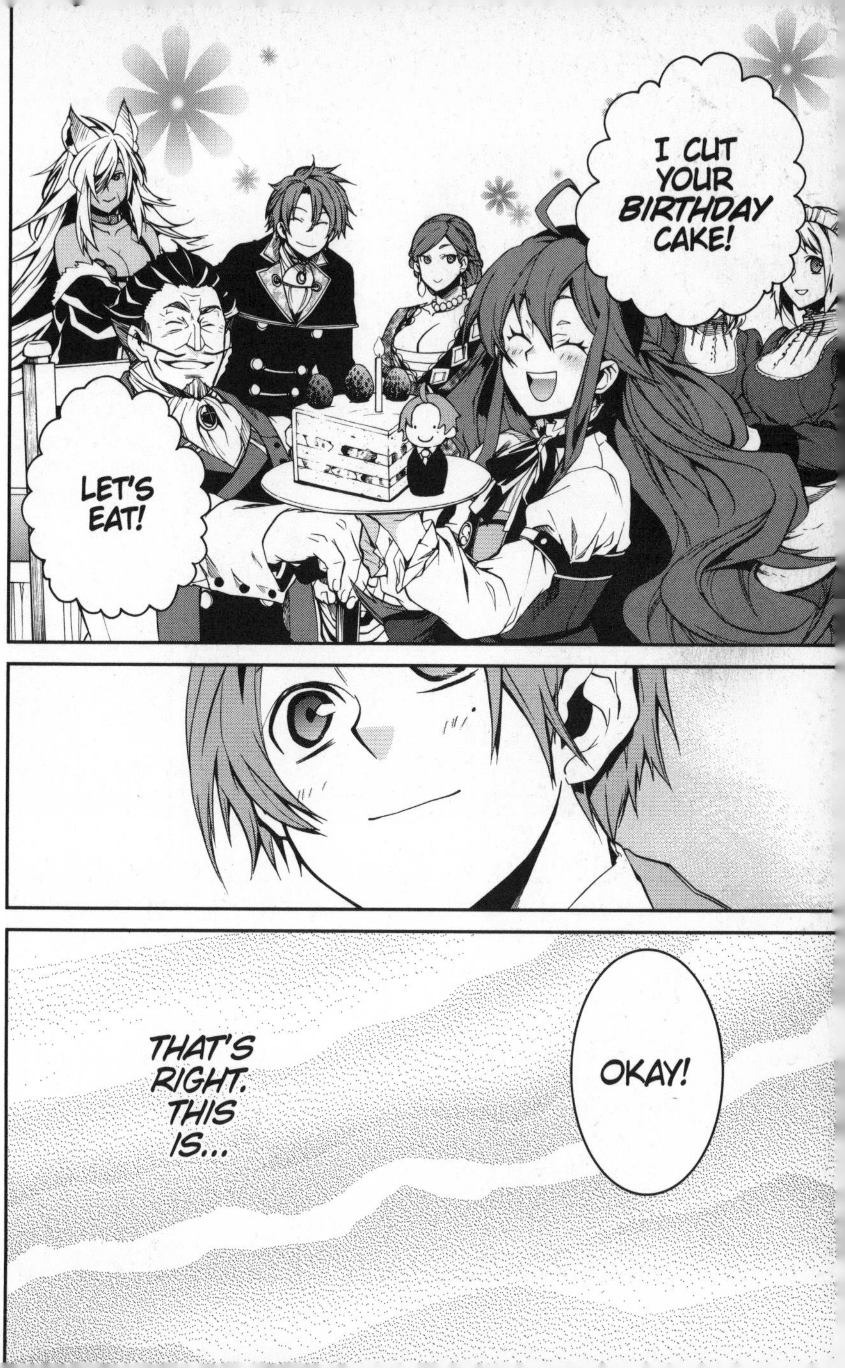
I CUT YOUR BIRTHDAY CAKE!
LET'S EAT!
OKAY!
THAT'S RIGHT. THIS IS...

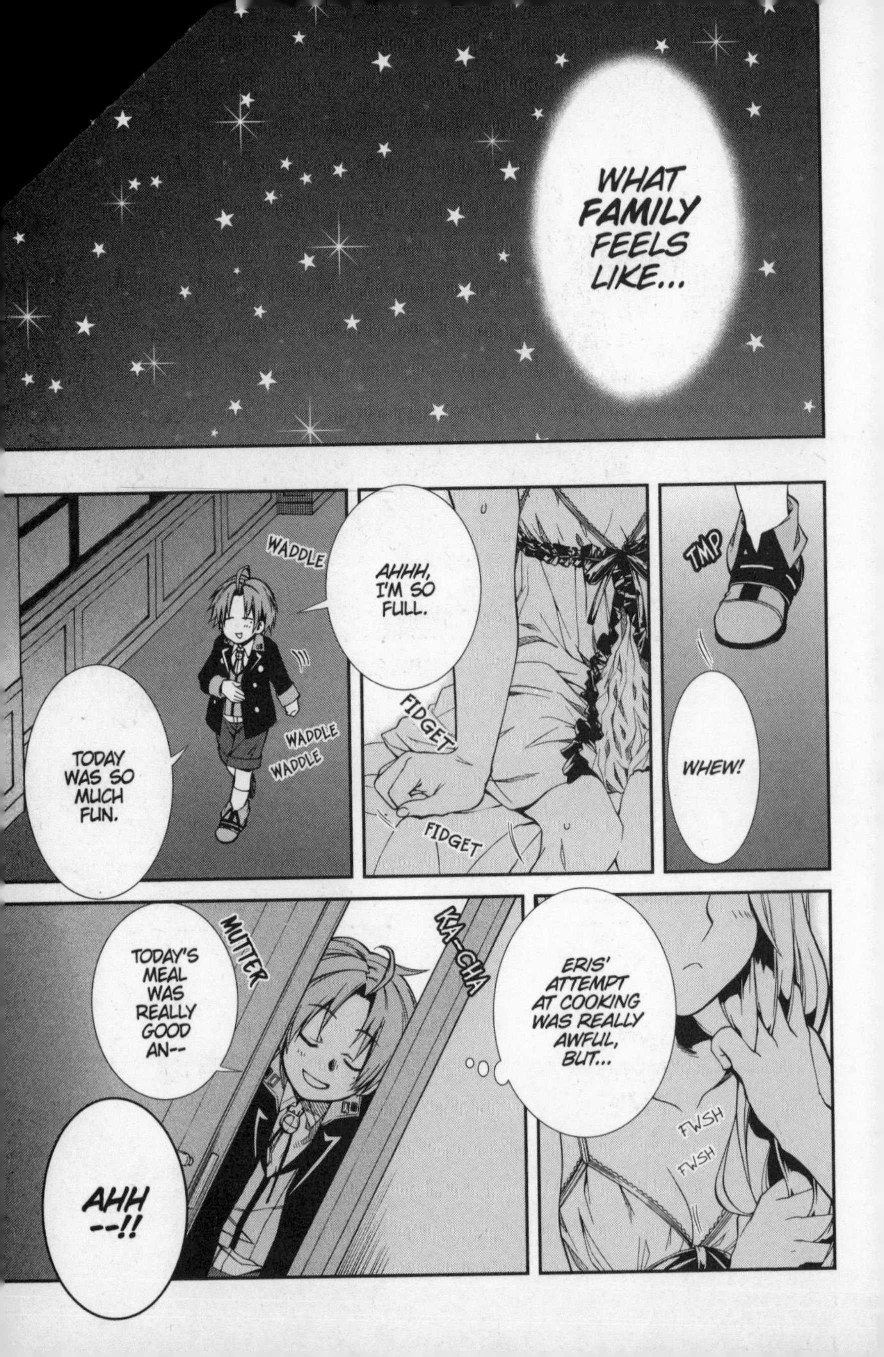
WHAT FAMILY FEELS LIKE...
TMP
WHEW!
FIDGET
FIDGET
WADDLE
AHHH, I'M SO FULL.
WADDLE WADDLE
TODAY WAS SO MUCH FUN.
ERIS' ATTEMPT AT COOKING WAS REALLY AWFUL, BUT...
FWSH
FWSH
KA-CHA
MUTTER
TODAY'S MEAL WAS REALLY GOOD AN--
AHH--!!

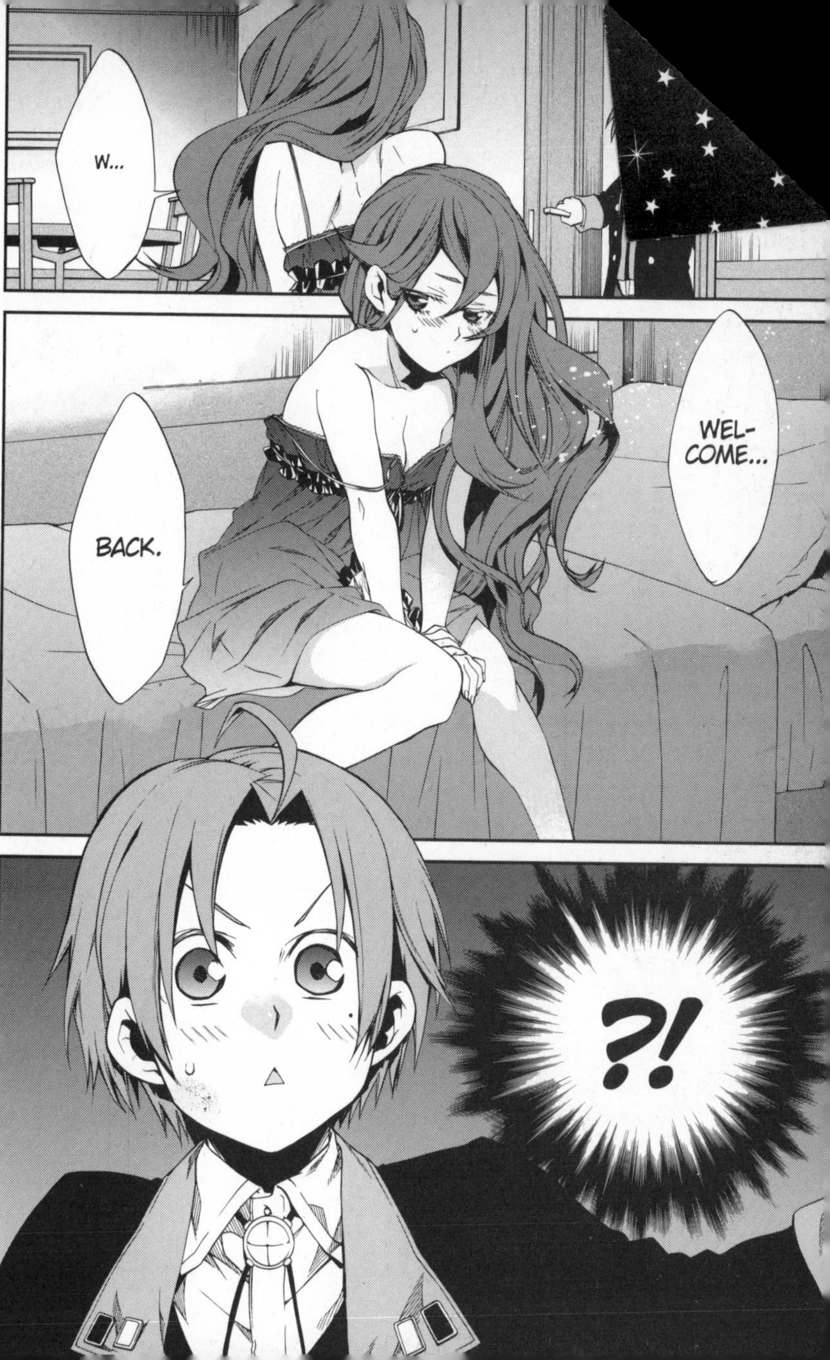
W...
WEL-
COME...
BACK.
?!

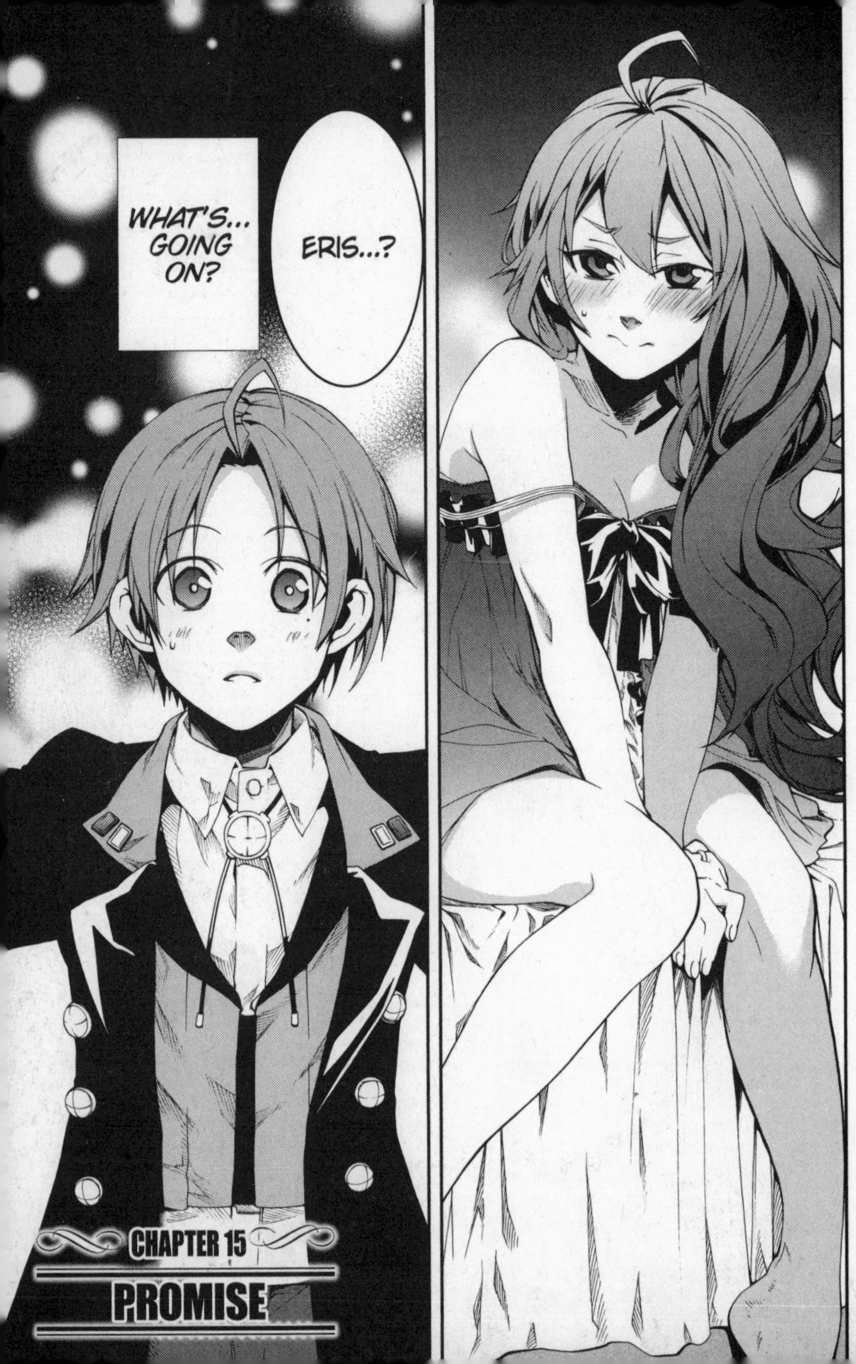
ERIS...?
WHAT'S... GOING ON?
CHAPTER 15
PROMISE

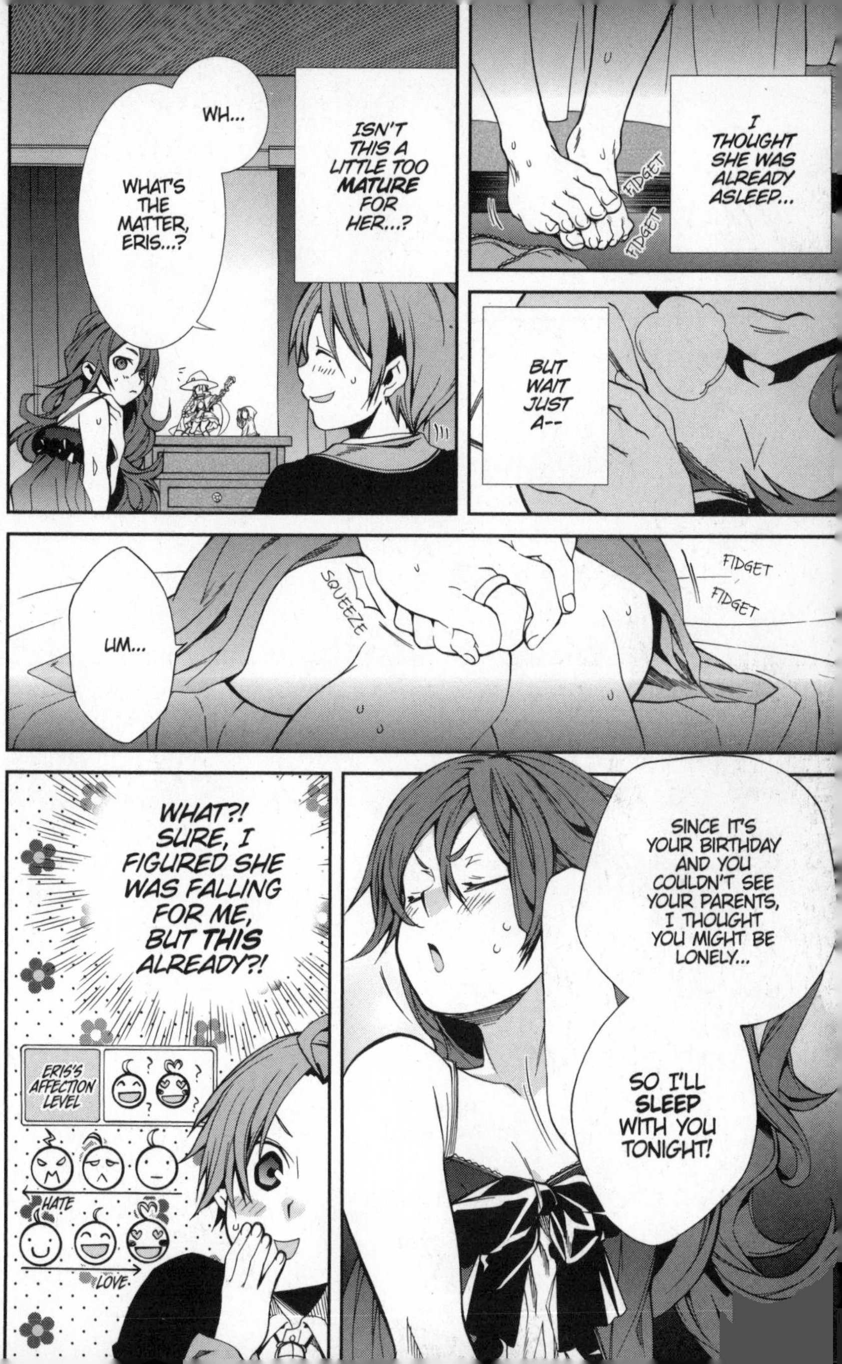

I THOUGHT SHE WAS ALREADY ASLEEP...
FIDGET
FIDGET
FIDGET
BUT WAIT JUST A--
ISN'T THIS A LITTLE TOO MATURE FOR HER...?
WH...
WHAT'S THE MATTER, ERIS...?
FIDGET
FIDGET
SQUEEZE
UM...
SINCE IT'S YOUR BIRTHDAY AND YOU COULDN'T SEE YOUR PARENTS, I THOUGHT YOU MIGHT BE LONELY...
SO I'LL SLEEP WITH YOU TONIGHT!
WHAT?! SURE, I FIGURED SHE WAS FALLING FOR ME, BUT THIS ALREADY?!
ERIS'S AFFECTION LEVEL
HATE
LOVE

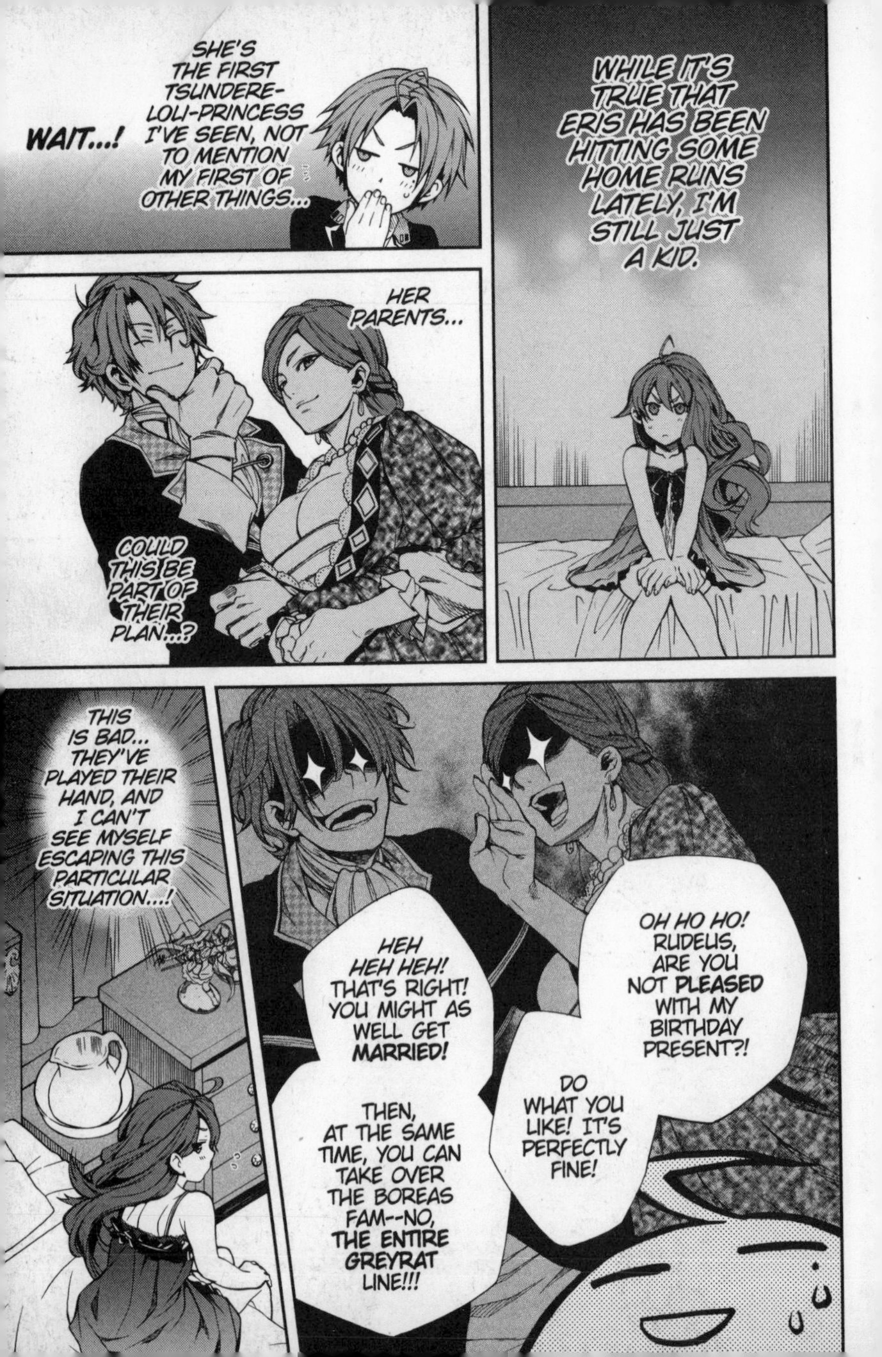
WHILE IT'S TRUE THAT ERIS HAS BEEN HITTING SOME HOME RUNS LATELY, I'M STILL JUST A KID.
SHE'S THE FIRST TSUNDERE-LOLI-PRINCESS I'VE SEEN, NOT TO MENTION MY FIRST OF OTHER THINGS...
WAIT...!
HER PARENTS...
COULD THIS BE PART OF THEIR PLAN...?
OH HO HO! RUDEUS, ARE YOU NOT PLEASED WITH MY BIRTHDAY PRESENT?!
HEH HEH HEH! THAT'S RIGHT! YOU MIGHT AS WELL GET MARRIED!
DO WHAT YOU LIKE! IT'S PERFECTLY FINE!
THEN, AT THE SAME TIME, YOU CAN TAKE OVER THE BOREAS FAM--NO, THE ENTIRE GREYRAT LINE!!!
THIS IS BAD... THEY'VE PLAYED THEIR HAND, AND I CAN'T SEE MYSELF ESCAPING THIS PARTICULAR SITUATION...!

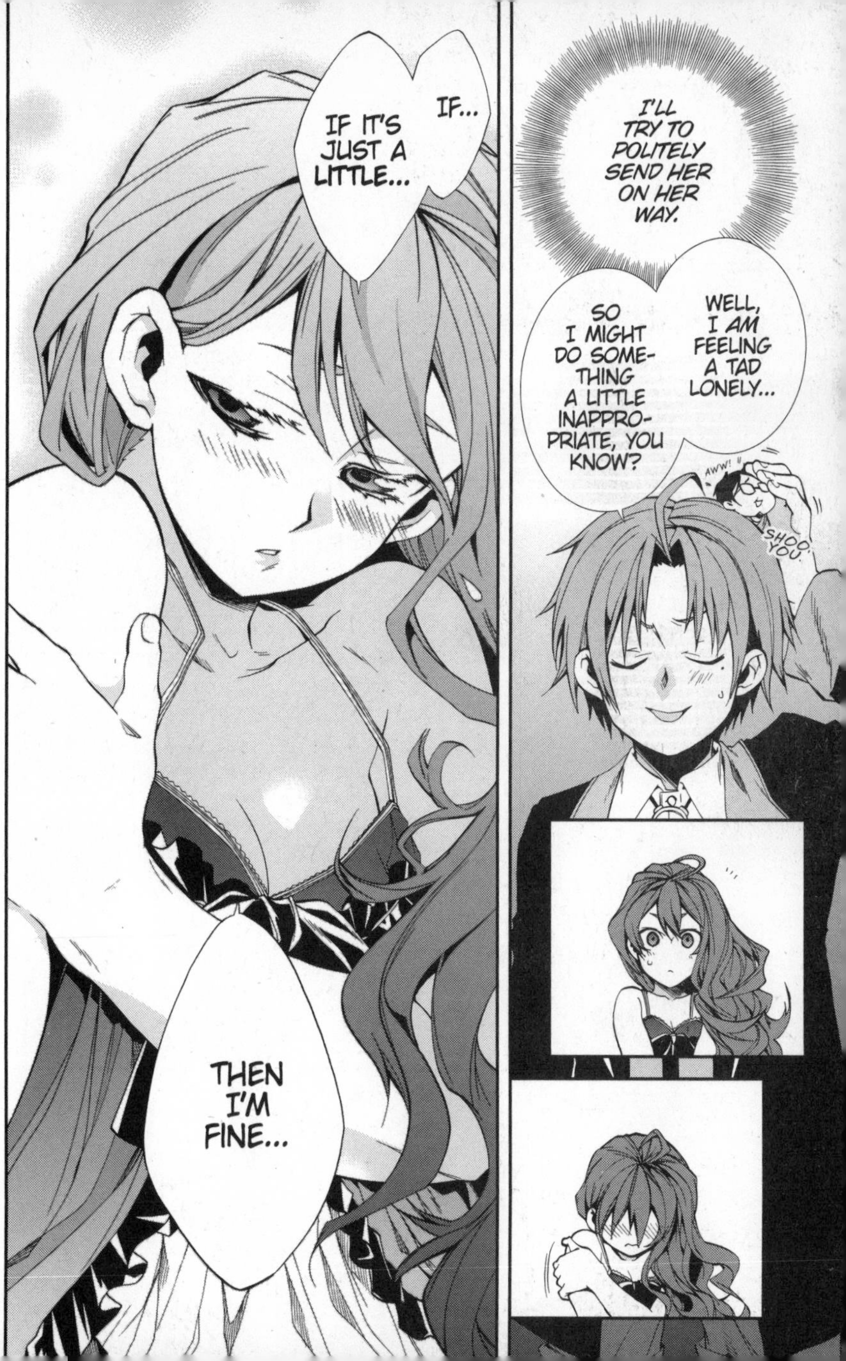
I'LL TRY TO POLITELY SEND HER ON HER WAY.
WELL, I AM FEELING A TAD LONELY...
SO I MIGHT DO SOME-THING A LITTLE INAPPRO-PRIATE, YOU KNOW?
AWW!
SHOO, YOU.
IF...
IF IT'S JUST A LITTLE...
THEN I'M FINE...

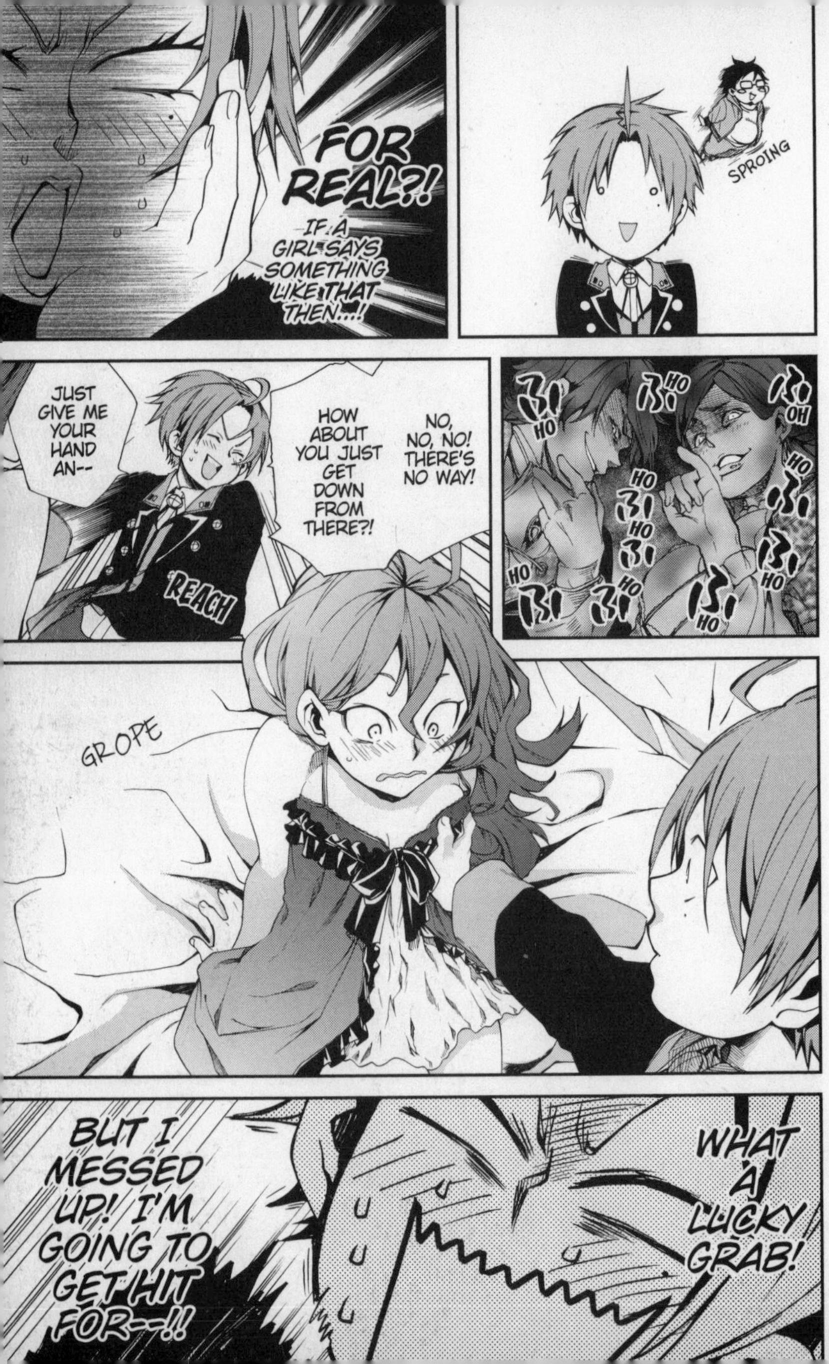
SPROING
FOR REAL?!
IF A GIRL SAYS SOMETHING LIKE THAT THEN...!
ふ OH
ふ HO
ふ HO
ふ HO
ふ HO
ふ HO
ふ HO
ふ HO
ふ HO
ふ HO
HOW ABOUT YOU JUST GET DOWN FROM THERE?!
NO, NO, NO! THERE'S NO WAY!
JUST GIVE ME YOUR HAND AN--
REACH
GROPE
WHAT A LUCKY GRAB!
BUT I MESSED UP! I'M GOING TO GET HIT FOR--!!

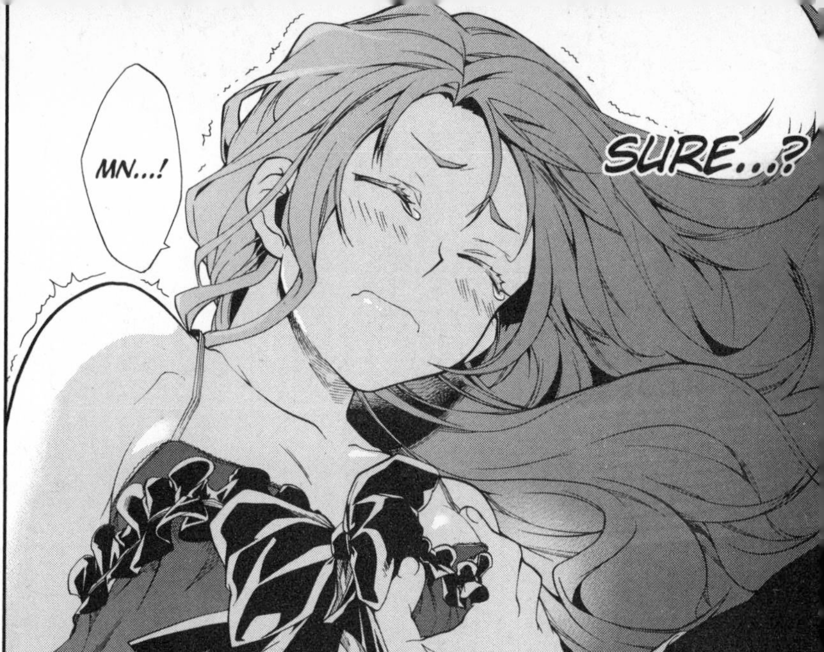
SURE...?
MN...!
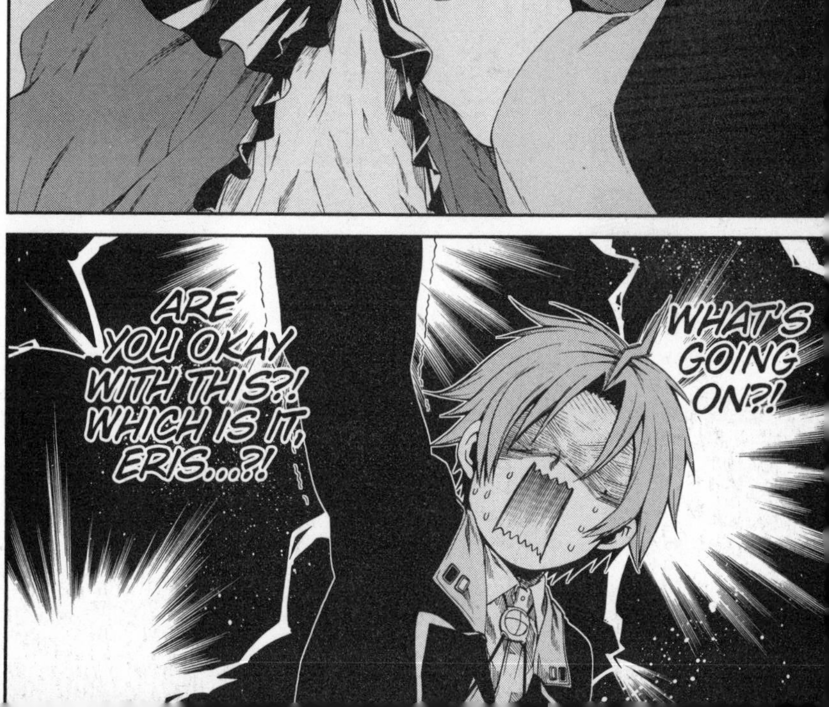
WHAT'S GOING ON?!
ARE YOU OKAY WITH THIS?! WHICH IS IT, ERIS...?!

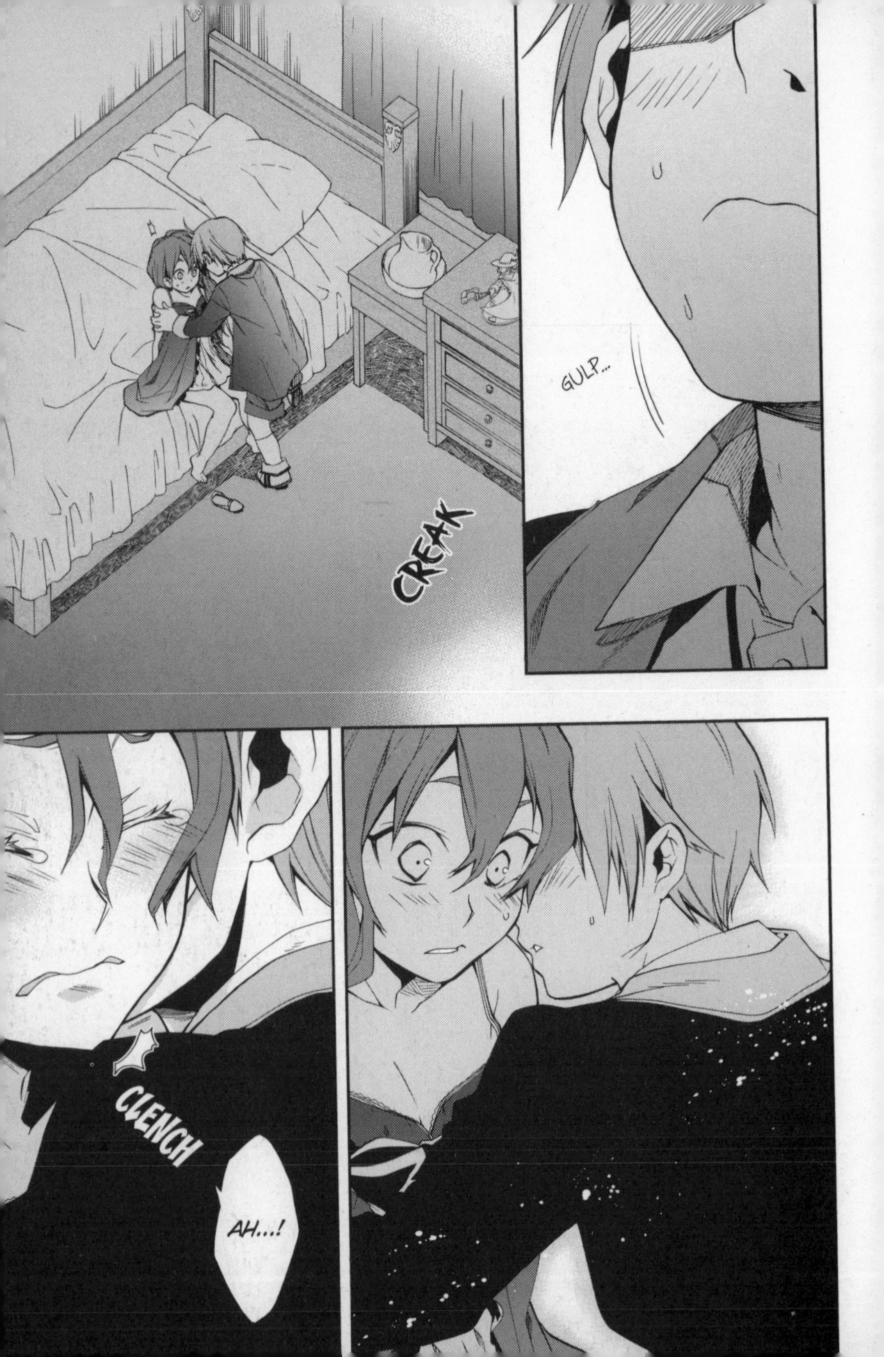
GULP...
CREAK
CLENCH
AH...!

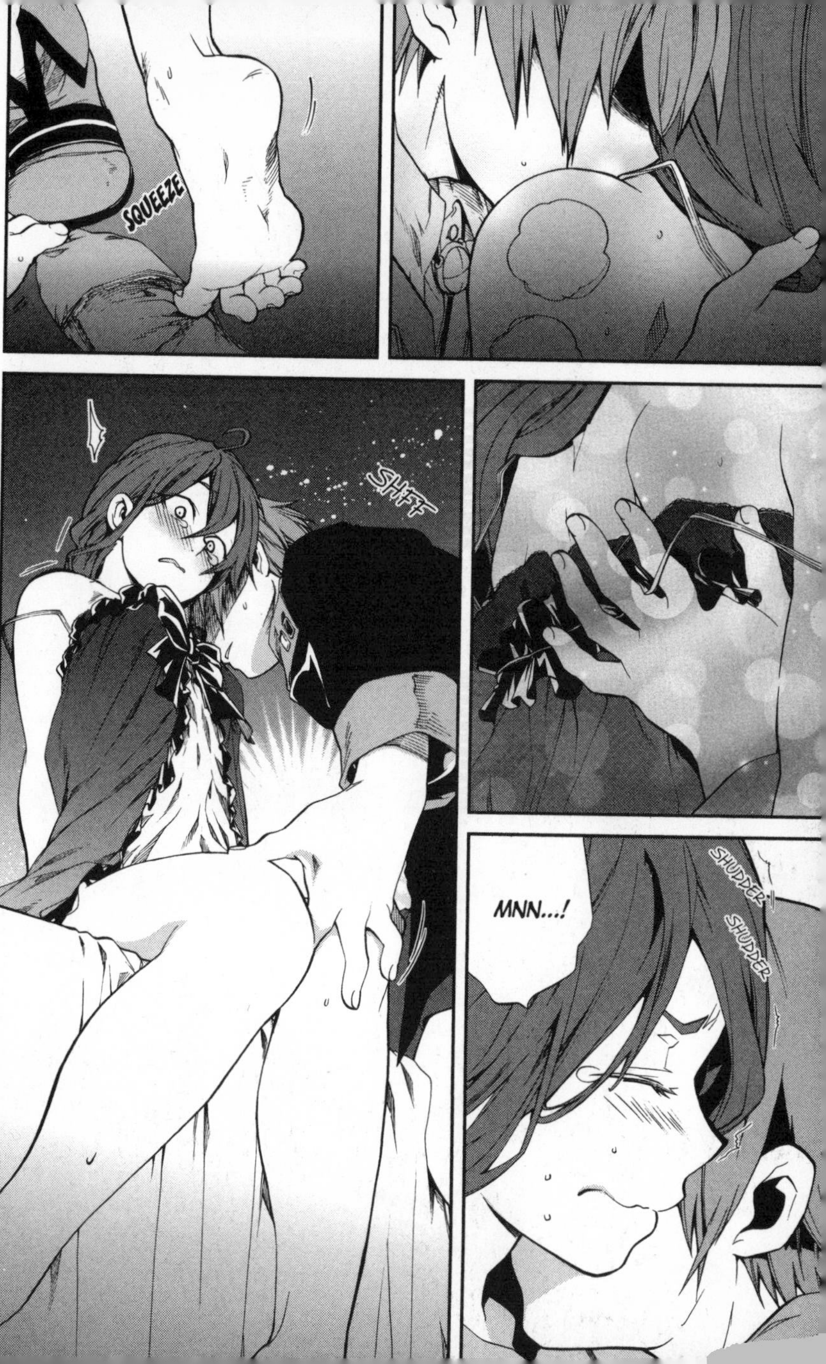
SQUEEZE
SHUDDER
SHUDDER
MNN...!
SHIFT

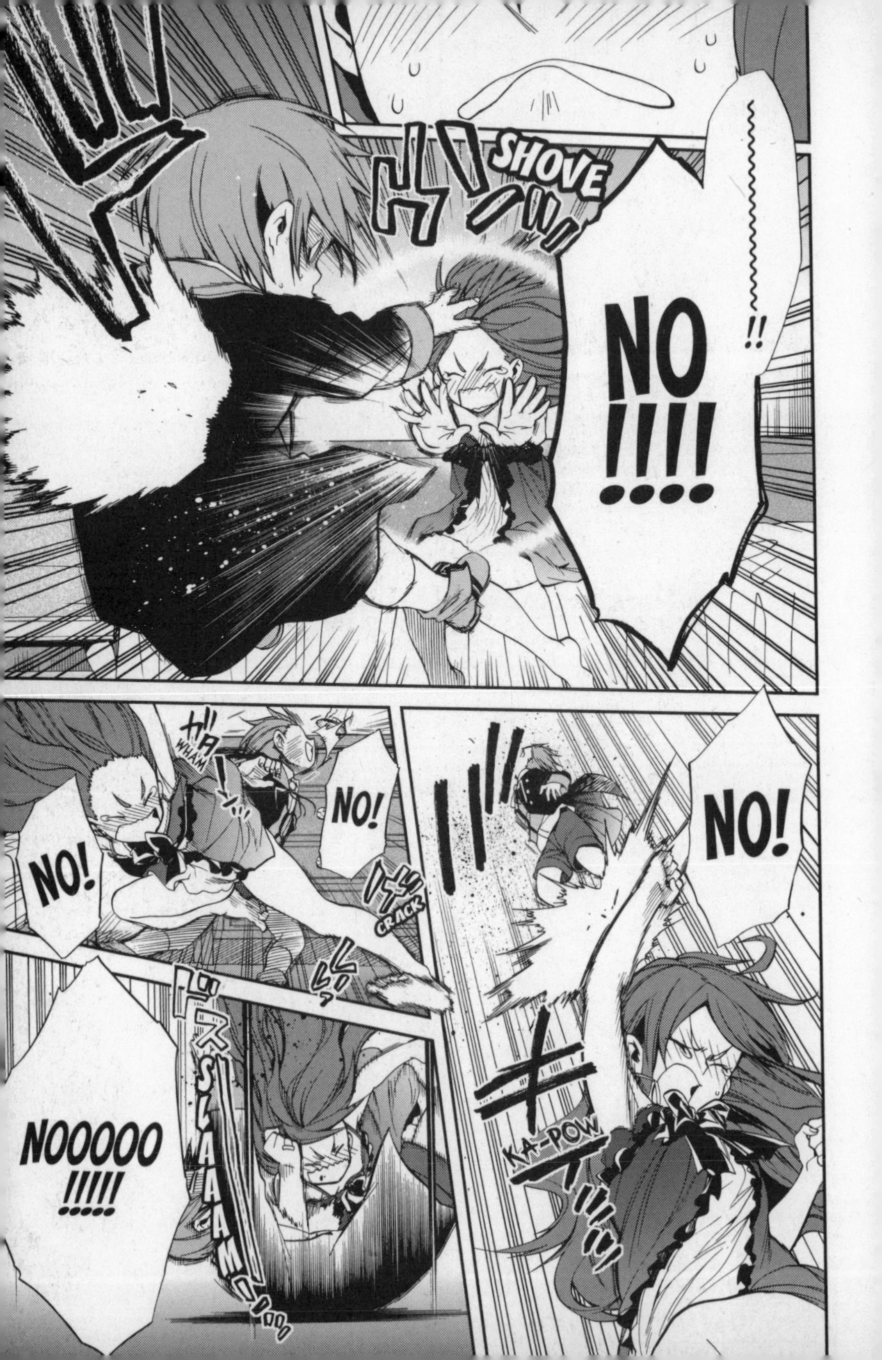
!!
SHOVE
NO!!!!
NO!
KA-POW
WHAM
NO!
CRACK
NO!
SLAAAAM
NOOOOO!!!!!

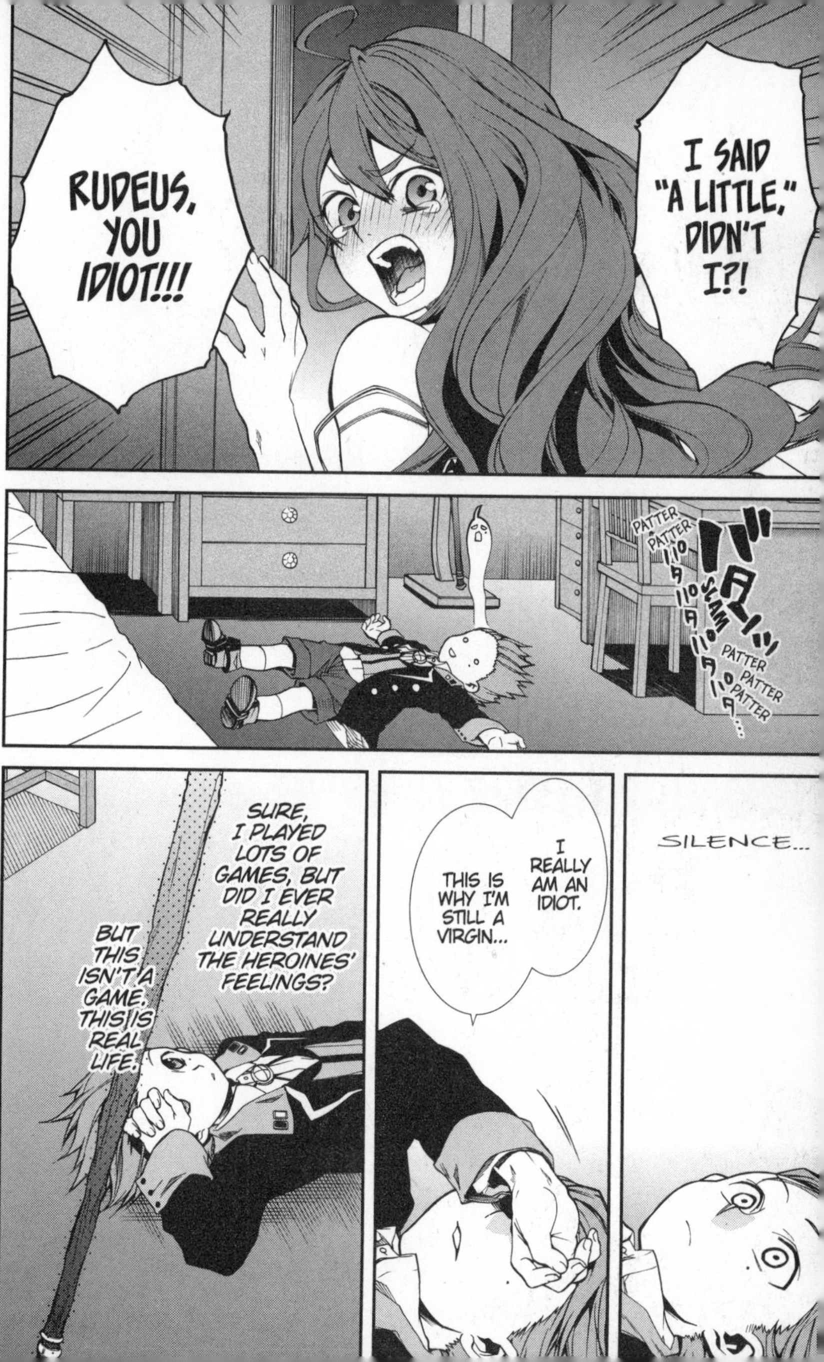
I SAID "A LITTLE," DIDN'T I?!
RUDEUS, YOU IDIOT!!!
バタンッ
SLAM
パタパタパタパタ…
PATTER PATTER
PATTER PATTER PATTER
SILENCE...
I REALLY AM AN IDIOT.
THIS IS WHY I'M STILL A VIRGIN...
SURE, I PLAYED LOTS OF GAMES, BUT DID I EVER REALLY UNDERSTAND THE HEROINES' FEELINGS?
BUT THIS ISN'T A GAME. THIS IS REAL LIFE.

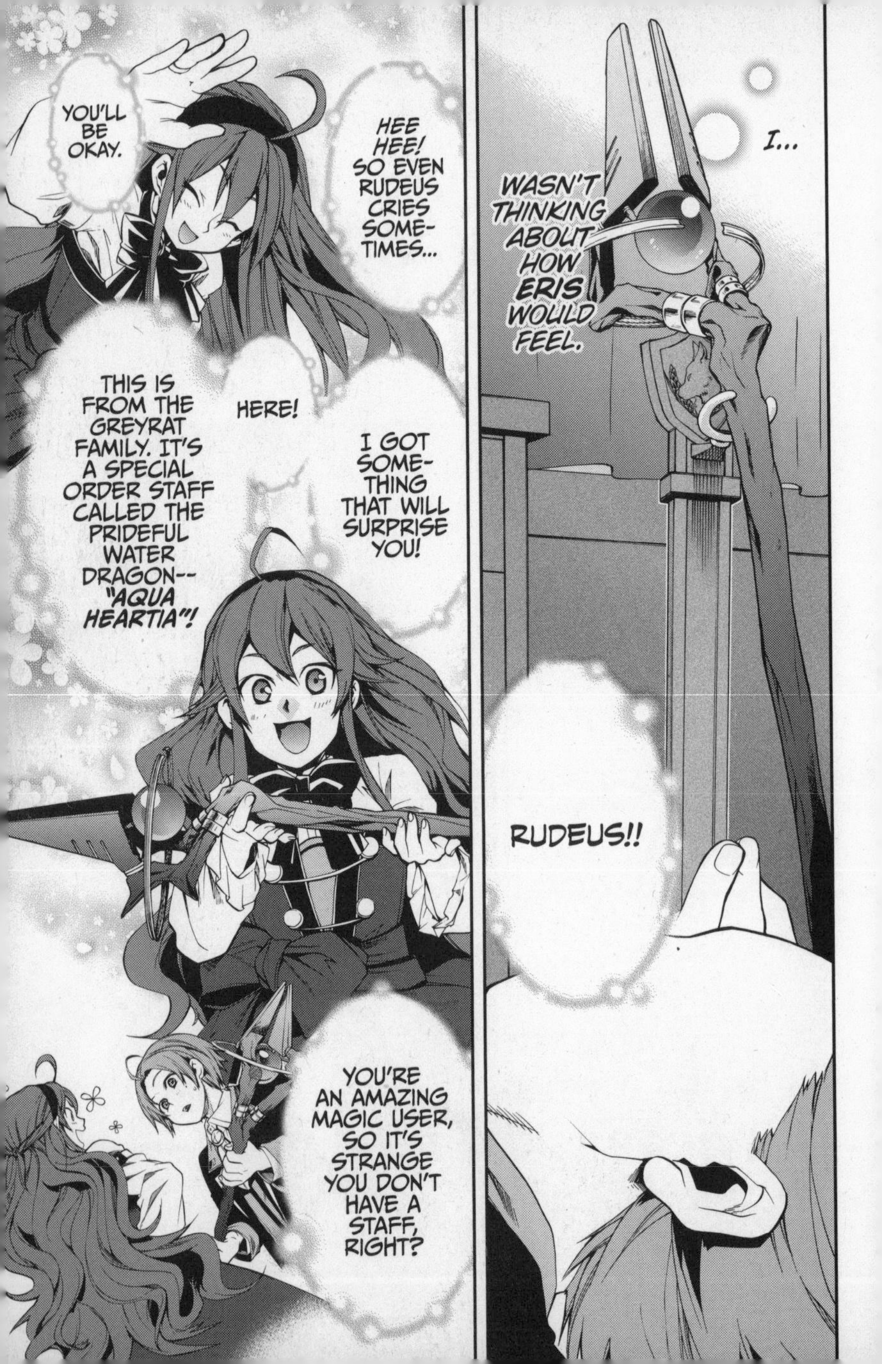

I...
WASN'T THINKING ABOUT HOW ERIS WOULD FEEL.
RUDEUS!!
HEE HEE! SO EVEN RUDEUS CRIES SOME-TIMES...
YOU'LL BE OKAY.
I GOT SOME-THING THAT WILL SURPRISE YOU!
HERE!
THIS IS FROM THE GREYRAT FAMILY. IT'S A SPECIAL ORDER STAFF CALLED THE PRIDEFUL WATER DRAGON-- "AQUA HEARTIA"!
YOU'RE AN AMAZING MAGIC USER, SO IT'S STRANGE YOU DON'T HAVE A STAFF, RIGHT?

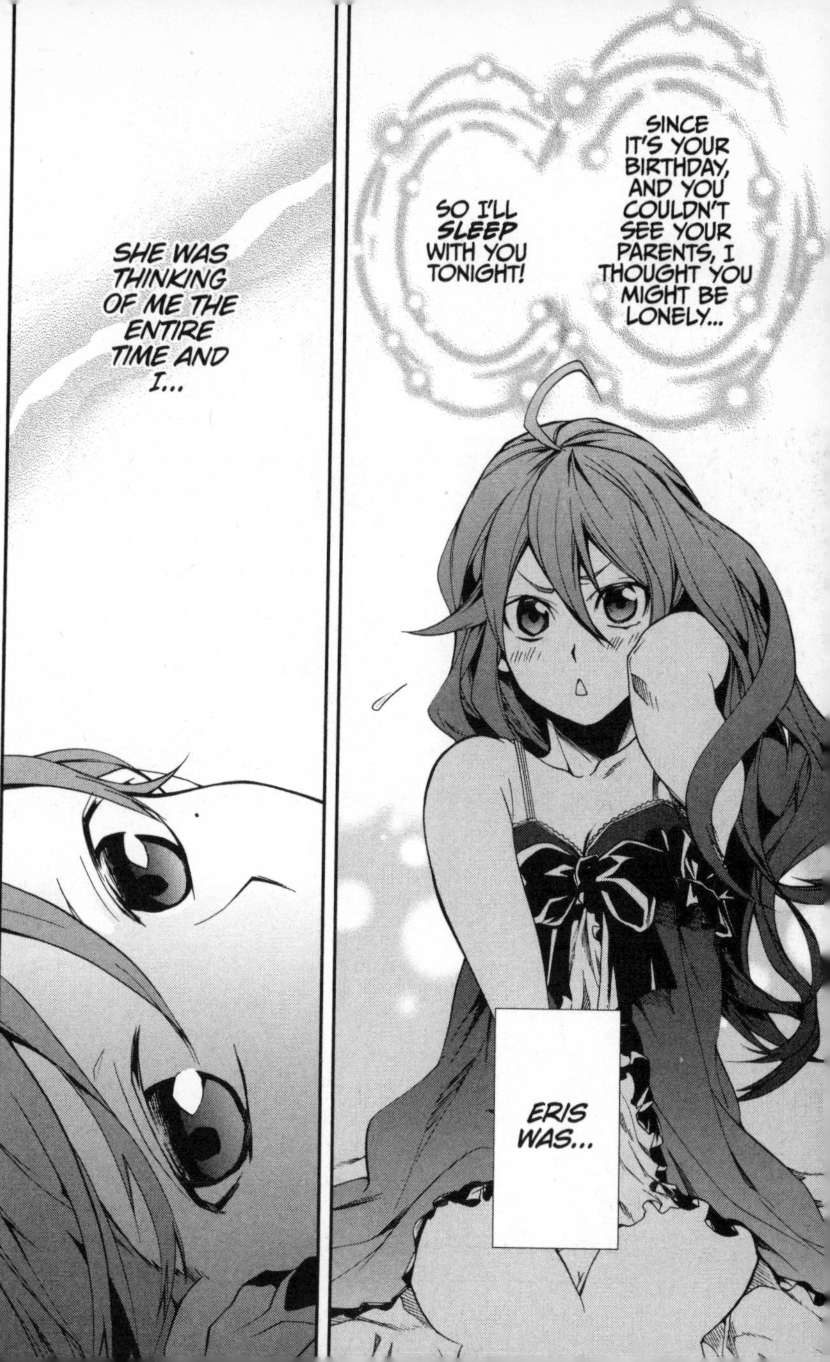
SINCE IT'S YOUR BIRTHDAY, AND YOU COULDN'T SEE YOUR PARENTS, I THOUGHT YOU MIGHT BE LONELY...
SO I'LL *SLEEP* WITH YOU TONIGHT!
ERIS WAS...
SHE WAS THINKING OF ME THE ENTIRE TIME AND I...

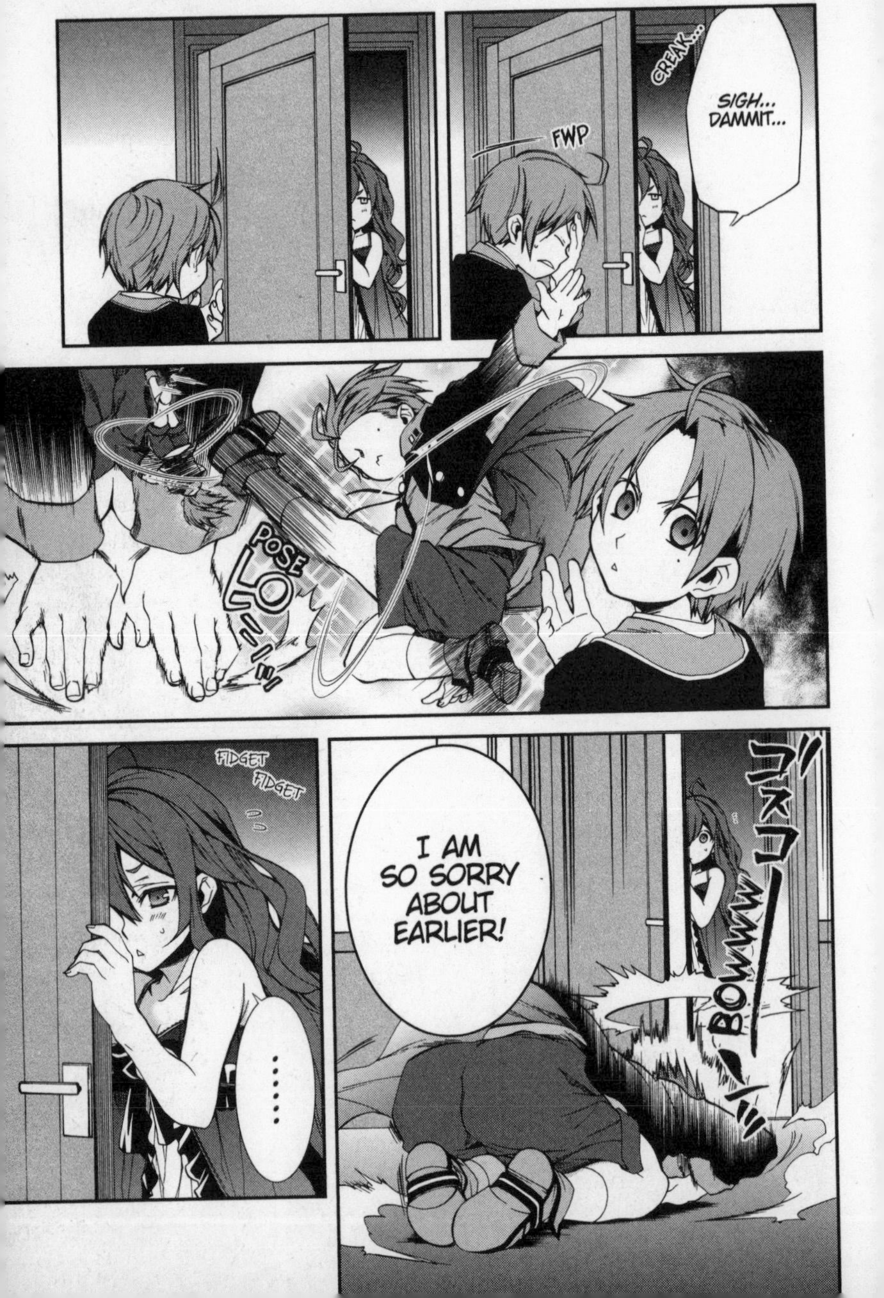
CREAK...
SIGH... DAMMIT...
FWP
POSE
LO
I AM SO SORRY ABOUT EARLIER!
BOWWW
FIDGET FIDGET
......

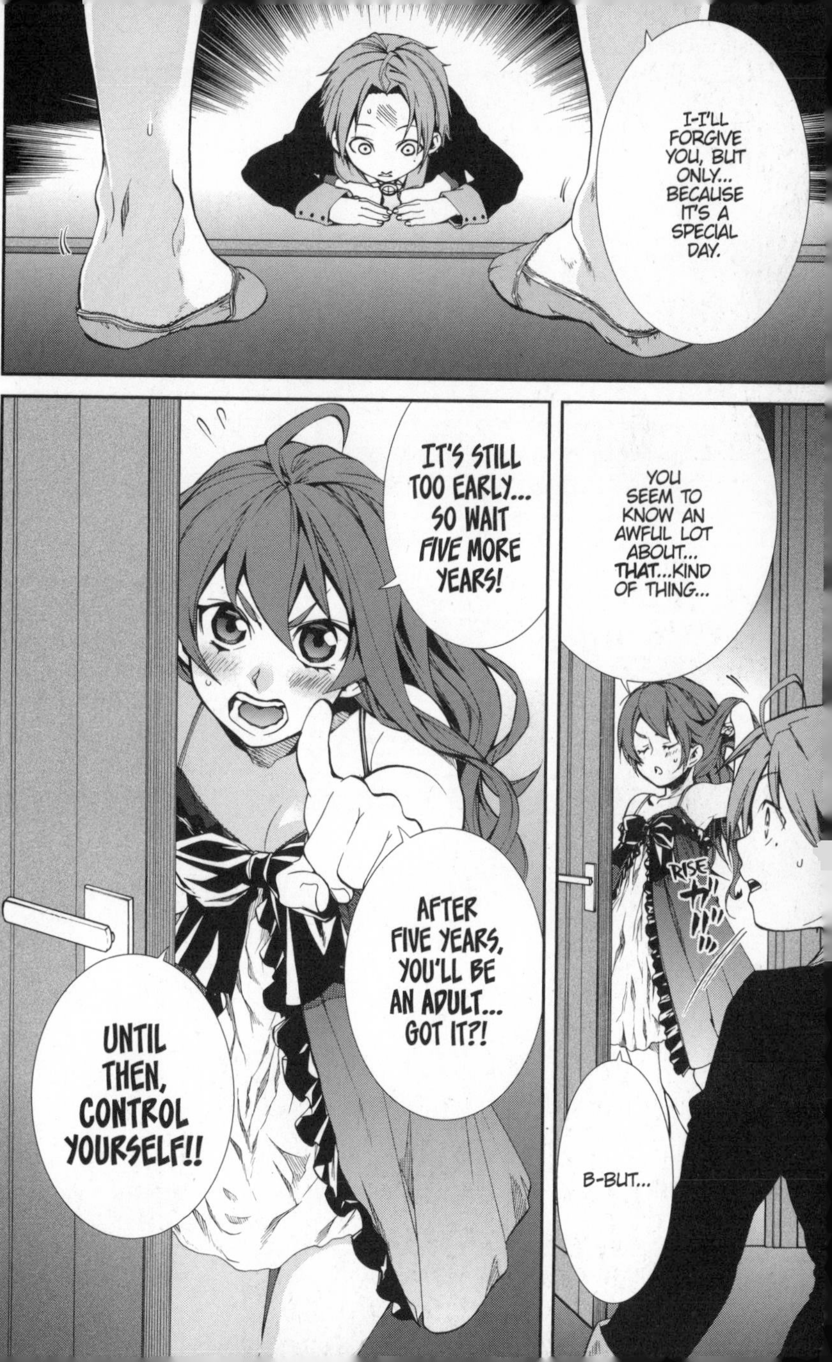
I-I'LL FORGIVE YOU, BUT ONLY... BECAUSE IT'S A SPECIAL DAY.
YOU SEEM TO KNOW AN AWFUL LOT ABOUT... THAT...KIND OF THING...
RISE
B-BUT...
IT'S STILL TOO EARLY... SO WAIT *FIVE* MORE YEARS!
AFTER FIVE YEARS, YOU'LL BE AN ADULT... GOT IT?!
UNTIL THEN, CONTROL YOURSELF!!

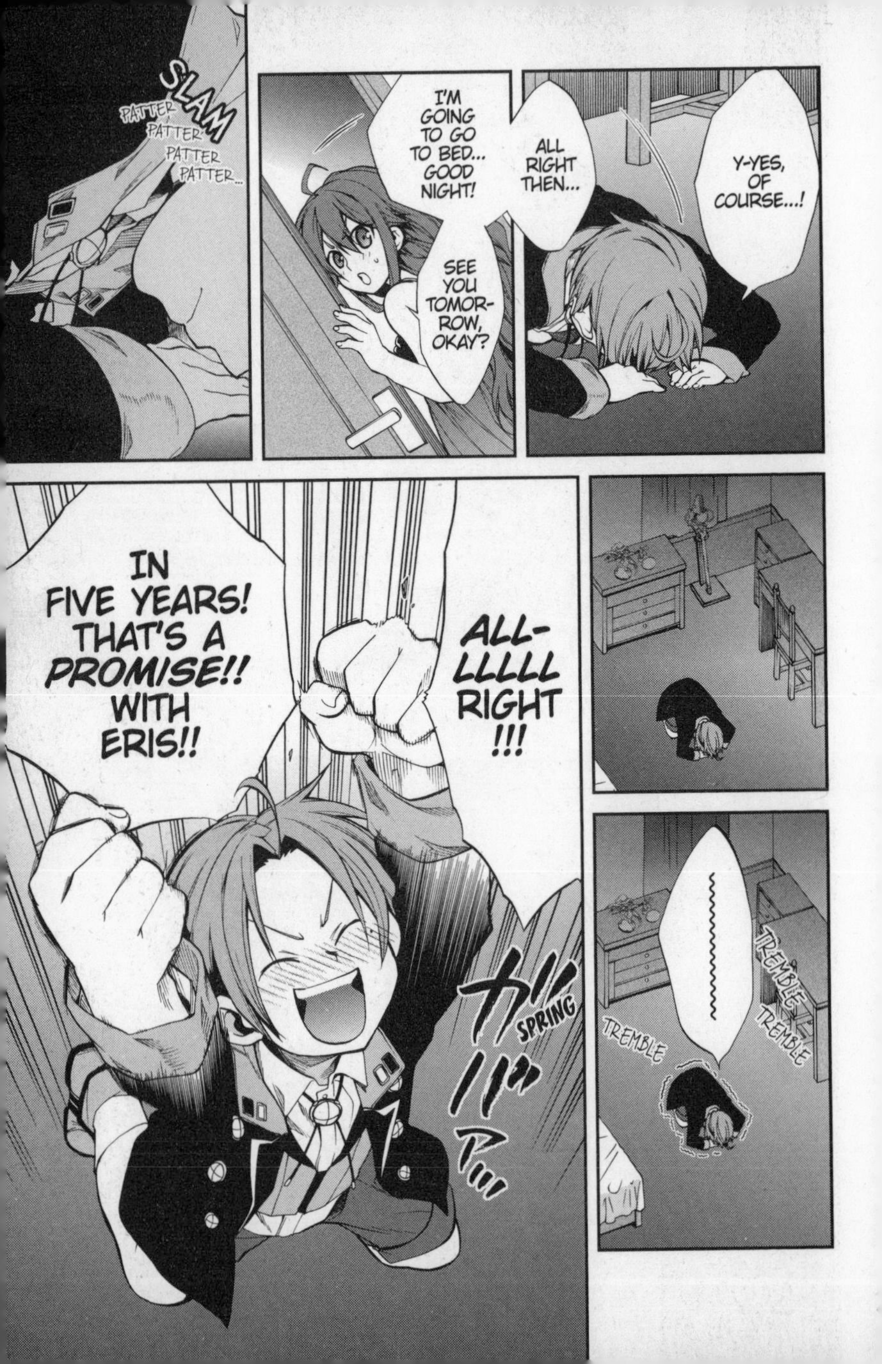
Y-YES, OF COURSE...!
ALL RIGHT THEN...
I'M GOING TO GO TO BED... GOOD NIGHT!
SEE YOU TOMORROW, OKAY?
SLAM
PATTER PATTER PATTER PATTER...
TREMBLE TREMBLE
TREMBLE
ALL-LLLLL RIGHT !!!
IN FIVE YEARS! THAT'S A PROMISE!! WITH ERIS!!
ガバァ...
SPRING

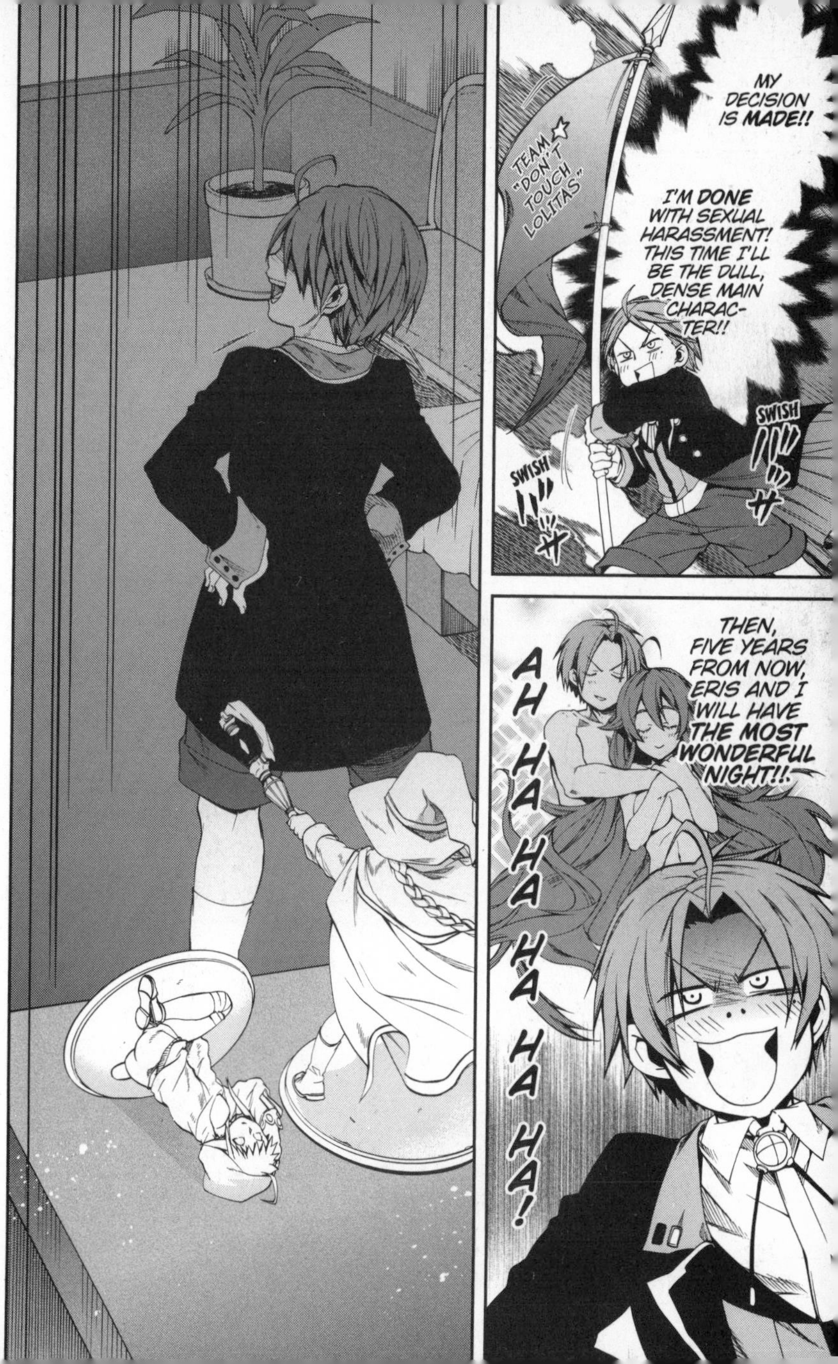
MY DECISION IS MADE!!
TEAM ☆ "DON'T TOUCH LOLITAS"
I'M DONE WITH SEXUAL HARASSMENT! THIS TIME I'LL BE THE DULL, DENSE MAIN CHARACTER!!
SWISH
SWISH
THEN, FIVE YEARS FROM NOW, ERIS AND I WILL HAVE THE MOST WONDERFUL NIGHT!!
AH HA HA HA HA HA HA!

CHAPTER 16

TURNING POINT

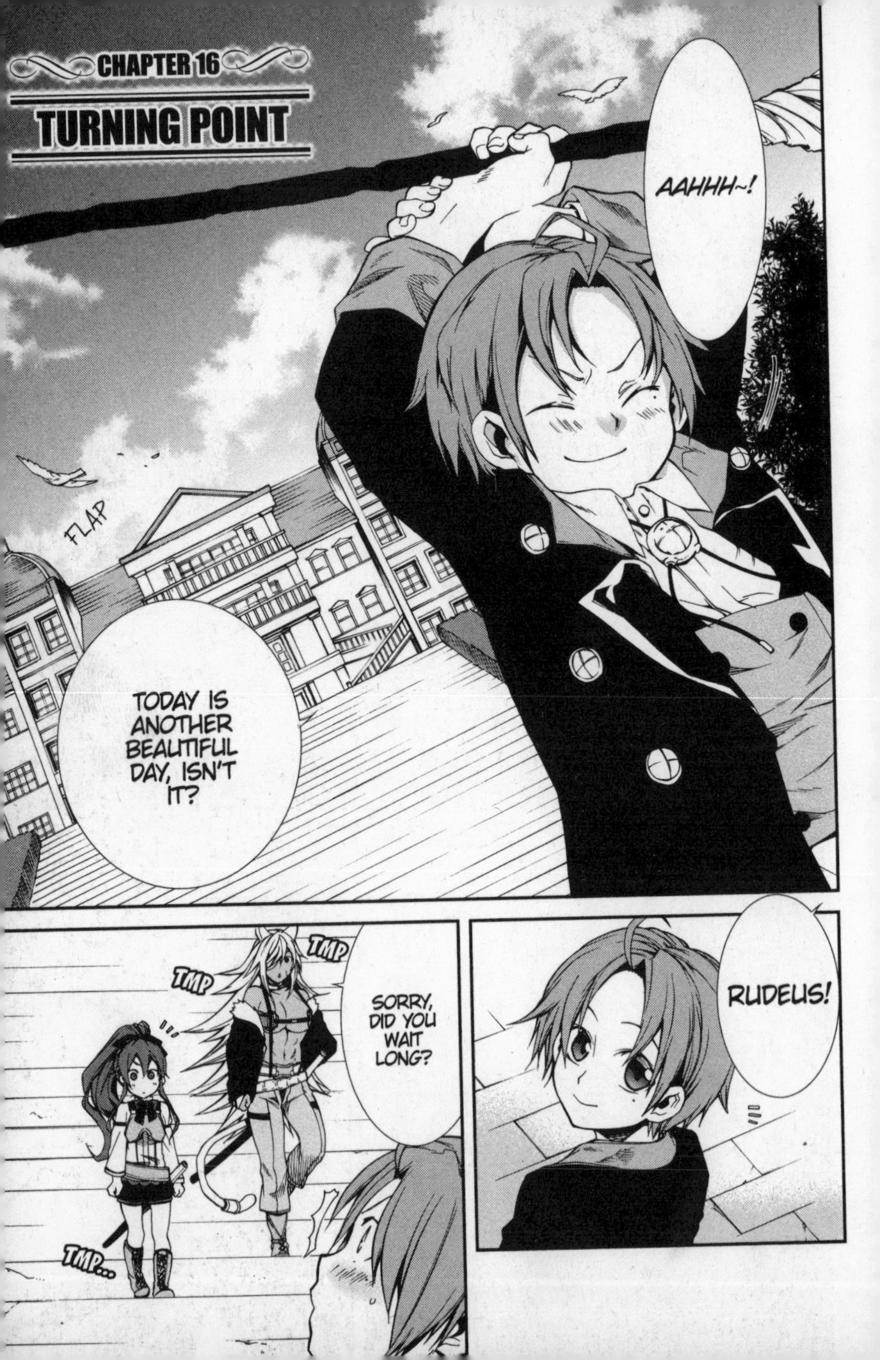
AAHHH~!
FLAP
TODAY IS ANOTHER BEAUTIFUL DAY, ISN'T IT?
RUDEUS!
SORRY, DID YOU WAIT LONG?
TMP
TMP
TMP...

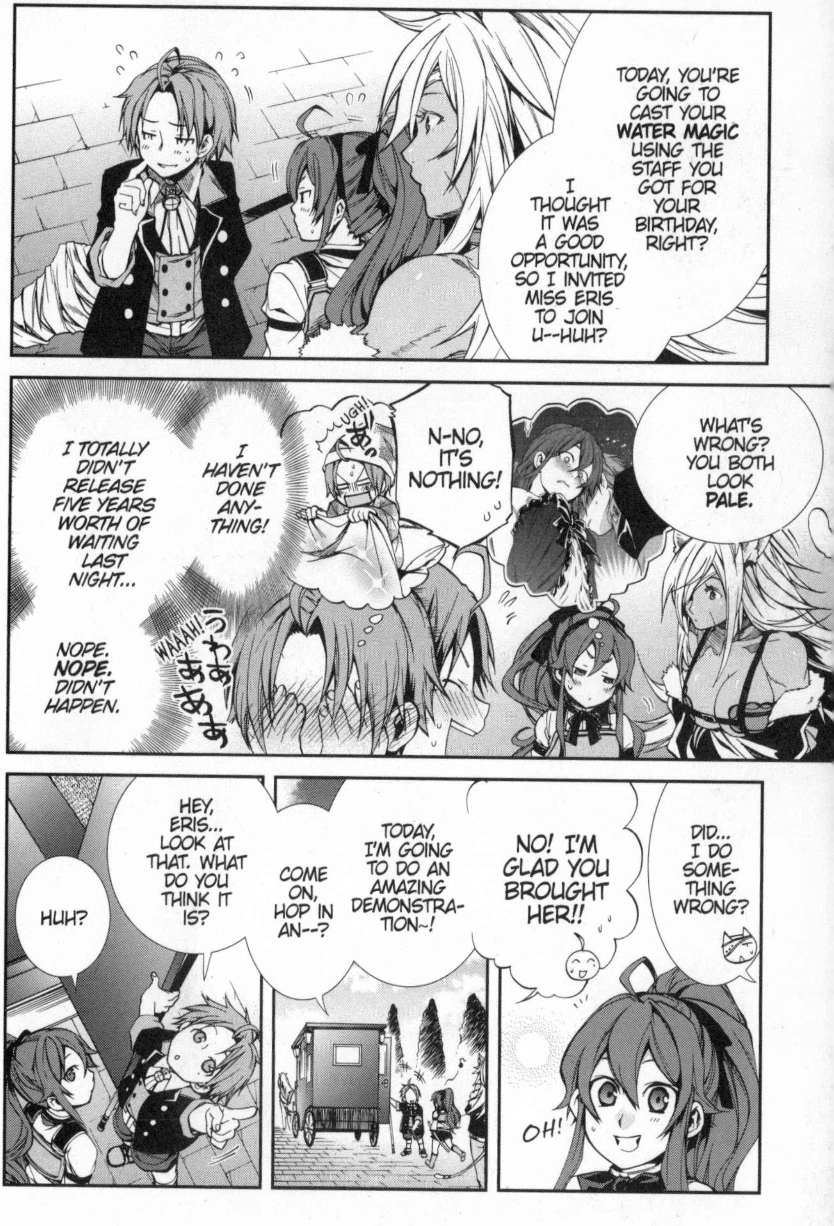
TODAY, YOU'RE GOING TO CAST YOUR WATER MAGIC USING THE STAFF YOU GOT FOR YOUR BIRTHDAY, RIGHT?
I THOUGHT IT WAS A GOOD OPPORTUNITY, SO I INVITED MISS ERIS TO JOIN U--HUH?
WHAT'S WRONG? YOU BOTH LOOK PALE.
N-NO, IT'S NOTHING!
UGH!
I HAVEN'T DONE ANYTHING!
I TOTALLY DIDN'T RELEASE FIVE YEARS WORTH OF WAITING LAST NIGHT...
WAAAH!
NOPE. NOPE. DIDN'T HAPPEN.
DID... I DO SOMETHING WRONG?
NO! I'M GLAD YOU BROUGHT HER!!
OH!
TODAY, I'M GOING TO DO AN AMAZING DEMONSTRATION~!
COME ON, HOP IN AN--?
HEY, ERIS... LOOK AT THAT. WHAT DO YOU THINK IT IS?
HUH?

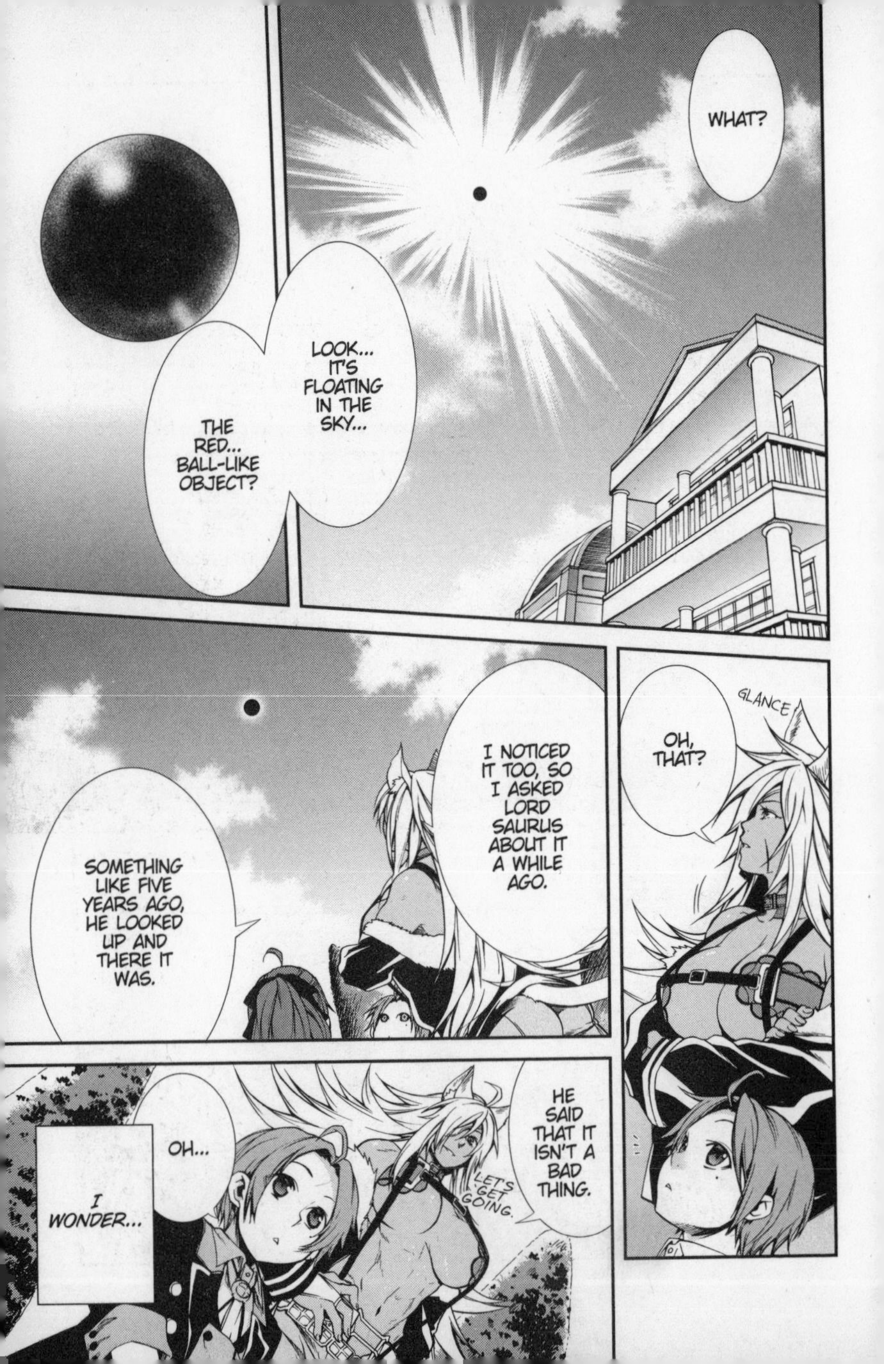
WHAT?
LOOK... IT'S FLOATING IN THE SKY...
THE RED... BALL-LIKE OBJECT?
GLANCE
OH, THAT?
I NOTICED IT TOO, SO I ASKED LORD SAURUS ABOUT IT A WHILE AGO.
SOMETHING LIKE FIVE YEARS AGO, HE LOOKED UP AND THERE IT WAS.
HE SAID THAT IT ISN'T A BAD THING.
LET'S GET GOING.
OH...
I WONDER...

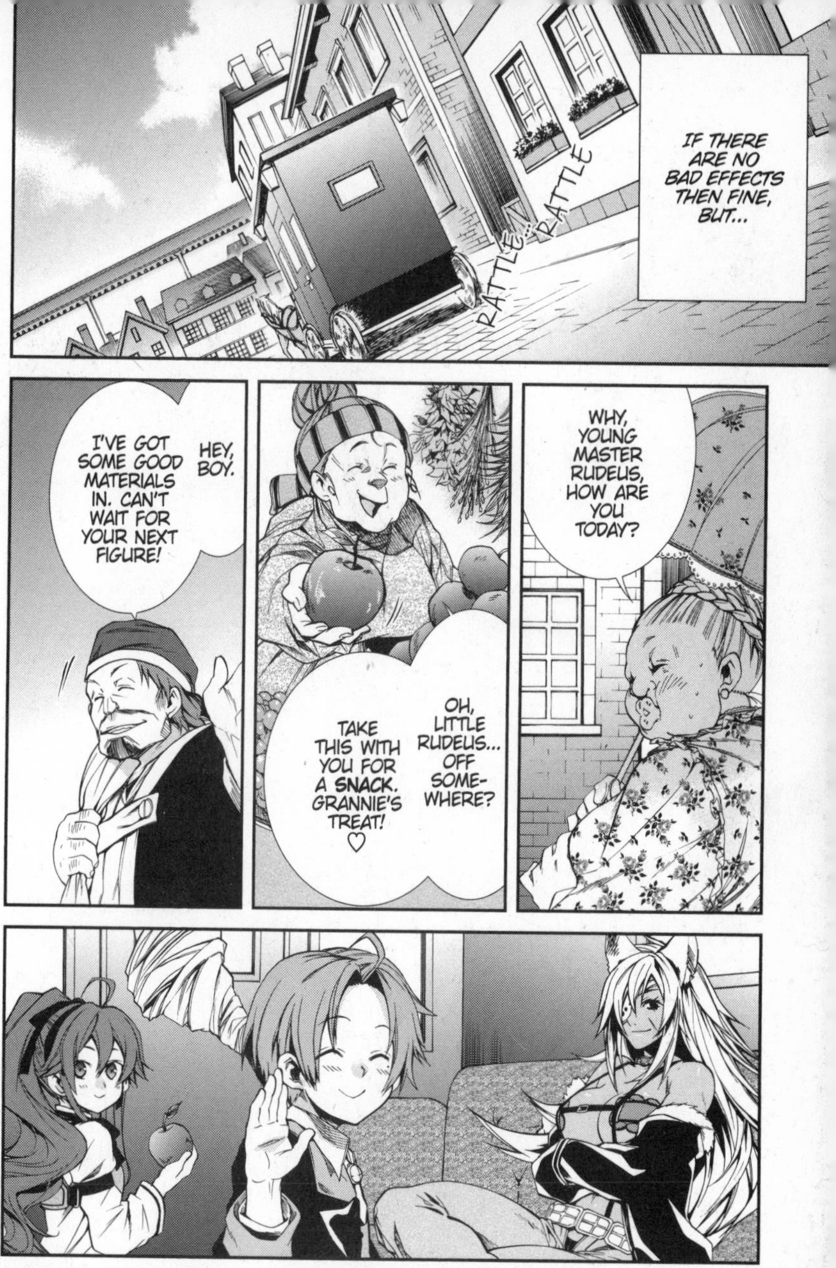
IF THERE ARE NO BAD EFFECTS THEN FINE, BUT...
RATTLE RATTLE
WHY, YOUNG MASTER RUDEUS, HOW ARE YOU TODAY?
OH, LITTLE RUDEUS... OFF SOME-WHERE?
TAKE THIS WITH YOU FOR A SNACK. GRANNIE'S TREAT! ♡
HEY, BOY.
I'VE GOT SOME GOOD MATERIALS IN. CAN'T WAIT FOR YOUR NEXT FIGURE!

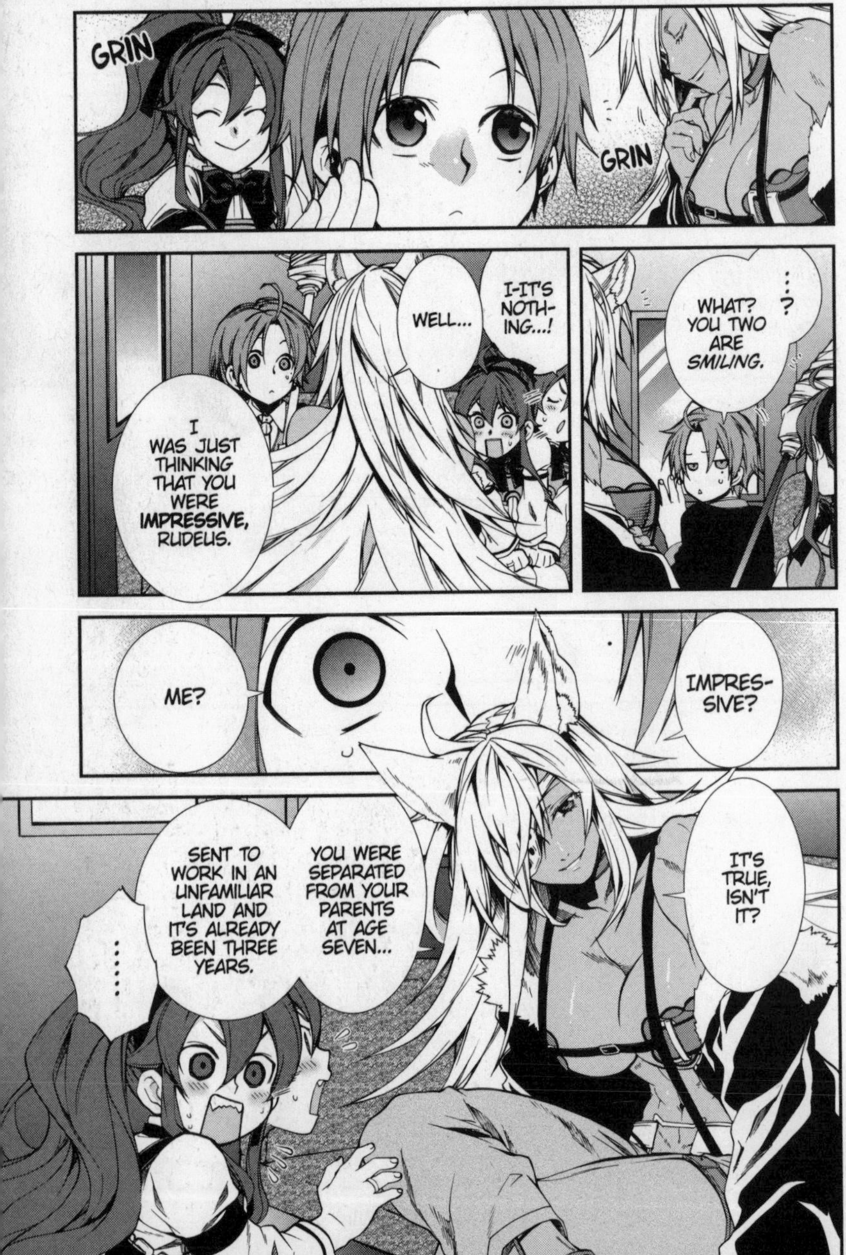
GRIN
GRIN
...?
WHAT? YOU TWO ARE SMILING.
I-IT'S NOTHING...!
WELL...
I WAS JUST THINKING THAT YOU WERE IMPRESSIVE, RUDEUS.
IMPRESSIVE?
ME?
IT'S TRUE, ISN'T IT?
YOU WERE SEPARATED FROM YOUR PARENTS AT AGE SEVEN...
SENT TO WORK IN AN UNFAMILIAR LAND AND IT'S ALREADY BEEN THREE YEARS.
......

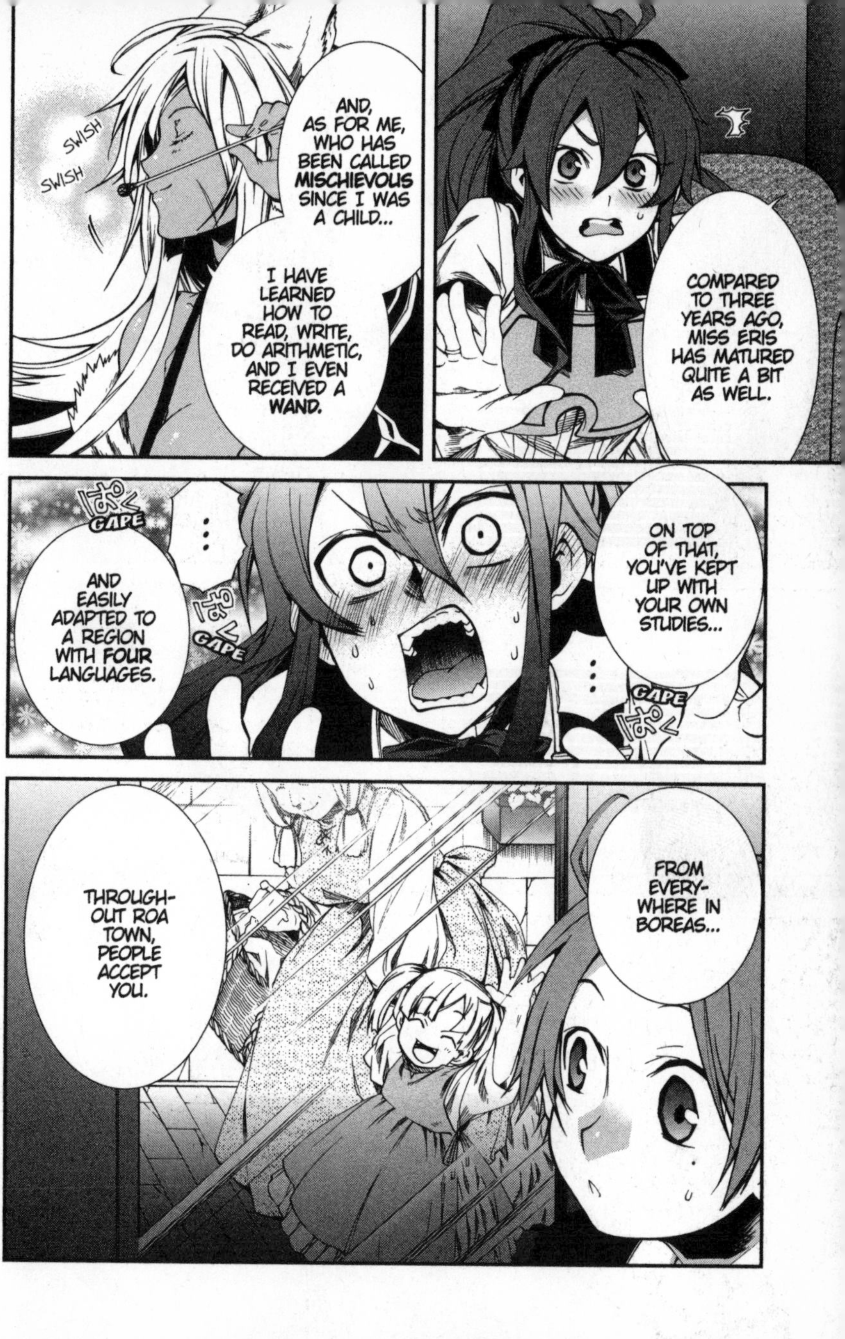
COMPARED TO THREE YEARS AGO, MISS ERIS HAS MATURED QUITE A BIT AS WELL.
AND, AS FOR ME, WHO HAS BEEN CALLED MISCHIEVOUS SINCE I WAS A CHILD...
SWISH
SWISH
I HAVE LEARNED HOW TO READ, WRITE, DO ARITHMETIC, AND I EVEN RECEIVED A WAND.
ON TOP OF THAT, YOU'VE KEPT UP WITH YOUR OWN STUDIES...
ぱく GAPE
...
ぱく GAPE
...
ぱく GAPE
AND EASILY ADAPTED TO A REGION WITH FOUR LANGUAGES.
FROM EVERY-WHERE IN BOREAS...
THROUGH-OUT ROA TOWN, PEOPLE ACCEPT YOU.

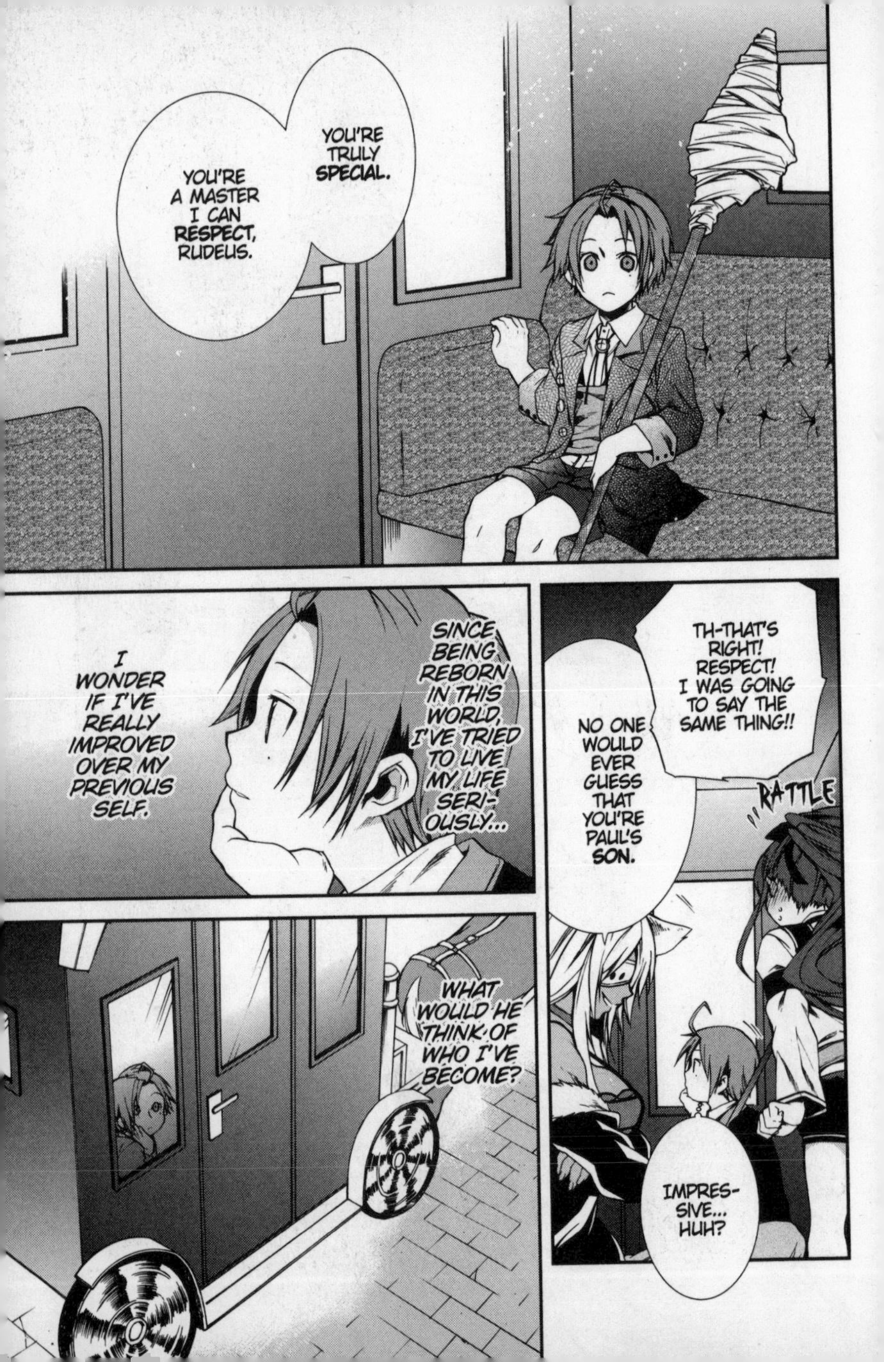
YOU'RE TRULY SPECIAL.
YOU'RE A MASTER I CAN RESPECT, RUDEUS.
TH-THAT'S RIGHT! RESPECT! I WAS GOING TO SAY THE SAME THING!!
NO ONE WOULD EVER GUESS THAT YOU'RE PAUL'S SON.
RATTLE
IMPRES-SIVE... HUH?
SINCE BEING REBORN IN THIS WORLD, I'VE TRIED TO LIVE MY LIFE SERI-OUSLY...
I WONDER IF I'VE REALLY IMPROVED OVER MY PREVIOUS SELF.
WHAT WOULD HE THINK OF WHO I'VE BECOME?

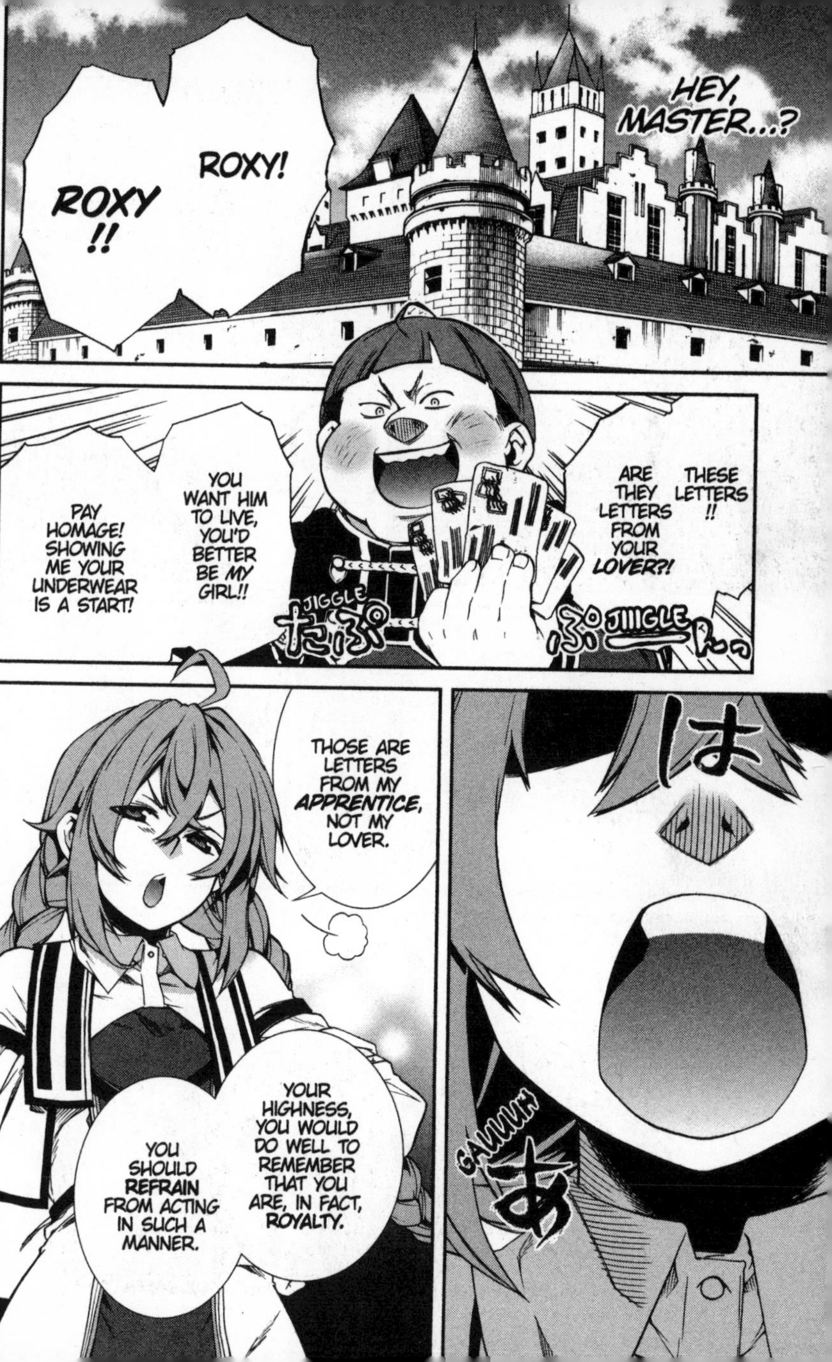
HEY, MASTER...?
ROXY!
ROXY !!
THESE LETTERS !!
ARE THEY LETTERS FROM YOUR LOVER?!
ぷ JIIIGLE ん
たぷ JIGGLE
YOU WANT HIM TO LIVE, YOU'D BETTER BE MY GIRL!!
PAY HOMAGE! SHOWING ME YOUR UNDERWEAR IS A START!
は
あ GAUUUH
THOSE ARE LETTERS FROM MY APPRENTICE, NOT MY LOVER.
YOUR HIGHNESS, YOU WOULD DO WELL TO REMEMBER THAT YOU ARE, IN FACT, ROYALTY.
YOU SHOULD REFRAIN FROM ACTING IN SUCH A MANNER.

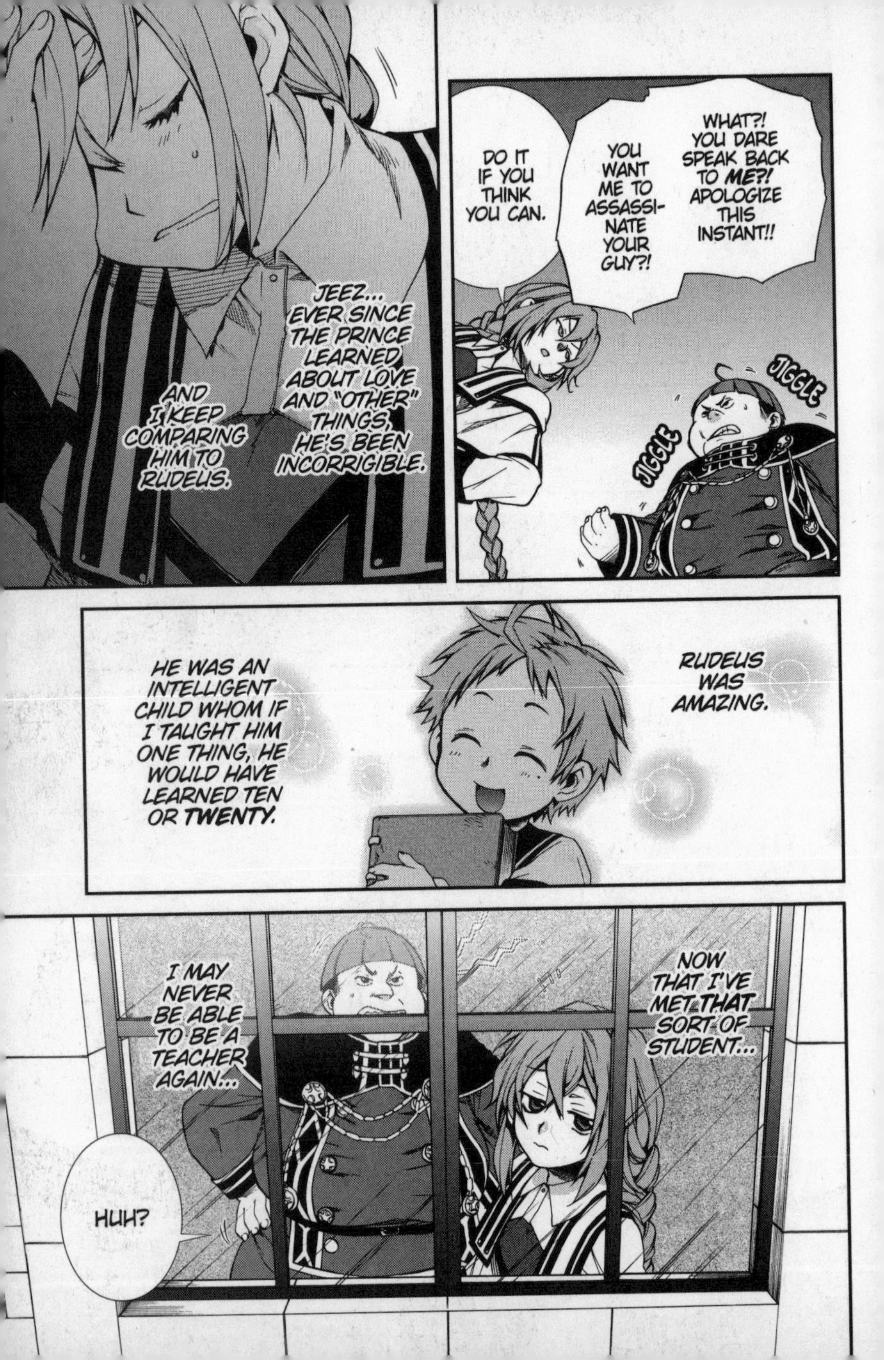
WHAT?! YOU DARE SPEAK BACK TO *ME?!* APOLOGIZE THIS INSTANT!!
YOU WANT ME TO ASSASSI-NATE YOUR GUY?!
DO IT IF YOU THINK YOU CAN.
JIGGLE
JIGGLE
JEEZ... EVER SINCE THE PRINCE LEARNED ABOUT LOVE AND "OTHER" THINGS, HE'S BEEN INCORRIGIBLE.
AND I KEEP COMPARING HIM TO RUDEUS.
RUDEUS WAS AMAZING.
HE WAS AN INTELLIGENT CHILD WHOM IF I TAUGHT HIM ONE THING, HE WOULD HAVE LEARNED TEN OR **TWENTY.**
NOW THAT I'VE MET **THAT** SORT OF STUDENT...
I MAY NEVER BE ABLE TO BE A TEACHER AGAIN...
HUH?

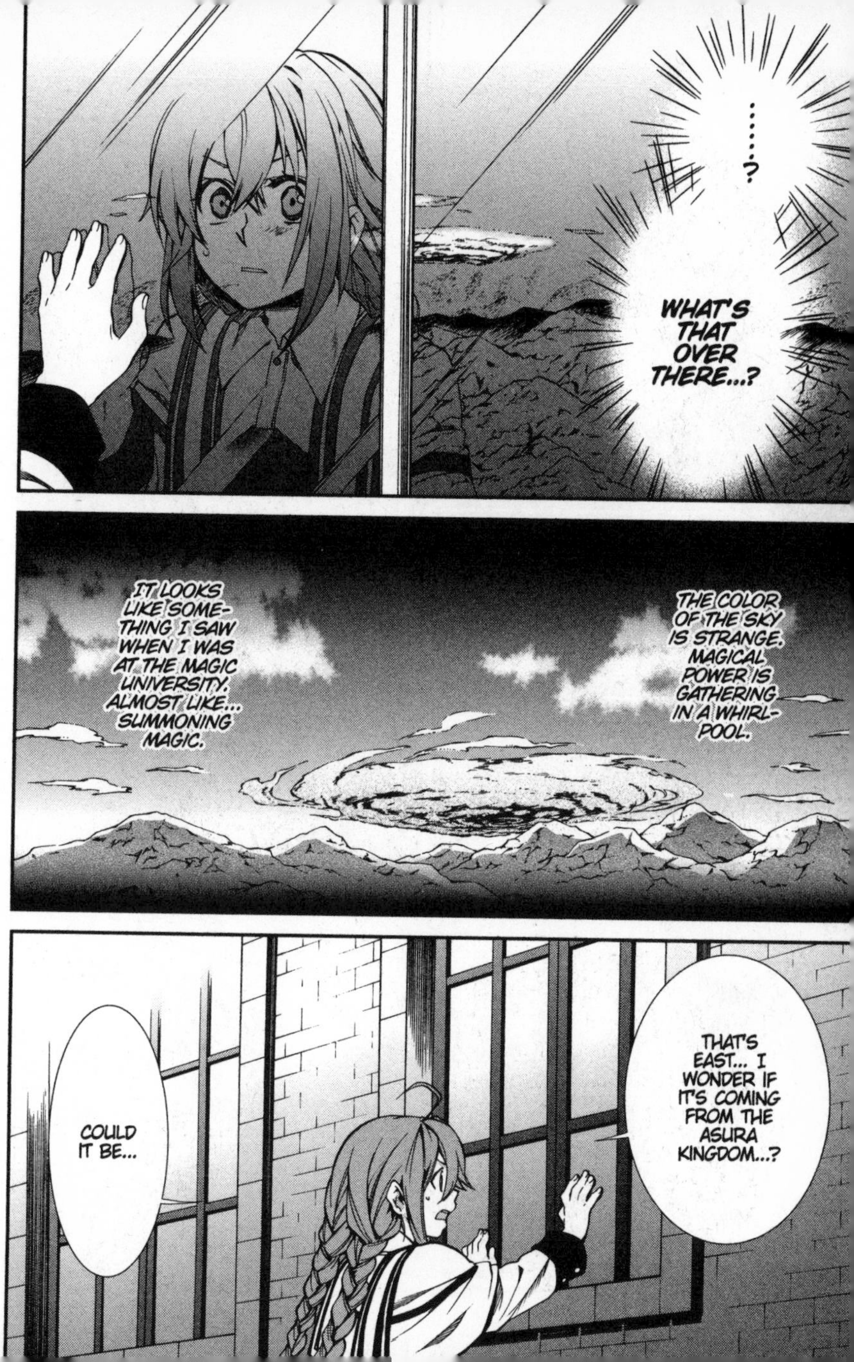
......?
WHAT'S THAT OVER THERE...?
THE COLOR OF THE SKY IS STRANGE. MAGICAL POWER IS GATHERING IN A WHIRL-POOL.
IT LOOKS LIKE SOME-THING I SAW WHEN I WAS AT THE MAGIC UNIVERSITY. ALMOST LIKE... SUMMONING MAGIC.
THAT'S EAST... I WONDER IF IT'S COMING FROM THE ASURA KINGDOM...?
COULD IT BE...

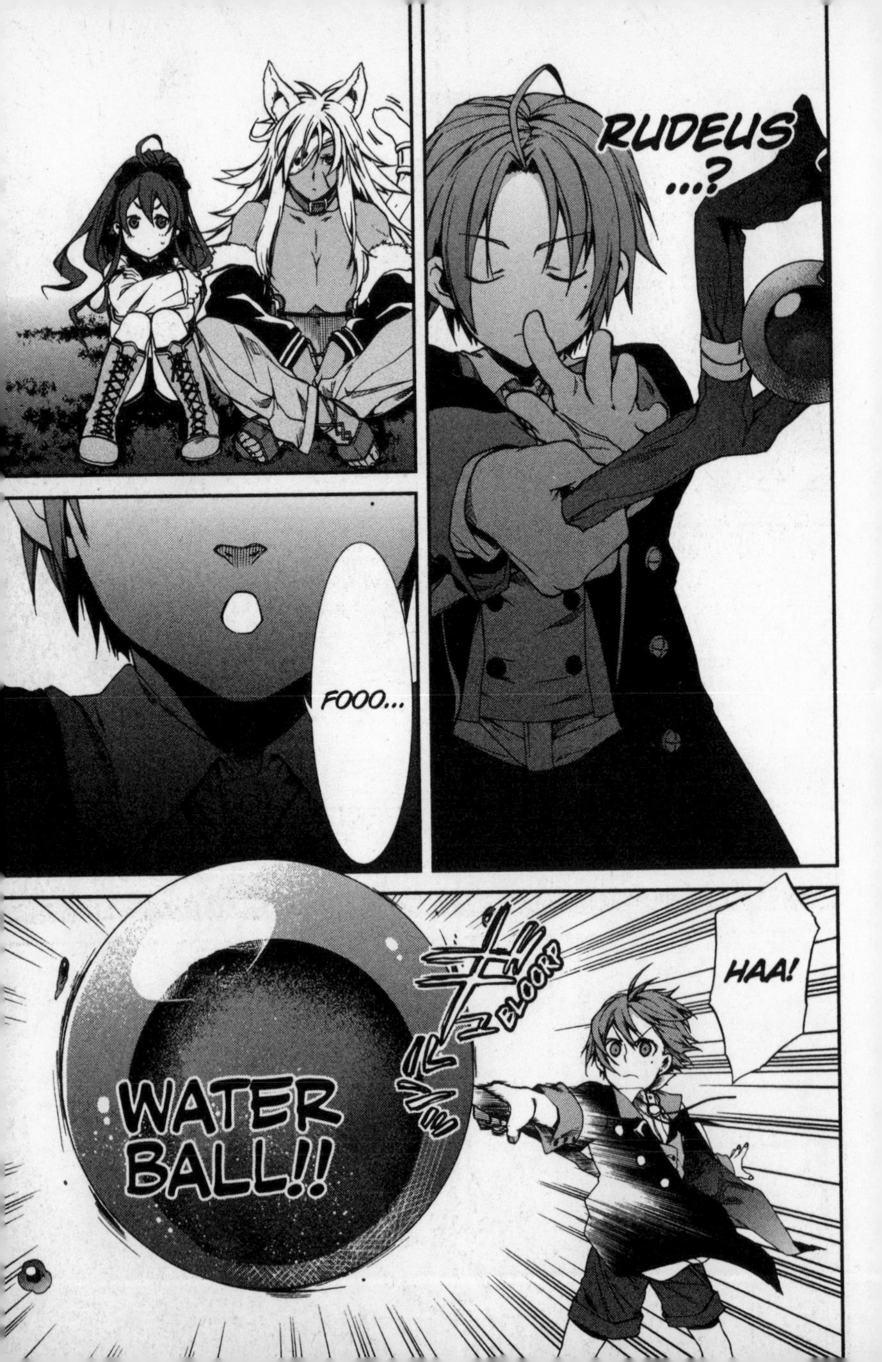
RUDEUS ...?
FOOO...
HAA!
BLOORP
WATER BALL!!

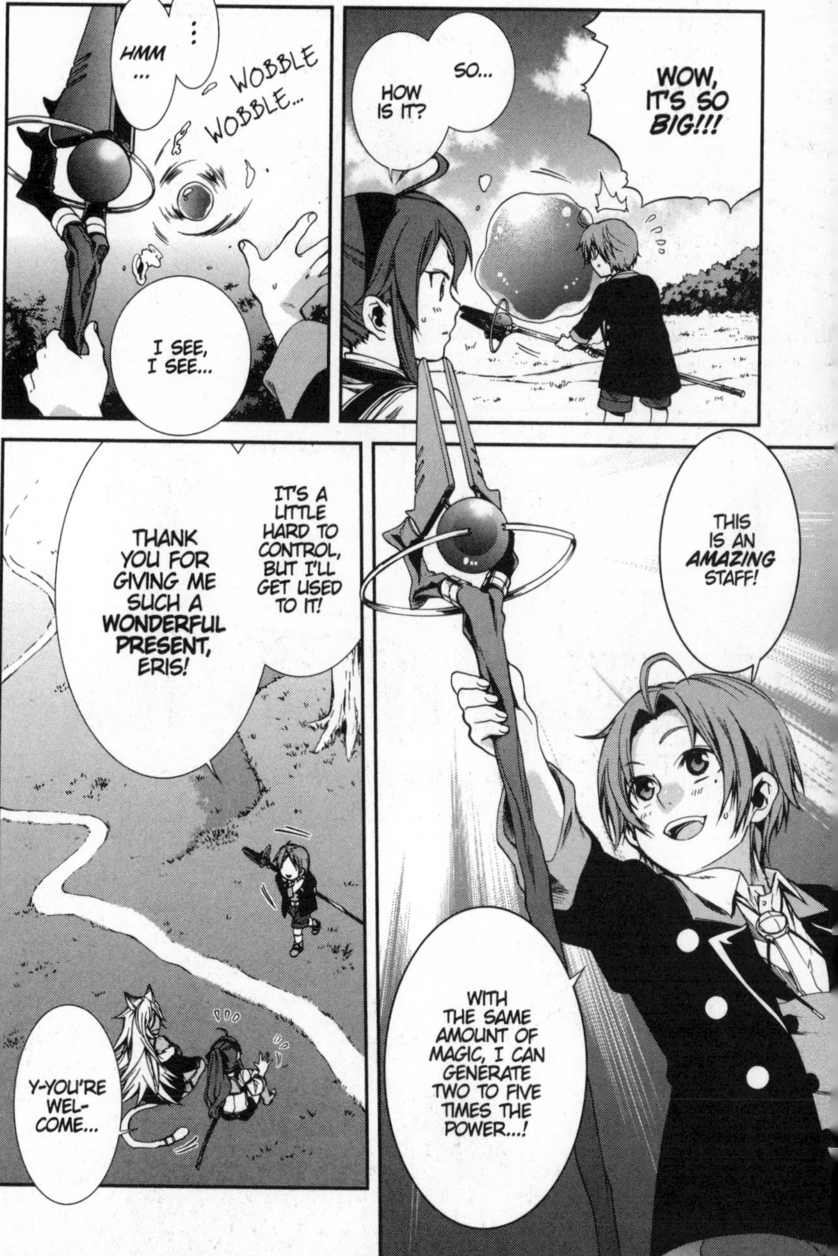
WOW, IT'S SO BIG!!!
SO... HOW IS IT?
... HMM...
WOBBLE WOBBLE...
I SEE, I SEE...
THIS IS AN AMAZING STAFF!
WITH THE SAME AMOUNT OF MAGIC, I CAN GENERATE TWO TO FIVE TIMES THE POWER...!
IT'S A LITTLE HARD TO CONTROL, BUT I'LL GET USED TO IT!
THANK YOU FOR GIVING ME SUCH A WONDERFUL PRESENT, ERIS!
Y-YOU'RE WEL-COME...

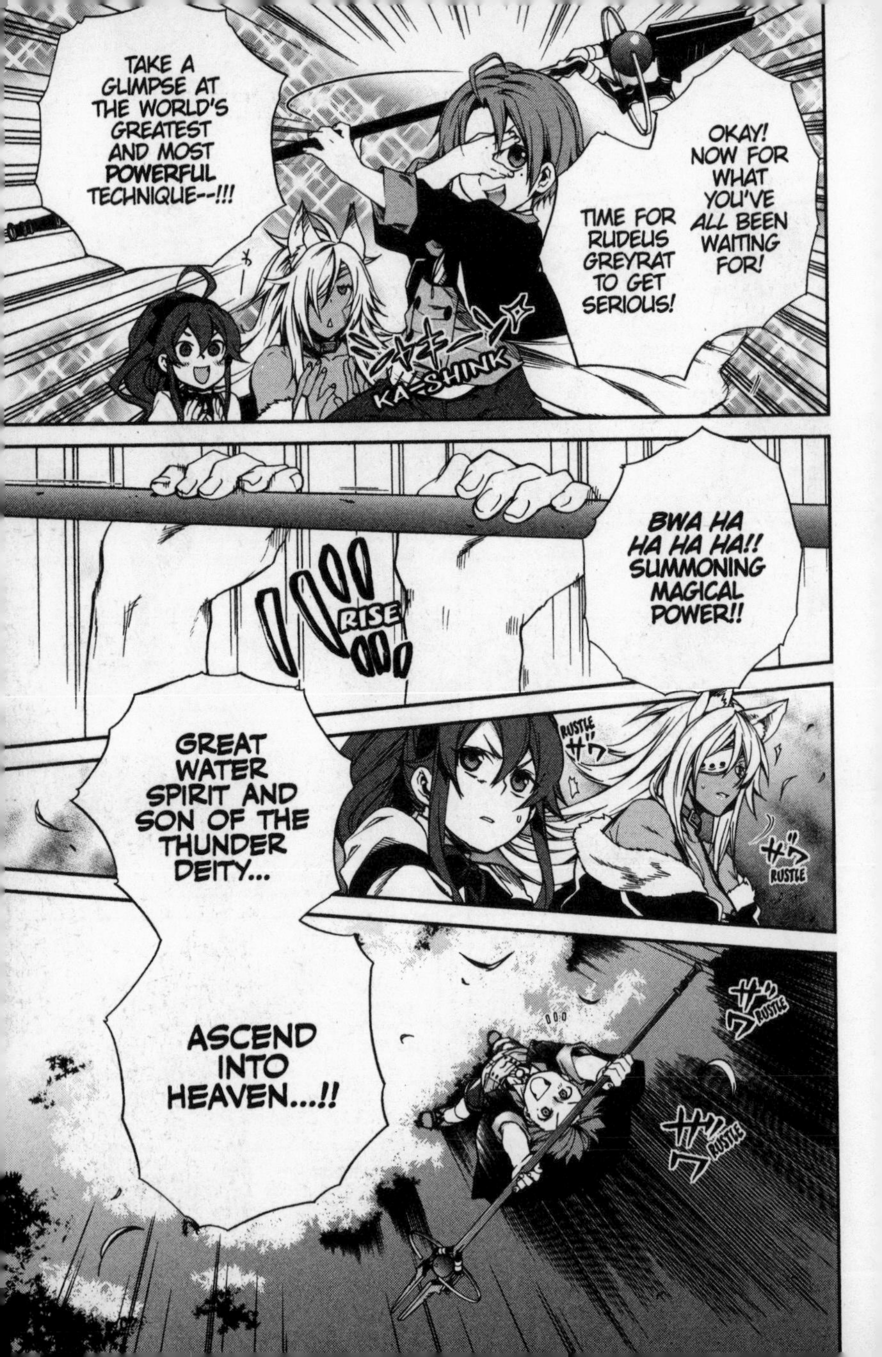
OKAY! NOW FOR WHAT YOU'VE ALL BEEN WAITING FOR!
TIME FOR RUDEUS GREYRAT TO GET SERIOUS!
KA-SHINK
TAKE A GLIMPSE AT THE WORLD'S GREATEST AND MOST POWERFUL TECHNIQUE--!!!
BWA HA HA HA HA!! SUMMONING MAGICAL POWER!!
RISE
RUSTLE
RUSTLE
GREAT WATER SPIRIT AND SON OF THE THUNDER DEITY...
RUSTLE
RUSTLE
ASCEND INTO HEAVEN...!!

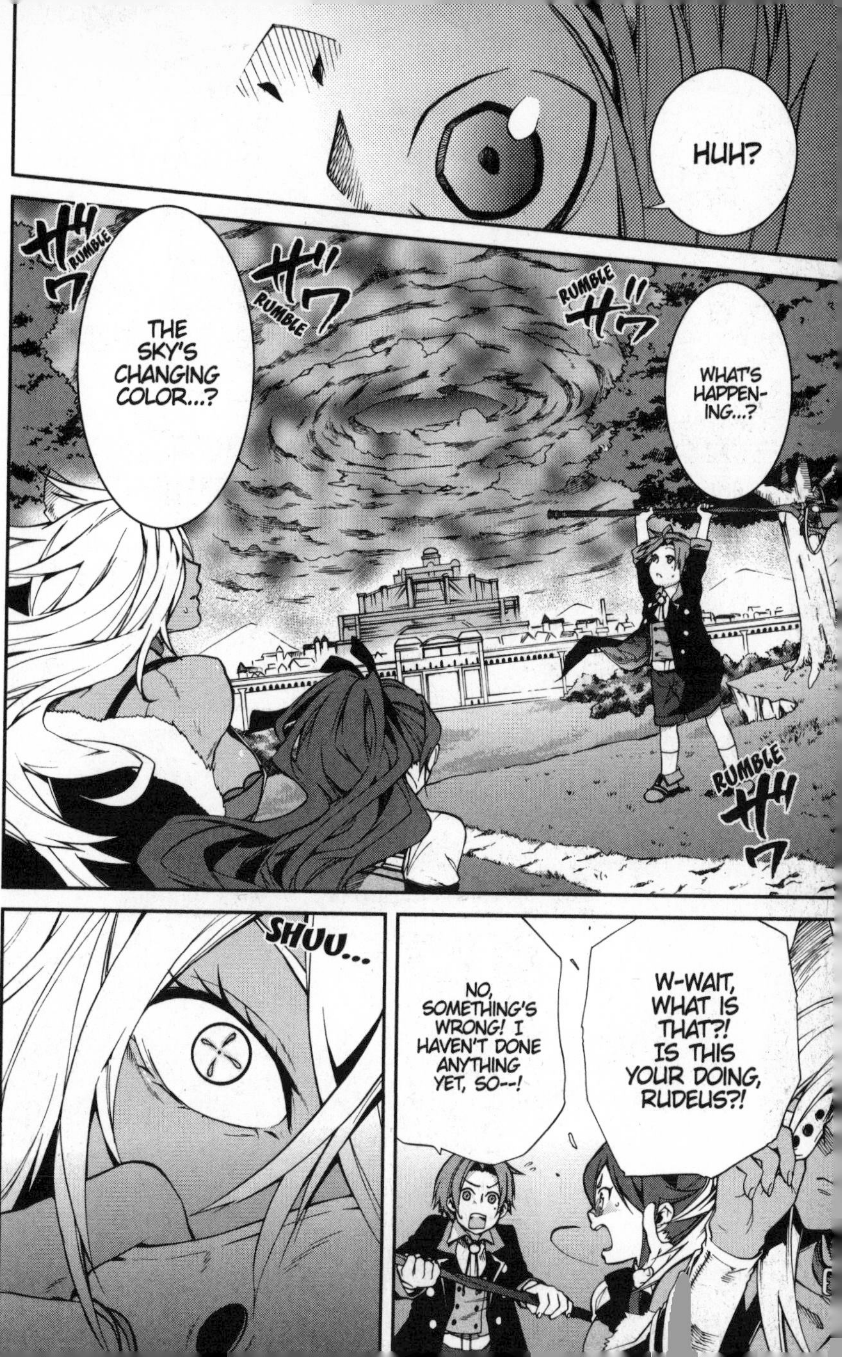
HUH?
RUMBLE
ザワ
WHAT'S HAPPENING...?
RUMBLE
ザワ
RUMBLE
ザワ
THE SKY'S CHANGING COLOR...?
RUMBLE
ザワ
W-WAIT, WHAT IS THAT?! IS THIS YOUR DOING, RUDEUS?!
NO, SOMETHING'S WRONG! I HAVEN'T DONE ANYTHING YET, SO--!
SHUU...

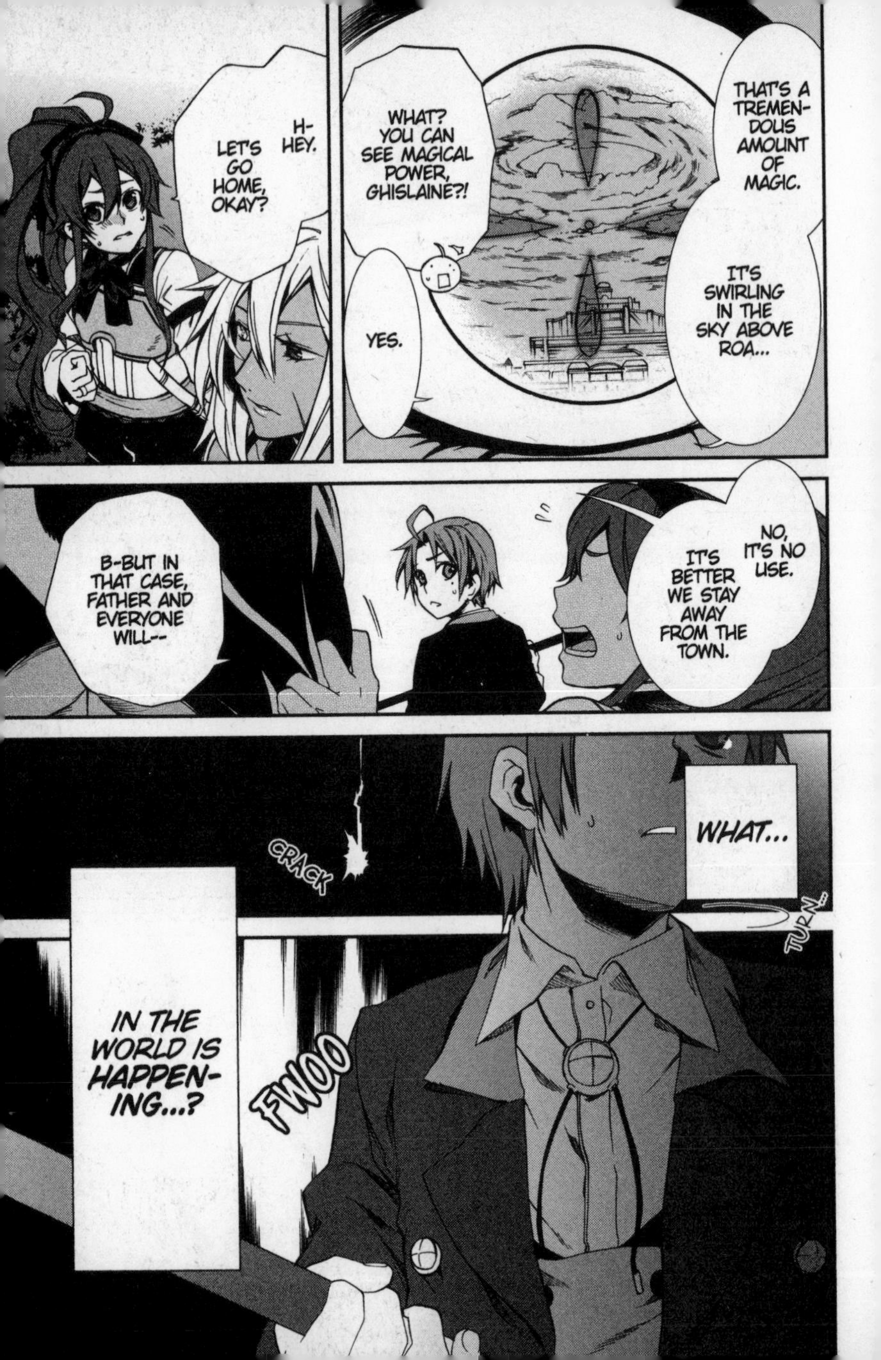
THAT'S A TREMENDOUS AMOUNT OF MAGIC.
IT'S SWIRLING IN THE SKY ABOVE ROA...
WHAT? YOU CAN SEE MAGICAL POWER, GHISLAINE?!
YES.
H-HEY.
LET'S GO HOME, OKAY?
NO, IT'S NO USE.
IT'S BETTER WE STAY AWAY FROM THE TOWN.
B-BUT IN THAT CASE, FATHER AND EVERYONE WILL--
WHAT...
TURN...
CRACK
FWOO
IN THE WORLD IS HAPPENING...?

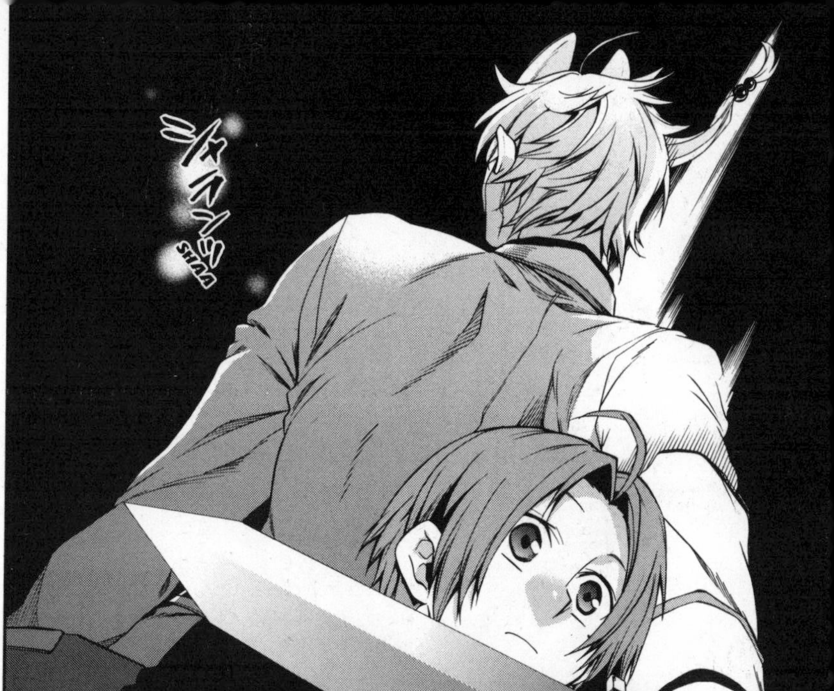
SHAA

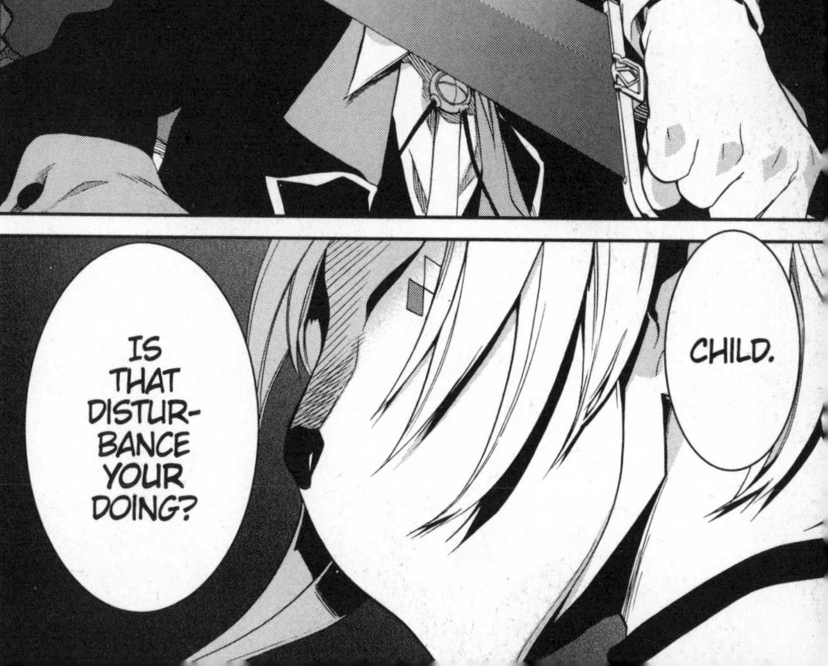
CHILD.
IS THAT DISTUR-BANCE YOUR DOING?

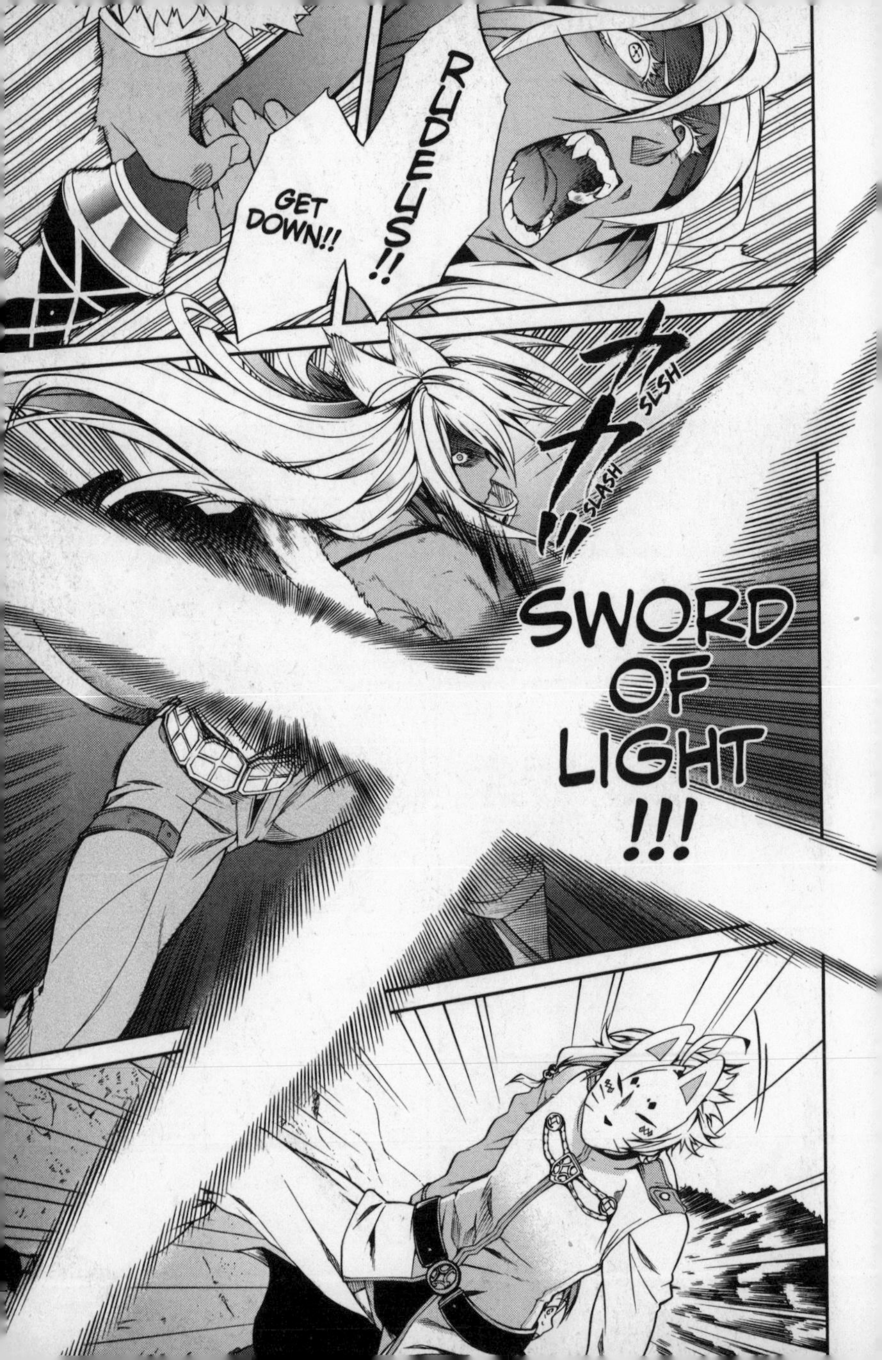
RUDEUS!!
GET DOWN!!
SLSH
SLASH
SWORD OF LIGHT!!!

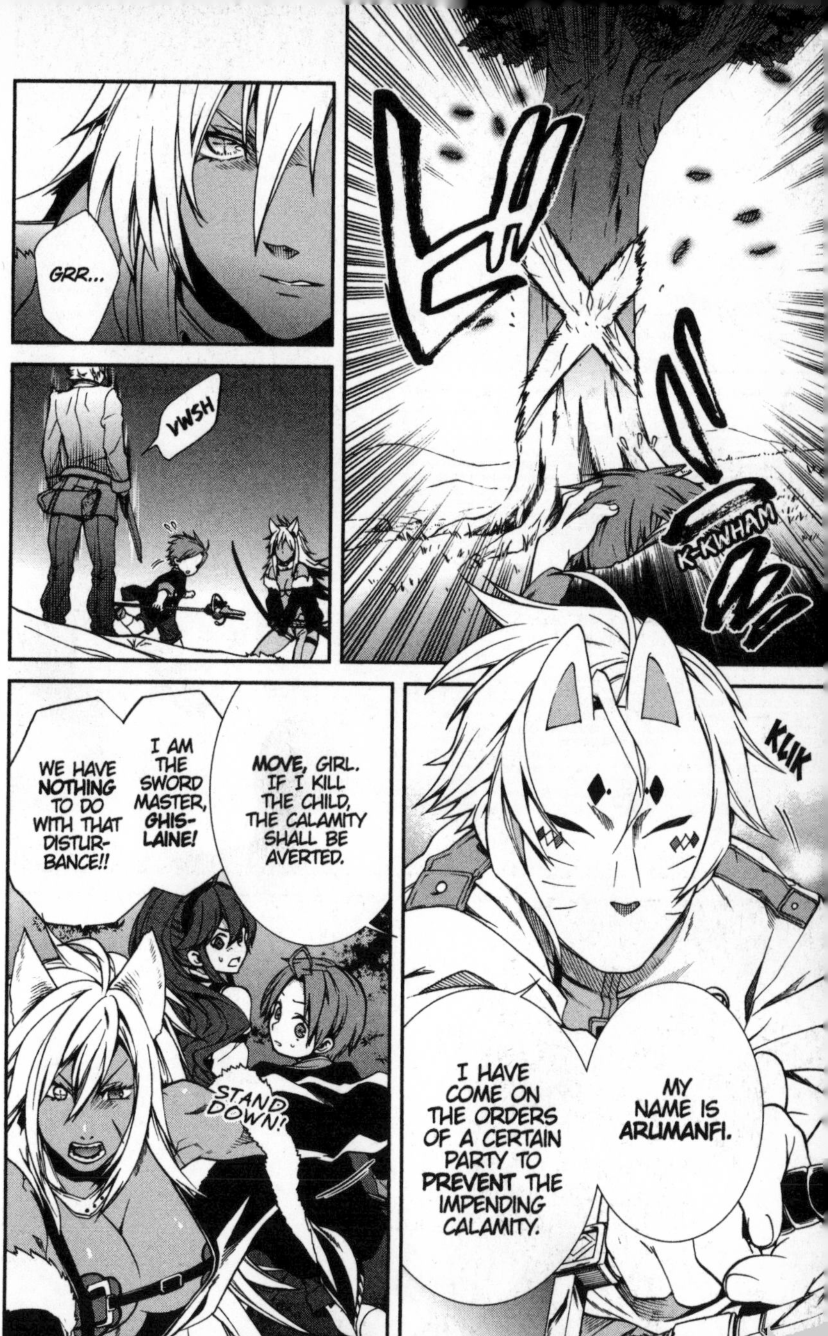
K-KWHAM
GRR...
VWSH
KLIK
MY NAME IS ARUMANFI.
I HAVE COME ON THE ORDERS OF A CERTAIN PARTY TO PREVENT THE IMPENDING CALAMITY.
MOVE, GIRL. IF I KILL THE CHILD, THE CALAMITY SHALL BE AVERTED.
I AM THE SWORD MASTER, GHISLAINE!
WE HAVE NOTHING TO DO WITH THAT DISTURBANCE!!
STAND DOWN!

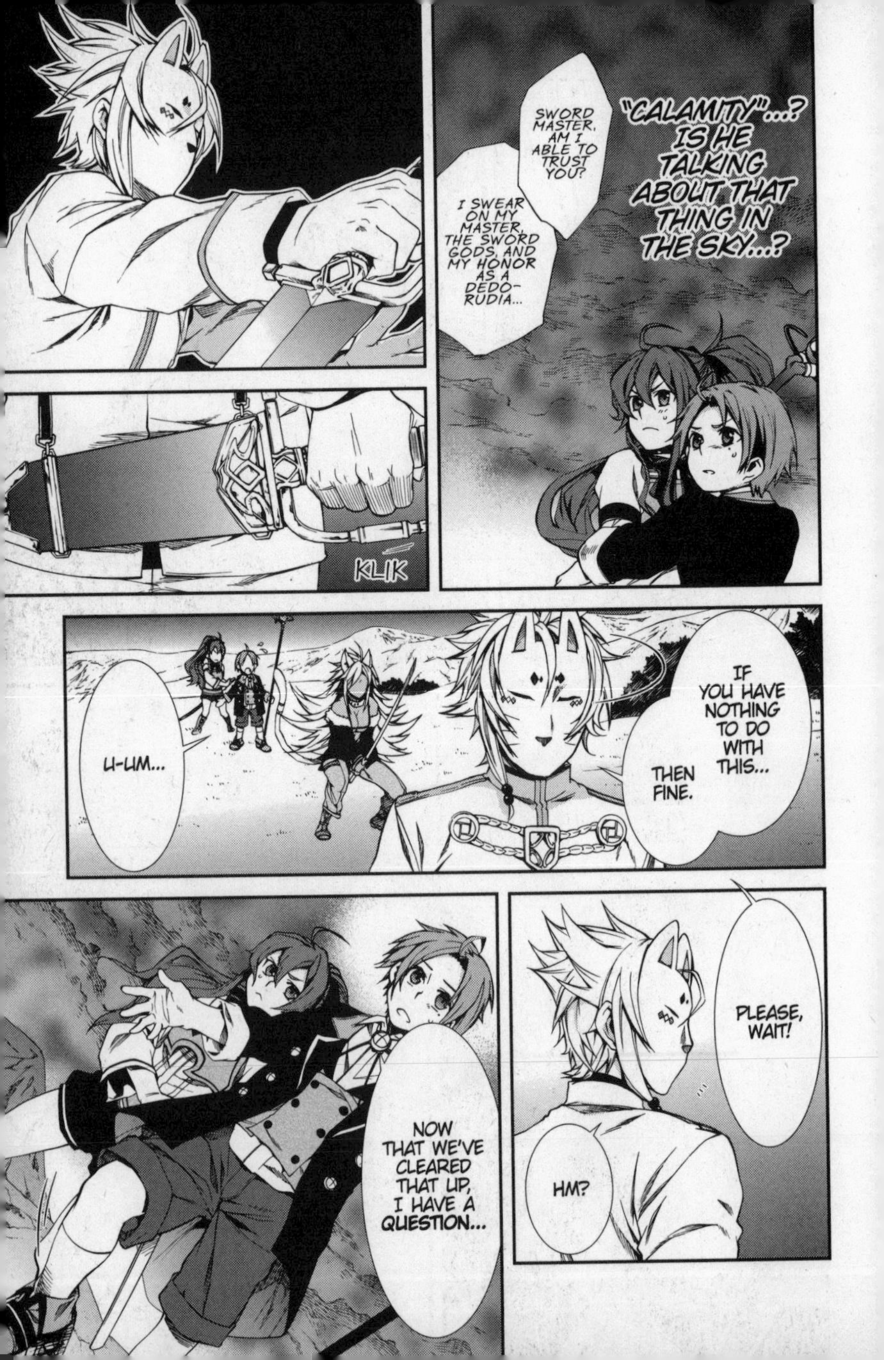
"CALAMITY"...? IS HE TALKING ABOUT THAT THING IN THE SKY...?
SWORD MASTER, AM I ABLE TO TRUST YOU?
I SWEAR ON MY MASTER, THE SWORD GODS, AND MY HONOR AS A DEDO-RUDIA...
KLIK
IF YOU HAVE NOTHING TO DO WITH THIS...
THEN FINE.
U-UM...
PLEASE, WAIT!
HM?
NOW THAT WE'VE CLEARED THAT UP, I HAVE A QUESTION...

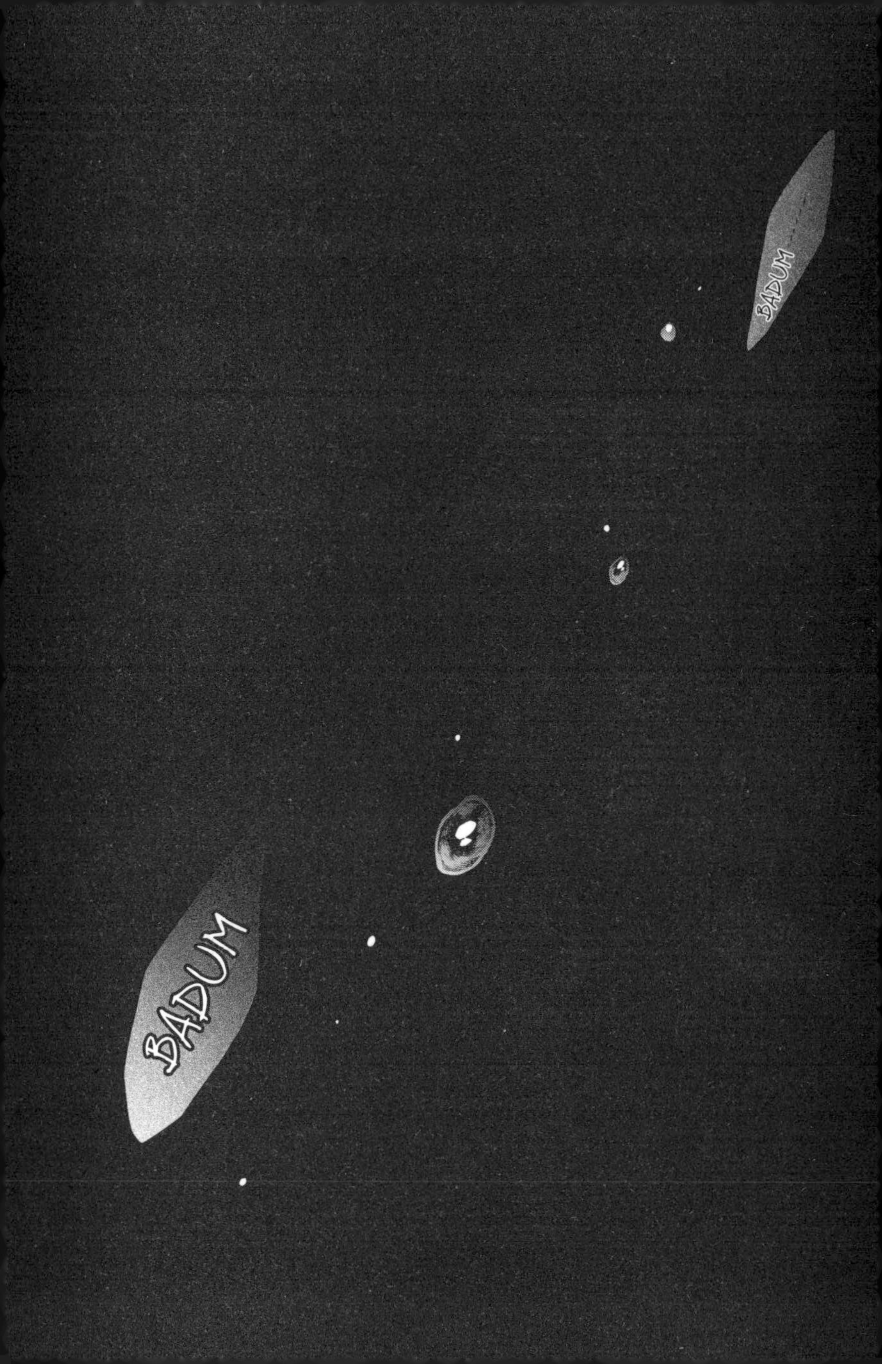
BADUM
BADUM

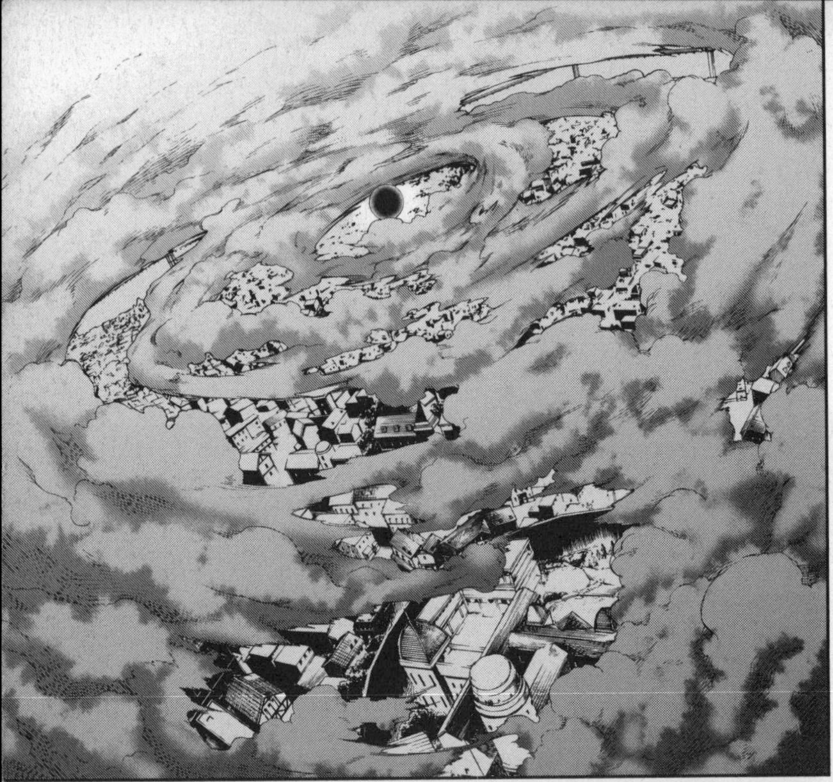
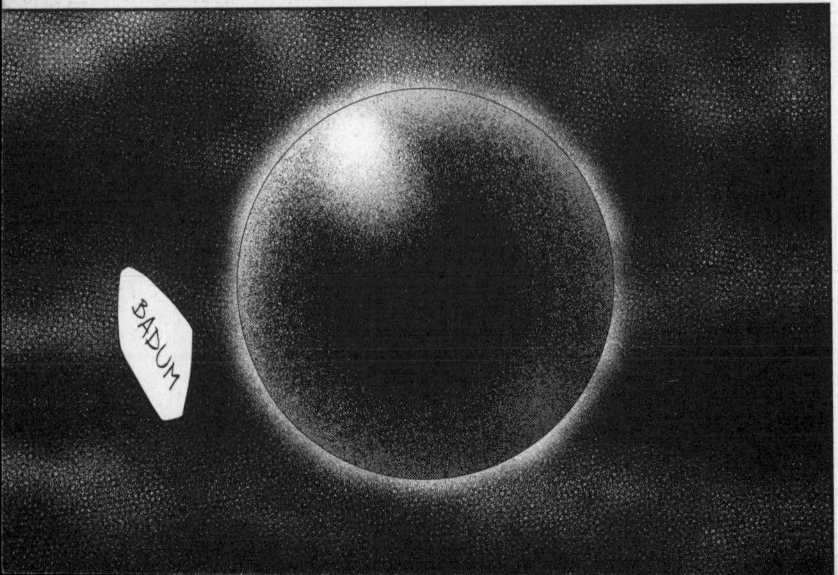
BADUM

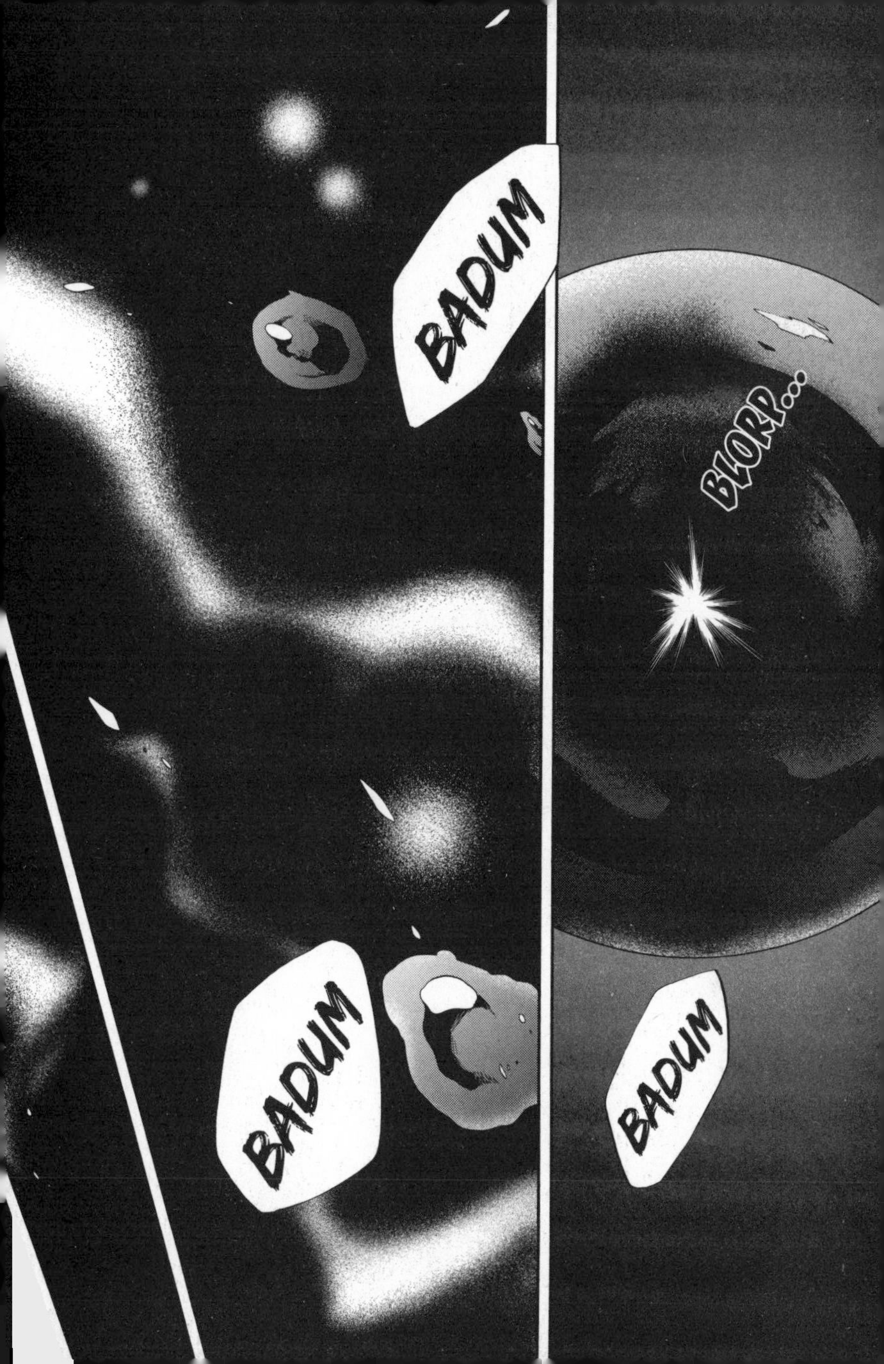
BLORP...
BADUM
BADUM
BADUM

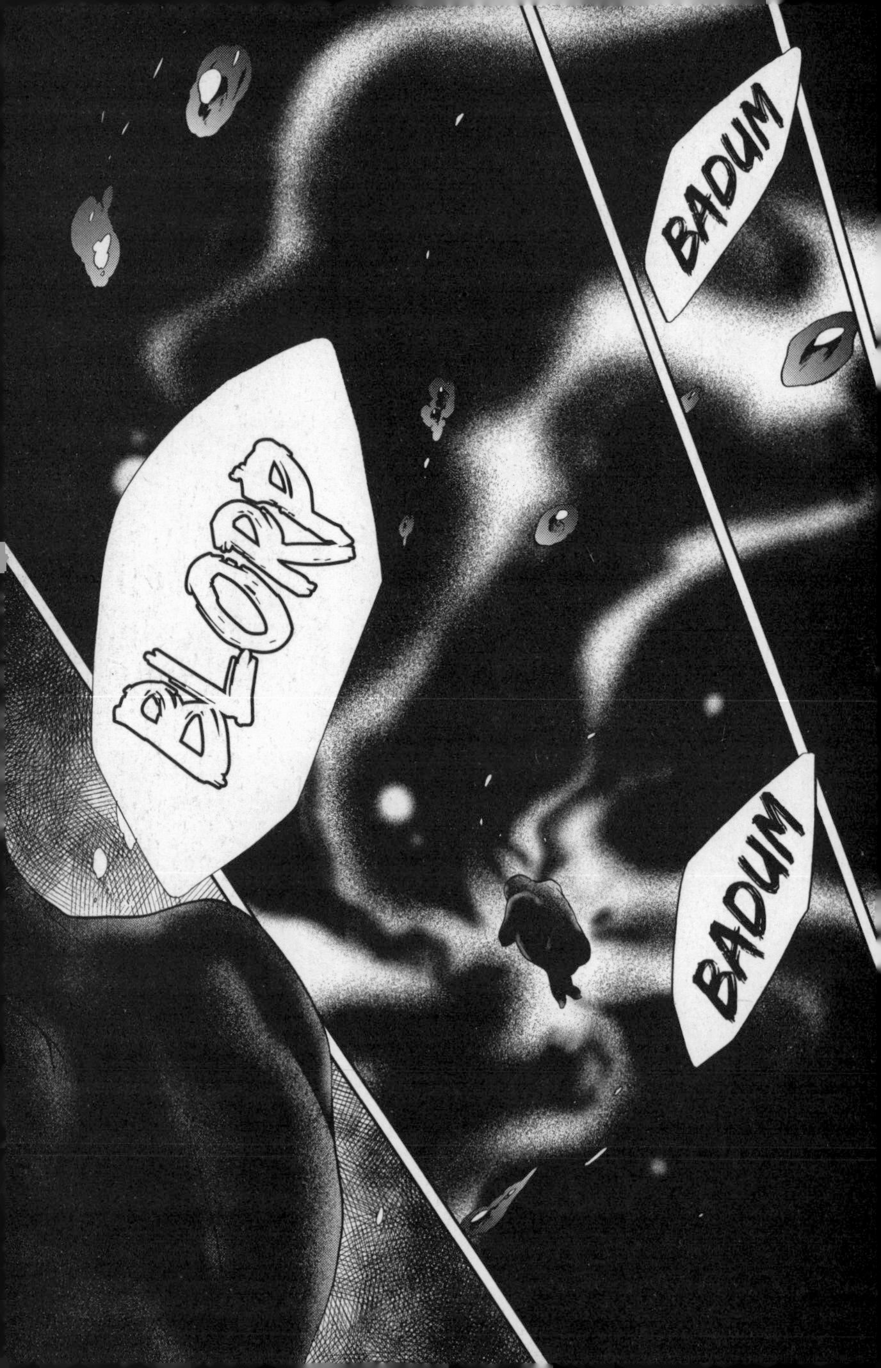
BADUM
BADUM
BLORP

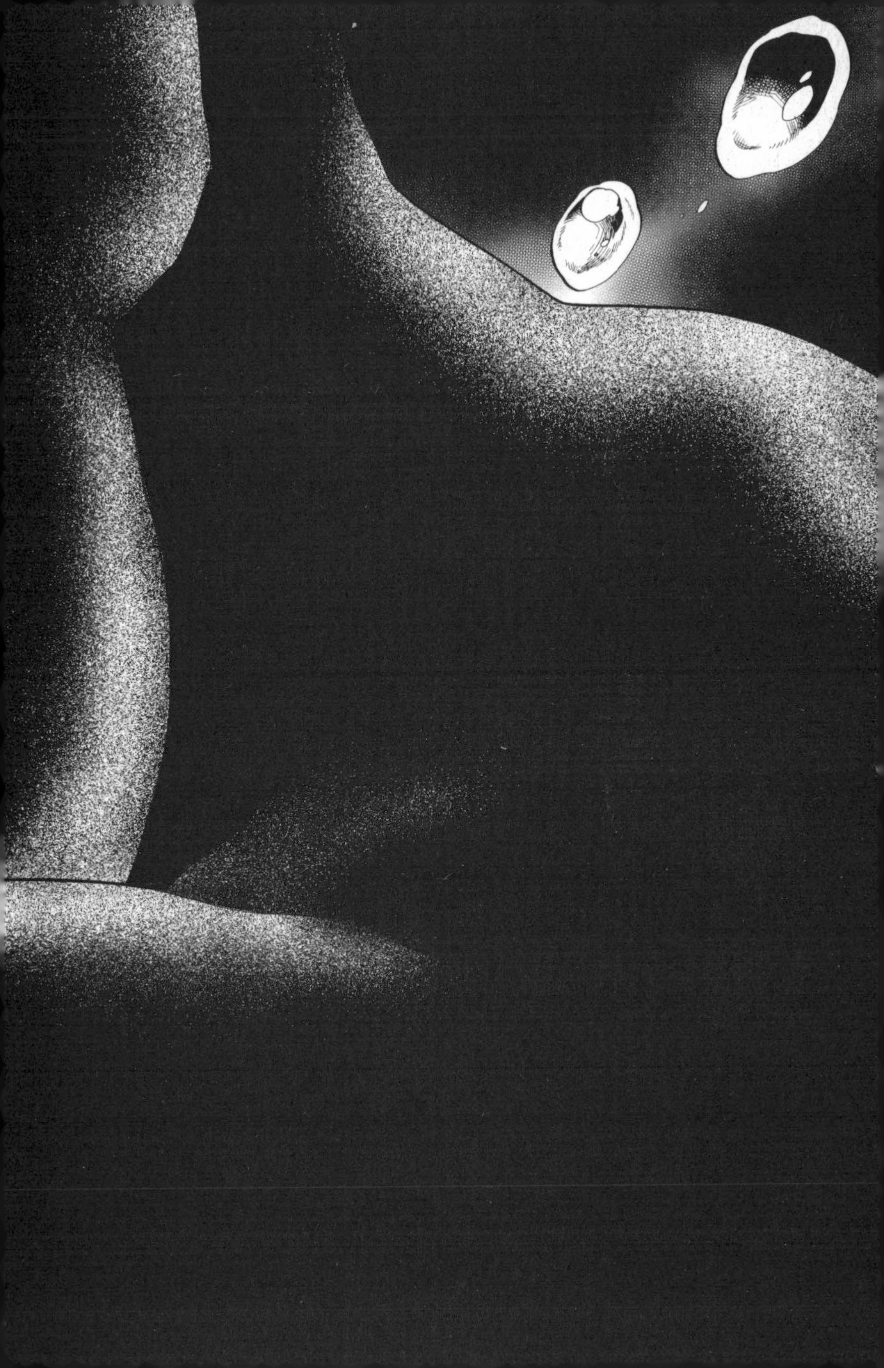

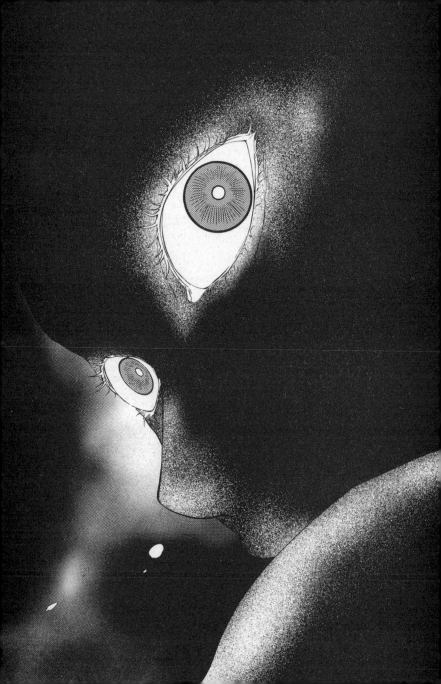

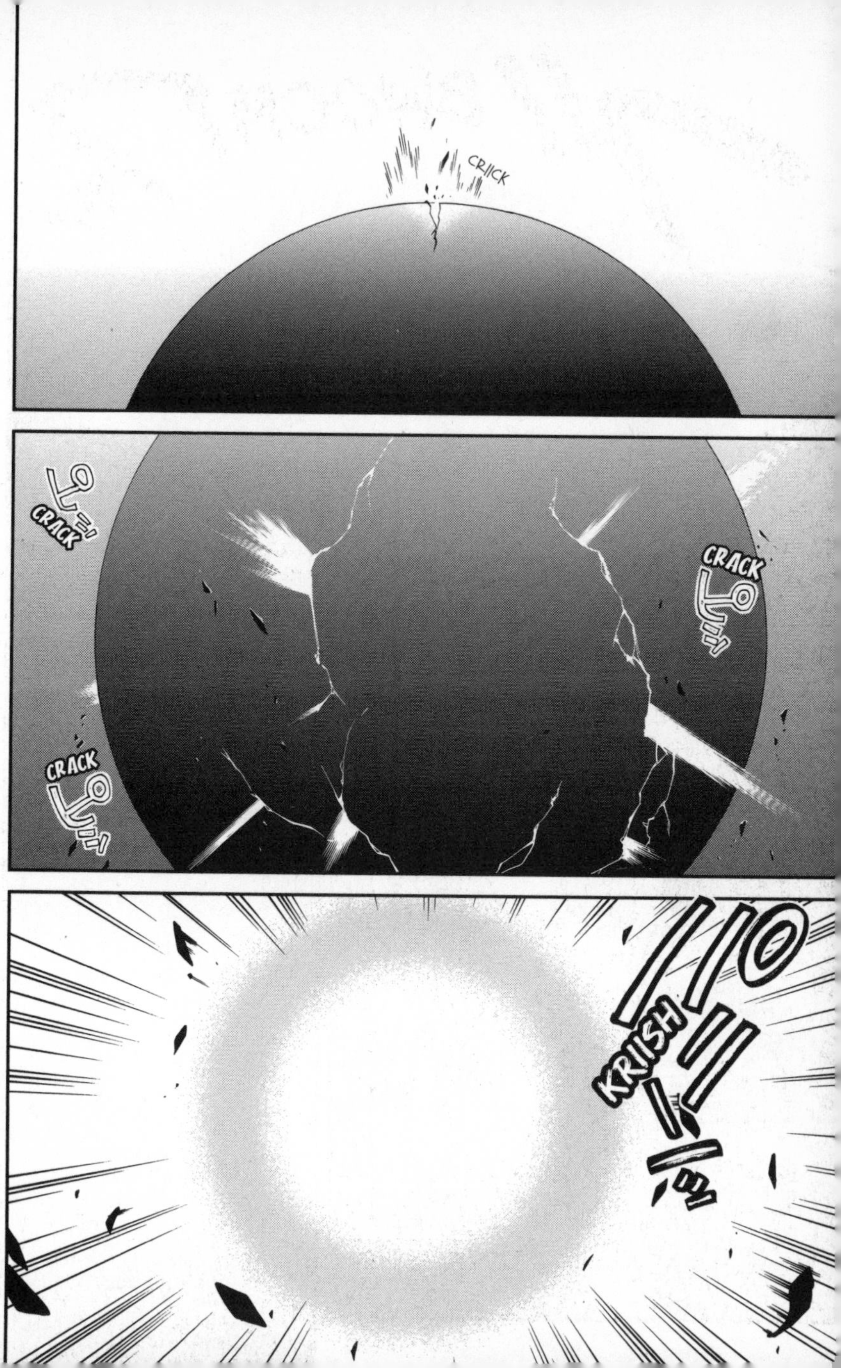
CRIICK
CRACK
CRACK
CRACK
KRIISH

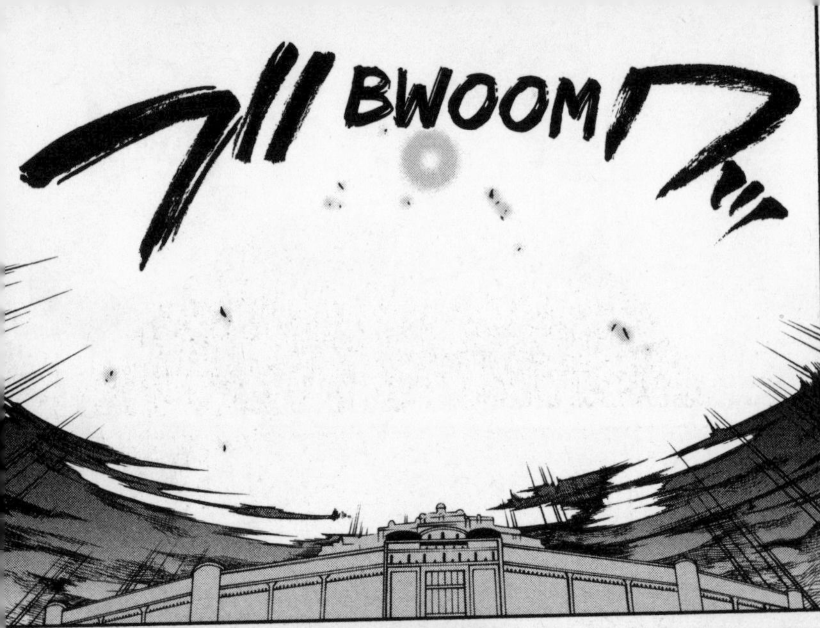
BWOOM
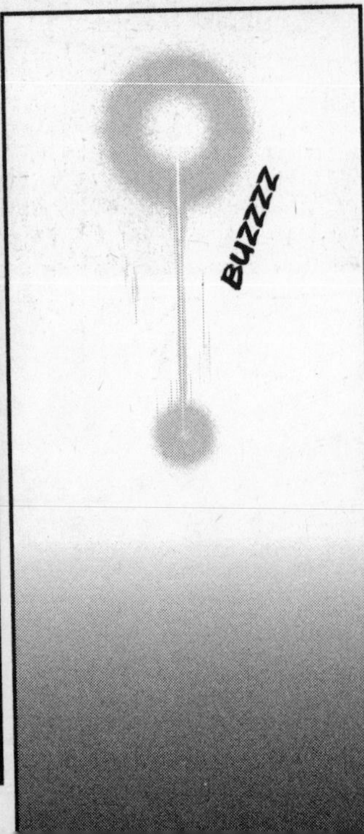
BUZZZZ
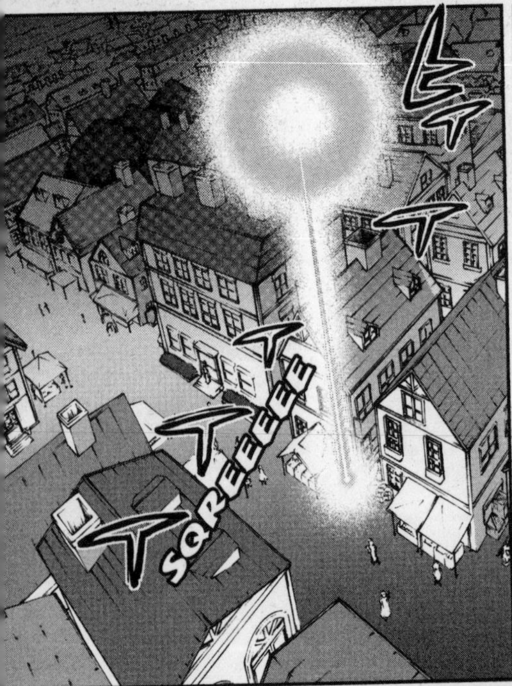
SQREEEEEE

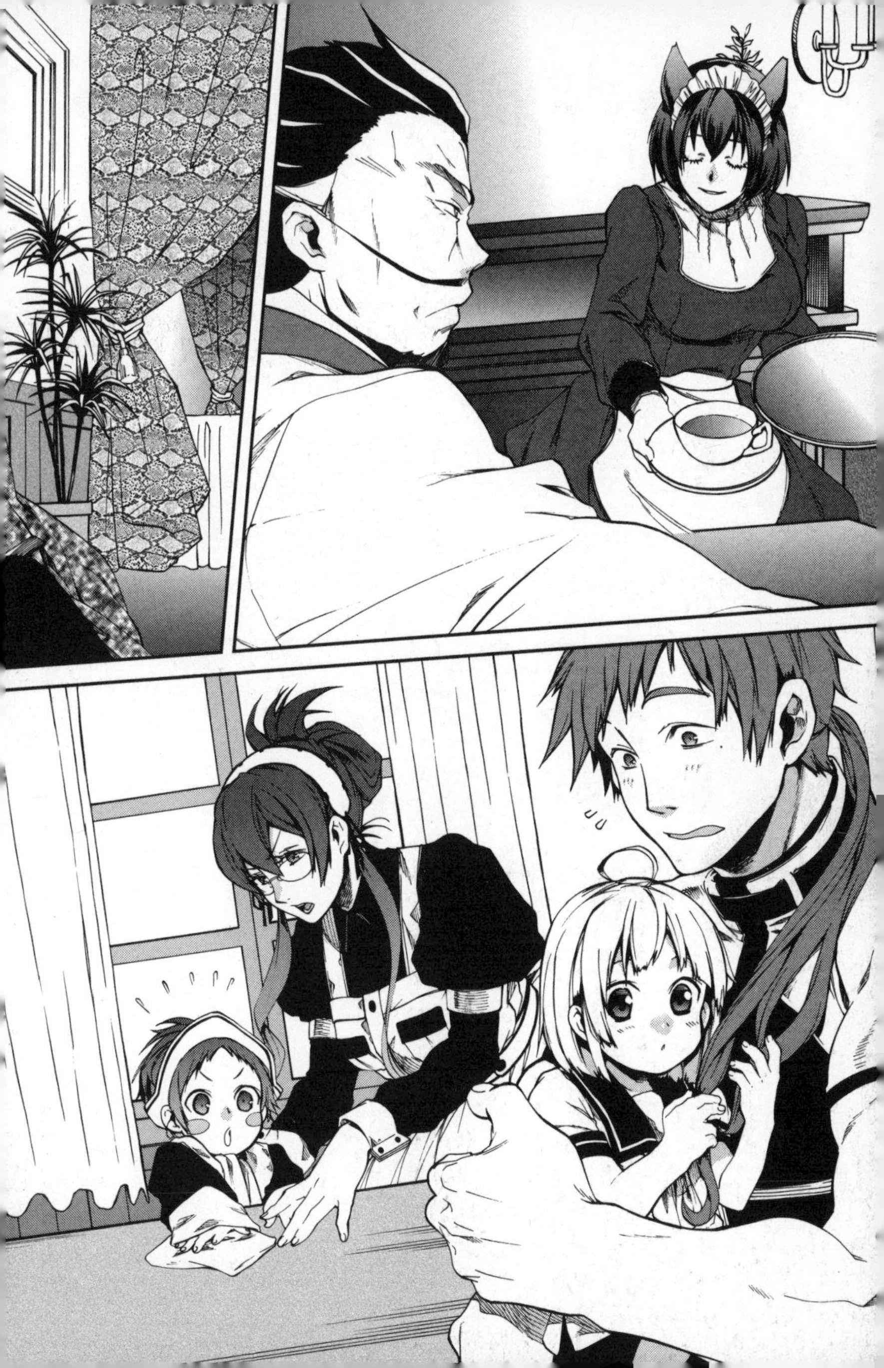

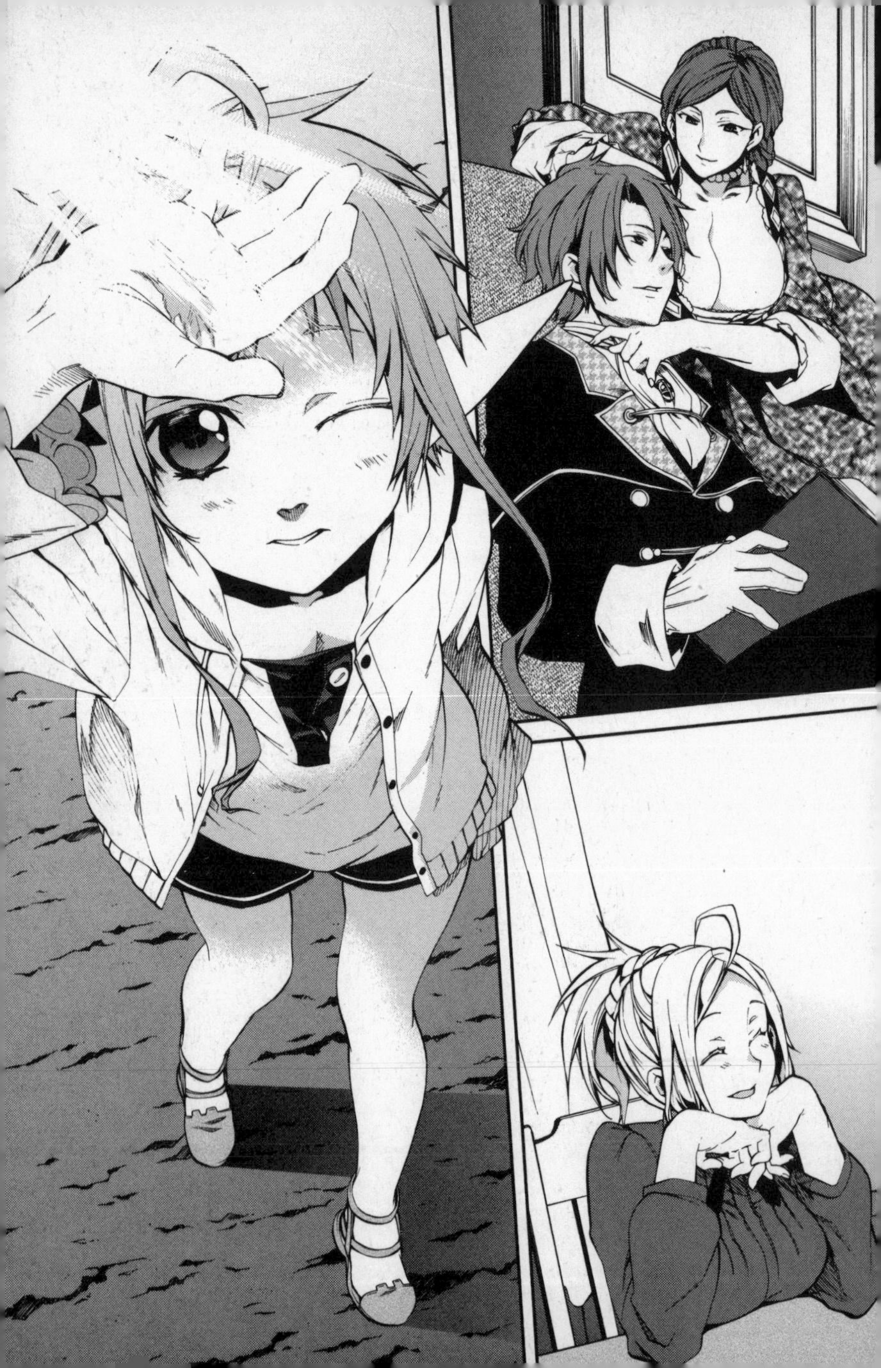

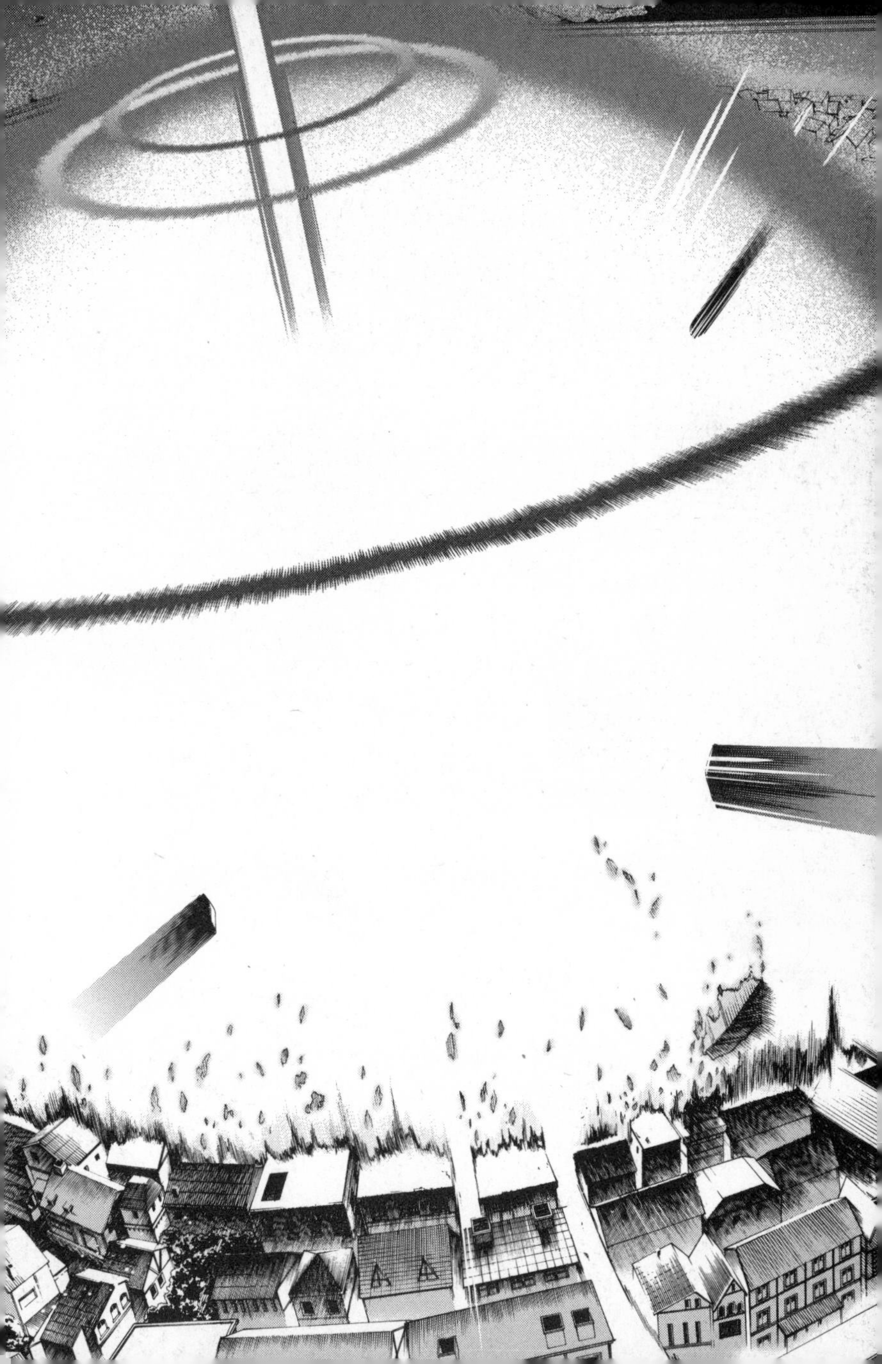

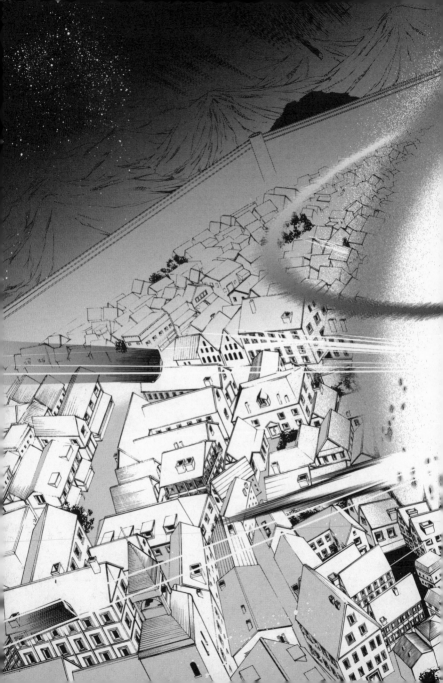

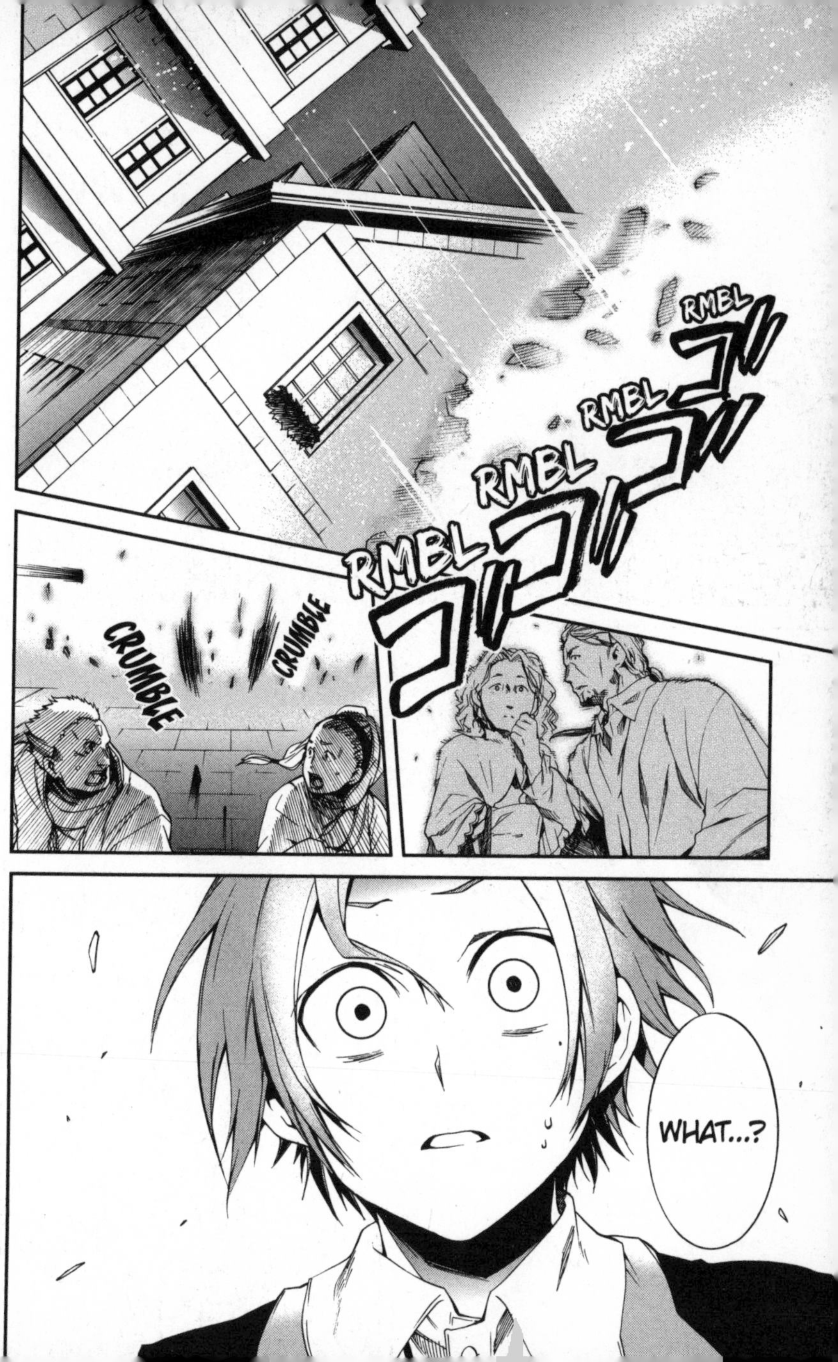
RMBL
RMBL
RMBL
RMBL
CRUMBLE
CRUMBLE
WHAT...?

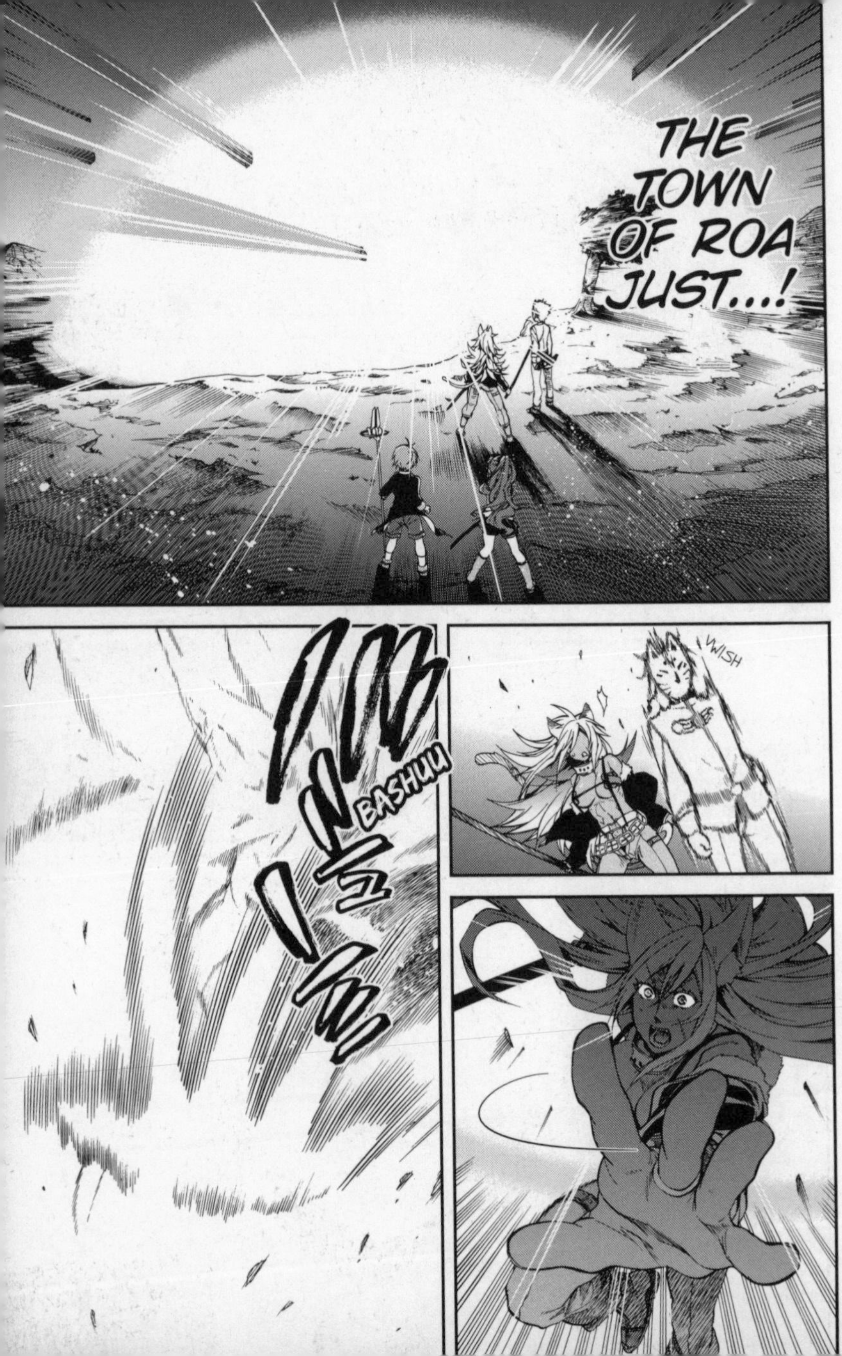
THE TOWN OF ROA JUST...!
VWISH
BASHUU

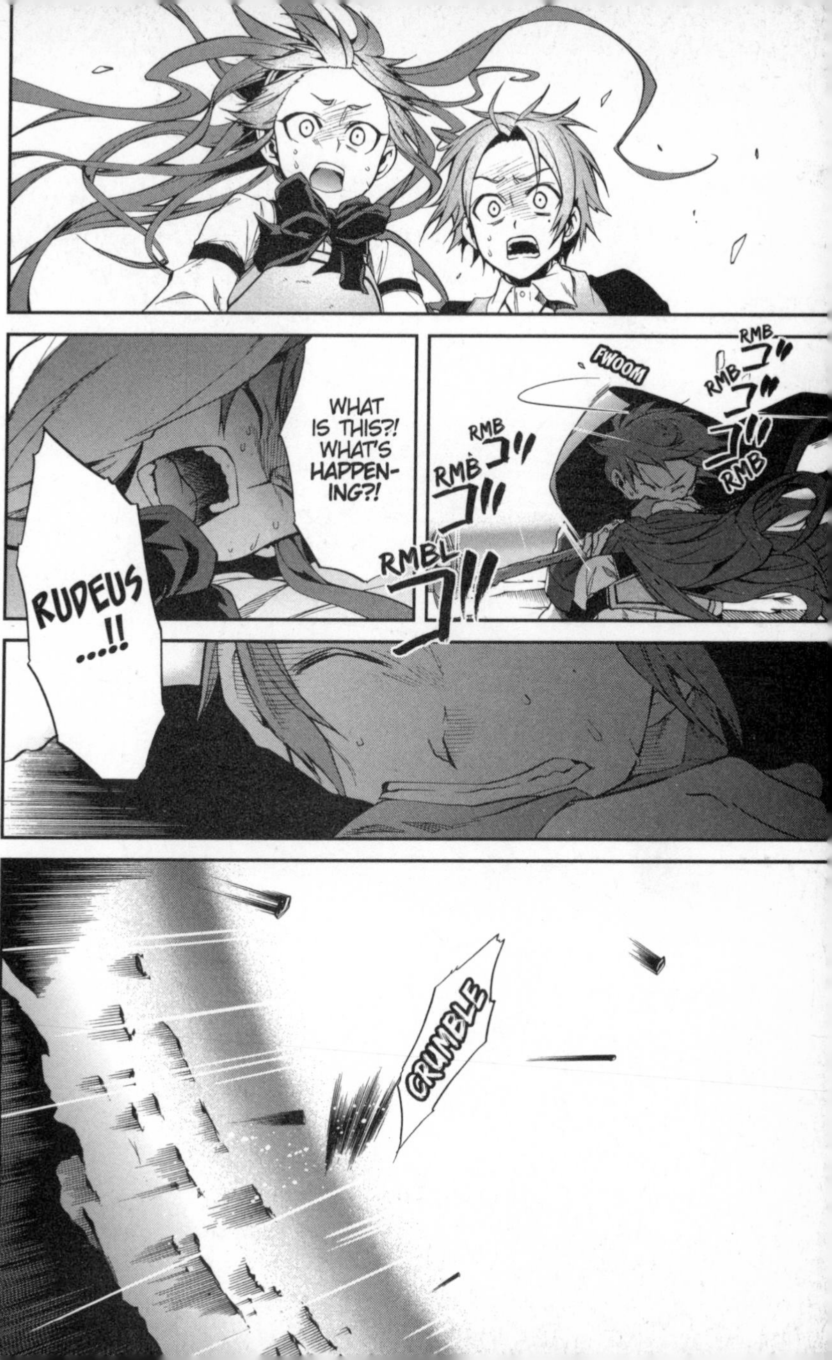
RMB
RMB
FWOOM
RMB
RMB
RMB
RMBL
WHAT IS THIS?! WHAT'S HAPPENING?!
RUDEUS ...!!
CRUMBLE

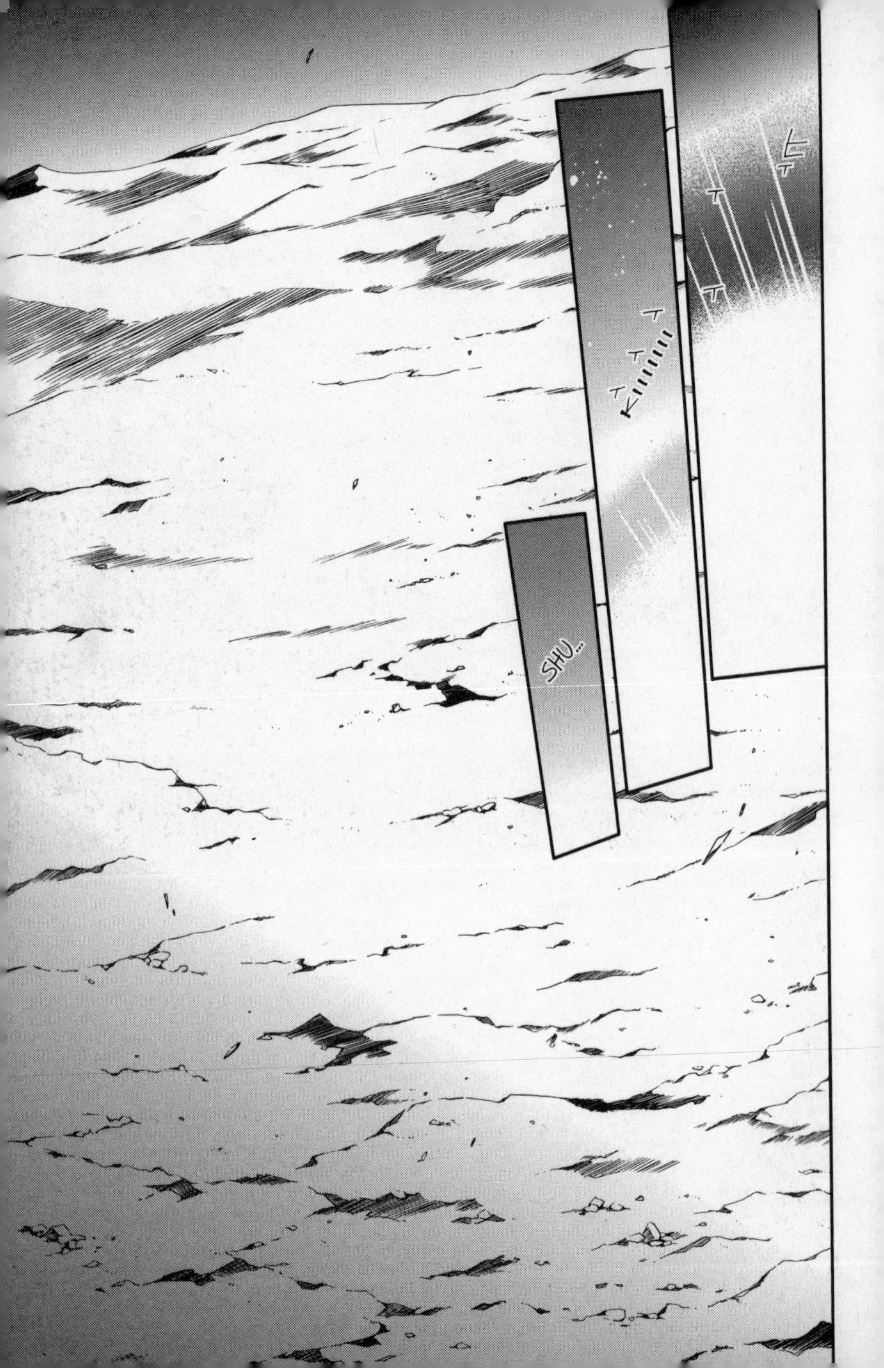
KIIIIIII
SHU...

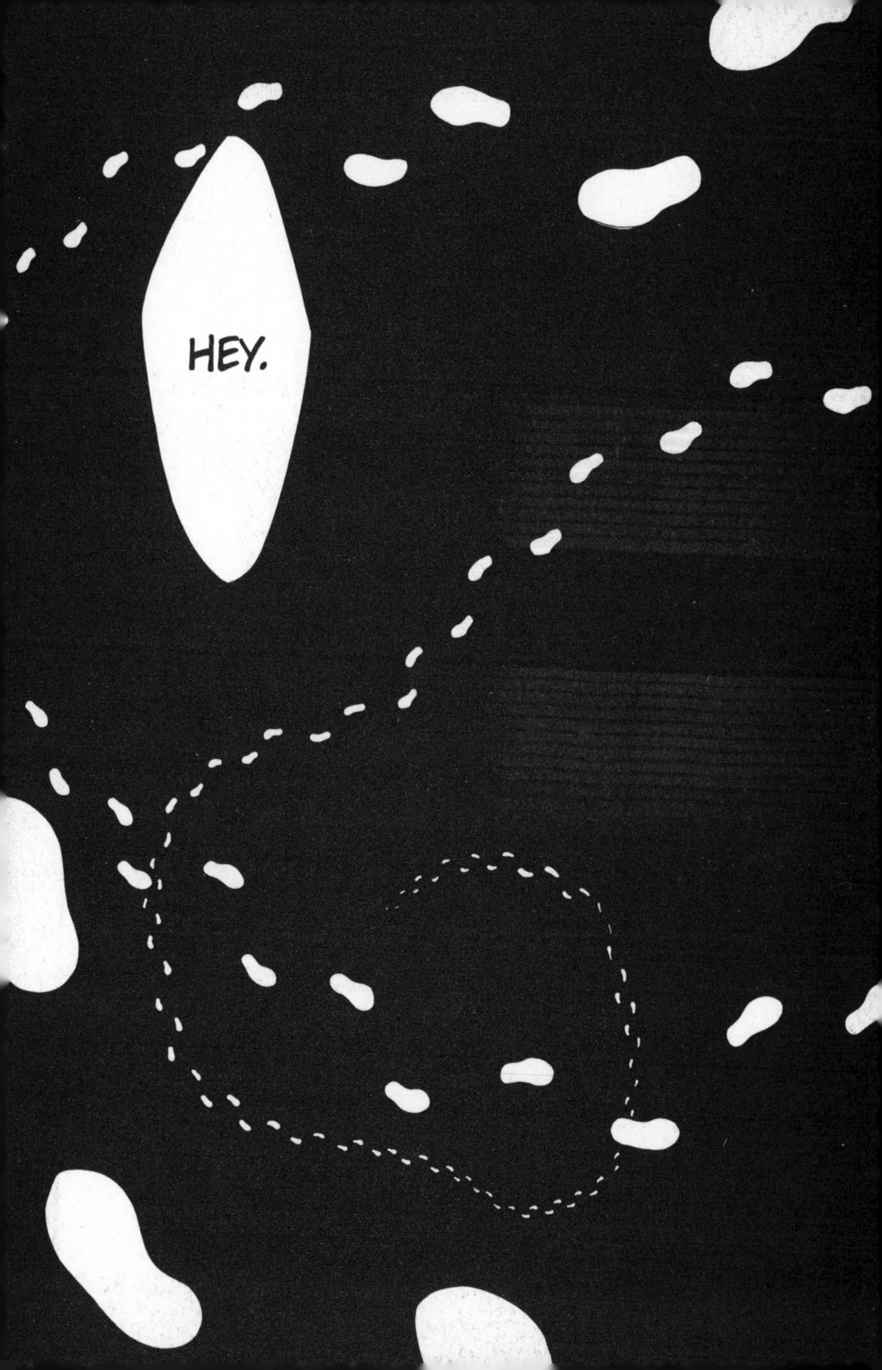
HEY.

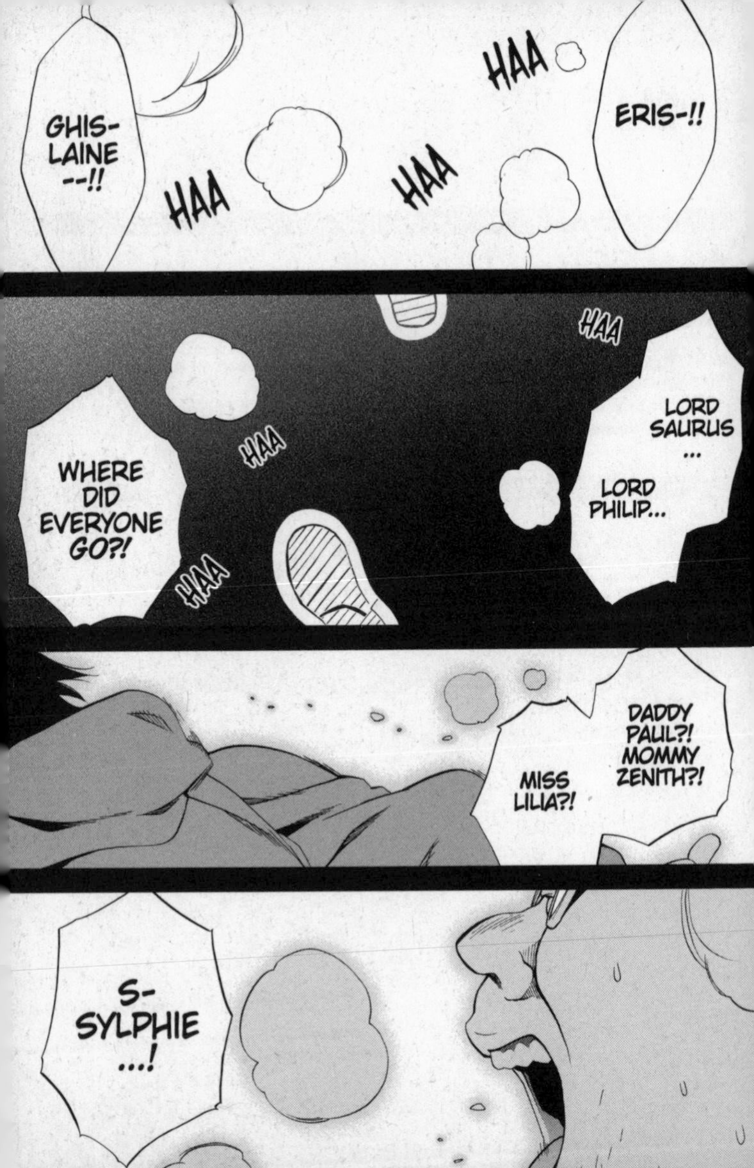
ERIS-!!
HAA
HAA
HAA
GHIS-LAINE--!!
HAA
LORD SAURUS...
LORD PHILIP...
HAA
HAA
WHERE DID EVERYONE GO?!
DADDY PAUL?! MOMMY ZENITH?!
MISS LILIA?!
S-SYLPHIE...!

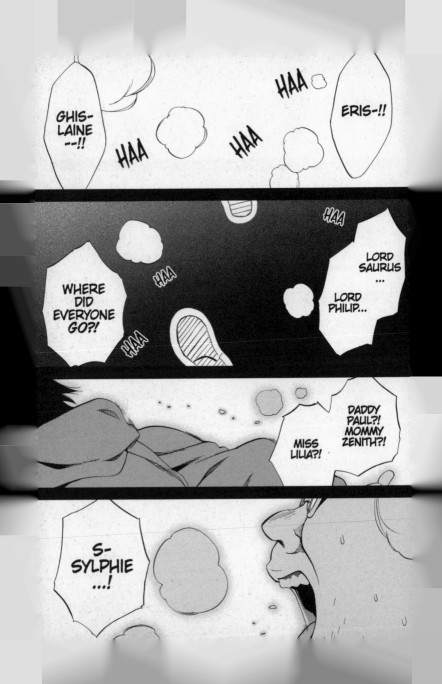

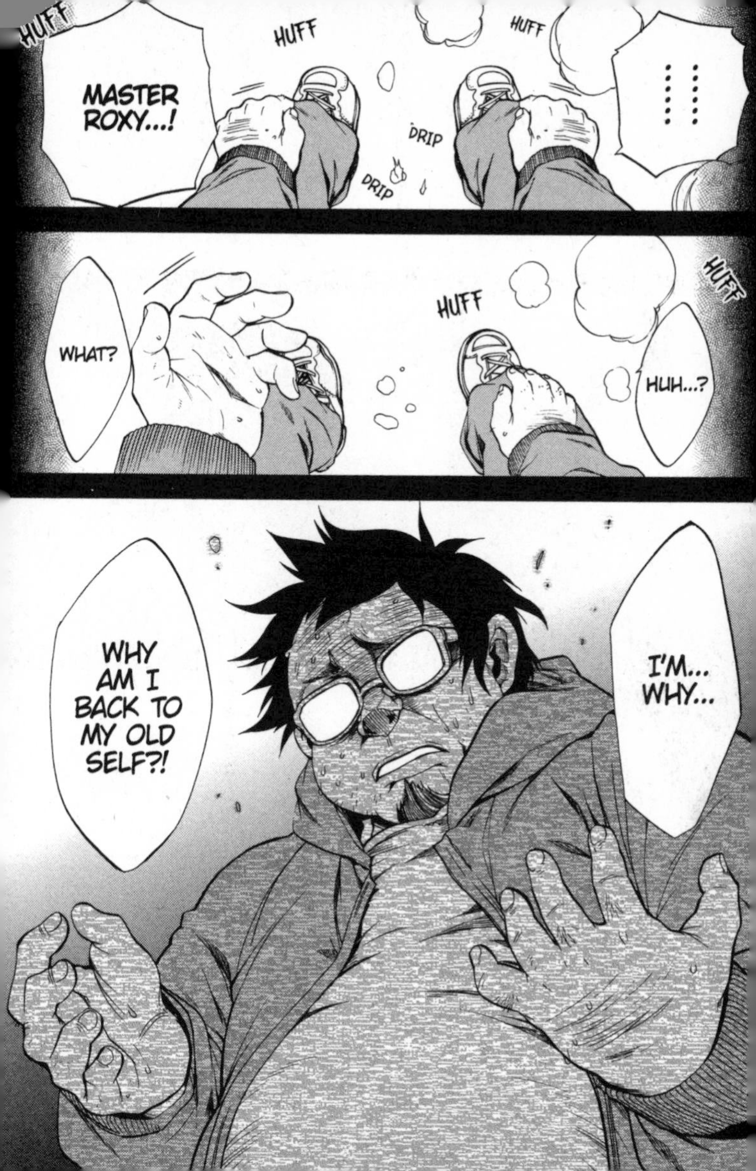
......
HUFF
DRIP
DRIP
HUFF
MASTER ROXY...!
HUFF
HUFF
HUH...?
HUFF
WHAT?
I'M... WHY...
WHY AM I BACK TO MY OLD SELF?!

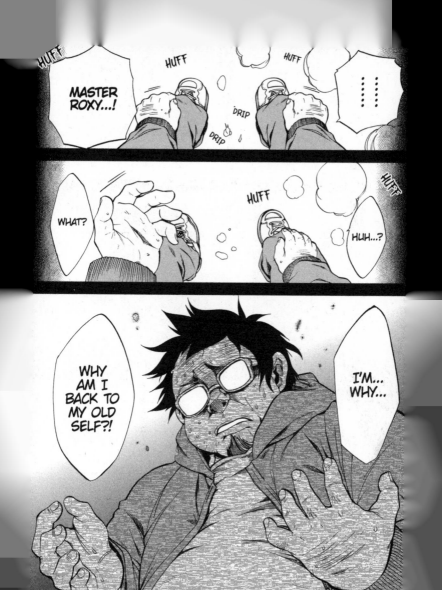

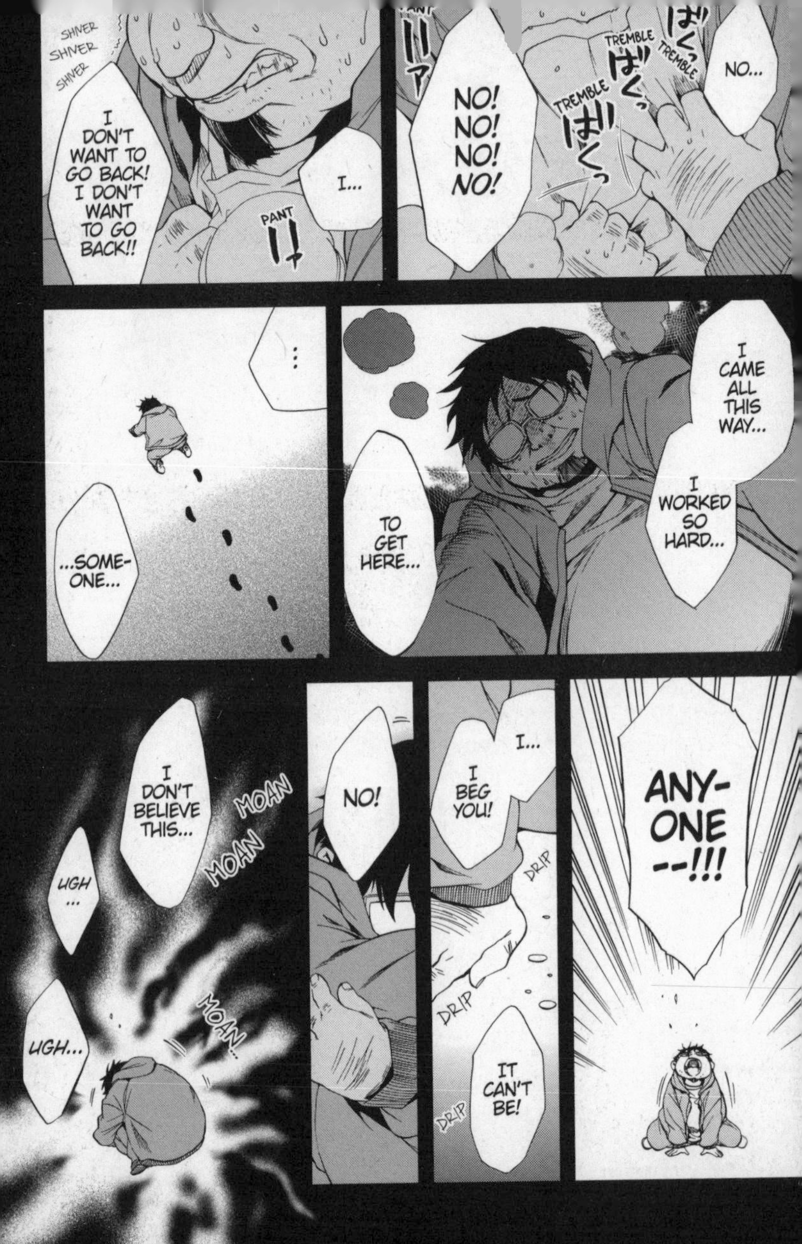
NO...
TREMBLE
ばくっ
TREMBLE
TREMBLE
ばくっ
ばくっ
NO! NO! NO! NO!
I...
PANT
I DON'T WANT TO GO BACK! I DON'T WANT TO GO BACK!!
SHIVER
SHIVER
SHIVER
I CAME ALL THIS WAY...
I WORKED SO HARD...
TO GET HERE...
...
...SOME-ONE...
ANY-ONE--!!!
I...
I BEG YOU!
DRIP
DRIP
IT CAN'T BE!
DRIP
NO!
I DON'T BELIEVE THIS...
MOAN
MOAN
UGH...
MOAN
UGH...

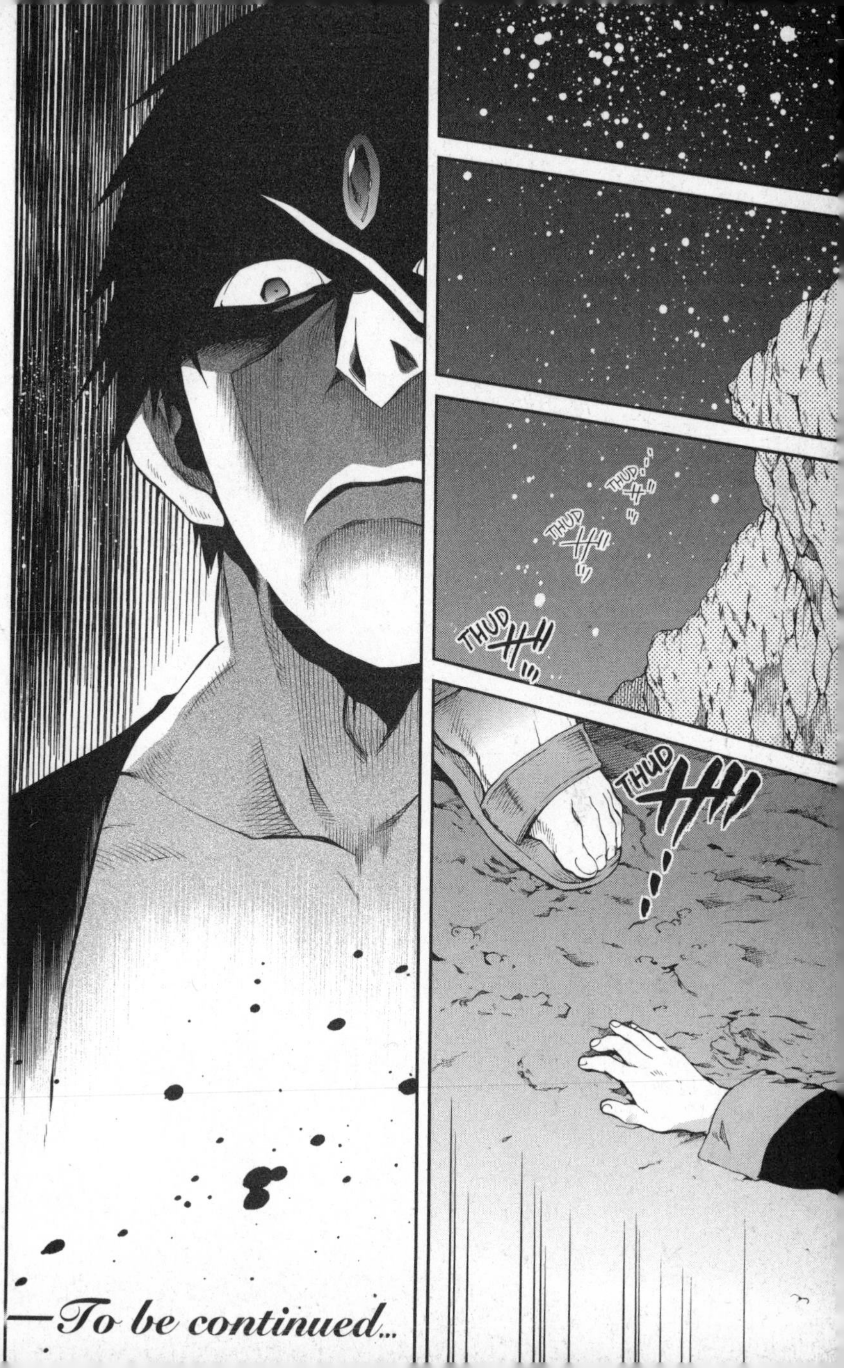
THUD
THUD
THUD
THUD
—To be continued...

MUSHOKU
TENSEI
jobless reincarnation

REUNION WITH AN ACQUAINTANCE

by: Rifujin Na Magonote

"It's interesting how people change over time," Philip thought to himself. His daughter, Eris, had grown so much in the past ten years. Philip thought back to when she was only two years old, when his days were an endless cycle of hopeless boredom. Due to political strife, he had been removed as head of the Boreas family almost a year before, and he was reduced to serving as mayor of Roa. Philip's life had become a monochrome blur of tedious mayoral tasks, attempts to pacify his neurotic wife, and enduring the daily orders and demands and verbal abuse of his father, Saurus.

Philip, who had been yelled at since childhood, was used to the latter of the three. He should

have been complacent, but he found himself growing anxious about the lack of opportunities to demonstrate his strength. Time seemed to crawl by without any significant improvement or variety.

One day, however, Paul Greyrat appeared at the door to the mayor's mansion. Philip saw that he was familiar, but something about him had completely changed from when he had last seen him, nearly ten years before.

When he saw Philip's face in the doorway, Paul bowed his head. "I come to you in hopes of finding a stable life. Please, give me some kind of work."

Philip stared at Paul in surprise. Paul explained that he had fled the Notos family almost a decade ago and became an adventurer. His travels took him to the Millis continent and the southern part of the Central continent, but along the way, he got a girl in his adventuring party pregnant. "The child is my responsibility," he stated. "That is why I have returned to the Asura Kingdom, where I hope to create a stable life."

Wide-eyed, Philip stared at the girl standing next to Paul. She was beautiful, with the facial contours

seen in the Millis aristocrats. Philip was silent and thoughtful as the girl cradled her swollen belly before him.

The Asura Kingdom was renowned as a desirable place for prospective parents to settle down. Paul was originally from the kingdom, but instead of returning to the Notos family, he had chosen to ask for the help of Boreas by seeking aid from his old friend, Philip. "I'm begging you. There's no one else I can ask."

Much to Philip's bewilderment, Paul took to his knee and bowed his head. This was the greeting used by villagers and craftsman—not the greeting of Asura nobility! Philip regarded Paul in scornful horror. Kneeling before him was Paul Notos Greyrat, the oldest son of Notos Greyrat, the intended head of the family. As soon as he had fled, he had been disinherited and was no longer considered a member of the nobility. To Philip, Paul was no better than trash.

Philip summoned his butler. "Tomas, escort him—" But before he was able to throw the two of them out, a loud *BAM!* reverberated through the

room as a door crashed open. Saurus stormed into the sitting room and glanced down at the kneeling Paul.

"*Hmph*, if it isn't Paul!"

"Lord Saurus, it's been a long time."

"You've grown so big! But it seems you still haven't learned how to greet people! Is that a greeting worthy of an Asura nobleman?"

Paul closed his eyes in shame. "I…no longer have any claim to Asura nobility."

The tips of Saurus's mustache seemed to take on a life of their own, as if they were channeling electricity generated by his rage. "You fool! If you truly had no relation to the Asura nobility, then I would not have allowed you to set foot in this mansion!"

Paul tried to hide his shock and remained on his knee with his head bowed. "Well…I understand that this is a bit absurd."

"*Hmph!* You got that from your father!"

At the mention of his estranged father, Paul cringed. Saurus unleashed a ranting recollection, shouting, "That man hated faulty logic, but he

was far too strict! Nearly fifteen years ago, when we were drinking together at his mansion, I recall he was trying to divide the contents of our bottle equally. When I informed him that I didn't like the wine and didn't want to drink it anyway, he replied that he also thought it was bad, and therefore we should split it! Once he opened the bottle, I couldn't be rude, so I—"

In the middle of Saurus's chaotic outburst, Philip's memories brought him back to an incident fifteen years ago, before he was old enough to attend school.

One day, Saurus was traveling to the Milbotts Region, which was part of Notos's territory. He had brought Philip along with him on his first long journey, his first excursion beyond the Fittoa Region. He remembered the thrill of seeing the grapevines and windmills in the Milbotts Region.

He was still excited when they arrived at the Notos estate. Around midday, Saurus and the head of the Notos family took to drinking wine, and Philip couldn't wait to explore. The estate was around the same size as his home, and as soon he was able to

escape Saurus's watchful gaze, Philip slipped away to investigate. Normally, Phillip was a well-behaved child, and he usually fought his boredom by asking a servant to bring him some toys or sweets. This time, emboldened by his curiosity, Philip set out on his first solo adventure. However, as he explored, he realized that the Notos estate was not nearly as interesting a building as the Boreas mansion. It had similar rooms that lined up in similar ways, and everything started to look the same. He wished he was tall enough to see out the windows. Finally, he saw a door at the end of a long hallway, but decided it wasn't worth checking out. He soon grew tired of searching for entertainment and suddenly thought of his father's angry face. If the short-tempered man found out that Philip had gone off on his own, he would probably drop his clenched fist on Philip's head! The young boy decided that he had to get back right away.

However, by the time he reached this conclusion, it was already too late. Philip was lost! He had no idea which room he had come from, nor what route he had taken. He recalled that the Notos estate had

been constructed to combat invaders with repetitive halls and no visible markers.

Philip searched his memory for the way back, but he found himself becoming more and more confused. Before long, he couldn't remember which floor he had started on. Disheartened, he roamed the estate forlornly, occasionally calling out, "Father… where are you… is anyone here?!"

He desperately wished that someone would appear to show him the way, but no one came, no matter how much he called out. It turned out the servants were all eating lunch, and Philip had ended up in a rarely used part of the estate. He had only been lost for about ten minutes, but to Philip, it felt like hours. "Uh… Ugh…" In his despair, Phillip sank to the floor at a dead end and began to cry. He cried and cried, but no one came. He began to worry that he might starve to death in the maze-like building.

Just as he realized he was hungry, something cast a shadow from behind him. He heard a voice. "Hi." Still crying, Philip twisted around to look up at the owner of the shadow. It was a young boy with light

brown hair, probably around Philip's age, maybe a bit older. He was well-dressed, but there was some mud on the cuff of his pants, and his shirt collar was slightly torn. He gave Philip a concerned look. "Why're you crying?"

"I was e-exploring and g-got lost… My father, I don't know where he is…"

"Oh, okay then. Follow me!" He gestured back down the hall with his chin.

"Uh, sure…" Philip wiped the tears from his eyes and started after the boy. This was Philip's first meeting with Paul Notos Greyrat.

After that, Philip thought that the boy would take him to his father, but he ended up accompanying him outside to play. When he returned in the evening, covered with mud, Saurus gave him a scolding, but that's another story.

Philip and Paul's meeting was nothing short of destiny. Following their first encounter, Saurus traveled to the Milbotts Region many times, and each time, Philip tagged along to play with Paul.

When Philip was seven, he began attending the school for nobility in the capital, and Paul was there,

too. Philip and Paul got along surprisingly well, and they considered each other soul mates. Though Paul lacked book smarts, Philip lacked physical strength. They worked on their opposing weaknesses together while causing all sorts of trouble. With Paul by his side, Philip was game for any mischief Paul might suggest, and they would execute devious plans without a care. They were best friends.

But at some point, Philip changed. As he grew up, he began to form relationships based solely on what he might gain from others. He wasn't sure when or how the change occurred. Maybe it happened when he heard that Paul, who had graduated from school and returned home, got into a fight with his father and ran away. It might have been when he and his older brother, James, found themselves in competition for the position of head of the Boreas family. Regardless, before he realized what was happening within him, Philip found that he tended to appraise and judge others based on their potential utility.

"……"

Philip snapped out of his reverie and looked down at Paul, whose head was still bowed before him. His name had long been removed from the ranks of the Asura nobility. Philip had thought he would never see Paul again, but here he was, chin lowered before him, pride swallowed for the sake of his unborn child. Philip observed his old friend. To him, the man who knelt before him appeared to have changed little from when they first met. Philip turned toward his butler. "Tomas, the resident knight of Buena Village recently died during an encounter with a monster, did he not? Paul is proficient with a sword. Let's leave it to him."

Paul's eyes snapped up in surprise. "Philip…"

"Your social status will be that of a low-grade noble. You'll be living in a remote village that doesn't even have a market of its own…but that will do, won't it?"

"Of course! I'm in your debt!" A smile full of joy spread across his face, and Paul bowed his head in gratitude.

Eight years from that day, Philip still didn't understand why he had made that choice. He was so

accustomed to judging others for their usefulness to him that he wondered why his memories of the past caused him to take pity on such a useless man. But as he watched his little girl's tenth birthday party draw to a conclusion, he thought to himself, Paul really did change.

Several months before, when he realized that Eris couldn't execute even the most basic dance steps, he thought that her tenth birthday party would be painful and humiliating for her. But on this day, she was able to do all of the steps with ease, and swept across the dance floor with relative grace. For a ten-year-old, there was still some awkwardness, but Philip could see that she truly looked happy while she was dancing.

A line of worry crossed his brow as he realized that Eris would mature into a lovely woman within the next few years. His eyes fell upon the boy standing next to Eris, Paul's son, Rudeus. It was Rudeus's influence that had brought about this change in his daughter. Paul had changed because of Rudeus, too, Philip noted. The neighborhood bully had become a father.

Philip realized that, from the moment he gave Paul work, he had changed a little, too. Although it was indirect, Rudeus had something to do with his own evolution, as well. Philip mused on the past few years as he watched Rudeus lead Eris and Ghislaine from the room.

During the party, Rudeus had some food brought to his room. Maybe it was another way to win Eris's favor. He was a wonderful teacher with a promising future, and despite his tenacity and patience, Philip found himself intrigued by Rudeus's frequent use of trickery to achieve his goals. Without his realizing it, an evil grin spread across his face. If Rudeus continued to develop at this rate, and he was able to manage his once-unruly daughter, he had potential as a future political tool…

Philip stopped himself. Before Rudeus came to him, he wouldn't have hesitated to groom him for use in his own quest for influence.

"Oh ho…" Philip realized how absurd his ideas were. He lost himself in thought. If Rudeus became the head of the Notos family, and he made Eris the head of the Boreas family, he would once again

be able to stand shoulder to shoulder with Paul. They could conspire like they used to, and—as a bonus—they might even be able to drink and laugh in each other's company again. He considered this possibility. "This seems more interesting than becoming the head myself."

Realizing the potential for these ideas, Philip chuckled quietly, and began plotting for the future.

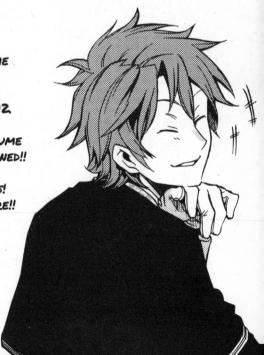

THE THIRD VOLUME OF THE COMIC IS ON SALE NOW!

I RECOMMEND CHAPTER 12. HILDA IS JUST LIKE THE ANNOYED ERIS FROM VOLUME 2! RUDEUS IS SO FRIGHTENED!!

HAIR LOSS DUE TO STRESS! HAIRS FLYING EVERYWHERE!! PLEASE ENJOY IT!!

理不尽な孫の手
RIFUJIN NA MAGONOTE

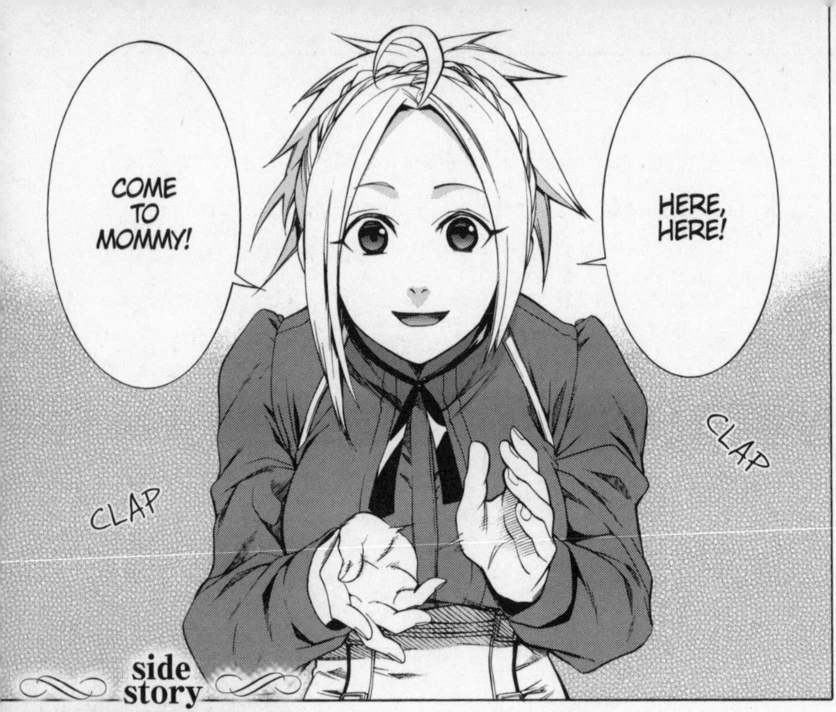
HERE, HERE!
COME TO MOMMY!
CLAP
CLAP

side story

THE LADY OF THE GREYRAT HOUSEHOLD

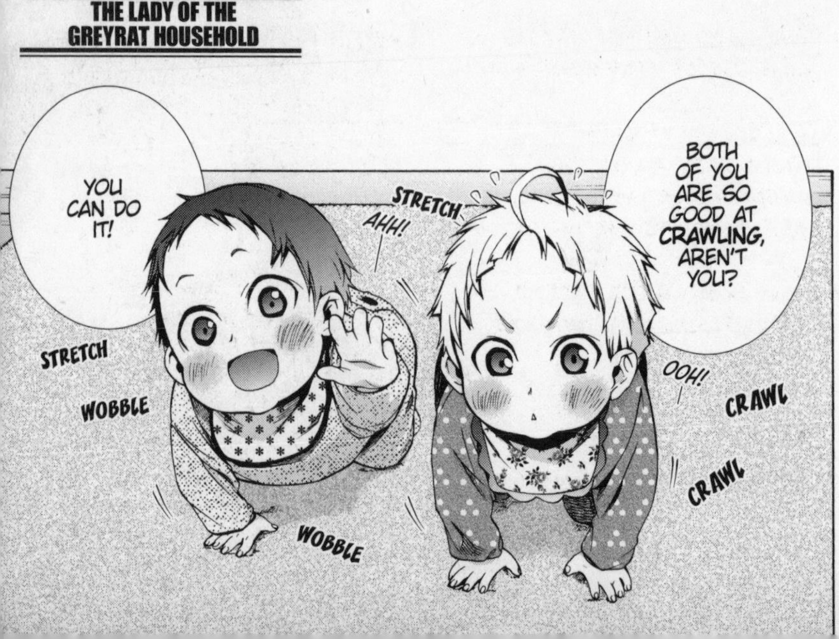
BOTH OF YOU ARE SO GOOD AT CRAWLING, AREN'T YOU?
YOU CAN DO IT!
STRETCH
AHH!
OOH!
CRAWL
CRAWL
STRETCH
WOBBLE
WOBBLE

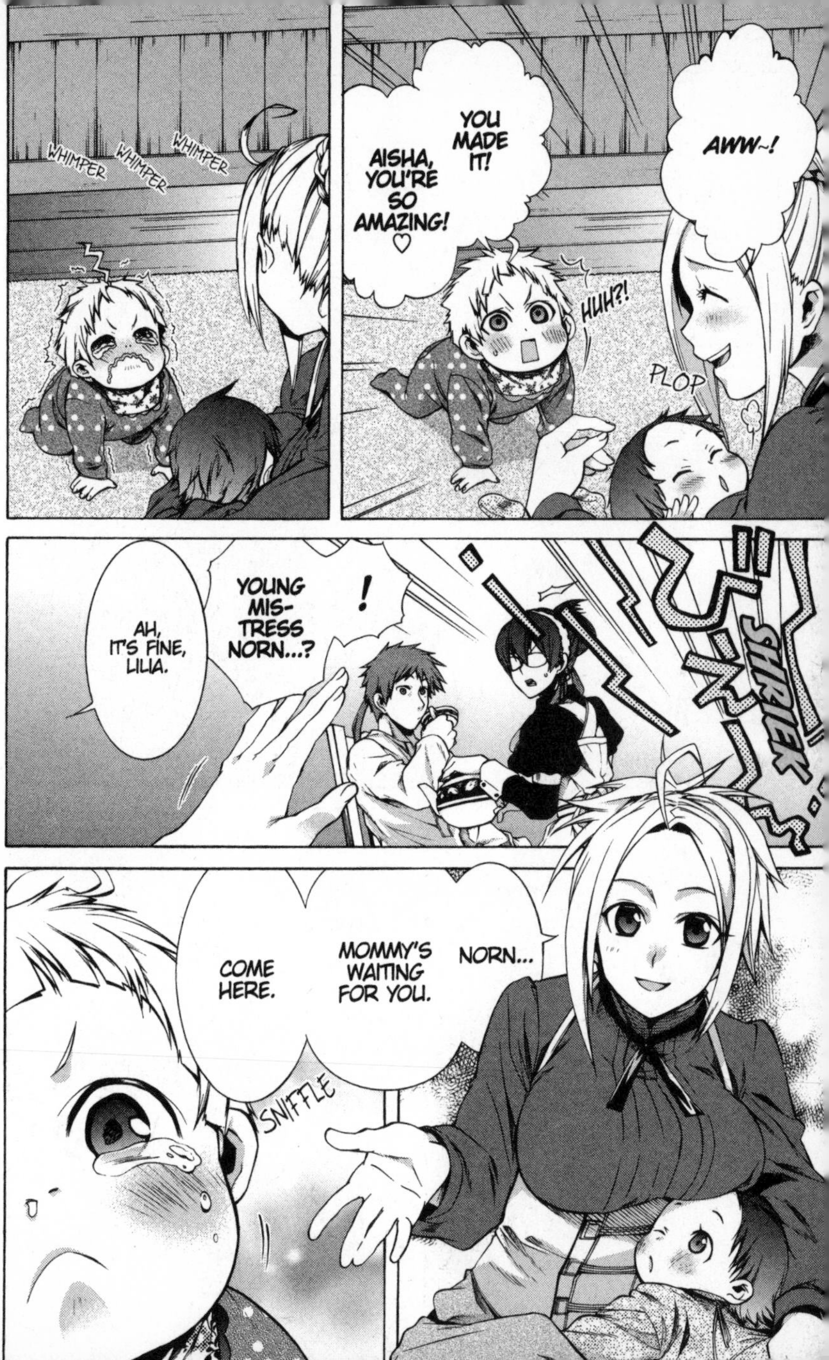
AWW~!
YOU MADE IT!
AISHA, YOU'RE SO AMAZING! ♡
HUH?!
PLOP
WHIMPER
WHIMPER
WHIMPER
SHRIEK
!
YOUNG MIS-TRESS NORN...?
AH, IT'S FINE, LILIA.
NORN...
MOMMY'S WAITING FOR YOU.
COME HERE.
SNIFFLE

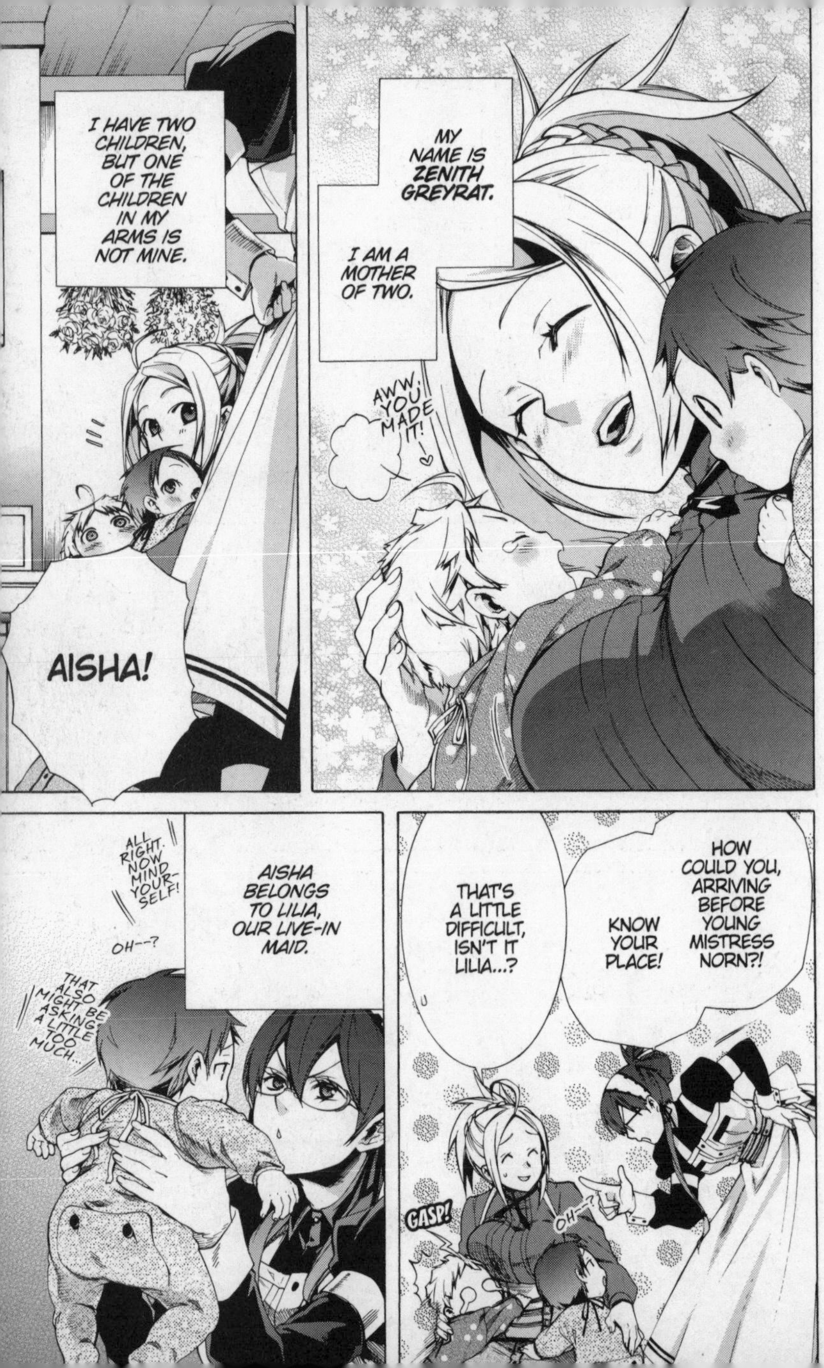
MY NAME IS ZENITH GREYRAT.
I AM A MOTHER OF TWO.
AWW, YOU MADE IT! ♥
I HAVE TWO CHILDREN, BUT ONE OF THE CHILDREN IN MY ARMS IS NOT MINE.
AISHA!
HOW COULD YOU, ARRIVING BEFORE YOUNG MISTRESS NORN?!
KNOW YOUR PLACE!
THAT'S A LITTLE DIFFICULT, ISN'T IT LILIA...?
OH--?
GASP!
AISHA BELONGS TO LILIA, OUR LIVE-IN MAID.
ALL RIGHT. NOW MIND YOUR-SELF!
OH--?
THAT ALSO MIGHT BE ASKING A LITTLE TOO MUCH...

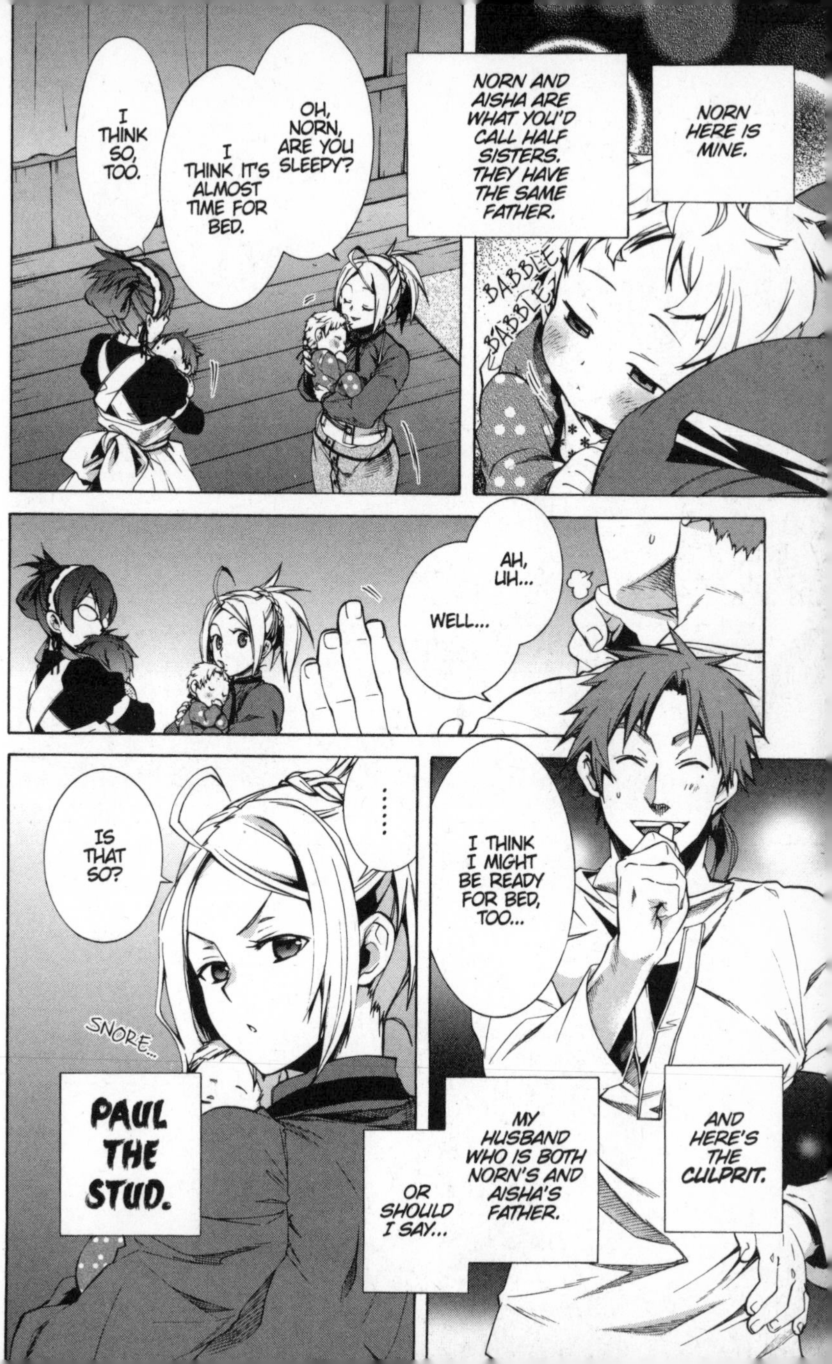

NORN HERE IS MINE.
NORN AND AISHA ARE WHAT YOU'D CALL HALF SISTERS. THEY HAVE THE SAME FATHER.
BABBLE BABBLE
OH, NORN, ARE YOU SLEEPY?
I THINK IT'S ALMOST TIME FOR BED.
I THINK SO, TOO.
AH, UH...
WELL...
AND HERE'S THE CULPRIT.
MY HUSBAND WHO IS BOTH NORN'S AND AISHA'S FATHER.
I THINK I MIGHT BE READY FOR BED, TOO...
OR SHOULD I SAY...
......
IS THAT SO?
SNORE...
PAUL THE STUD.

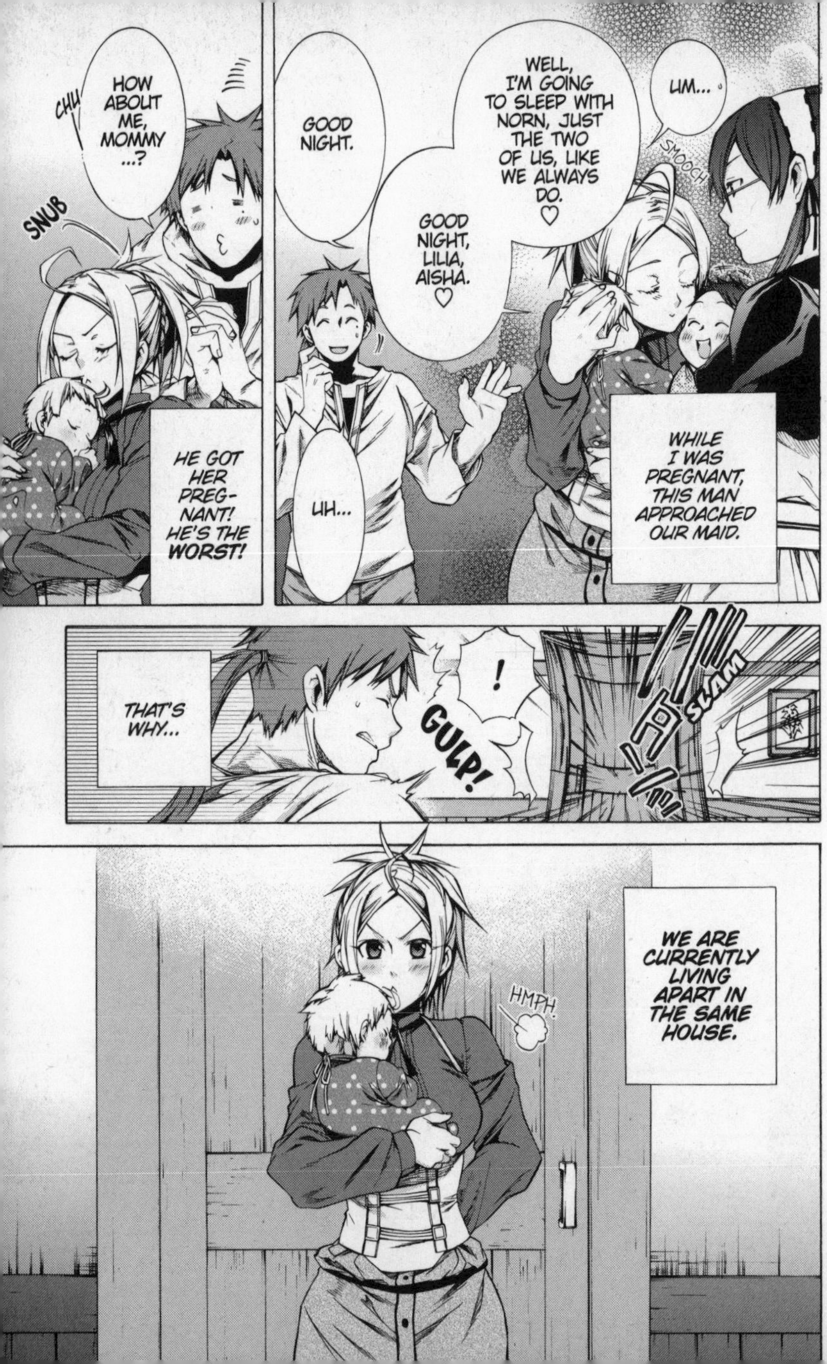
UM...
SMOOCH
WELL, I'M GOING TO SLEEP WITH NORN, JUST THE TWO OF US, LIKE WE ALWAYS DO. ♡
GOOD NIGHT, LILIA, AISHA. ♡
GOOD NIGHT.
WHILE I WAS PREGNANT, THIS MAN APPROACHED OUR MAID.
UH...
HOW ABOUT ME, MOMMY ...?
CHU
SNUB
HE GOT HER PREG-NANT! HE'S THE WORST!
SLAM
!
GULP!
THAT'S WHY...
WE ARE CURRENTLY LIVING APART IN THE SAME HOUSE.
HMPH.

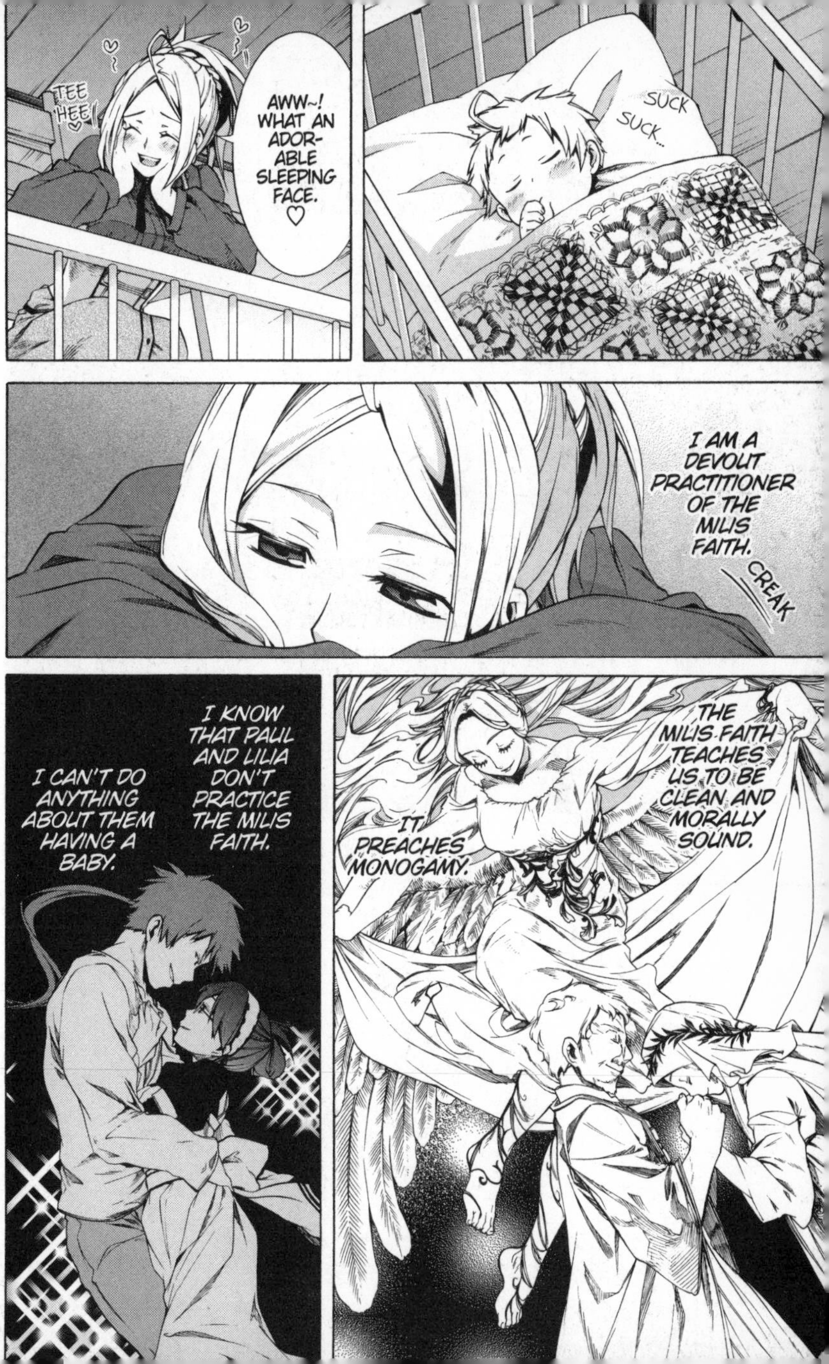
SUCK SUCK...
AWW~! WHAT AN ADORABLE SLEEPING FACE. ♡
TEE HEE ♡
I AM A DEVOUT PRACTITIONER OF THE MILIS FAITH.
CREAK
THE MILIS FAITH TEACHES US TO BE CLEAN AND MORALLY SOUND.
IT PREACHES MONOGAMY.
I KNOW THAT PAUL AND LILIA DON'T PRACTICE THE MILIS FAITH.
I CAN'T DO ANYTHING ABOUT THEM HAVING A BABY.

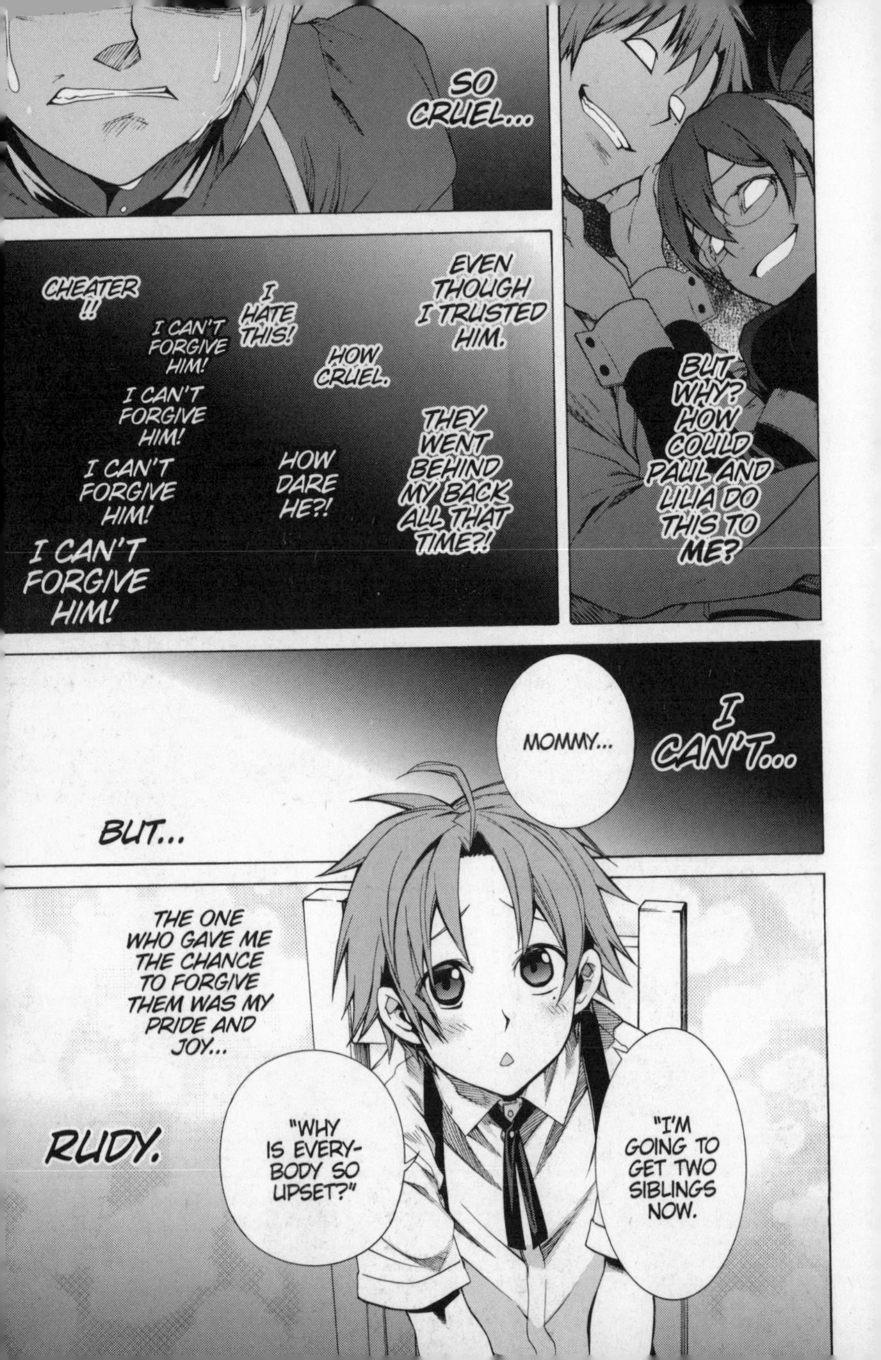
BUT WHY? HOW COULD PAUL AND LILIA DO THIS TO ME?
SO CRUEL...
EVEN THOUGH I TRUSTED HIM.
THEY WENT BEHIND MY BACK ALL THAT TIME?!
HOW CRUEL.
HOW DARE HE?!
I HATE THIS!
I CAN'T FORGIVE HIM!
I CAN'T FORGIVE HIM!
I CAN'T FORGIVE HIM!
I CAN'T FORGIVE HIM!
CHEATER!!
I CAN'T...
MOMMY...
BUT...
"I'M GOING TO GET TWO SIBLINGS NOW.
"WHY IS EVERYBODY SO UPSET?"
THE ONE WHO GAVE ME THE CHANCE TO FORGIVE THEM WAS MY PRIDE AND JOY...
RUDY.

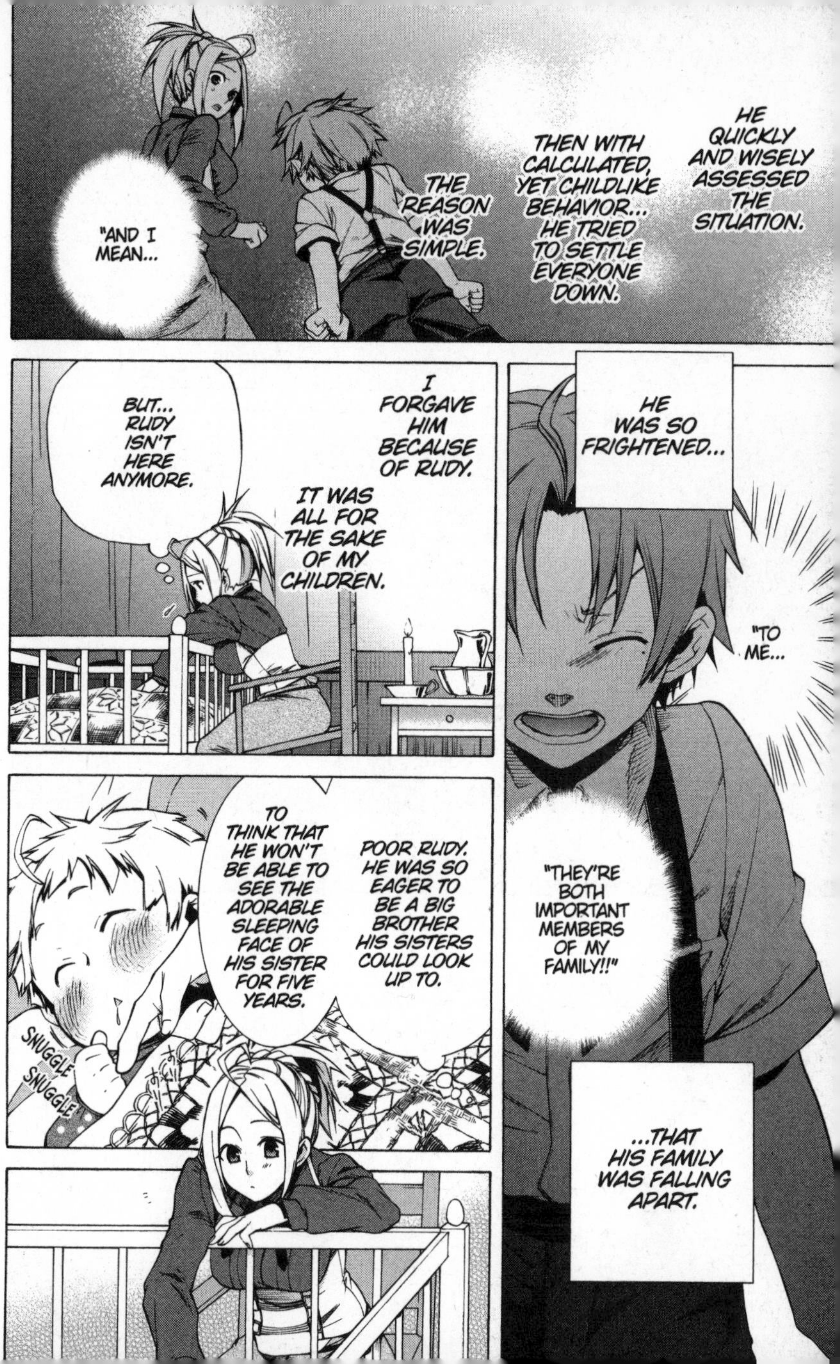
HE QUICKLY AND WISELY ASSESSED THE SITUATION.
THEN WITH CALCULATED, YET CHILDLIKE BEHAVIOR... HE TRIED TO SETTLE EVERYONE DOWN.
THE REASON WAS SIMPLE.
"AND I MEAN...
HE WAS SO FRIGHTENED...
"TO ME...
"THEY'RE BOTH IMPORTANT MEMBERS OF MY FAMILY!!"
...THAT HIS FAMILY WAS FALLING APART.
I FORGAVE HIM BECAUSE OF RUDY.
IT WAS ALL FOR THE SAKE OF MY CHILDREN.
BUT... RUDY ISN'T HERE ANYMORE.
POOR RUDY. HE WAS SO EAGER TO BE A BIG BROTHER HIS SISTERS COULD LOOK UP TO.
TO THINK THAT HE WON'T BE ABLE TO SEE THE ADORABLE SLEEPING FACE OF HIS SISTER FOR FIVE YEARS.
SNUGGLE SNUGGLE

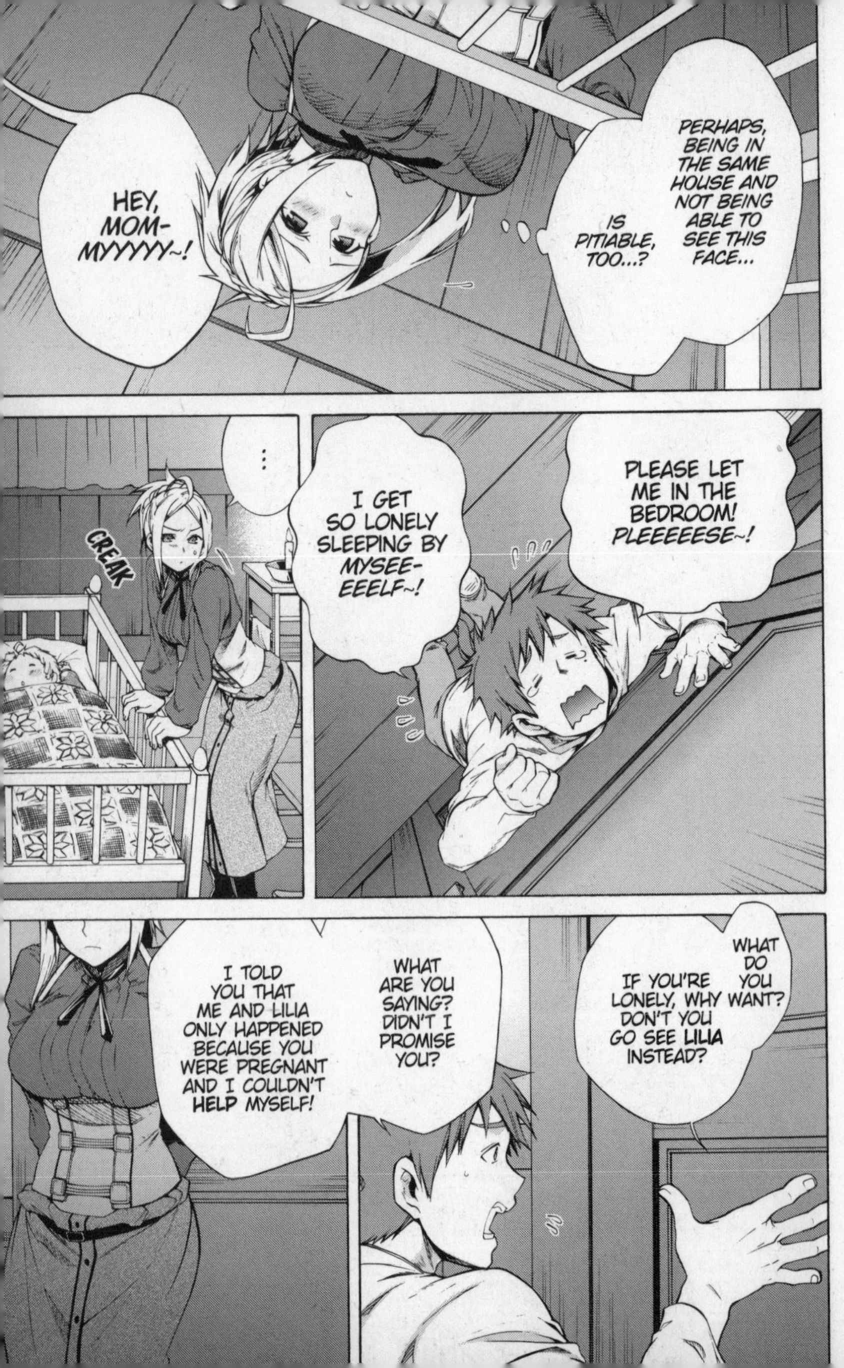
PERHAPS, BEING IN THE SAME HOUSE AND NOT BEING ABLE TO SEE THIS FACE...
IS PITIABLE, TOO...?
HEY, MOM-MYYYYY~!
PLEASE LET ME IN THE BEDROOM! PLEEEEESE~!
I GET SO LONELY SLEEPING BY MYSEE-EEELF~!
...
CREAK
WHAT DO YOU WANT?
IF YOU'RE LONELY, WHY DON'T YOU GO SEE LILIA INSTEAD?
WHAT ARE YOU SAYING? DIDN'T I PROMISE YOU?
I TOLD YOU THAT ME AND LILIA ONLY HAPPENED BECAUSE YOU WERE PREGNANT AND I COULDN'T HELP MYSELF!

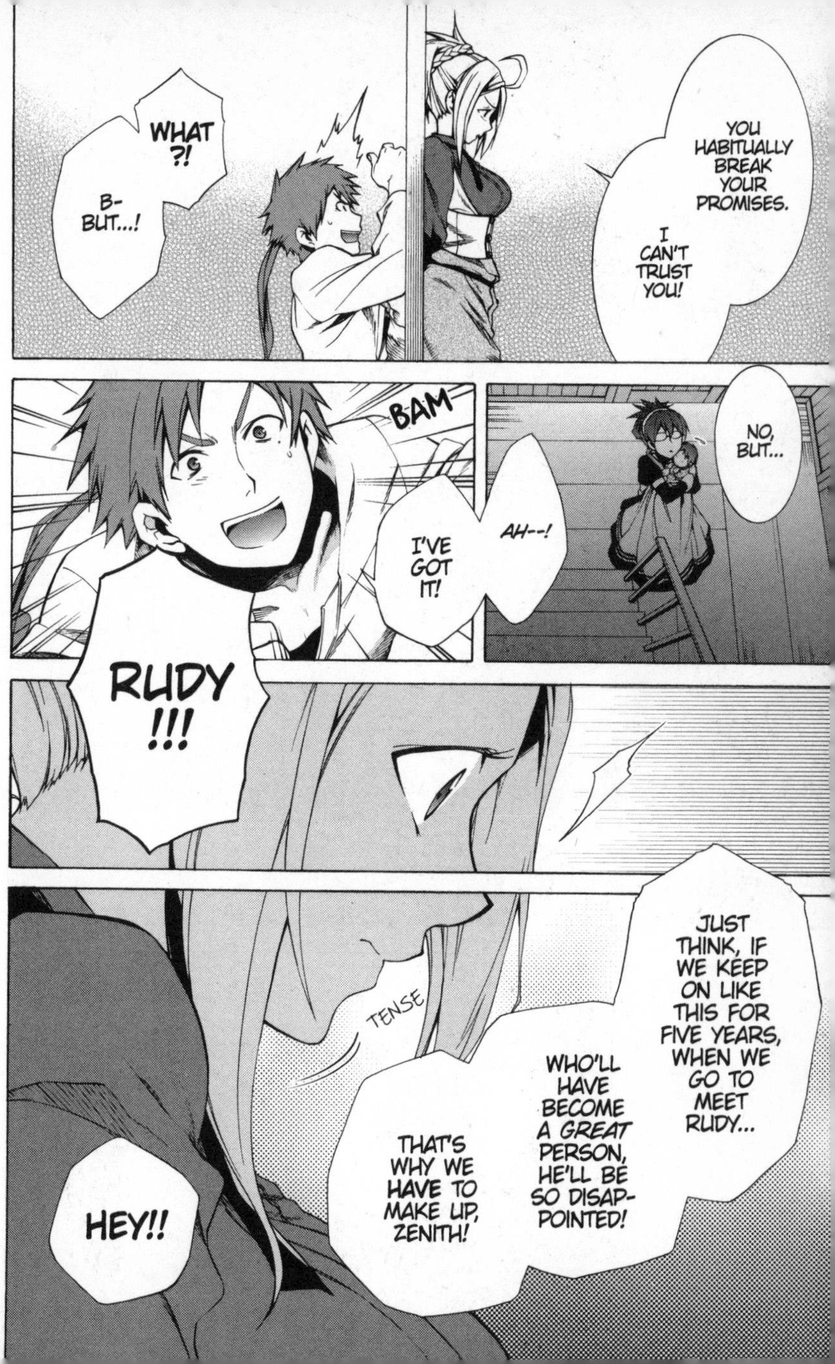
YOU HABITUALLY BREAK YOUR PROMISES.
I CAN'T TRUST YOU!
WHAT?!
B-BUT...!
NO, BUT...
AH--!
I'VE GOT IT!
BAM
RUDY!!!
JUST THINK, IF WE KEEP ON LIKE THIS FOR FIVE YEARS, WHEN WE GO TO MEET RUDY...
WHO'LL HAVE BECOME A GREAT PERSON, HE'LL BE SO DISAPPOINTED!
THAT'S WHY WE HAVE TO MAKE UP, ZENITH!
TENSE
HEY!!

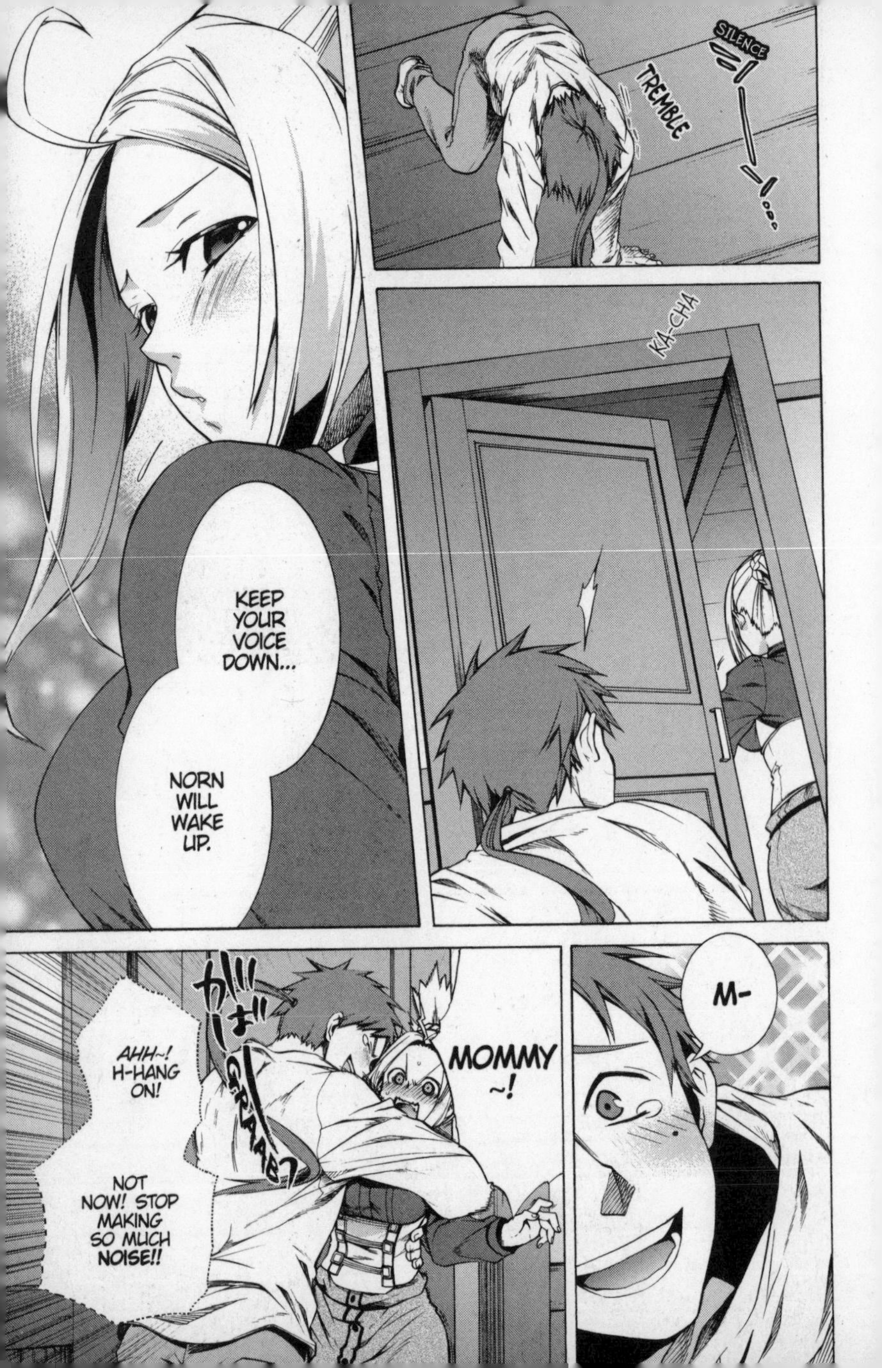
SILENCE
TREMBLE
KA-CHA
KEEP YOUR VOICE DOWN...
NORN WILL WAKE UP.
M-
MOMMY ~!
GRAAB
AHH~! H-HANG ON!
NOT NOW! STOP MAKING SO MUCH NOISE!!

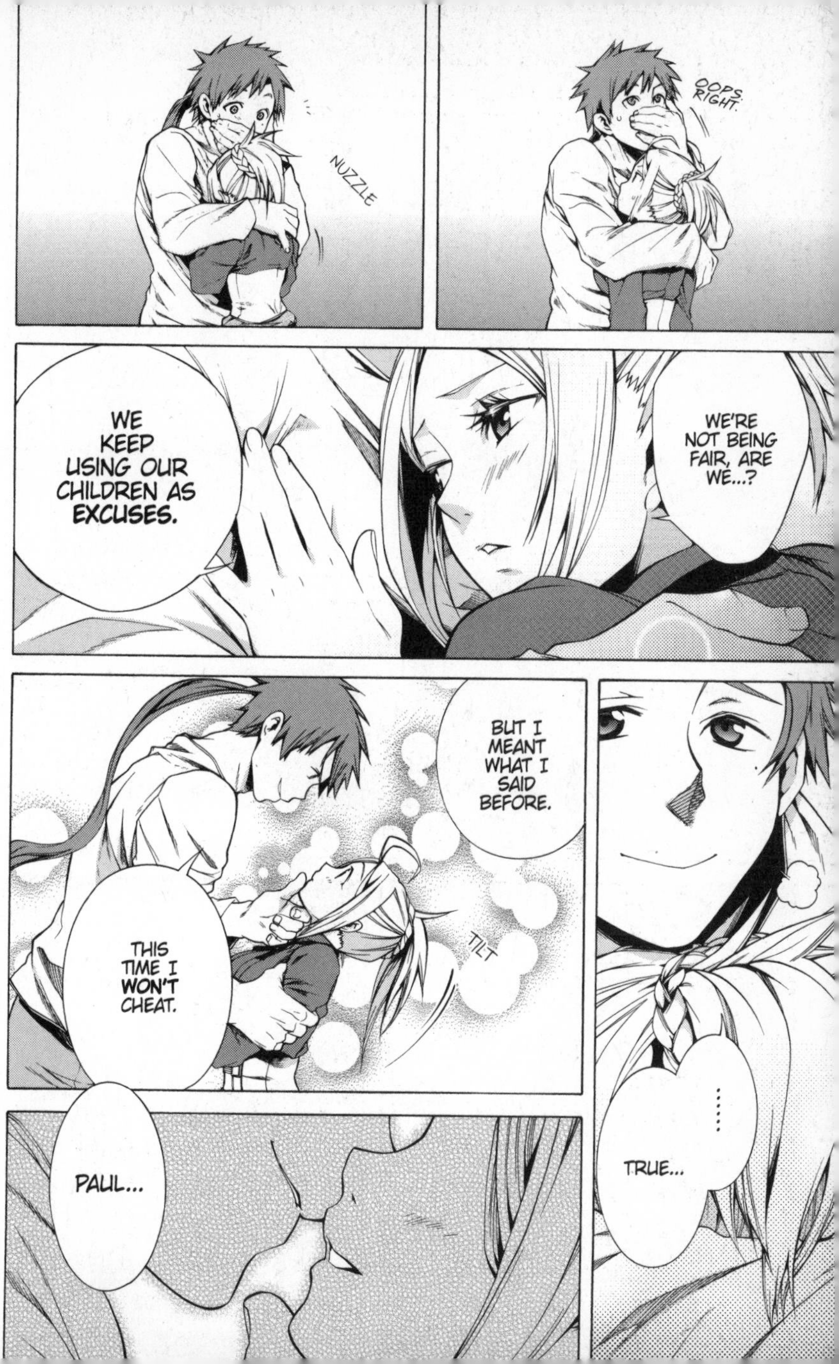
OOPS. RIGHT.
NUZZLE
WE'RE NOT BEING FAIR, ARE WE...?
WE KEEP USING OUR CHILDREN AS EXCUSES.
......
TRUE...
BUT I MEANT WHAT I SAID BEFORE.
TILT
THIS TIME I WON'T CHEAT.
PAUL...

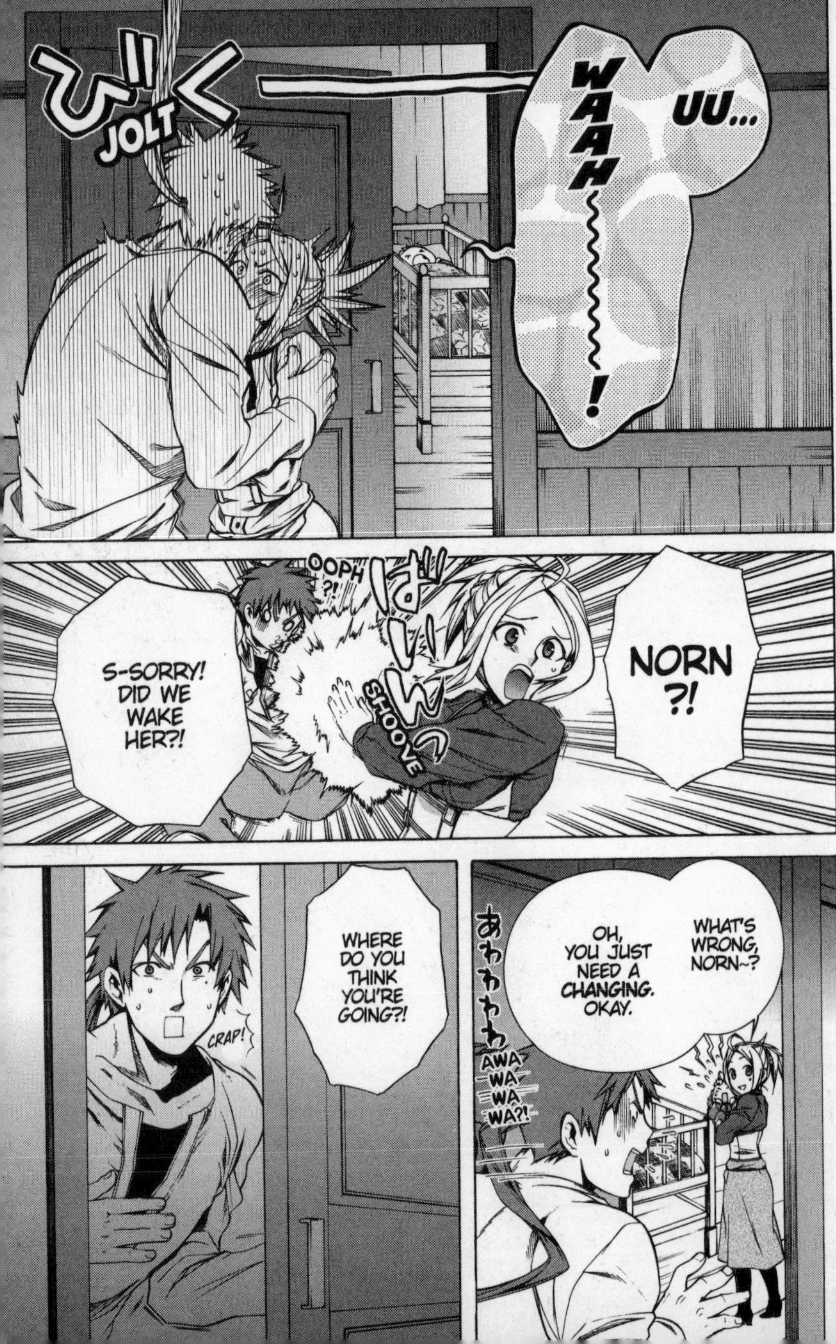
UU...
WAAAH~~~!
ひっく
JOLT
NORN ?!
ばいんっ
SHOOVE
OOPH ?!
S-SORRY! DID WE WAKE HER?!
WHAT'S WRONG, NORN~?
OH, YOU JUST NEED A CHANGING. OKAY.
あわわわわ
AWA WA WA WA?!
WHERE DO YOU THINK YOU'RE GOING?!
CRAP!

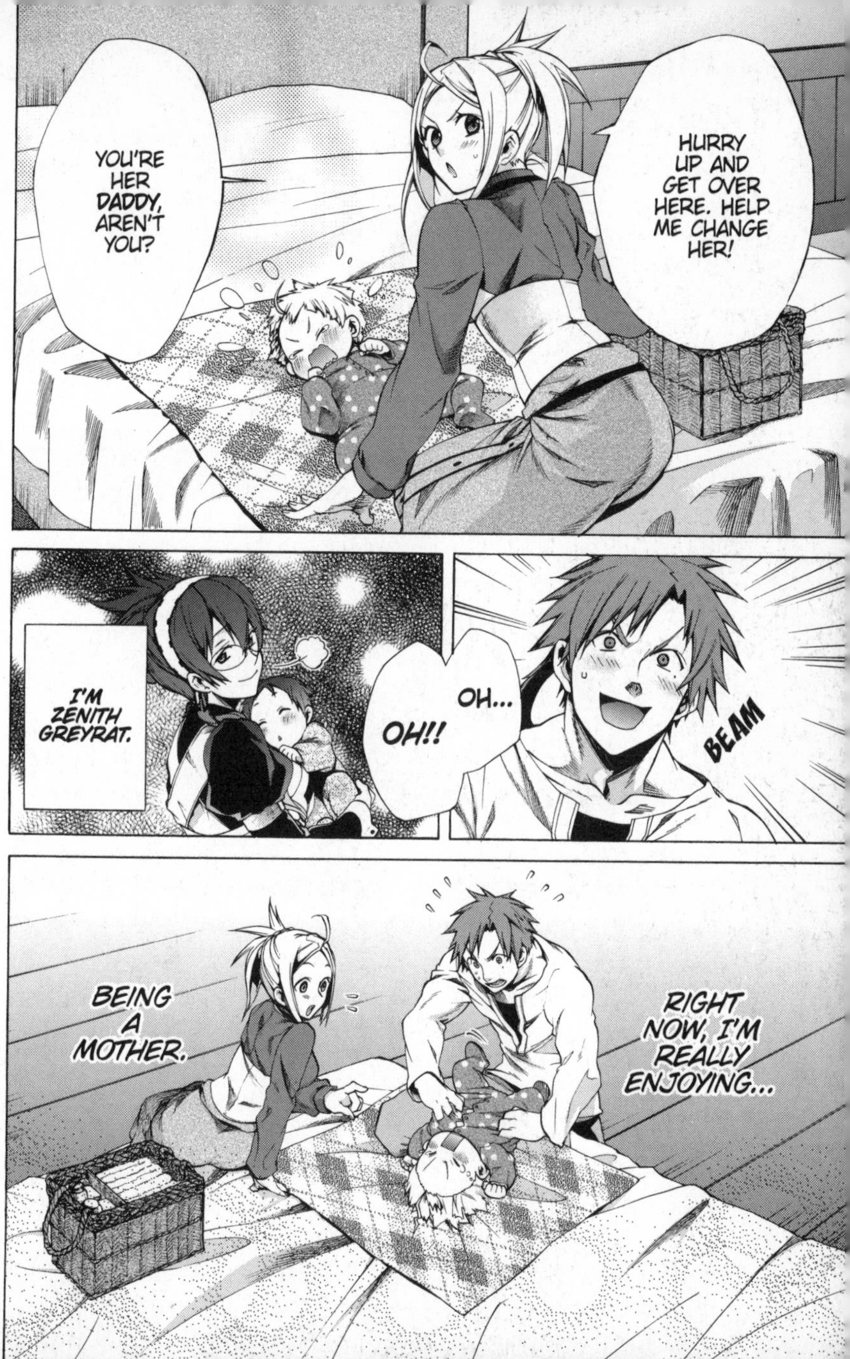
HURRY UP AND GET OVER HERE. HELP ME CHANGE HER!
YOU'RE HER DADDY, AREN'T YOU?
OH...
OH!!
BEAM
I'M ZENITH GREYRAT.
RIGHT NOW, I'M REALLY ENJOYING...
BEING A MOTHER.

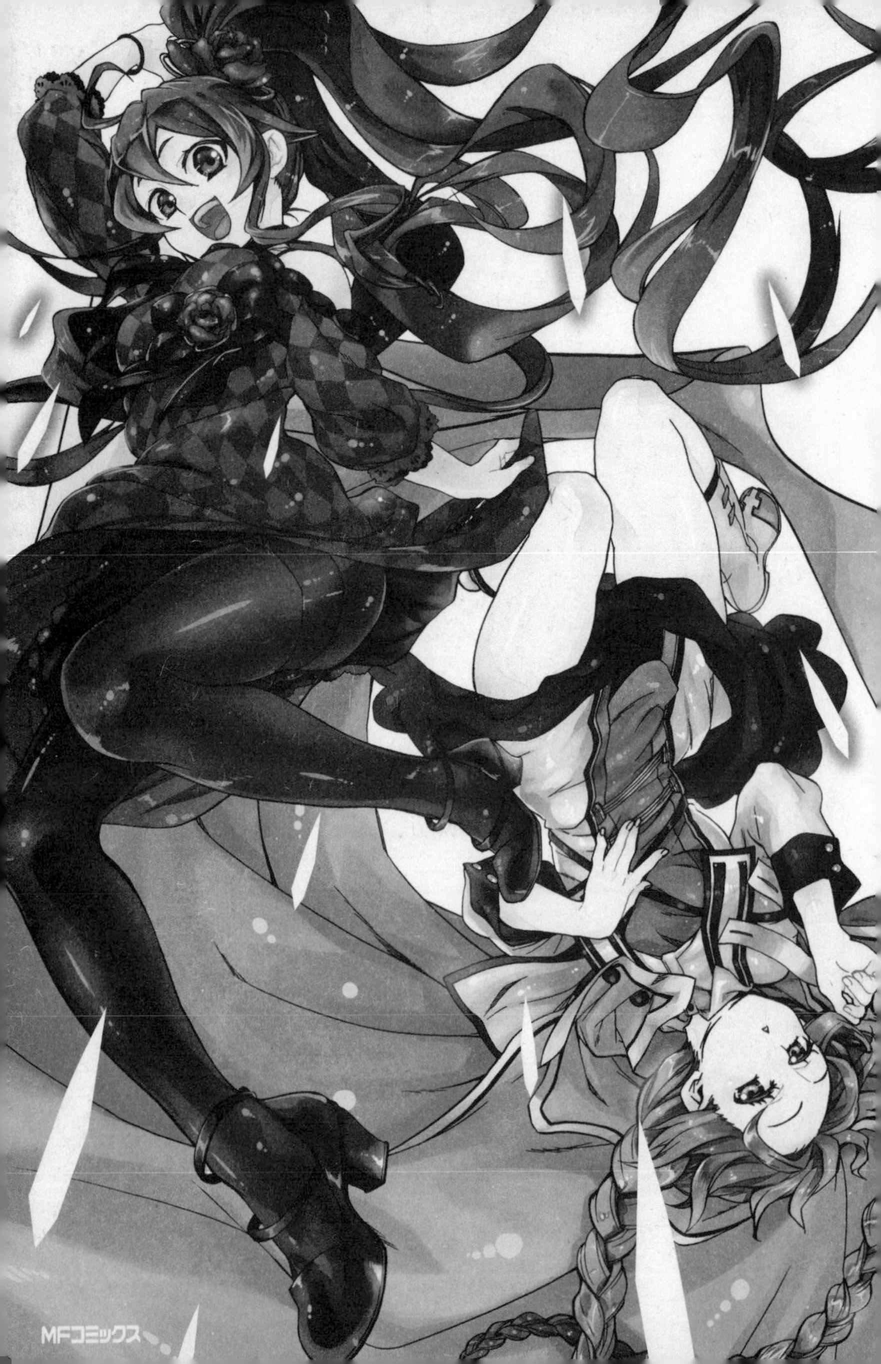
MFコミックス

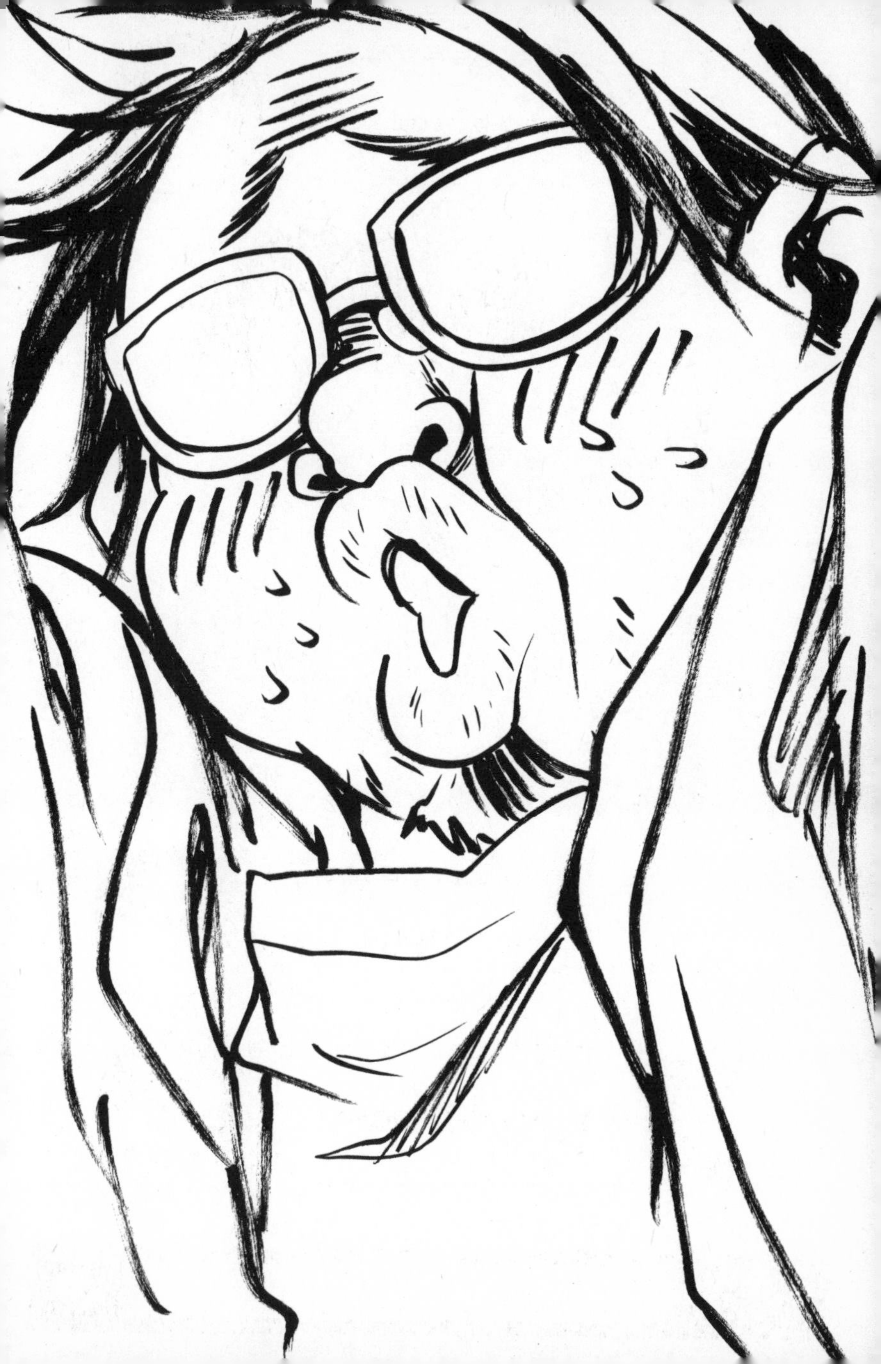

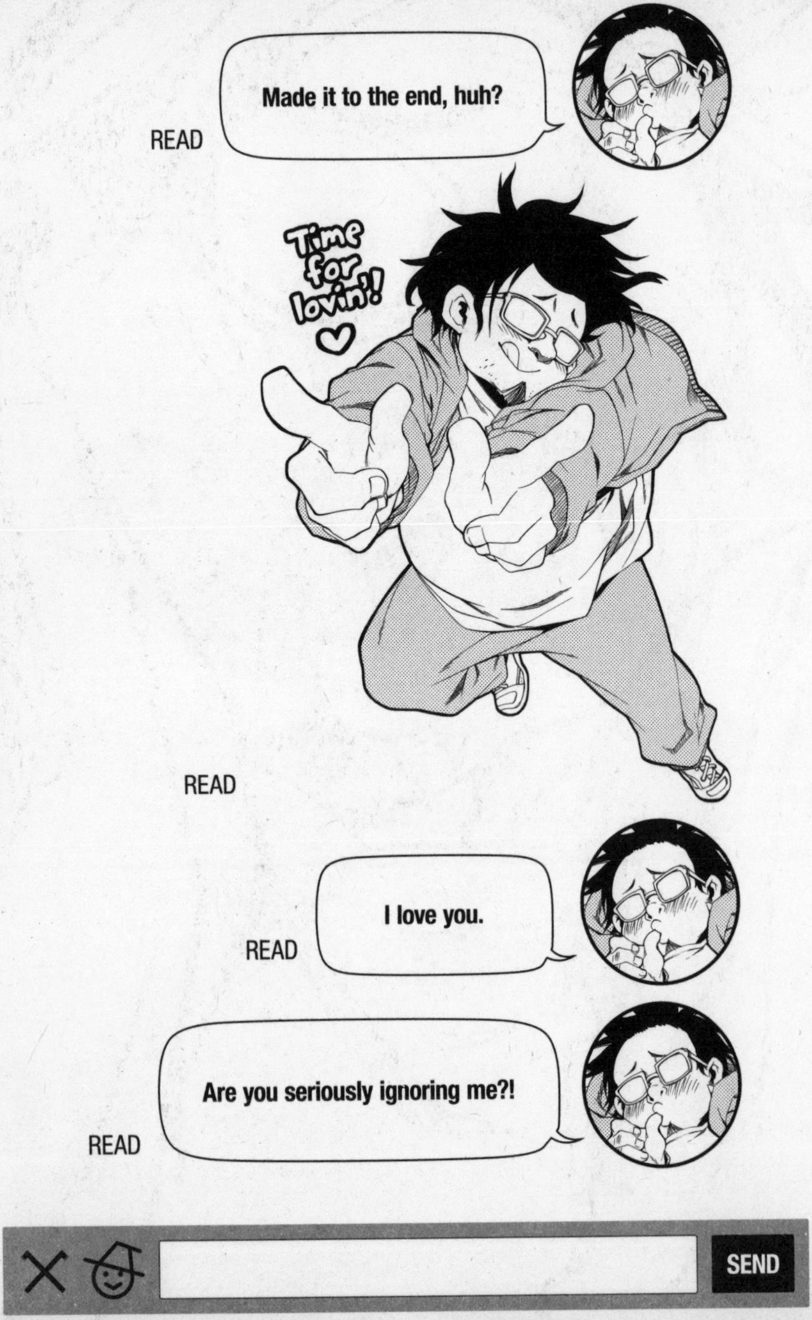
Made it to the end, huh?
READ
Time for lovin'!
READ
I love you.
READ
Are you seriously ignoring me?!
READ
SEND

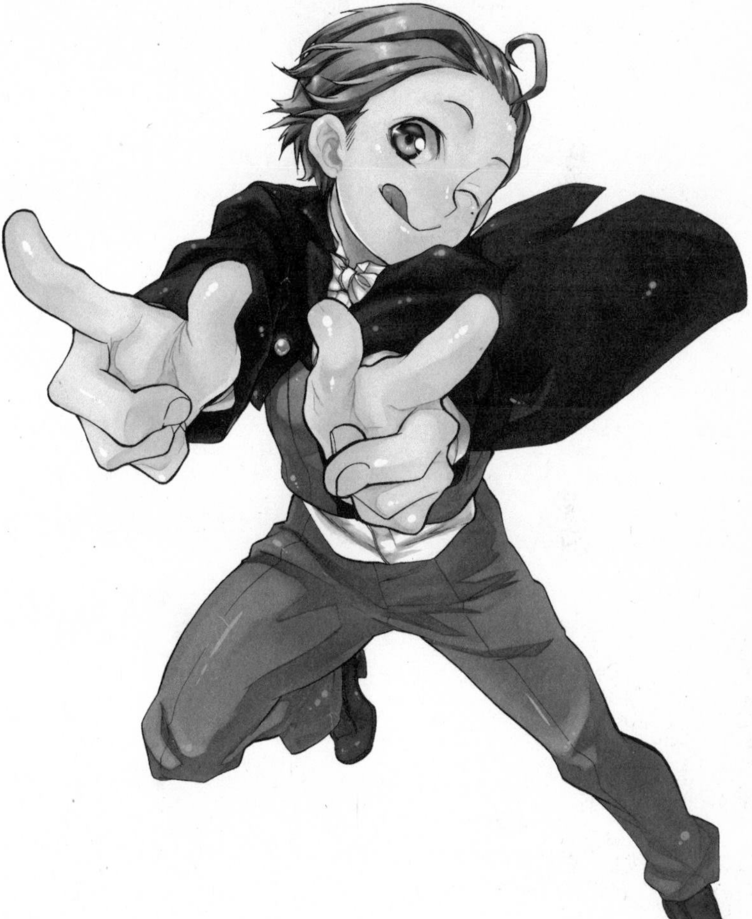

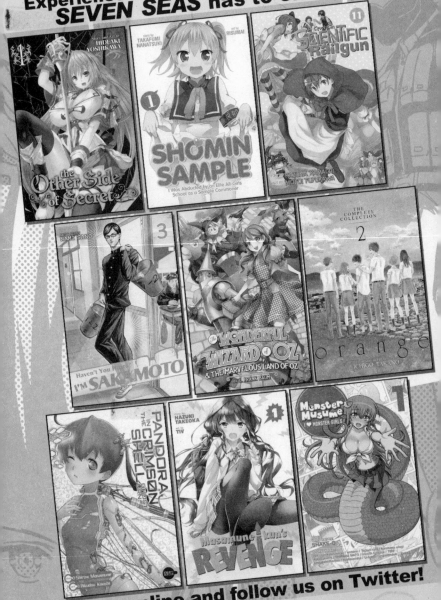

SEVEN SEAS ENTERTAINMENT PRESENTS

Mushoku Tensei
jobless reincarnation
volume 3

story by RIFUJIN NA MAGONOTE / art by YUKA FUJIKAWA

TRANSLATION
Jill Morita

ADAPTATION
Karis Page

LETTERING AND LAYOUT
Laura Scoville

COVER DESIGN
Nicky Lim

PROOFREADER
Danielle King
Lee Otter

PRODUCTION MANAGER
Lissa Pattillo

EDITOR-IN-CHIEF
Adam Arnold

PUBLISHER
Jason DeAngelis

MUSHOKU TENSEI: JOBLESS REINCARNATION VOL. 3
© Yuka Fujikawa 2015, © Rifujin na Magonote 2015
Edited by MEDIA FACTORY.
First published in Japan in 2015 by KADOKAWA CORPORATION, Tokyo.
English translation rights reserved by Seven Seas Entertainment, LLC.
under the license from KADOKAWA CORPORATION, Tokyo.

Seven Seas books may be purchased in bulk for educational, business, or
promotional use. For information on bulk purchases, please contact Macmillan
Corporate & Premium Sales Department at 1-800-221-7945 (ext 5442)
or write specialmarkets@macmillan.com.

Seven Seas and the Seven Seas logo are trademarks of
Seven Seas Entertainment, LLC. All rights reserved.

ISBN: 978-1-626922-79-2
Printed in Canada
First Printing: June 2016
10 9 8 7 6 5 4 3 2 1

FOLLOW US ONLINE: *www.gomanga.com*

READING DIRECTIONS

This book reads from *right to left*, Japanese style. If this is your first time reading manga, you start reading from the top right panel on each page and take it from there. If you get lost, just follow the numbered diagram here. It may seem backwards at first, but you'll get the hang of it! Have fun!!

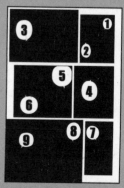

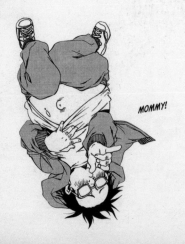

MOMMY!

Mushoku Tensei

jobless reincarnation

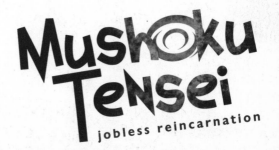